D1559755

Understanding Types, Shadows, and Names

A Biblical Guide

Volume 2
D–F

Understanding Types, Shadows, and Names

A Biblical Guide

Volume 2
D–F

Kelley Varner

Destiny Image® **Publishers, Inc.**
P.O. Box 310
Shippensburg, PA 17257-0310

"We Publish the Prophets"

ISBN 1-56043-197-0

For Worldwide Distribution
Printed in the U.S.A.

This book and all other Destiny Image, Revival Press,
and Treasure House books are available
at Christian bookstores and distributors worldwide.

For a U.S. bookstore nearest you, call **1-800-722-6774**.
For more information on foreign distributors, call **717-532-3040**.
Or reach us on the Internet: **http://www.reapernet.com**

Table of Contents

Preface
Introduction

Preface

These are unprecedented days of harvest and ingathering. A new generation of redeemed people, a vast army of raw recruits, have encountered the Person of the Lord Jesus Christ and the power of His Holy Spirit.

This is God's finest hour. A glorious Church, like a sleeping giant, is shaking herself. As the Queen of Sheba in the days of Solomon, the nations are coming to Zion with their praise, their awe, and their finance (1 Kings 10). We must be prepared and equipped to give them answers.

To that end, *Understanding Types, Shadows, and Names: A Biblical Guide* was born. We must all learn to speak the same thing: the language of the Bible (1 Cor. 1:10), "the tongue of the learned" (Is. 50:4). As we discovered how to talk in the natural realm, so we have begun to find out the spiritual language of God's Kingdom. A man's speech will betray him (Mt. 26:73).

The word "Hebrews" means "to cross over; crossing the river." God has brought His people out of Egypt by the blood of the Passover Lamb Christ Jesus. He has led us through the wilderness and brought us to the edge of Jordan. It is time for the Joshua generation to cross over, to go in and possess the land.

There is a powerful Old Testament story that illustrates this. In the times of the judges, the warrior Jephthah was leading the Gileadites into victorious battle against the Ephraimites (Judg. 12:1-6). The Gileadites took the passages of the Jordan River ahead of their enemies. To prevent any Ephraimites from crossing the river by disguise, Jephthah's men made them say the word "Shibboleth." The Ephraimites "could not frame to pronounce it right" (Judg. 12:6). They could only say "Sibboleth." In other words, they did not know the language of the people of God.

"Shibboleth" means "to flow like a river or stream." As we flow with Him who is the River, as we cross Jordan to inherit the promises, we must learn how to talk. Those who are not moving with what God is doing in the earth today have not learned the language of the Bible. Like the Ephraimites in Judges, they will be destroyed for lack of knowledge (Hos. 4:6).

Introduction

I did not write this biblical guide from scratch. It is a compilation of almost 30 years of Bible study. Before I share its format, I want you to hear and understand my heart.

First, I am not attempting to make the people of God become mere intellectuals. When Eve reached for knowledge in the beginning, the heavens closed. A man can only learn the Bible by having a personal experience with its Author, the Holy Ghost. Merely knowing a vast storehouse of information does not qualify one for the ministry. We can only be a blessing to others on the basis of who we are in Christ as a new creature empowered by His Spirit. It is on the basis of whom we know, not what we know.

Second, I am not presuming to limit God or the things of His Spirit to what is covered in this "Biblical Guide." Much more will be said and written by the ministries that Jesus has sent to equip the Church (Eph. 4:11). All of us are still being guided into all truth by the Holy Spirit (Jn. 16:13). But we must build our lives, homes, and ministries upon the solid, foundational, Christological truths contained herein. My purpose is not meant to be exhaustive but introductory, to stimulate the student to further study and prayer.

Third, *Understanding Types, Shadows, and Names* is not the product of one man. Every ministry, both oral and literary, that has ever spoken into my life is about to speak into yours. The concepts set before you are sure and sound, for they are scriptural. God is speaking these things through apostles, prophets, evangelists, pastors, and teachers all over the earth. These many voices blend into one—the voice of the Head of the Church. We have not arrived. Only One has arrived, and He sits enthroned as our Anchor within the veil, expecting until His enemies be made His footstool (Heb. 6:19-20; 10:12-13), until His end-time Church crosses the river!

This work was a mammoth undertaking. Its writing is simple, succinct, and to the point. It is Christ-centered and intensely evangelical. It is devotional and inspirational, as well as a challenge to serious Bible students.

All that is before you. Dig as deep as you want, from a cursory glance at the simple meaning of a Bible term to hours of investigative Bible exegesis. The names of every significant person, place, or thing in the Bible have been alphabetically treated in the same manner, broken down into six simple categories:

1. **Primary Meaning.** This first definition is the heart, the gist, the intent, the spiritual sense of each term, interpreted in the light of the New Testament. I have cut

to the main point and declared its meaning, which may include more than one application.

2. **Key Scriptures.** This list of references contains from three to seven major Old and New Testament passages for each term, geared for quick Bible reference.

3. **Foundational Information.** This section is like an abridged Bible dictionary. It includes the original Hebrew or Greek meaning of each term from *Strong's Exhaustive Concordance of the Bible* (including its number), and its translation in the King James Version.

4. **Fulfilled in Christ.** This section shows how each term finds its primary and consummate meaning in the Person and work of the Messiah, the Lord Jesus Christ. His incarnation, death, burial, resurrection, ascension, exaltation, and coronation are emphasized throughout.

5. **Applied to the Christian.** This section is an extension of the previous one, showing how each term relates personally and collectively in three practical areas: the individual, the home, and the local church.

6. **Go Deeper.** This final section is for the serious Bible student. It lists between 20 and 30 cross-references for each term, based on the usage of the same Hebrew or Greek word, as well as on broad sweeping themes of topical Bible study.

The utility of this biblical guide is multifaceted; it can be used for:
- General and personal Bible study.
- Group Bible study.
- Lesson preparation for Sunday school teachers.
- Sermon preparation for pastors.
- Resource and research material for Bible schools.
- Resource and research material for writers.

The biblical mandate for my life and ministry as a literary apostle is found in the last book of the Bible:

...What thou seest, write in a book, and send it unto the seven churches... (Revelation 1:11).

Understanding Types, Shadows, and Names: A Biblical Guide is for the "seven churches," the whole Body of Christ. We're crossing the river together. Let the Lord and me teach you how to say "Shibboleth"!

Kelley Varner, B.S., Th.B., D.D.
Senior Pastor
Praise Tabernacle
Richlands, North Carolina

𝔇agon

Satan, the god of this world

Key Scriptures: Judg. 16:23; 1 Sam. 5:1-7; 1 Chron. 10:10; 2 Cor. 4:4.

Foundational Information ✑

Dagon was the chief national god of the ancient Philistines, whose most famous temples were at Gaza and Ashdod. "Dagon" is from the Hebrew *Dagown* (Strong's #1712) which means "the fish-god; Dagon, a Philistine deity." It is taken from *dag* (Strong's #1709) which means "a fish (in the sense of squirming, moving by the vibratory action of the tail)." Dagon is the diminutive (expressing affection) of *dag*—"dear little fish."

Fulfilled in Christ ⵣ

Just as the Ark of the Covenant was three days in the temple of Dagon at Ashdod, so the Lord Jesus Christ was three days and three nights in the heart of the earth (Mt. 12:40; see also Mt. 26:61; 27:63). Jesus led captivity captive and ascended, giving gifts unto men (Eph. 4:8-9). Our victorious Lord made the devil squirm like a fish for three-and-one-half years, then cut off his head and his hands at Calvary—only the "stump" was left (1 Sam. 5:4; see also Col. 2:15; Heb. 2:14)! John declared, "For this purpose the Son of God was manifested, that He might destroy the works of the devil" (1 Jn. 3:8b). Moses' song foretold Messiah's triumph, "Thy right hand, O Lord, is become glorious in power: Thy right hand, O Lord, hath dashed in pieces the enemy" (Ex. 15:6; see also Mt. 28:18; Eph. 1:20; Heb. 12:2).

Applied to the Christian ⚖

Believers are not to give place to the devil by worshiping other gods (Ex. 20:3-5; Eph. 4:27). Christians are the temple of the living God, and are to have no fellowship with unrighteousness, no communion with darkness (2 Cor. 6:14-16). We are to abstain from idolatry, part of "the works of the flesh" (Gal. 5:19-21; compare Acts 15:20). The apostle John confirmed, "Little children, keep yourselves from idols…" (1 Jn. 5:21). Like the Ark of the Lord, let us "…cut off the pride of the Philistines" (Zech. 9:6; see also Prov. 16:18; 1 Jn. 2:16). Satan may be the "god of this world" (2 Cor. 4:4), but he's not the god of our world!

Go Deeper 📖

See 1 Sam. 15:23; Ps. 78:61; 96:5; 97:7; 106:36; 115:4; Dan. 1:2; Joel 3:5; Hab. 1:11; Zech. 10:2; 13:2; Lk. 11:22; Jn. 12:31; 16:11; 19:30; Acts 15:29; 17:16; 21:25; 1 Cor. 8:1,4; 10:14; 12:2; Col. 3:5; 1 Thess. 1:9; Jas. 4:7; Rev. 2:14,20; 9:20.

∞ ∞ ∞

𝔇ainties

That which is delightsome or desirous

Key Scriptures: Gen. 49:20; Ps. 40:7-8; Mal. 3:12; Rom. 7:22.

Foundational Information ✐

There are different Hebrew words for "dainties." *Ma'adan* (Strong's #4574) means "a delicacy or (abstractly) pleasure (adverbially, cheerfully)." *Ta'avah* (Strong's #8378) means "a longing; by implication, a delight (subjectively, satisfaction)," and comes from a root that means "to wish for." Other Hebrew roots for "dainty" mean "to be agreeable" and "to taste; figuratively, to perceive." The Greek word for "dainty" is *liparos* (Strong's #3045), which means "grease, fat, (figuratively) sumptuous." *Liparos* also signifies "oily, or anointed with oil." It is derived from *lipos* ("grease") and connected with *aleipho* ("to anoint"); it is used of things that pertain to delicate and sumptuous living.

Fulfilled in Christ ☀

Jesus Christ, the Bread of life (Jn. 6:48), is the Messiah ("the anointed One"), the royal Dainty from Heaven who delighted to do the will of the Father (Gen. 49:20; Ps. 40:7-8). The Son, the Wisdom from above (Jas. 3:17; see also 1 Cor. 1:30), was daily the "delight" of His Father (Prov. 8:30). Jesus is the genuine Vine (Jn. 15:1-5), the Tree of life, mankind's only true desire (Prov. 13:12). He is the Messenger of the New Covenant in whom we delight (Mal. 3:1). Jesus, the Messiah, "the desire of all nations," has come (Hag. 2:7).

Applied to the Christian ⚖

As with the Psalmists, true believers:

1. Delight in the law of the Lord (Ps. 1:2).
2. Delight in the Lord (Ps. 37:4).
3. Delight in the abundance of peace (Ps. 37:11).
4. Delight in His comforts (Ps. 94:19).
5. Delight in His statutes, testimonies, and commandments (Ps. 119:16, 24, 35, 47).

"The desire of the righteous" is granted (Prov. 10:24) as we "delight in the law of God after the inward man" (Rom. 7:22). Our inheritance is a "delightsome land" (Mal. 3:12), the "heavenly places" of the New Testament (Eph. 1:3; 2:6). Negatively, we are to avoid the sweet pleasures of sin (Heb. 11:25). Christians are not to eat the dainties of wicked men who work iniquity (Ps. 141:4). Like the aged Isaac, men can be blinded by the taste of "savoury meat" (Gen. 27:4), the works of the flesh, the traditional dainties of religious Babylon (Rev. 18:14; see also Gal. 5:19-21).

Go Deeper 📖

See Ex. 20:17; 1 Sam. 15:22; Neh. 9:35; Job 22:26; 33:20; 38:31; Ps. 10:17; 16:3; 21:2; 38:9; 62:4; 68:30; Prov. 11:23; 13:19; 23:3,6; 29:17; Song 2:3; 7:6; Is. 1:11; 26:8; 30:23; 55:2; 58:3; Jer. 9:24; Lam. 4:5; Rom. 7:7; 13:9; 1 Cor. 12:31; 14:39.

∾ ∾ ∾

Damascus

Religious and intellectual pride

Key Scriptures: Gen. 15:2; Prov. 16:18; Acts 9:1-27; 17:16-23; 2 Cor. 10:3-5.

Foundational Information 📎

Damascus, the oldest continually-inhabited city in the world, is the capital of Syria. "Syria" means "highland, elevated, a citadel (from its height)." "Damascus" is from the Hebrew *Dammeseq* and the Greek *Damaskos*. Of foreign origin, "Damascus" has been rendered as "activity, alertness (with reference to trade or possessions); sack of blood, red sack, red sackcloth; silent is the sackcloth weaver." Three major caravan routes through Damascus made it become a trade center. Syria came to power shortly after David's rule, and the Syrians were later Israel's enemies. All references to Damascus in the New Testament are associated with the apostle Paul's conversion and ministry.

Fulfilled in Christ ☦

Jesus Christ went to Damascus to encounter Saul of Tarsus, a proud man who personified religious intellectualism (Acts 9:5,17). Our Savior is the "light from heaven" who has conquered the dark ignorance of man's wisdom (Acts 9:3; see also Jn. 8:12; Acts 22:11; 1 Jn. 1:5). He is the heavenly David who subdued the citizens of Damascus (2 Sam. 8:5-6). Jesus, the true "wisdom that is from above" (Jas. 3:17; see also 1 Cor. 1:30), has been exalted above all religious and intellectual activity (Acts 17:16-23; Col. 2:8,16-23). The Last Adam identified with the first man Adam—who was "a sack of blood"—and overcame all things (1 Cor. 15:44-49; see also Heb. 4:15; Rev. 3:21).

Applied to the Christian ⚖

The first man Adam is but "a sack of blood." As new creatures, "Abraham's seed" (Gal. 3:29), we now understand that God's promise can never be produced by any religious or intellectual activity that comes out of the lower nature (Gen. 15:2). We cast down imaginations and every "high thing that exalteth itself" against the knowledge of God (2 Cor. 10:5). A religious spirit of antichrist opposes and exalts itself above all that is called God (2 Thess. 2:3-4). We are not to make agreements with the pride of Damascus (1 Kings 15:18-20). As the Bride of Christ, we must discern (with the "nose" of Song of Solomon 7:4) what took place on the highway to Damascus (Acts 9:1-27). Christians are to beware the "couch" of Damascus (Amos 3:12; see also Amos 6:1). Solomon cautioned, "Pride goeth before destruction, and an haughty spirit before a fall" (Prov. 16:18).

Damascus has also been translated as "silent is the sackcloth weaver." Saul, who became the Apostle Paul, was the epitome of religious and intellectual pride prior to his conversion (Phil. 3:4-7). Like Paul, we have been delivered from the deadly sackcloth and ashes of the law into the wonderful liberty of the grace of God (Rom. 8:1-2; 2 Cor. 3:12-17; Gal. 5:1). The literary apostle was transformed from making natural tents (Acts 18:1-3) to weaving a true understanding of our robes of righteousness (Rev. 6:11; 7:9-14; 19:8,14).

Go Deeper 📖

See Gen. 14:15; 2 Sam. 8:5-6; 1 Kings 19:15; 2 Kings 8:7; 2 Chron. 24:23; Prov. 17:19; Is. 7:8; 17:1-3; Jer. 49:23-27; Ezek. 27:18; 47:16-18; 48:1; Amos 1:3-5; 5:27; Zech. 9:1; Mk. 7:22; Acts 22:5-11; 26:12,20; 2 Cor. 11:32; Gal. 1:17; 1 Tim. 3:6; 1 Jn. 2:16.

∞   ∞   ∞

𝕯𝖆𝖓

Judge; judgment

Key Scriptures: Gen. 30:1-6; 49:16-18; Ex. 28:20; Deut. 33:22; Ps. 75:7; Jn. 5:22; 7:24; 1 Cor. 6:1-3.

Foundational Information ✎

Dan was the fifth son of Jacob and the first born to Rachel's handmaid Bilhah. "Dan" is transliterated from the Hebrew *Dan* (Strong's #1835) and means "judge." It is akin to *diyn* (Strong's #1777), which means "a straight course, sail direct." "Dan" has also been rendered as "rule of righteous judgment, a defender, an advocate." The name of the tribe of Dan was engraved upon the tenth stone (beryl) of the high priest's breastplate.

Fulfilled in Christ ✝

Jesus Christ is the Judge of all the earth (Gen. 18:25; see also Judg. 11:27; Ps. 75:7; Jn. 5:22). John declared, "...We have an Advocate with the Father, Jesus Christ the righteous"

(1 Jn. 2:1). The "gospel of God" (Rom. 1:1) is the judgment written—the Scriptures—the criterion of all judgment, the infallible rule of faith and practice. The "gospel of His Son" is the judgment personified in the Lord Jesus, the Word made flesh; His life is now the standard by which all men are to be judged (Rom. 1:9). The "gospel of [the] Christ" is His Body's execution of the judgment which He is (Rom. 1:16; see also 1 Jn. 4:17). Jesus did not tell us not to judge, but how to judge (Mt. 7:1-5; see also Jn. 7:24).

Applied to the Christian ⚖

Judgment is past—our sins were judged in Christ (Jn. 19:30), presently progressive (1 Cor. 11:28-32), and future (Rom. 14:10-12; see also 2 Cor. 5:10). The Church, conformed to the image of her glorious Head, will judge the world and judge angels (1 Cor. 6:1-3). The standard of the camp of Dan was on the "north side" (Num. 2:25)—judgment flows from Zion (Ps. 48:2). Judgment must begin "at" (*apo*, or "away from") the House of God, the Church (1 Pet. 4:17; compare Heb. 12:22-23). In the Old Testament, priests were judges (Deut. 17:9); in the New Testament, the Church is a priesthood of believers, destined to be "...perfectly joined together in the same mind and in the same judgment" (1 Cor. 1:10; see also 1 Pet. 2:9).

Go Deeper 📖

See Gen. 14:14; 35:25; 46:23; Ex. 1:4; 31:6; Num. 26:42; Josh. 19:40-48; Judg. 1:34; 2:18-19; 1 Sam. 3:20; 1 Kings 4:25; 12:29-30; 2 Kings 10:29; 1 Chron. 2:2; 27:22; 2 Chron. 2:14; 30:5; Jer. 4:15; 8:16; Ezek. 48:1-2; Amos 8:14; Mt. 5:25; Acts 10:42; Rom. 2:1-5; Phil. 1:9; Heb. 6:2; 9:27; 10:27; Jas. 5:9; Rev. 14:7; 20:4.

∞ ∞ ∞

𝕯𝖆𝖓𝖈𝖎𝖓𝖌

Celebration, jubilation

Key Scriptures: 2 Sam. 6:14; Ps. 30:11; 149:3; 150:4; Eccles. 3:4; Lk. 15:25.

Foundational Information ✐

Dancing is the rhythmic movement of the body, usually done with musical accompaniment, such as the tambourine. Dancing was not meant to be a sensual art form; rather it was to be an act of worship, a celebration of joy. The original Hebrew words reveal that this dancing involved skipping about, whirling, and leaping. *Chuwl* (Strong's #2342) means "to twist or whirl (in a circular or spiral manner), (specifically) to dance." *Raqad* (Strong's #7540) means "to stamp, to spring about (wildly or for joy)." It is rendered in the King James Version as "dance, jump, leap, skip." The Greek *orcheomai* (Strong's #3738) means "(a row or ring); to dance (from the ranklike or regular motion)." Compare the English *orchestra*. It probably originally signified "to lift up," as of the feet; hence, "to leap with regularity of motion." Another Greek word, *choros* (Strong's #5525), primarily denoted "an enclosure for dancing"; hence, "a company of dancers and singers." Compare the English *chorus*.

Fulfilled in Christ   ✝

Jesus Christ is the heavenly David, our King-priest, who rejoiced before Jehovah with all His might (2 Sam. 6:14; see also Ps. 18:29,33-36). His joy is our strength (Neh. 8:10). Our glorious King is to be praised as His people sing to one another of Him and dance before Him (1 Sam. 21:11). His eternal victory over sin and satan has turned earth's mourning into dancing (Ps. 30:11; see also Is. 61:1-3). His blood has redeemed the lost sheep, the lost coin, and the lost son; because of His finished work, the house of the Father is filled with "musick and dancing" (Lk. 15:25). The voice of our beloved Savior comes "leaping" upon the mountains and "skipping" upon the hills (Song 2:8). The Word walks on the stormy waters of life (Mt. 14:25-26).

Applied to the Christian   ⚖

The saints are exhorted by the psalmist, "Let them praise His name in the dance...Praise Him with the timbrel and dance..." (Ps. 149:3; 150:4). As exampled by Miriam, the prophetic ministry is expressed in the dance following great victories (Ex. 15:20). For individuals, families, and local churches, such seasons are "a time to dance" (Eccles. 3:4). Jeremiah prophesied of these New Testament days, "Then shall the virgin rejoice in the dance, both young men and old together: for I will turn their mourning into joy, and will comfort them, and make them rejoice from their sorrow" (Jer. 31:13). Michal, David's wife, is a picture of local churches who were birthed in an old order (Saul's house)—those who despise dancing become barren (2 Sam. 6:16-23).

Go Deeper   📖

See Ex. 32:19; Judg. 11:34; 21:21-23; 1 Sam. 18:6; 29:5; 30:16; 1 Chron. 15:29; Neh. 12:27,43; Job 21:11; Ps. 28:7; 29:6; 51:8; 118:15; Is. 13:21; 35:6; 38:20; 43:19; 55:12; 61:11; Jer. 31:4; Lam. 5:15; Mt. 11:17; 14:6; Mk. 6:22; Lk. 6:23; 7:32; Acts 3:8-9; 14:10.

∞   ∞   ∞

𝔇aniel

A judge who interprets divine secrets; Kingdom-seer

Key Scriptures: Ezek. 14:14,20; 28:3; Dan. 1–12; Mt. 24:15; Mk. 13:14.

Foundational Information ✐

Daniel, author of the Old Testament book that bears his name, ministered for 60 years during the period of the captivity of God's people in Babylon and Persia. "Daniel" is derived from the Hebrew *Daniye'l* (Strong's #1840) and means "judge of God." *'El* (Strong's #410) means "strength; mighty; a ram; a pilaster; an oak." "Daniel" has also been rendered as "God is my Judge, the judgment of God."

Fulfilled in Christ ☼

The heavenly Daniel brought faith, grace, and truth (Jn. 1:17); He interpreted the Father and dissolved every doubt (Dan. 5:12-17). Jesus is the Judge (Jn. 5:22), the Wisdom that is from above (Jas. 3:17; see also 1 Cor. 1:30). Typified by the integrity of the ancient prophet, He is the King of righteousness (Heb. 7:2; see also Ezek. 14:14,20; 28:3). Jesus has been crowned with glory, honor, and favor (Heb. 2:9; see also Dan. 1:9; 6:2). This Revealer of secrets is the King of kings and the Lord of lords (Rev. 19:16; see also Dan. 2:47). He is "chief of the governors" (Dan. 2:48), set over the whole realm of the Kingdom (Dan. 6:3). As with the prophet (Dan. 6:4), there was "no fault" found in Jesus (Lk. 23:4; Jn. 18:38). Daniel was thrown into a den of lions sealed with a stone (Dan. 6:16-23); Jesus was placed in a tomb sealed with a stone (Mt. 27:57-66). The archangel Gabriel, who announced Jesus' birth to Mary, prophesied Jesus' death to Daniel (Dan. 9:20-27; Lk. 1:19,26)! The Old Testament Daniel sealed up the book (Dan. 12:4); the worthy Lamb of the New Covenant has prevailed to open the book and loose its seals (Rev. 5:1-5).

Applied to the Christian ⚖

Through the power of the same Spirit that energized Daniel (Dan. 1:17), Christians can interpret the mysteries of God, being filled with supernatural knowledge and wisdom (1 Cor. 12:8-10). The Spirit of the Son has been sent into our hearts (Gal. 4:6; see also Dan. 4:8; Col. 1:27). We are not to defile ourselves at the table of the world (Dan. 1:8). Like Daniel, we are to pray without ceasing (Dan. 6:10-13; 1 Thess. 5:17). We serve the "living God" whose Kingdom shall not be destroyed (Dan. 6:26; see also Heb. 12:26-28), the One who works signs and wonders in Heaven and in earth (Dan. 6:27; see also Mk. 15:16-20). We are the "saints of the most High" who shall "possess the Kingdom" and be given dominion (Dan. 7:18-27; see also Gen. 1:26-28; 22:17; Rev. 2:26-28).

Go Deeper 📖

See Gen. 40:5-8; 41:1-16; Deut. 29:29; Judg. 7:15; 1 Sam. 3:7,21; Job 15:8; 29:4; Ps. 25:14; 81:7; Prov. 1:6; 3:32; Eccles. 8:1; Jer. 33:6; Amos 3:7; Mt. 11:25-27; 16:17; Jn. 7:10; Rom. 1:17; 16:25; 1 Cor. 2:9-10; 12:30; 14:5,13,26-28; Gal. 1:16; 3:23; Eph. 3:5; Phil. 3:15; 1 Pet. 1:5; 2 Pet. 1:20.

∞ ∞ ∞

𝔇arkness

Ignorance, mourning, perplexity, death; God's dwelling-place

Key Scriptures: 1 Kings 8:12; Ps. 97:2; Acts 26:18; Rom. 13:12; 1 Pet. 2:9.

Foundational Information ✐

Darkness is the absence of light. "Darkness" is from the Hebrew *choshek* (Strong's #2822) which means "the dark; hence (literally) darkness; figuratively, misery, destruction, death, ignorance, sorrow, wickedness." Two related Old Testament words are *'araphel* (Strong's #6205), which means "gloom (as of a lowering sky)" and comes from a root meaning "to droop; hence, to drip"; and *'aphel* (Strong's #651), meaning "to set as the sun; dusky." In the New Testament, "darkness" is from the Greek *skoteinos* (Strong's #4652), which means "opaque, (figuratively) benighted." It is taken from *skotos* (Strong's #4655), meaning "shadiness, obscurity (literally or figuratively)." To the Oriental mind, light is an object of desire, and darkness something to be greatly dreaded: A lamp is usually kept burning in the Eastern house all night.

Fulfilled in Christ ✝

Jesus Christ is the Light of the world (Jn. 8:12; see also John 1:5; 3:19; 12:46); in Him is no darkness at all (1 Jn. 1:5). The light of the knowledge of God's glory is revealed in the face of Jesus Christ (2 Cor. 4:6). Jesus fulfilled Isaiah's Messianic prophecy, "The people that walked in darkness have seen a great light" (Is. 9:2a; see also Mt. 4:16). He is typified by the glory cloud of the Exodus, which was darkness to the Egyptians but light to the children of God (Num. 9:15-23). From another perspective, the Lord dwells in the thick darkness (1 Kings 8:12); the Psalmist declared, "Clouds and darkness are round about Him: righteousness and judgment are the habitation of His throne" (Ps. 97:2). This divine light of the Most Holy Place seems like darkness to the natural mind (1 Cor. 2:14).

Applied to the Christian ⚖

Believers are the light of the world, sons of the day who are to have no fellowship with the unfruitful works of darkness (Mt. 5:14; Eph. 5:8-11). The Lord has brought us out of the chaos of the land of darkness and the shadow of death (Job 10:21-22; see also Lk. 1:79; Acts 26:18; Col. 1:13; 1 Pet. 2:9). Because of religious traditions (Mk. 7:13), men cannot order their speech by reason of darkness (Job 37:19). Solomon explained, "The way of the wicked is as darkness: they know not at what they stumble" (Prov. 4:19). The Day of the Lord is day (light) and night (darkness) at the same time: Isaiah explained, "For, behold, the darkness shall cover the earth, and gross darkness the people: but the Lord shall arise upon thee, and His glory shall be seen upon thee" (Is. 60:2; see also Joel 2:2; Mal. 4:1-2). He who hates his brother walks in darkness (1 Jn. 2:11). Paul taught, "The night is far spent, the day is at hand: let us therefore cast off the works of darkness, and let us put on the armour of light" (Rom. 13:12).

Go Deeper 📖

See Gen. 1:2-5; 15:12; Ex. 10:21; Deut. 4:11; 5:22; 28:29; Josh. 24:7; 2 Sam. 22:10-12; 2 Chron. 6:1; Ps. 18:28; 82:5; 91:6; 107:10; 112:4; 139:12; Prov. 13:9; 20:20; Eccles. 2:14; 6:4; Is. 5:20; 42:7; 45:3; 47:5; 58:10; Dan. 2:22; Amos 5:18; Zeph. 1:15; Mt. 6:23; 8:12; 27:45; Acts 13:11; 2 Cor. 6:14; Eph. 6:12; 1 Thess. 5:4-5.

∞ ∞ ∞

𝔇arts

Devilish accusations; condemnation

Key Scriptures: Jn. 3:17; Rom. 8:1; Eph. 6:16; Heb. 12:20; Rev. 12:10.

Foundational Information ✐

"Darts" refers to javelins or spears—weapons with a long, slender shaft and a metal point. There are different Hebrew words translated in the King James Version as "dart." *Shebet* (Strong's #7626) means "to branch off; a scion, a stick," and is the Hebrew word for "rod, tribe." *Shelach* (Strong's #7973) means "a missile of attack, spear." *Chets* (Strong's #2671) means "a piercer, an arrow; by implication, a wound." The Greek word for "dart" is *belos* (Strong's #956) and means "a missile, spear or arrow." It comes from the primary verb *ballo* (Strong's #906), which means "to throw" (with violence and intensity). "Fiery darts" (Eph. 6:16) were hollow reeds filled with combustible material and then shot from bows.

Fulfilled in Christ 🕇

Paul declared, "There is therefore now no condemnation to them which are in Christ Jesus…" (Rom. 8:1; see also Jn. 5:24). Jesus Christ came not to condemn the world but to destroy the works of the devil, the "accuser" of the brethren (Rev. 12:10; see also Jn. 3:17; 1 Jn. 3:8). He says to all who come to Him, "Neither do I condemn thee; go, and sin no more" (Jn. 8:11b). Jesus mediated grace and truth; the law came through Moses (Jn. 1:17). That first mountain (Sinai) was marked by the administration of condemnation of that law (2 Cor. 3:9; see also Jn. 5:45; Heb. 12:20). Jesus taught that the tongue is a creative force, "For by thy words thou shalt be justified, and by thy words thou shalt be condemned" (Mt. 12:37; see also Prov. 18:21; Is. 57:19).

Applied to the Christian ⚖

Believers are to wear the shield of faith, whereby we are to quench all the "fiery darts" of the wicked one (Eph. 6:16). The prophet Joel foresaw the unity of the end-time Church, "Neither shall one thrust another; they shall walk every one in his path: and when they fall upon the sword, they shall not be wounded" (Joel 2:8). Those who shoot darts at their brethren commit the abomination of condemnation (Prov. 17:15). But those who hear and believe Him shall not come into condemnation, but have passed from death unto life (Jn. 5:24; see also Rom. 14:22). The psalmist pictured the wicked as those "…whose teeth are spears and arrows, and their tongue a sharp sword" (Ps. 57:4). Solomon described these accusers as men who bear false witness against their neighbors (Prov. 25:18).

Go Deeper 📖

See 2 Sam. 18:14; 2 Chron. 32:5; Job 41:26,29; Ps. 64:3; 91:5; Prov. 7:23; 26:18; 30:10; Dan. 6:24; Mt. 12:10; 27:12,37; Mk. 3:2; 15:3; Lk. 3:14; 23:10-14; Jn. 3:19; Rom. 5:16-18; 8:34; Acts 22:30; 24:2; 26:7; 1 Tim. 3:6; 5:19; Tit. 1:6; Jas. 5:12; 1 Pet. 3:16; 1 Jn. 3:20-21.

∞ ∞ ∞

𝔇aughters of 𝔷ion

Local churches

Key Scriptures: Is. 4:3-6; Eph. 5:22-33; Heb. 12:22-23; Rev. 19:7; 21:2,9.

Foundational Information ✎

"Zion" in the Old Testament was the religious (priestly) and political (kingly) center of David's kingdom, and it was a type of the New Testament Church. The Hebrew word for "daughter" is *bath* (Strong's #1323); it is taken from *banah* (Strong's #1129), which means "to build." It is the feminine form of *ben* (Strong's #1121), the Hebrew word for "son." The term "daughters of Zion" is used to describe a circle of female relatives.

Fulfilled in Christ ☥

Jesus Christ is the Head of the woman, the Church, His Bride (Eph. 5:22-33; Rev. 19:7; 21:2,9). With respect to His corporate Body with its many local expressions, He declared, "I will build My Church" (Mt. 16:18). Jeremiah described the Bride of Christ, "I have likened the daughter of Zion to a comely and delicate woman" (Jer. 6:2). Jesus is the "salvation" who has come to us (Is. 62:11; see also Mt. 1:21). He has been given all authority (Mt. 28:18), the "first dominion" (Mic. 4:8). Jesus fulfilled Zechariah's prophecy, "Rejoice greatly, O daughter of Zion; shout, O daughter of Jerusalem: behold, thy King cometh unto thee: He is just, and having salvation; lowly, and riding upon an ass, and upon a colt the foal of an ass" (Zech. 9:9; see also Mt. 21:4-5).

Applied to the Christian ⚖

The writer to the Hebrews proclaims a New Testament people to be as Mount Sion, the city of the living God, the heavenly Jerusalem—"the Church of the firstborn" (Heb. 12:22-23; see also Gal. 4:21-31). Every believer who is a part of Christ's universal Body should be a functioning member of a local body, a local church (1 Cor. 12:12-27). We are not to forsake the assembling of ourselves together (Heb. 10:25). Christians show forth His praise in the gates of their gatherings (Ps. 9:14; see also Zeph. 3:14), for He has redeemed us from the hand of our enemies (Mic. 4:10; see also Gal. 3:13-14). Isaiah described this season of the Church's restoration as a time "when the Lord shall have washed away the filth of the daughters of Zion, and shall have purged the blood of Jerusalem from the midst thereof by the spirit of judgment, and by the spirit of burning" (Is. 4:4).

Go Deeper 📖

See 2 Kings 19:21; Song 3:11; Is. 3:16-17; 10:32; 16:1; 37:22; 52:2; 61:10; Jer. 2:32; 4:31; 6:23; 33:11; Lam. 1:6; 2:1,4,8,10,13,18; 4:22; Joel 2:16,28; Mic. 1:13; 4:13; Zeph. 3:14; Zech. 2:10; Lk. 1:5; 23:28; Acts 2:17; 21:9; 2 Cor. 6:18; Rev. 22:17.

∞ ∞ ∞

𝔇𝔞𝔳𝔦𝔡

Jesus Christ, the Shepherd-king, the King of kings

Key Scriptures: Ruth 4:17,22; 1 Sam. 16–31; 2 Sam. 1–24; 1 Kings 1–2; 1 Chron. 10–29; Mt. 28:18; Lk. 1:30-33; Jn. 10:1-11; Rev. 3:7; 5:5; 22:16.

Foundational Information ✐

David was the second king of the United Kingdom of the Hebrew people, ancestor of Jesus Christ, and writer of numerous psalms. "David" is transliterated from the Hebrew *Daviyd* (Strong's #1732) and means "loving." It is taken from an unused root meaning "to boil, (figuratively) to love; by implication, a lovetoken, lover, friend." "David" is translated in the King James Version as "(well-) beloved, father's brother, love, uncle."

David grew up in Bethlehem-Judah as the youngest of Jesse's eight sons. A keeper of sheep and a talented minstrel, he was anointed by the prophet Samuel to be King Saul's successor. The lad David slew the giant Goliath, champion of the Philistines. Saul's ensuing jealousy forced David to leave the royal court to become a fugitive and exile. This rejected heir proved his greatness by a godly attitude toward his enemies, sparing Saul on two occasions. After Saul's sad death at the hand of the Philistines, the tribe of Judah (first at Hebron) and eventually all Israel crowned David king. The new monarch established his capital at Jerusalem and brought the Ark of the Covenant to Mount Zion. This great king later strayed in his sin with Bathsheba and through engineering the consequent death of her Hittite husband Uriah. He reaped the folly of this sin in his sons with Amnon's violation of Tamar and Absalom's consequent revenge and open rebellion. David prepared for the building of the Temple before his death. The sweet psalmist of Israel wrote almost half the Book of Psalms. Much more could be said about:

1. The house of David (2 Sam. 3:1).
2. The city of David (2 Sam. 5:7).
3. The throne of David (1 Kings 2:24).
4. The way of David (2 Kings 22:2).
5. The acts of David (1 Chron. 29:29).
6. The instruments of David (Neh. 12:36).
7. The prayers of David (Ps. 72:20).
8. The horn of David (Ps. 132:17).
9. The tower of David (Song 4:4).
10. The tabernacle of David (Is. 16:5).
11. The sure mercies of David (Is. 55:3).
12. The key of David (Rev. 3:7).

Fulfilled in Christ ☀

Jesus Christ is the greatest "son of David" (Mt. 1:1), the shepherd-king (Jn. 10:1-11). Our "great shepherd" (Heb. 13:20) and "chief shepherd" (1 Pet. 5:4) is the royal Seed who was appointed "heir of all things" (Heb. 1:2) according to the Davidic Covenant of Second Samuel 7 and First Chronicles 17. This great covenant of kingship, based on a father-son relationship, establishes the Lord Jesus Christ as the ultimate Ruler of the earth, providing Him:

1. A house—a posterity, family (Mt. 1:1,16).
2. A throne—a royal position and authority (Rev. 3:21).
3. A kingdom—a sphere of rule (Rom. 14:17; Eph. 1:20-23).
4. Forever—without cessation (Is. 9:6-7; Lk. 1:31-33).

Jesus is "King of kings, and Lord of lords" (Rev. 19:16), the "...root and the off-spring of David, and the bright and morning star" (Rev. 22:16). The "Lion of the tribe of Juda" has prevailed over all enemies (Rev. 5:5). The Messiah has been given all executive authority in Heaven and in earth (Mt. 28:18). He has inherited the throne of David, and of His Kingdom there shall be no end (Lk. 1:32-33). As with David (Ps. 89:20), King Jesus has been anointed with the oil of gladness above His fellows (Heb. 1:9). He fulfilled the type of David's three-fold anointing (Prov. 22:20): as exalted son (1 Sam. 16:13; Mt. 3:17; 17:5), as king over Judah (2 Sam. 2:4; Mt. 2:6; Heb. 7:14), and as head over all things (2 Sam. 5:3; Eph. 1:22; Col. 1:18). Isaiah heralded Jesus' reign, "Of the increase of His government and peace there shall be no end, upon the throne of David, and upon His kingdom, to order it, and to establish it with judgment and with justice..." (Is. 9:7).

Applied to the Christian   ⚖

Like Jesus, the Church is the seed of Abraham and the seed of David (Mt. 1:1; 1 Jn. 4:17). In Christ, we have been made kings unto God (Rev. 1:6; 5:10) and given the right-ful privilege to become the sons of God (Jn. 1:12). The "throne" of the Davidic Covenant is the legal authority to rule in the name of the Lord Jesus Christ (see Mt. 10:1; Mk. 16:15-20; Lk. 9:1-2; 10:19). The Church (His called-out ones) is the New Testament ful-fillment of the Tabernacle of David—"a people for His name" (Acts 15:14; compare Amos 9:11; Acts 15:16). We are the many-membered "Branch of righteousness" who are to grow up to the stature of our heavenly King (Jer. 33:15; see also Jn. 15:1-5; Eph. 4:13-16). Like David, we are to be men and women after God's own heart, those who fulfill His will (Acts 13:22). Our ultimate destiny as the "house of David" is to be conformed to the likeness of God (Zech. 12:8; see also Rom. 8:29; 1 Cor. 15:49; 2 Cor. 3:18; 1 Jn. 3:2).

Go Deeper   📖

See 1 Kings 2:4; 1 Chron. 22:8-10; 2 Chron. 7:17-18; Ps. 18:50; 72:20; 78:70; 89:1; 122:5; 132:11; Is. 11:1-10; Jer. 23:5-6; 33:21-26; Amos 6:5; Zech. 3:8-9; 6:12-13; 9:10; 13:1; Mt. 9:27; 15:22; 20:30-31; 21:9; Lk. 1:27,69; 3:31; Jn. 7:42; Acts 1:16; 2:34-36; 4:25; 7:45; Rom. 1:3; 4:6; 11:9; 2 Tim. 2:8; Heb. 4:7; 11:32.

∞ ∞ ∞

𝔇𝔞𝔴𝔫 (𝔇𝔞𝔶𝔰𝔭𝔯𝔦𝔫𝔤)

A new day, new hope, new promise

Key Scriptures: Job 38:12; Is. 60:1; Lk. 1:78-79; 2 Pet. 1:19.

Foundational Information ✎

Dawn is the first appearance of light in the morning as the sun rises. "Dawn" is from the Hebrew *'alah* (Strong's #5927), which means "to ascend." This is the same word used to describe the "burnt offering," and it is akin to *El-Elyon*, the "Most High God." Other Old Testament words for "dawn" are *panah* ("to turn, to face"), *'aph'aph* ("an eyelash, as fluttering; morning ray"), and *nesheph* ("a breeze"). Two New Testament words for "dawn" are *epiphosko* (Strong's #2020), which means "to begin to grow light;" and *diaugazo* (Strong's #1306), which means "to glimmer through" or "to shine through."

The Hebrew word for "dayspring" is taken from the root *shachar* (Strong's #7836), which means "to dawn, (figuratively) be (up) early at any task (with the implication of earnestness); by extension, to search for (with painstaking)." The Greek word for "dayspring" is *anatole* (Strong's #395), which means "a rising of light, dawn; by implication, the east." *Anatole* also means "a rising up" or "a shoot, branch," and is so used in the Septuagint (Jer. 23:5; Zech. 6:12).

Fulfilled in Christ ☦

Jesus Christ is the "day star" (2 Pet. 1:19), the "Sun of righteousness" who arises with healing in His rays (Mal. 4:2), the "light of the world" (Jn. 8:12). Zacharias, the father of John the Baptist, described Him as "the dayspring from on high" who has mercifully visited this planet "to give light" to them who sit in darkness (Lk. 1:78-79). The wise men followed His star in the east (Mt. 2:1-9). Jesus rose from the dead "as it began to dawn toward the first day of the week" (Mt. 28:1). He was the first to rise from the dead to show light to all the nations (Acts 26:23). Heaven's "dayspring" was under the commandment of the Father (Job 38:12; see also Jn. 8:29; Heb. 5:7-9). Hosea prophesied that His "...going forth is prepared as the morning" (Hos. 6:3a).

Applied to the Christian ⚖

Peter admonished, "We have also a more sure word of prophecy; whereunto ye do well that ye take heed, as unto a light that shineth in a dark place, until the day dawn, and the day star arise in your hearts" (2 Pet. 1:19). The glorious Church is arising in the earth, conformed to His image, "clear as the sun" (Song 6:10). This great army of people is like "the morning spread upon the mountains" (Joel 2:2). As sons of light, we have begun to arise and shine in this new day (Is. 60:1; Eph. 5:8,14). We are prisoners of new expectation (Zech. 9:12; Col. 1:27). Isaiah prophesied to us, "Then shall thy light break forth as the morning, and thine health shall spring forth speedily: and thy righteousness shall go before thee; the glory of the Lord shall be thy rereward" (Is. 58:8; see also Job 11:17; Ps. 37:6; Prov. 4:18).

Go Deeper 📖

See Gen. 32:24; Num. 2:3; Josh. 6:15; 1 Sam. 9:26; 29:10; Job 3:9; 7:4; 41:18; Ps. 50:1; 57:8; 108:2; 113:3; 119:147; 139:9; Is. 9:2; 45:6; 59:19; Dan. 12:3; Jon. 4:7; Mal. 1:11; Mt. 4:16; 5:16,45; 13:43; 17:2; 24:27; Mk. 16:2; Lk. 23:54; 2 Cor. 4:4-6; Phil. 2:15; Rev. 16:12.

∾ ∾ ∾

Day of Atonement

The cleansing of the Church, individually and corporately

Key Scriptures: Lev. 16:1-34; 23:27-32; Num. 29:7-11; Heb. 8–10.

Foundational Information ✏

The feast Day of Atonement, or Yom Kippur, the tenth day of the seventh month, was the annual cleansing of the nation and the sanctuary, set aside as a day of public fasting and humiliation when Israel sought atonement for its sins. "Atonement" is from the Hebrew *kaphar* (Strong's #3722), which means "to cover (specifically with bitumen); figuratively, to expiate or condone, to placate or cancel." *Kaphar* is translated in the King James Version as "appease, make (an atonement), cleanse, disannul, forgive, be merciful, pacify, pardon, purge (away), put off, (make) reconcile (-liation)."

The high priest who officiated on the Day of Atonement first sanctified himself by taking a ceremonial bath and putting on white linen garments, then made atonement for himself and the other priests by sacrificing a bullock. A goat was chosen for a sin offering, and its blood sprinkled on and about the mercy seat within the veil. The scapegoat, symbolically bearing the sins of the people, was afterward sent into the wilderness.

Fulfilled in Christ ✝

Jesus Christ is our great High Priest (Heb. 5–7) who appeared "…to put away sin by the sacrifice of Himself" (Heb. 9:26). Jesus typifies both goats on the Day of Atonement: He is the Lord's goat who died to reconcile (Heb. 9:1-14; 13:11-13), and the scapegoat who lived to reconcile (Rom. 5:10). He is our sin offering, the Lord's goat, who was killed at the cross (Jn. 3:14-16). Isaiah prophesied of Heaven's scapegoat, "All we like sheep have gone astray; we have turned every one to his own way; and the Lord hath laid on Him the iniquity of us all" (Is. 53:6). The Savior died for our sins and then carried them away (Jn. 1:29). We find joy in God through our Lord Jesus Christ, "…by whom we have now received the atonement" (Rom. 5:11).

Jesus cleansed the temple two times, at the beginning (Jn. 2:13-17) and at the end (Mt. 21:12-14) of His public ministry. Similarly, God cleansed His people at the beginning of this age (during the ministry of Jesus), and He will purify His Church in the Day of Atonement at the end of this age. In His ongoing purposes, the Lord sanctifies the Church by His blood in the Feast of Passover, and then by a baptism of fire in the Feast Day of Atonement (Is. 4:3-6; Mt. 3:11; 20:21-23). The former includes an outward washing with water; the latter, an inward purging with fire (Is. 33:11-14; Heb. 12:29).

Applied to the Christian ⚖

The Day of Atonement was fulfilled historically in Jesus Christ and will be consummated experientially in His Body, the Church. This time of holy convocation was a day of fasting (Acts 27:9)—the afflicting of the soul (intellect, emotions, and will) and the subjugation of the bodily appetites. The Day of Atonement was a time of mourning, humiliation, repentance, purification, cleansing, intercession, and forgiveness.

The overall scheme of the seven Feasts of the Lord (Lev. 23) can be reduced to three: Passover, Pentecost, and Tabernacles. In Passover, Jesus is our Savior (1 Cor. 5:7); in Pentecost, He baptizes us with the Holy Ghost (Acts 1:5; 2:4). In Tabernacles, Jesus is Lord and King over a mature people (Eph. 4:13). Believers are initially cleansed by the blood of the Passover Lamb, but the Church is to be purged in the Feast Day of Atonement, preparing them for the global harvest of Tabernacles and the subsequent coming of the Lord. It is noteworthy that the high priest went beyond the veil that day (the tenth day of the seventh month) with both hands full of incense (Lev. 16:12), a picture of prayer and praise matured within the veil—the Jubilee trumpet blew on the same day every fiftieth year (Lev. 25:8-10; Rom. 8:14-23).

As individuals, our transgression and guilt were transferred to the head of the divine Goat who gave Himself as a ransom for all (Lev. 16:21-22; Gal. 1:4; 1 Tim. 2:6). Moses explained the basis of blood covenant, "For the life of the flesh is in the blood: and I have given it to you upon the altar to make an atonement for your souls: for it is the blood that maketh an atonement for the soul" (Lev. 17:11; see also Heb. 9:22). Like the two goats, there are two kinds of Christians: Some are like the goat for the sin offering, whose blood (or life) was unselfishly poured out for others; others are like the scapegoat, who was dealt with by the breakings of the "wilderness" (Lev. 16:10; see also Hos. 2:3,14; Rev. 12:6,14).

Go Deeper 📖

See Gen. 6:14; 32:20; Ex. 29:33-37; 30:10-16; 32:20; Lev. 1:4; 5:6; 14:18-21,53; 15:15,30; Num. 5:8; 1 Chron. 6:49; 2 Chron. 29:24; Ps. 65:3; 78:38; 79:9; 119:9; Prov. 16:6; Is. 6:7; 58:6-12; Jer. 33:6; Lam. 2:13; Ezek. 36:25; 43:20,26; Dan. 9:24; Joel 3:21; Zech. 12:9-14; 13:1; Mt. 5:48; Jn. 17:20-24; Rom. 6:1-14; 8:2; Gal. 5:24; Eph. 5:25-27; 1 Jn. 3:1-9.

∾ ∾ ∾

𝔇ay of the 𝔏ord

The day of reversals, when the Lord is exalted and all
else is brought low; the day of His vengeance, when
God judges the earth; the third day, the seventh day

Key Scriptures: Ps. 126; Is. 60:1-5; Joel 2:1,11,31; Mal. 4:1-6; 1 Thess. 5:2.

Foundational Information ✐

The Day of the Lord is that season in the overall purposes of God wherein the wisdom and strength of men comes to an end and the Lord reigns supreme. "Day" is from the Hebrew *yowm* (Strong's #3117), which means "to be hot; a day (as the warm hours), whether literal (from sunrise to sunset, or from one sunset to the next), or figurative (a space of time defined by an associated term)." *Yowm* can also mean "daylight; day; time; moment; year." This word represents the period of daylight, as contrasted with nighttime.

"Lord" is from the Hebrew *Yehovah* (Strong's #3068), which means "(the) self-Existent or Eternal; Jehovah, Jewish national name of God." The Greek word for "Lord" is *kurios* (Strong's #2962); it means "supreme in authority, (as noun) controller; by implication, Mr. (as a respectful title)," and is translated in the King James Version as "God, Lord, master, Sir." *Kurios* signifies One with power and authority and could also be rendered as "owner."

Fulfilled in Christ ✝

Jesus is "both Lord and Christ" in the Day of the Lord (Acts 2:36; see also Lk. 2:11). Jesus' finished work reversed the curse (Gal. 3:13-14). His "day" is expressed by the New Testament as:

1. The Day of Christ (Phil. 1:10).
2. The Day of Jesus Christ (Phil. 1:6).
3. The Day of our Lord Jesus Christ (1 Cor. 1:8).
4. The Day of the Lord Jesus (2 Cor. 1:14).
5. The Day of the Lord (1 Thess. 5:2).

One day is with the Lord as a thousand years (2 Pet. 3:8). The Day of the Lord is the "seventh day" (sabbath) from the time of Adam (see Gen. 2:2-3; Ex. 24:16; Josh. 6:15; Heb. 4:4) and the "third day" from Jesus' earthly ministry (see Hos. 6:1-3; Lk. 13:32; Jn. 2:1; 1 Cor. 15:4). The truth of God's Word is revealed in "excellent" or "threefold" things (Prov. 22:20; see also Jn. 17:17). In the Feast of Passover, Jesus is our Savior (Deut. 16:16; Acts 4:12). In the Feast of Pentecost, Jesus is the One who baptizes us with the Holy Ghost (Acts 1:5; 2:4). In the Feast of Tabernacles, within the veil in the Most Holy Place, the realm of maturity, Jesus is Lord (Eph. 4:13; Heb. 6:19-20).

Applied to the Christian ⚖

The Day of the Lord is both "great and terrible" (Joel 2:31), and "great and dreadful" (Mal. 4:5) at the same time, just as there is natural light and darkness in the earth simultaneously (based upon one's relationship to the sun). Both the day and the night belong to the Lord (Ps. 74:16), as confirmed by the prophets (Is. 60:1-5; Joel 2:1-11; Mal. 4:1-6). While there was dense darkness in Egypt, there was light in Goshen (Ex. 10:21-23). The same flood that destroyed wicked men elevated Noah's family to inherit the earth (Gen. 6–8). The same fire that consumed the mighty men of Babylon delivered and promoted the three Hebrew children (Dan. 3).

The key difference is one's relationship to the Son, the "Sun of righteousness" (Mal. 4:2), who said, "I am the light of the world: he that followeth Me shall not walk in darkness, but shall have the light of life" (Jn. 8:12; see also Ps. 27:1; 36:9; Prov. 4:18). Believers are sons of light (Eph. 5:8-14; 1 Thess. 5:1-9). Our focus, emphasis, and vision is expressed by Isaiah, "…Watchman, what of the night? The watchman said, The morning cometh, and also the night" (Is. 21:11-12a). We walk not after the flesh (the darkness), but after the Spirit (the Word) as we fulfill the righteousness of the law (Rom. 8:4).

Go Deeper

See Ex. 12:15-16; 13:6; 16:26-30; Lev. 23:3; Deut. 16:8; 2 Sam. 1:2; Ezra 6:15; Esther 5:1; Is. 2:12; 13:6, 9; Jer. 46:10; Ezek. 13:5; 30:3; 45:20; Joel 1:15; 3:14; Amos 5:18, 20; Obad. 15; Zeph. 1:7,14; Zech. 14:1; Mt. 16:21; Acts 2:20; 1 Cor. 5:5; 2 Pet. 3:10.

∞   ∞   ∞

Daysman (Mediator)

Jesus Christ, the Mediator, Advocate, Intercessor, Judge, and Surety of the New Testament

Key Scriptures: Job 9:33; 16:21; 1 Tim. 2:5; Heb. 8:6; 9:15; 12:24.

Foundational Information

A daysman is a mediator or umpire. "Daysman" is from the Hebrew *yakach* (Strong's #3198), which means "to be right (correct); reciprocal, to argue; causatively, to decide, justify or convict." It is rendered in the King James Version as "argue, chasten, convince, correct (-ion), daysman, dispute, judge, maintain, plead, reason (together), rebuke, reprove (-r)."

"Mediator" is from the Greek word *mesites* (Strong's #3316), which means "a go-between, (simply) an internunciator, or (by implication) a reconciler (intercessor)." *Mesites* is taken from *mesos* ("middle") and *eimi* ("to go"). It speaks of one who mediates between two parties with a view to producing peace, or one who acts as a guarantee to secure something that could not be otherwise obtained.

Fulfilled in Christ

Jesus Christ is the Daysman for whom Job cried, the One who laid His hand on both God and man (Job 9:33). The Word was made flesh and tabernacled "among" us (Jn. 1:14). Paul declared, "For there is one God, and one mediator between God and men, the man Christ Jesus" (1 Tim. 2:5). Jesus brought reconciliation by arbitration; He was "very God" and "very man," fully qualified to represent both parties. Jesus is the "surety" (Heb. 7:22) and "mediator of a better covenant," the New Covenant, guaranteeing its terms for His people (Heb. 8:6; see also Heb. 9:15; 12:24). Moses mediated the law (Gal. 3:19); Jesus came to adjudicate grace and truth (Jn. 1:17).

Applied to the Christian

The ancient patriarch cried, "Surely I would speak to the Almighty, and I desire to reason with God" (Job 13:3)."O that one might plead for a man with God, as a man pleadeth for his neighbour" (Job 16:21)! John affirmed that "we have an advocate with the Father, Jesus Christ the righteous" (1 Jn. 2:1). He ever lives to make intercession for us (Heb. 7:25; see also Rom. 8:26-27,34). Our great High Priest was "...in all points tempted like as we are, yet without sin" (Heb. 4:15; see also Ezek. 3:15; Heb. 2:14-18). The One who reconciled us back to God has committed to the Church the same word and ministry of reconciliation (2 Cor. 5:17-21).

Go Deeper

See Gen. 17:11; 22:4; 26:28; 31:37; 43:9; 44:32; Ex. 19:11; Job 5:17; Ps. 106:23; Prov. 3:12; 25:12; Is. 1:18; 2:4; 11:3-4; 53:12; 59:16; Ezek. 3:15; Amos 5:10; Mic. 4:3; 6:2; Jn. 3:35; 5:22; Acts 10:42; 1 Cor. 10:13; Gal. 3:20; Heb. 9:24.

∞ ∞ ∞

Dead Sea (Salt Sea)

Death; the lowest point; no flow, no life

Key Scriptures: Gen. 14:3; Ezek. 47:8-11; Joel 2:20; Eph. 4:9.

Foundational Information

The Dead Sea is a "salt sea" in southern Palestine at the lowest point on earth— 1,300 feet below sea level. Water flows in but nothing flows out. "Salt" is from the Hebrew *melach* (Strong's #4417), which means "powder, (specifically) salt (as easily pulverized and dissolved)." It is akin to *malach* (Strong's #4408), which means "a rag or old garment," whose root means "to rub to pieces."

Fulfilled in Christ

Jesus Christ, the Word made flesh, descended from Heaven into "...the lower parts of the earth," (Eph. 4:9), the "lowest hell" (Deut. 32:22; Ps. 86:13). He came to loose those who were "appointed to death" (Ps. 102:20), mercifully remembering us in our "low estate" (Ps. 136:23; see also Lk. 1:52). Our Savior "...humbled Himself, and became obedient unto death, even the death of the cross" (Phil. 2:8). Jesus is "the resurrection, and the life" (Jn. 11:25), the One who swallowed up death in victory (Is. 25:8; 1 Cor. 15:51-57). He has "abolished death," and He has brought life and immortality to light through the gospel (2 Tim. 1:10), having tasted the salt of death for every man (Heb. 2:9). Paul declared, "Knowing that Christ being raised from the dead dieth no more; death hath no more dominion over Him...For the law of the Spirit of life in Christ Jesus hath made me free from the law of sin and death" (Rom. 6:9; 8:2).

Applied to the Christian

We have been delivered from the barren desolation and stench of being "dead in trespasses and sins" (Eph. 2:1; see also Ps. 56:13; 116:8; Joel 2:20). Jesus declared that those who heard and believed His word would pass "from death unto life" (Jn. 5:24; see also 1 Jn. 3:14). Those still dead in their sins live in the parched places of the wilderness, in a "salt land" not inhabited by God (Jer. 17:6). The prophet Ezekiel described those areas of our lives that refuse to be impacted by the flow of the living water of the Holy Spirit, "But the miry places thereof and the marishes thereof shall not be healed; they shall be given to salt" (Ezek. 47:11). We are not to be like Lot's wife, who looked back upon worldly things, and "became a pillar of salt" (Gen. 19:26). The redeemed speak words of life, not bitter words like "salt water" (Jas. 3:12). Like the Pattern Son, we are to humbly "condescend to men of low estate" (Rom. 12:16), allowing the "rivers of living water" to flow in and out (Jn. 7:38; see also Song 4:16; Jer. 31:12).

Go Deeper

See Gen. 14:3; Num. 34:3,12; Deut. 3:17; Josh. 3:16; 12:3; 15:2,5; 18:19; Ezek. 47:18; Amos 8:12; Zech. 14:8; Mt. 4:16; Acts 2:24; Rom. 5:10-21; 8:6; 1 Cor. 15:21,26; 2 Cor. 1:10; 2:16; Eph. 5:14; Col. 1:18; Heb. 2:14; 5:7; 9:14-16; 11:5; Jas. 2:20; Rev. 1:18.

∞ ∞ ∞

𝔇eafness

The inability or refusal to hear the voice of God

Key Scriptures: Ex. 4:11; Mt. 13:15; Mk. 7:32-35; Lk. 7:22; 2 Tim. 4:4.

Foundational Information ✎

Deafness is the condition of one who is dull of hearing, unable to hear, or not willing to hear. "Deaf" is from the Hebrew *cheresh* (Strong's #2795), which means "deaf (whether literally or spiritually)." It comes from a root meaning "to fabricate, to devise; hence (from the idea of secrecy) to be silent, to let alone; hence (by implication) to be deaf (as an accompaniment of dumbness)." The Greek word is *kophos* (Strong's #2974), which means "blunted, (figuratively) of hearing (deaf) or speech (dumb)." It comes from the root *kopto* (Strong's #2875), which means "to chop; specially, to beat the breast in grief." Compare *kopiao,* which means "to be tired."

Fulfilled in Christ ✝

Jesus Christ, whose ear was always open to the Father's voice (Ps. 40:6; Is. 50:5; Jn. 8:29), announced, "I can of mine own self do nothing: as I hear, I judge: and My judgment is just; because I seek not mine own will, but the will of the Father which hath sent Me" (Jn. 5:30). The Savior came to make "...both the deaf to hear, and the dumb to speak" (Mk. 7:37). Mark recounts, "And they bring unto Him one that was deaf...And He took him aside from the multitude, and put His fingers into his ears...And straightway his ears were opened..." (Mk. 7:32-35). Jesus also healed a child who was dumb and deaf because of an evil spirit (Mk. 9:17-29). Solomon declared, "The hearing ear, and the seeing eye, the Lord hath made even both of them" (Prov. 20:12).

Applied to the Christian ⚖

Those who are physically deaf can be healed by the power of Jesus' name (Lk. 7:22). Before we were converted and healed of our sins, our spiritual ears were "dull of hearing" (Mt. 13:15; see also Ps. 38:13). But we heard "the words of the book" (the Bible) and were brought out of darkness (Is. 28:18). New Testament priests have blood on their ears (Ex. 29:20; see also Rev. 1:6)! Jeremiah vividly described men who refuse to hear the Word of the Lord as those who "...walk in the imagination of their heart, and walk after other gods, to serve them, and to worship them...which is good for nothing" (Jer. 13:10). The apostle Paul warned, "For the time will come when they will not endure sound doctrine; but after their own lusts heap to themselves teachers, having itching ears; and they shall turn away their ears from the truth, and shall be turned unto fables" (2 Tim. 4:3-4). Amos prophesied of a time in the earth when there would be a famine "...of hearing the words of the Lord" (Amos 8:11).

Go Deeper 📖

See Lev. 19:14; 2 Kings 4:31; Ps. 58:4; 115:6; 135:17; Prov. 28:9; Is. 6:10; 11:3; 33:15; 35:5; 42:18-19; 43:8; Jer. 5:21; 11:10; Ezek. 12:2; Zech. 7:11; Mt. 11:5; 13:13-15; Mk. 4:12; Lk. 16:31; Acts 7:57; 28:27; Rom. 10:17; Gal. 3:2,5; Heb. 5:11; 10:5-9.

∾ ∾ ∾

𝔇eborah

Order; righteous judgment by the wisdom of the Spirit

Key Scriptures: Judg. 4–5; Is. 9:6-7; Jn. 5:30; 1 Cor. 2:9-16; 2 Tim. 4:8; Heb. 11:32.

Foundational Information ✐

Deborah was the fifth judge of Israel, a prophetess and the only female judge. "Deborah" is transliterated from the Hebrew *Debowrah* (Strong's #1682), which means "(in the sense of orderly motion); the bee (from its systematic instincts)." Its root is *dabar* (Strong's #1696), which means "to arrange; but used figuratively (of words), to speak; rarely (in a destructive sense) to subdue." "Deborah" has also been translated as "wasp; a leader of the flock." She was the wife of "Lapidoth," taken from the Hebrew *lappiyd* (Strong's #3940), which means "to shine; a flambeau, lamp or flame," and translated in the King James Version as "(fire-) brand, (burning) lamp, lightning, torch."

Fulfilled in Christ ✝

Jesus Christ is the Bee of Heaven who took the sting out of death (1 Cor. 15:55)! The Lord is the "righteous judge" (2 Tim. 4:8). His Kingdom has been ordered and established with judgment and with justice (Is. 9:7). "Greater than Solomon" (Mt. 12:42), the righteous Judge has a living understanding by the Spirit (Is. 11:3-4; see also Jn. 5:30; 7:24). In the story and song of Deborah, Jesus is revealed as:

1. "The palm tree" under which the prophetess dwelled (Judg. 4:5; see also Ps. 92:12; Song 7:7-8; Jer. 10:5).
2. The "nail" and "hammer" who smote the enemy (Judg. 4:21; see also Judg. 5:26; Jer. 23:29; Zech. 10:4).
3. The heavenly Barak (whose name means "lightning, a flashing sword") who led "captivity captive" (Judg. 5:12; see also Eph. 4:8; Heb. 4:12).
4. "The sun" who went forth in His might (Judg. 5:31; see also Ps. 19:4-5; Mal. 4:2).

Applied to the Christian ⚖

The Church, the Bride of Christ, is married to the heavenly Lapidoth, "the light of the world" (Jn. 8:12; see also Rev. 21:2,9). Like Deborah who sang (Judg. 5:1), we extol our victorious Lord and King (Ps. 98:1; Eph. 5:19). We are to seek Him after the "due order" (1 Chron. 5:13; see also 1 Cor. 14:40). We are to "order" our steps in His Word (Ps. 119:133). The believer is to be busy as a "bee" in diligent, systematic study of the "word of truth" (2 Tim. 2:15; see also Ps. 19:9-11; 119:103; Ezek. 3:3). The Church is destined to judge the world and angels (1 Cor. 6:1-3). Deborah was "a mother in Israel" (Judg. 5:7); the true Church, the heavenly Jerusalem which is above, "is the mother of us all" (Gal. 4:26). The corporate Christ within His people is the "wisdom of God" (1 Cor. 1:24; compare Eph. 3:10; Col. 1:27). The psalmist declared, "The mouth of the righteous speaketh wisdom, and his tongue talketh of judgment" (Ps. 37:30).

Go Deeper 📖

See Gen. 22:9; Ex. 26:17; 27:21; 39:37; 40:4,23; 1 Kings 3:28; 1 Chron. 23:31; 2 Chron. 8:14; Job 10:22; Ps. 9:8; 110:4; Prov. 1:1-5; 2:9; 31:10-31; Is. 56:1; Jer. 33:15; Amos 5:24; Jn. 16:8; Rom. 2:5; 1 Cor. 2:7; 11:34; 15:23; Col. 2:5; 2 Thess. 1:5; Tit. 1:5; Heb. 5:6.

∾ ∾ ∾

Debt

That which is owed to God or man; trespasses, that which needs to be forgiven

Key Scriptures: Lev. 25:10; Deut. 15:1-3; Mt. 6:12; 18:15-35; Lk. 7:36-50; Rom. 1:14.

Foundational Information 📎

Debt is borrowed money or property that a person is bound by law to pay back. Every sabbatical year (seventh year) and year of jubilee (every 50th year), debts were to be forgiven and all pledges or security returned. "Debt" is from the Hebrew *nasha'* (Strong's #5378), which means "to lend on interest; to dun for debt." Compare *nashah* (Strong's #5383) which means "to lend or (by reciprocity) borrow on security or interest," and is rendered in the King James Version as "creditor, exact, extortioner, lend, usurer, lend on (taker on) usury."

The Greek word for "debt" is *opheilema* (Strong's #3783), which means "something owed, (figuratively) a due; morally, a fault." It is akin to *opheilo* (Strong's #3784), which means "to owe (pecuniarily); figuratively, to be under obligation (ought, must, should); morally, to fail in duty." The Mosaic law gave the creditor the right to claim the person and the children of the debtor for service until the Year of Jubilee (Lev. 25:39-41).

Fulfilled in Christ ⅄

Jesus Christ, our Jubilee, paid the sin-debt He did not owe for those who owed a debt they could not pay (Lk. 4:18-19). He is the Pledge and "...surety of a better testament" (Heb. 7:22). The King taught us to pray, "And forgive us our debts, as we forgive our debtors" (Mt. 6:12). Jesus explained about forgiveness and cancelled debts to Simon the Pharisee (Lk. 7:36-50), and later to his disciples with the story of the unjust steward (Lk. 16:1-10). The true meaning of the authority to bind and loose has to do with the power of forgiving men their trespasses (Mt. 18:15-35). Paul revealed, "...God was in Christ, reconciling the world unto Himself, not imputing their trespasses unto them..." (2 Cor. 5:19).

Applied to the Christian ⚖

Those whose lives were marked by distress, debt, and discontent have gathered themselves unto the Captain of their salvation (1 Sam. 22:2; Heb. 2:10). Grateful for being forgiven, we can say with the apostle Paul, "I am debtor both to the Greeks, and to the Barbarians; both to the wise, and to the unwise...Therefore, brethren, we are debtors, not to the flesh, to live after the flesh" (Rom. 1:14; 8:12). We are under obligation to proclaim the gospel with our lips and our lives. The Master taught His disciples, "For if ye forgive men their trespasses, your heavenly Father will also forgive you" (Mt. 6:14). God wants His people to live free of debt. All of creation is groaning for the ultimate year of release from every debt of sin (Rom. 8:19-23).

Go Deeper 📖

See Ex. 22:9,25; Lev. 25:35-38; Deut. 23:19-20; 24:10-11; 2 Kings 4:1-7; Neh. 5:6-13; 10:31; Job 24:9; Ps. 89:22; Prov. 22:26; Eccles. 5:4-5; Is. 24:2; Ezek. 18:1-18; Mt. 5:25-26; 23:16; Mk. 11:25-26; Rom. 4:4; 13:8; 15:27; Gal. 5:3; Eph. 2:1; Col. 2:13; Philem. 19.

∞ ∞ ∞

𝔇eep

Mysterious, profound, unsearchable, hidden things

Key Scriptures: Gen. 1:2; Ps. 36:6; 92:5; Prov. 25:2; Rom. 11:33;
1 Cor. 2:9-10; Eph. 3:8-9,18; Col. 1:26-27; 2:3.

Foundational Information

The "deep" is a vast space, expanse, or abyss. "Deep" is from the Hebrew *tehowm* (Strong's #8415),which means "an abyss (as a surging mass of water), especially the deep (the main sea or the subterranean water-supply)." The Greek word is *bathos* (Strong's #899), which means "profundity, (by implication) extent; (figuratively) mystery." Its root is *basis* (Strong's #939), which means "a pace ('base'), (by implication) the foot." The Greek word for "hidden" is *krupto* and means "to cover, conceal, keep secret." Compare the English *crypt* and *cryptic*.

Fulfilled in Christ

Solomon described the pre-incarnate Christ and the creation of the depths (Prov. 8:24-28). Jesus Christ was the "hidden wisdom" (1 Cor. 2:7) and the "hidden manna" (Rev. 2:17) held deep within the Father's heart until the time of His incarnation. The Father is the deep Thinker who spoke and "the Word was made flesh" (Jn. 1:14). The psalmist revealed Jesus, the personification of the Father's thoughts, "Thy righteousness is like the great mountains; thy judgments are a great deep..." (Ps. 36:6; see also Ps. 92:5; 1 Cor. 1:30). Paul added, "O the depth of the riches both of the wisdom and knowledge of God!..." (Rom. 11:33). In Christ are hidden "...all the treasures of wisdom and knowledge" (Col. 2:3). All the deep is to praise Him (Ps. 148:7). Job said that God does "...great things and unsearchable; great things without number" (Job 5:9).

Applied to the Christian

Deep calls to deep when fervent worshipers commune with a loving God (Ps. 42:7; see also 1 Cor. 14:2). The sovereign God has done whatsoever He has pleased in the "deep places" of our hearts (Ps. 135:6; see also Phil. 2:13). The psalmist David declared, "Behold, thou desirest truth in the inward parts: and in the hidden part thou shalt make me to know wisdom" (Ps. 51:6). Isaiah spoke of these "hidden riches of secret places" (Is. 45:3). When a believer is filled with the Holy Spirit, the "fountains of the great deep" are broken up, and the "windows of heaven" are opened (Gen. 7:11). Like Simon, we are called to "launch out into the deep," to let the shore line go (Lk. 5:4). Believers have been called to fellowship and comprehend the mystery of the gospel (Eph. 3:9, 18; Col. 1:26-27). We must dig deep to lay the foundation for our lives (Lk. 6:48), removing all the dirt between ourselves and the Rock! Paul explained, "...Eye hath not seen, nor ear heard, neither have entered into the heart of man, the things which God hath prepared for them that love Him. But God hath revealed them unto us by His Spirit: for the Spirit searcheth all things, yea, the deep things of God" (1 Cor. 2:9-10).

Go Deeper 📖

See Gen. 1:2; 49:25; Deut. 8:7; 33:13; Job 12:22; 38:16; Ps. 33:7; 64:6; 78:15; 80:9; 95:4; 104:6; 107:24; 145:5; Prov. 3:20; 18:4; 20:5; 25:3; Eccles. 7:24; Is. 33:19; 48:6; 51:10; Dan. 2:22; Jon. 2:5; Hab. 3:10; Jn. 4:11; Rom. 10:7; 1 Cor. 4:5; 1 Pet. 3:4.

∾ ∾ ∾

𝔇egrees

Ascension or decension; promotion

Key Scriptures: 2 Kings 20:9; Ps. 120–134; Jn. 12:32; Eph. 4:8-11.

Foundational Information ✐

"Degree(s)" is from the Hebrew *ma'alah* (Strong's #4609), which means "elevation, the act (literally, a journey to a higher place, figuratively, a thought arising), or (concretely) the condition (literally, a step or grade-mark, figuratively, a superiority of station); specifically a climactic progression (in certain Psalms)." It is translated in the King James Version as "things that come up, (high) degree, go up, stair, step, story." Its root *'alah* (Strong's #5927) means "to ascend," and is akin to *El-Elyon*, or "the Most High God." The Greek word for "ascend" is *anabaino* (Strong's #305), which means "to go up; to walk up."

The "Songs of Degrees" are 15 psalms (Ps. 120–134) sung by worshipers "going up" the hill to Jerusalem and priests "ascending" the steps of the temple. These psalms are also known as the Songs of the Steps, the Songs of the Goings Up, the Gradual Psalms, and the Pilgrim Psalms.

Fulfilled in Christ ✝

Jesus said, "And I, if I be lifted up from the earth, will draw all men unto Me" (Jn. 12:32). The Savior ascended the hill of Jerusalem (Lk. 19:28) and was "lifted up" in His crucifixion and subsequent resurrection and ascension (Acts 1:1-11). The greatest son of David was "a man of high degree" (1 Chron. 17:17; see also Mt. 1:1; Lk. 1:32). Jesus told Nathanael that he would "...see heaven open, and the angels of God ascending and descending upon the Son of man" (Jn. 1:51). Mary magnified her Lord and Savior, "He hath put down the mighty from their seats, and exalted them of low degree" (Lk. 1:52; see also Ps. 113:6-8). All true promotion comes from the Lord; He puts down one, and sets up another (Ps. 75:6-7).

Applied to the Christian ⚖

The psalmist asked, "Who shall ascend into the hill of the Lord? or who shall stand in His holy place?" (Ps. 24:3) A glorious Church is stepping up into the full stature of Jesus (Eph. 4:13-15). Our growth in grace is progressive (2 Pet. 3:18)—from strength to strength (Ps. 84:7), from faith to faith (Rom. 1:17), and from glory to glory (2 Cor. 3:18). Like Jesus in John 20:17, we have been resurrected, but are not yet fully ascended. Wisdom is the secret of all promotion (Prov. 4:8). The 15 Songs of Degrees (Ps. 120–134) could be compared with the 15 steps up into Ezekiel's temple by which the priests ascended (Ezek. 40:6, 22-31). The Shulamite, a picture of the Bride of Christ, was found to be in "the secret places of the stairs" (Song 2:14). Christians are called to follow the example of the "steps" of the Pattern Son (1 Pet. 2:21; see also Ps. 37:23; 119:133; Rom. 4:12; 2 Cor. 12:18).

Go Deeper 📖

See Gen. 28:12; Ex. 19:18; 1 Sam. 2:30; 3:1; 1 Kings 6:8; 2 Kings 20:10-11; 1 Chron. 15:18; Ps. 62:9; 113:7; 135:7; 139:8; Prov. 3:35; Is. 5:14; 14:13-14; 30:29; 38:8; Jer. 10:13; Dan. 2:21; 4:17; Mk. 15:32; Jn. 6:62; 20:17; Acts 11:15; Rom. 10:6; 1 Tim. 3:13; Jas. 1:9; Rev. 21:10.

∾ ∾ ∾

Delilah

Harlotry, seduction, lies, deception; the strange woman

Key Scriptures: Judg. 16; Prov. 7; Rev. 17–18.

Foundational Information ✐

Delilah was the Philistine woman loved by the mighty judge Samson, who betrayed him to the Philistine lords for 1,100 pieces of silver. "Delilah" is transliterated from the Hebrew *Deliylah* (Strong's #1807), which means "languishing." Its root *dalal* (Strong's #1809) means "to slacken or be feeble; figuratively, to be oppressed." "Delilah" has also been translated as "dainty one, delicate, poured out, exhausted, weak, brought low, pining with desire, lustful pining, longing."

The Greek word for "seduce" is *apoplanao* (Strong's #635), meaning "to lead astray (figuratively); passively, to stray (from truth)." Compare *planao* ("to roam from safety, truth, or virtue"), *plane* ("fraudulence; a straying from orthodoxy or piety"), and *planos* ("roving as a tramp; an imposter or misleader").

Fulfilled in Christ ✝

Jesus Christ is the true Judge, the Husband of the New Testament "virtuous woman," His Church (Prov. 31:10; see also Jn. 5:22; Eph. 5:23). There is a purity and "simplicity" that is in Christ (2 Cor. 11:2-3), the "faithful witness" (Rev. 1:5). Jesus warned about the "Delilahs" of this day, "For false Christs and false prophets shall rise, and shall shew signs and wonders, to seduce, if it were possible, even the elect" (Mk. 13:22). Our great High Priest has compassion on those who have been deceived, "…and on them that are out of the way; for that he himself also is compassed with infirmity" (Heb. 5:2; see also Heb. 2:17-18; 4:15). Sheep that stray from the truth can return to the Shepherd and Bishop of their souls (1 Pet. 2:25).

Applied to the Christian ⚖

Believers are not to marry non-believers (2 Cor. 6:14–7:1). Moreover, we are to keep ourselves from the "strange woman" (Prov. 7:5), who pictures evil religious systems rooted in the "love of money," whose sorceries have deceived all nations (1 Tim. 6:10; compare Rev. 18:23). Delilah represents anything that "mocks" and saps the spiritual strength of the Christian (Judg. 16:10,13). With regard to false prophets who seduce God's people (Ezek. 13:10), Paul warned, "Beware lest any man spoil you through philosophy and vain deceit, after the tradition of men, after the rudiments of the world, and not after Christ" (Col. 2:8). He later alerted Timothy about "…seducing spirits, and doctrines of devils" (1 Tim. 4:1). Those who are rocked to sleep on the lap of the old harlot are captured by demons (typified by the Philistines) and end up bound, blind, and going in circles (Judg. 16:21).

Go Deeper 📖

See 1 Kings 11:1; Prov. 2:16; 5:3,20; 6:24; 20:16; 22:14; 23:27,33; 27:13; Is. 24:4; Jer. 50–52; Hos. 4:3; Mt. 18:12; 22:29; 24:4,11,24; 1 Cor. 6:9; 15:33; Gal. 6:7; 2 Tim. 3:13; Tit. 3:3; Heb. 3:10; Jas. 1:16; 5:19; 2 Pet. 2:15; 1 Jn. 2:26; 3:7; Rev. 2:20; 12:9; 13:14.

∞   ∞   ∞

Den (of Lions)

A hiding place, a refuge; an abiding place, a habitation; the savage violence of worldly men

Key Scriptures: Job 37:8; Ps. 57:4; 90:1; 91:1-2,9; Dan. 6; Heb. 11:33.

Foundational Information ✐

A den is the lair of a wild animal. A den of lions is the lair, thicket, or cave where lions live. "Den" is from the Hebrew *ma'own* (Strong's #4583), which means "an abode, of God (the Tabernacle or the Temple), men (their home) or animals (their lair); hence, a retreat (asylum)." It is translated in the King James Version as "den, dwelling, dwelling-place, habitation." Compare the Aramaic word *gob* (Strong's #1358), which means "a pit (for wild animals) (as cut out)." The Greek word for "den" or "cave" is *spelaion* (Strong's #4693), which means "(a grotto); a cavern; by implication, a hiding-place or resort."

Fulfilled in Christ ☦

Jesus Christ was the "Den" in which the Father lived (Col. 1:19; 2:9). The Lion of the tribe of Juda is our "strong habitation," our Rock and fortress to whom we continually resort (Ps. 71:3; compare Rev. 5:5). The Lord is the strong consolation and living hope to whom we have fled for refuge (Heb. 6:18). The psalmist exclaimed, "God is our refuge and strength, a very present help in trouble" (Ps. 46:1). Jesus declared, "...Is it not written, My house shall be called of all nations the house of prayer? but ye have made it a den of thieves" (Mk. 11:17). The One who is "the resurrection, and the life" has raised more than one Lazarus out of the cave and pit of death (Jn. 11:25,38)!

Applied to the Christian ⚖

The Church, the Body of Christ, is a "den of lions." As the Sun rises in this new day (Mal. 4:2), we are gathering together in the place of rest (Ps. 104:21-22). The Lord has been the dwelling place of His people in every generation (Ps. 90:1). We can say with the psalmist, "A father of the fatherless, and a judge of the widows, is God in his holy habitation" (Ps. 68:5). Those once wild in sin have been tamed by the power of forgiveness (Eph. 2:1-3). Covenantal commitment is "stronger than lions" (2 Sam. 1:23). Like Paul, we believe in the God who enables us to rest without hurt in the den of lions (Dan. 6:22-23; see also Lk. 10:19; 1 Cor.15:32; Heb. 11:33). Our lives should be a "house of prayer," not a "den of thieves" (Lk. 19:46).

Go Deeper 📖

See Ex. 15:2,13; Judg. 6:2; 1 Chron. 12:8; Job 38:40; Ps. 10:9; 15:1; 26:8; 35:17; 58:6; 59:16; Prov. 3:33; Song 4:8; Is. 4:6; 11:8; 25:4; 32:14; 33:20; Jer. 7:11; 9:11; 10:22;

16:19; Amos 3:4; Nahum 2:11-13; Zeph. 3:3; Zech. 2:13; Jn. 14:23; Eph. 2:22; Heb. 11:38; Rev. 6:15.

∞ ∞ ∞

𝔇esert

A dry place, wilderness; loneliness; rebellion
Key Scriptures: Ps. 68:6; Is. 35:1,6; 51:3; Lk. 4:42; 9:10-12.

Foundational Information

A desert is a dry and barren wasteland, a solitary place which is only inhabited by wild beasts, an arid pastureland. "Desert" is from the Hebrew *midbar* (Strong's #4057), which means "a pasture (open field, whither cattle are driven); by implication, a desert." Compare *'arabah* (Strong's #6160), which means "(in the sense of sterility); a desert." Its root *'arab* (Strong's #6148) means "to braid, intermix; technically, to traffic (as if by barter)." The Greek word for "desert" is *eremos* (Strong's #2048) and means "lonesome, waste." It is also translated in the King James Version as "desolate, solitary, wilderness."

Fulfilled in Christ

Jesus left the glory of Heaven and entered the human wasteland to make His grave with the wicked (Is. 53:9). Like Moses, He chose "the backside of the desert" to identify with the sufferings of the people of God (Ex. 3:1; compare Heb. 11:25-26). Jesus was tested in the wilderness for 40 days and nights with regard to the lust of the flesh, the lust of the eyes, and the pride of life (Lk. 4:1-14; 1 Jn. 2:15-17). In His earthly ministry, the Pattern Son often resorted to the private loneliness of the desert to pray and minister (Lk. 4:42; 9:10-12). Moses also described how the Lord keeps His people, "He found him in a desert land, and in the waste howling wilderness; He led him about, He instructed him, He kept him as the apple of His eye" (Deut. 32:10).

Applied to the Christian

The psalmist declared, "God setteth the solitary in families: He bringeth out those which are bound with chains: but the rebellious dwell in a dry land" (Ps. 68:6). There is no spiritual food in the desert place (Job 24:5). Men provoke and grieve God in the wilderness (Ps. 78:40), but a fresh prophetic ministry has begun to prepare the way of the Lord (Is. 40:3). Isaiah described the glory of the end-time Church, "The wilderness and the solitary place shall be glad for them; and the desert shall rejoice, and blossom as the rose...Then shall the lame man leap as an hart, and the tongue of the dumb sing: for in the wilderness shall waters break out, and streams in the desert" (Is. 35:1,6; see also Is. 41:19; 43:19; 51:3).

Go Deeper 📖

See Ex. 3:1; Num. 27:14; 1 Sam. 15:22-23; 2 Chron. 26:10; Ps. 102:6; 106:14; Is. 13:21; 21:1; 34:14; 43:20; 48:21; Jer. 2:6; 17:6; 23:10-12; 50:39; Ezek. 13:4; 47:8; Joel 1:19-20; Mt. 4:13-15; 24:26; Mk. 1:45; 6:31-35; Lk. 1:80; Jn. 6:10,31; Acts 8:26; 2 Cor. 5:21; Heb. 11:38.

∞ ∞ ∞

𝔇esire of 𝔄ll 𝔑ations

The Messiah; the manifestation of the sons of God

Key Scriptures: Ps. 145:16; Hag. 2:7; Rom. 8:14-23; Heb. 2:6-13.

Foundational Information ✎

"The desire of all nations" is a phrase interpreted by some translations of the Bible as a prophecy of the Messiah. "Desire" is from the Hebrew *chemdah* (Strong's #2532), which means "delight." It is also translated in the King James Version as "goodly, pleasant, precious." The verb form emphasizes the sense of choice (Is. 53:2). *Chemdah*, which also means "long for, covet," is applied to the Bible to refer to:

1. The king (1 Sam. 9:20).
2. Stones and jewels (2 Chron. 32:27).
3. The land (Ps. 106:24; Jer. 3:19; Zech. 7:14).
4. Ships (Is. 2:16).
5. Plants (Is. 17:10).
6. Houses (Ezek. 26:12).
7. Vessels of silver and gold (Dan. 11:8).
8. Furniture (Nahum 2:9).

The Greek word for "desire" is *thelo*, and means "to choose or prefer, to will, to wish," implying volition and purpose, frequently a determination. It is most usually rendered "to will."

Fulfilled in Christ ✝

Jesus Christ is the Messiah, the "desire of all nations" (Hag. 2:7). Jesus, the wisdom of God, is "more precious than rubies"; all that we could desire cannot be compared to Him (Prov. 3:15; compare 1 Cor. 1:30). Jesus, man's desire, is the "tree of life" (Prov. 13:12), the true and genuine Vine (Jn. 15:1-5). The Messiah prophesied through the psalmist, "I delight to do Thy will, O God: yea, Thy law is within my heart" (Ps. 40:8; see also Heb. 10:5-10). At His baptism and later transfiguration, Jesus was affirmed by His Father, "This is My beloved Son, in whom I am well pleased" (Mt. 3:17; 17:5). The Master taught, "Therefore I say unto you, What things soever ye desire, when ye pray, believe that ye receive them, and ye shall have them" (Mk. 11:24).

Applied to the Christian ⚖

In Haggai 2:7, "desire" is a singular subject and "shall come" is a plural verb! It literally reads, "the desire of all nations, they shall come." The Desire of all nations is our precious Savior, but the singular subject includes His Body in union with Him (1 Cor. 6:17; 1 Jn. 4:17). Together, Christ in the fullness of His Body, "they shall come." The plural predicate of Haggai 2:7 denotes His elect out of all nations, those whom God has from eternity foreknown and predestinated, and whom in time He calls, justifies, and glorifies (Rom. 8:29-30; 1 Pet. 1:2).

Christ in and among all of us is the hope of glory (Col. 1:27). Paul's apostolic burden and desire was for Christ to be fully "formed" in a people (Gal. 4:19), a "nation" from among the nations (1 Pet. 2:9)—"a people for His name" (Acts 15:14). The "desire of all nations" is the manifestation and unveiling of the Pattern Son in His sons (Rom. 8:19). The Book of Revelation, the unveiling of the slain Lamb, presents these "brethren" of Jesus (Heb. 2:6-13) as one new Man—"He that overcometh" (Rev. 2:26-27; 3:21; 21:7).

Go Deeper 📖

See Ps. 10:17; 21:2; 37:4; 40:6; 45:11; 73:25; Prov. 10:24; 11:23; Song 7:10; Is. 26:8; Jer. 12:10; 25:34; Ezek. 24:16,21,25; Dan. 2:18; 11:37; Hos. 13:15; Mk. 9:35; Lk. 17:22; 22:15; Acts 28:22; Rom. 10:1; 15:23; 1 Cor. 14:1; 2 Cor. 7:7,11; Eph. 2:3; 3:13; Phil. 1:23; 4:17; Col. 1:9; 1 Tim. 3:1; Heb. 11:16; 1 Pet. 1:12; 2:2.

∞ ∞ ∞

𝔇estroyer

Satan, the devil; death

Key Scriptures: Ex. 12:23; Mal. 3:11; Jn. 10:10; Heb. 2:14; 1 Jn. 3:8.

Foundational Information ✐

The destroyer is the enemy that invades the land. It is also used to mean a special agent used by God to accomplish judgment. "Destroyer" is from the Hebrew *shachath* (Strong's #7843), which means "to decay, (causatively) ruin (literally or figuratively)." This word can also mean "to corrupt, mar." Compare *shamad*, which means "to destroy, annihilate, exterminate; to desolate." The Greek word for "destroyer" is *olothreutes* (Strong's #3644), meaning "a ruiner, (specifically) a venomous serpent." It is derived from *olothreuo* ("to spoil, slay") and *olethros* ("to destroy; ruin, death, punishment").

Fulfilled in Christ ⍓

Jesus Christ is the New Testament Passover Lamb whose blood protects us from "the destroyer" (Ex. 12:23; see also Jn. 1:29; 1 Cor. 5:7; 1 Pet. 1:18-19; Rev. 13:8). The Son of God was manifested that He might destroy the works of the devil (1 Jn. 3:8; see also Mk. 1:24; Heb. 2:14). He is called a "lion" and "destroyer" by the prophet Jeremiah (Jer. 4:7). Through his death, our Lord destroyed "...him that had the power of death, that is, the devil" (Heb. 2:14). The evil one tried to destroy the young child Jesus through wicked King Herod, but failed (Mt. 2:13). Later, "...the chief priests and elders persuaded the multitude that they should ask Barabbas, and destroy Jesus" (Mt. 27:20). The Son of man came not to "destroy men's lives, but to save them" (Lk. 9:56). Jesus said, "The thief cometh not, but for to steal, and to kill, and to destroy: I am come that they might have life, and that they might have it more abundantly" (Jn. 10:10).

Applied to the Christian ⚔

We who have received forgiveness of sins have been delivered "from the power of satan" (Acts 26:18). The law of the spirit of life in Christ Jesus has made us free from the law of sin and death (Rom. 8:2). Paul warned the Christians at Corinth, "Neither murmur ye, as some of them also murmured, and were destroyed of the destroyer" (1 Cor. 10:10). God promised the faithful tither and offerer that He would rebuke the devourer so that the enemy would not "destroy the fruits of your ground" (Mal. 3:11). John prophesied that the time would come when God would "...destroy them which destroy the earth" (Rev. 11:18). Isaiah declared of that day, "The wolf and the lamb shall feed together, and the lion shall eat straw like the bullock...They shall not hurt nor destroy in all My holy mountain, saith the Lord" (Is. 65:25).

Go Deeper 📖

See Judg. 16:24; Job 15:21; Ps. 5:6; 28:5; 101:8; 106:23; 144:6; 145:20; Prov. 11:3; 15:25; 17:4; 28:34; Jer. 1:10; Hag. 2:22; Mt. 10:28; 12:14; 21:41; Mk. 3:6; 9:22; 11:18; Lk. 4:34; 6:9; 19:47; Acts 6:14; Rom. 14:15,20; 1 Cor. 1:19; 3:17; 6:13; 2 Thess. 2:8; Jas. 4:12.

∞ ∞ ∞

𝔇euteronomy

Remembrance; the second law

Key Scriptures: Deut. 1–34; Mt. 5:17; Jn. 14:26; Gal. 6:2; Jas. 2:8.

Foundational Information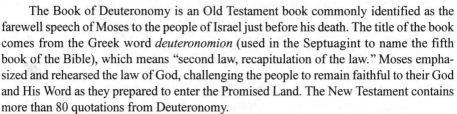

The Book of Deuteronomy is an Old Testament book commonly identified as the farewell speech of Moses to the people of Israel just before his death. The title of the book comes from the Greek word *deuteronomion* (used in the Septuagint to name the fifth book of the Bible), which means "second law, recapitulation of the law." Moses emphasized and rehearsed the law of God, challenging the people to remain faithful to their God and His Word as they prepared to enter the Promised Land. The New Testament contains more than 80 quotations from Deuteronomy.

"Remembrance" is from the Hebrew *zeker* (Strong's #2143), which means "a memento; by implication, commemoration." It is rendered in the King James Version as "memorial, memory, remembrance, scent." Its root *zakar* (Strong's #2142) means "to mark (so as to be recognized), to remember; by implication, to mention." The Greek word for "remembrance" is *anamimnesko* (Strong's #363), which means "to remind; to recollect."

Fulfilled in Christ

Jesus Christ is the fulfillment of the law (Mt. 5:17). The Pattern Son quoted from Deuteronomy during His temptation, answering satan with three quotations from this key Old Testament book (see Mt. 4:4; Lk. 4:4 [Deut. 8:3]; Mt. 4:7; Lk. 4:12 [Deut. 6:16]; and Mt. 4:10; Lk. 4:8 [Deut. 6:13]). When asked to name the most important commandment in the Law, our Teacher responded, "And thou shalt love the Lord thy God with all thy heart, and with all thine soul, and with all thy might" (Deut. 6:5; see also Mt. 22:37; Mk. 12:30; Lk. 10:27). "The Lord our God is one Lord" (Deut. 6:4; see also Mk. 12:29; 1 Cor. 8:6; Gal. 3:20; Eph. 4:5). Jesus Christ is the one Mediator between God and men (1 Tim. 2:5).

Applied to the Christian

Paul declared, "Bear ye one another's burdens, and so fulfil the law of Christ" (Gal. 6:2). James added, "If ye fulfil the royal law according to the scripture, Thou shalt love thy neighbor as thyself, ye do well" (Jas. 2:8). There are 14 things that believers need to "remember" from the Book of Deuteronomy:

1. God brought us out of Egypt (sin) (Deut. 5:15).
2. God defeated Pharaoh (satan) for us (Deut. 7:18).
3. God led us through the wilderness (Deut. 8:2).
4. God gave us power to get wealth (Deut. 8:18).

5. God revealed His mercy unto us (Deut. 9:7).
6. God made us part of His covenant family (Deut. 9:27).
7. God redeemed us, and now we belong to Him (Deut. 15:15).
8. God suffered and was afflicted for us (Deut. 16:3).
9. God gave us His Word and His statutes (Deut. 16:12).
10. God judged rebellious leadership (Deut. 24:9).
11. God always moved with righteous judgment (Deut. 24:18).
12. God had compassion for orphans and widows (Deut. 24:22).
13. God dealt with Amalek (the flesh)(Deut. 25:17).
14. God has always been faithful (Deut. 32:7).

The "second law" for the Christian is the New Testament law of "the spirit of life in Christ Jesus" (Rom. 8:2). This inward "law of liberty" (Jas. 1:25; 2:12), the law of a new nature, has been written on the fleshly tables on our hearts by the Holy Ghost, who will bring all things to our "remembrance" (Jn. 14:26; see also 2 Cor. 3:3).

Go Deeper

See Ex. 17:14; Ps. 30:4; 97:12; 102:12; 112:6; 135:13; 145:7; Prov. 10:7; Is. 26:8, 13-14; Hos. 12:5; 14:7; Mal. 3:16; Lk. 1:54,72; 22:19; 23:42; Jn. 14:26; Acts 10:31; 20:35; 1 Cor. 4:17; 11:24-25; Gal. 2:10; Eph. 2:11; Col. 4:18; 1 Thess. 2:9; 2 Thess. 2:5; 2 Tim. 1:6; 2:8; Heb. 10:32; 13:3,7; Jude 17; Rev. 2:5; 3:3.

∾ ∾ ∾

Dew

The blessing of the Holy Spirit; the unity of the Spirit; the Word of God

Key Scriptures: Gen. 27:28; Deut. 32:2; Ps. 133; Prov. 19:12.

Foundational Information

Dew is water that condenses upon vegetation during the night and early morning hours. "Dew" is from the Hebrew *tal* (Strong's #2919), which means "dew (as covering vegetation)." Its root is *tahal* (Strong's #2926), meaning "to strew over, (by implication) to cover in or plate (with beams)." The Hebrew word for "unity" is *yachad* (Strong's #3162), and it means "together; alike; all at once; all together." Its root means "to be or become one." The Greek word *henotes* means "oneness, unanimity."

Fulfilled in Christ ✝

Jesus Christ, "the Word" of God, is Heaven's Dew unto His people (Jn. 1:1; compare Hos. 14:5). He personified the Father's doctrine and speech, and came to earth "…as the small rain upon the tender herb, and as the showers upon the grass" (Deut. 32:2). The Spirit of the Lord was upon Jesus (see Lk. 3:22; 4:18; Jn. 3:34; Acts 10:38) just as the dew covered the manna, a type of Him who is the "bread of life" (Jn. 6:48; compare Ex. 16:13-14). Jesus' intercession in the Garden of Gethsemane was like the dew, "the drops of the night" (Song 5:2; see also Lk. 22:44). Gideon's soaking fleece reveals the life of Jesus wrung out on the cross, like "a bowl full of water" (Judg. 6:38; see also Jn. 19:34).

Applied to the Christian ⚖

Believers have been filled with the Holy Spirit, "the dew of heaven" (Gen. 27:28; see also Eph. 5:17-19). The absence of the dew's anointing, depicting the King's favor and blessing (Prov. 19:12), will result in a spiritual famine (1 Kings 17:1). We are like "drops of dew" (Job 38:28) begotten by the Father of spirits (Heb. 12:9; Jas. 3:17-18). The unity of the Spirit (Eph. 4:3) was described by the psalmist to be like dew, "Behold, how good and how pleasant it is for brethren to dwell together in unity! It is like…the dew of Hermon, and as the dew that descended upon the mountains of Zion…" (Ps. 133:1-3). Micah prophesied about the end-time Church, "And the remnant of Jacob shall be in the midst of many people as a dew from the Lord, as the showers upon the grass…" (Mic. 5:7).

Go Deeper 📖

See Gen. 27:39; Num. 11:9; Deut. 33:13,28; 2 Sam. 1:21; 17:12; Job 29:19; Ps. 110:3; Prov. 3:20; Is. 18:4; 26:19; Jer. 32:38-39; Dan. 4:15,23,25,33; 5:21; Hos. 6:4; 13:3; Zeph. 3:9; Hag. 1:10; Zech. 8:12; Jn. 17:21-23; Acts 4:32; Rom. 12:10,16; 1 Cor. 1:10; 12:12-13; Eph. 4:1-13; Phil. 2:1-3; Heb. 12:14.

∞ ∞ ∞

𝔇𝔦𝔞𝔡𝔢𝔪

Crown; kingly or priestly honor and glory; the mind of Christ

Key Scriptures: Job 29:14; Is. 28:5; 62:3; Ezek. 21:26; 1 Cor. 2:16.

Foundational Information ✎

A diadem was a band or wrapping around the king's or queen's turban. It was often studded with gems, signifying their royal authority. A diadem was also the headpiece of the high priest. In the New Testament world, the crown could also be a garland or a wreath awarded for faithfulness in service, whereas the diadem always symbolized royal authority.

There are different Hebrew words for "diadem." *Tsaniyph* (Strong's #6797) means "a head-dress (piece of cloth wrapped around)," and is translated in the King James Version as "diadem, hood, mitre." Its root is *tsanaph* (Strong's #6801), which means "to wrap, i.e. roll or dress." Compare *mitsnepheth* (Strong's #4701) meaning "a tiara, official turban (of a king or high priest)," taken from the same root. "Diadem" is also from the Hebrew *tsephiyrah* (Strong's #6843), which means "a crown (as encircling the head)." It is derived from a word meaning "a male goat (as prancing)," and the root *tsaphar* ("to skip about").

Fulfilled in Christ ✝

Jesus Christ, our great King-Priest, was crowned by mother earth with a crown of thorns (Song 3:11; Jn. 19:1-5). Then He was exalted and crowned by the heavenly Father with glory and honor (Heb. 2:9; Rev. 14:14; 19:12). Isaiah prophesied of Him, "In that day shall the Lord of hosts be for a crown of glory, and for a diadem of beauty, unto the residue of His people" (Is. 28:5). King Jesus has been wrapped with the robes of royal judgment (Job 29:14; see also Is. 11:1-5; Jn. 5:22). The priestly "diadem" and kingly crown of the tribe of Judah, the house of David, was retained and given to Him "whose right it is" (Ezek. 21:26-27; see also Mt. 28:18; Heb. 7:14). Jesus is a living, flourishing Crown (Ps. 132:18; see also Jn. 11:25).

Applied to the Christian ⚖

We have been made kings and priests unto God (Rev. 1:6; 5:10). Isaiah prophesied that Zion, the New Testament Church (Heb. 12:22-23), would be called "...a crown of glory in the hand of the Lord, and a royal diadem in the hand of thy God" (Is. 62:3). The Lord is cleansing and changing our priestly garments that He might give us a diadem of beauty—"the mind of Christ" (1 Cor. 2:16; see also Zech. 3:4-5; Phil. 2:5). Jesus' blood has washed away our sins, qualifying us to enter the Christian race. Those who are faithful to the end will be given the following:

1. A crown of incorruption (1 Cor. 9:24-26).
2. A crown of rejoicing (1 Thess. 2:19).
3. A crown of righteousness (2 Tim. 4:8).
4. A crown of life (Jas. 1:12; Rev. 2:10).
5. A crown of glory (1 Pet. 5:4).

Go Deeper 📖

See Gen. 49:26; Ex. 28:4,37,39; 29:6; 39:28,31; Lev. 8:9; 16:4; Esther 2:17; 8:15; Ps. 8:5; 21:3; Prov. 4:9; 12:4; 14:18; 16:31; Is. 3:23; Ezek. 16:12; Zech. 9:16; Mt. 27:29; Rom. 11:34; 1 Cor. 6:17; Eph. 3:3-4; Phil. 4:1; 2 Tim. 2:5; Rev. 3:11; 6:2; 12:1; 14:14.

𝔇𝔦𝔞𝔪𝔬𝔫𝔡

A predestined troop; the army of God in conquest

Key Scriptures: Gen. 30:9-11; Ex. 28:18; 39:11; Jer. 17:1; Ezek. 28:13; 2 Tim. 2:3.

Foundational Information

A diamond is pure crystallized carbon, the hardest known substance. When transparent and without flaws, it is one of the most highly valued gemstones. "Diamond" is from the Hebrew *yahalom* (Strong's #3095), which means "(in the sense of hardness); a precious stone, probably onyx." Its root *halam* (Strong's #1986) means "to strike down; by implication, to hammer, stamp, conquer, disband." Compare *shamiyr* (Strong's #8068), which means "(in the original sense of pricking) a thorn; also (from its keenness for scratching) a gem, probably the diamond."

The diamond was the third stone in the second row of Aaron's breastplate—on this sixth stone was engraved the name of the tribe of Gad. "Gad" comes the Hebrew root *guwd* (Strong's #1464), which means "to crowd upon, attack." It is translated in the King James Version as "invade, overcome." Compare *gadad* (Strong's #1413), which means "to crowd; also to gash (as if by pressing into)." "Gad" has also been rendered as "to assemble by troops, organized division, assembly; good fortune, lot, seer."

Fulfilled in Christ

Jesus Christ, Heaven's flawless, sinless Diamond (see 2 Cor. 5:21; Heb. 4:15; 7:26; 1 Pet. 2:22), is the Overcomer and conquering King (Rev. 3:21). He said to His disciples, "...be of good cheer; I have overcome the world" (Jn. 16:33). Jesus subdued satan, the strong man, because He was the stronger Man (Lk. 11:22)! The Captain and General of God's army (Heb. 2:10) was not overcome with evil, but overcame evil with good (Rom. 12:21; see also Mt. 4:23-25; Acts 10:38). Our Savior was the point of the diamond who came to show man the folly of sin and remove us from sin's snare (Jer. 17:1; see also Jn. 1:29; Rom. 5:12-21). Jesus' forehead is an adamant or diamond harder (stronger) than flint (Ezek. 3:9). His resolve to please the Father was hard and firm, impenetrable.

Applied to the Christian

The Church is God's army (Joel 2:1-11; Eph. 6:10-18). It is our lot to have been "predestinated" according to His purpose (Eph. 1:5,11). Leah foresaw the end-time Church when she named Gad, "A troop cometh" (Gen. 30:11). We "...shall overcome at the last" (Gen. 49:19; see also Rev. 3:21; 21:7). Diamonds were in the Garden of Eden in the day when Adam was created (Ezek. 28:13). "Diamond" Christians who overcome will eat of the tree of life, "...which is in the midst of the paradise of God" (Rev. 2:7). The diamond was on the breastplate of judgment (Ex. 28:18; 39:11); one should not expect to obtain the privilege of ruling and reigning with Christ who has not learned to "rule over his own spirit" (Prov. 25:28). Some points and facets of overcoming in our walk with God (like the diamond) take years to crystallize into full and complete victory. Every believer is to "...endure hardness, as a good soldier of Jesus Christ" (2 Tim. 2:3).

Go Deeper 📖

See Gen. 35:26; 46:16; Ex. 1:4; Num. 1:14,24; Deut. 33:20-21; Josh. 13:24; 2 Sam. 2:25; 1 Chron. 6:63; 12:14; Ps. 60:12; 118:15-16; Song 6:4,10; Ezek. 48:27-28; Amos 9:6; Mic. 5:1; Rom. 3:4; 2 Tim. 2:12; 1 Jn. 2:13-14; 4:4; 5:4-5; Rev. 2:26-27; 7:5; 12:11; 19:19.

∞ ∞ ∞

𝔇ill (𝔄nise, ℭummin)

Providential preservation

Key Scriptures: Is. 28:25,27; Hos. 12:13; Mt. 23:23; 1 Thess. 5:23; Jude 1.

Foundational Information ✐

Dill (also known as anise, cummin) is an annual herb that bears yellow flowers and fragrant seeds. It is used as medicine and for cooking. The Greek word for "anise" is *anathon* (Strong's #432), which means "dill." "Cummin" is from the Hebrew *kammon* (Strong's #3646), which means "to store up or preserve; 'cummin' (from its use as a condiment)." The Greek word is *kuminon* (Strong's #2951); it means "dill or fennel ('cummin')." Most aromatic, dill is crushed and mixed with bread, added as flavoring to the meat pot, or used in pickling. Its small, tender seeds are harvested with a rod, not a threshing instrument.

"Preserve" is taken from two primary Hebrew words (used mostly in the Books of Psalms and Proverbs): *Natsar* (Strong's #5341) means "to guard (to protect, maintain);" and *salmah* (Strong's #8008) means "a dress." The root of the latter means "a cover or mantle." In the New Testament, the word "preserved" is from *tereo* (Strong's #5083), meaning "(a watch); to guard (from loss or injury, properly, by keeping the eye upon)."

Fulfilled in Christ ✝

Jesus, the great Preserver under the governmental rod of the Father, came to earth and mixed His life with ours, tasting death for every man (Heb. 2:9). He favored us and flavored us with Himself—"the sweet savour of Christ...the savour of life" (2 Cor. 2:15-16). Like Joseph, Jesus was sent ahead of His brethren "to preserve life" (Gen. 45:5,7; see also

Rom. 8:29; Heb. 2:11-15). Life without the spice Christ Jesus is bland (1 Jn. 5:12). The great Teacher used the anise as an illustration when He scolded the Pharisees for preserving part of the law in detail while ignoring the rest (Mt. 23:23). The psalmist prophesied of Him, "The Lord shall preserve thee from all evil: He shall preserve thy soul. The Lord shall preserve thy going out and thy coming in from this time forth, and even for evermore" (Ps. 121:7-8).

Applied to the Christian ⚖

Believers are sanctified and preserved in Jesus Christ (Jude 1). Paul interceded, "And the very God of peace sanctify you wholly; and I pray God your whole spirit and soul and body be preserved blameless unto the coming of our Lord Jesus Christ" (1 Thess. 5:23). Isaiah, speaking of God's loving care and providence, notes that the cart wheel is not turned about upon the cummin (dill), "...but the fitches are beaten out with a staff, and the cummin with a rod" (Is. 28:27; see also Ps. 23:4; Mic. 6:9; 7:14). The self-life must be crushed before we are mixed with the "bread of life" (Jn. 6:48); the wise God gently works His Word into us, moving very carefully so as not to bruise us in the process (Mt. 12:20; Jas. 3:17). Hosea instructed God's people, "And by a prophet the Lord brought Israel out of Egypt, and by a prophet was he preserved" (Hos. 12:13; see also 2 Chron. 20:20; Amos 3:7).

Go Deeper 📖

See Gen. 32:30; 43:11; Ex. 25:6; 30:23,34; Deut. 6:24; Josh. 24:17; 2 Sam. 8:14; Job 10:12; Ps. 12:7; 16:1; 25:21; 32:7; 79:11; Prov. 2:11; 4:6; 14:3; 20:28; 22:12; Song 4:10,14,16; 5:1,13; 6:2; 8:14; Is. 31:5; 49:6-8; Mt. 5:13; Mk. 16:1; Lk. 5:38; 14:34; 17:33; 23:56; 24:1; Jn. 19:40; Eph. 5:2; 2 Tim. 4:18.

∞ ∞ ∞

Dish

Holding forth the Word of life with excellence; medicine

Key Scriptures: Judg. 5:25; Ps. 8:1,9; Mt. 26:23; Phil. 2:16.

Foundational Information ✎

A dish was a utensil for holding or serving food, usually made of earthenware. "Dish" is from the Hebrew *qe'arah* (Strong's #7086), which means "a bowl (as cut out hollow)." Compare *cephel* (Strong's #5602), meaning "to depress; a basin (as deepened out)," and *tsallachath* (Strong's #6747), meaning "something advanced or deep, a bowl; figuratively, the bosom." The Greek word for "dish" is *trublion* (Strong's #5165), which means "a bowl." Among the Greeks the "dish" was a measure in medical prescriptions.

The Hebrew word for "medicine" is *gehah* (Strong's #1456), which means "a cure." Its root is *gahah* (Strong's #1455), which means "to remove (a bandage from a wound, heal it)." Compare *teruwphah* (Strong's #8644), which means "a remedy." The similar root of the latter is *rapha'* (Strong's #7495), which means "to mend (by stitching), (figuratively) to cure." Compare *marpe'* (Strong's #4832), which means "a medicine, or a cure; deliverance." The Greek word for "cure" is *therapeuo* and signifies "to serve as a therapon, an attendant"; then, "to care for the sick, to treat, cure, heal." Compare the English word *therapeutics*.

Fulfilled in Christ

Jesus Christ, cut out of the bosom of the Father, was the "lordly dish" from Heaven who held the One who sent Him (Judg. 5:25; see also Col. 1:19; 2:9; Jn. 1:18). The Hebrew word for "lordly" in Judges 5:25 describes the Lord Jesus and means "wide, large, powerful; expansive, great, magnificent; noble, principal, stately one." Isaiah used that same word to describe the Messiah's expansive influence, "But there [in Zion] the glorious Lord will be unto us a place of broad rivers and streams..." (Is. 33:21; see also Jn. 14:2-3; Eph. 1:3; 2:6; 3:10). Jesus dished out the life of the Father, having obtained a more excellent name and ministry (Heb. 1:4; 8:6). His life style was the "more excellent way," the way of love (1 Cor. 12:31; see also Jn. 14:6; Heb. 10:19-20), climaxed by His "more excellent sacrifice" on the cross (Heb. 11:4). Luke records that our great Physician "...cured many of their infirmities and plagues, and of evil spirits; and unto many that were blind He gave sight" (Lk. 7:21). The psalmist exclaimed, "O Lord, our Lord, how excellent is Thy name in all the earth..." (Ps. 8:1,9)!

Applied to the Christian

The apostle Paul admonished the Church to hold forth "the word of life" (Phil. 2:16; see also Tit. 1:9). Together, we constitute a dish that holds the Head (Col. 2:19). The dishes of "pure gold" in the Tabernacle of Moses (Ex. 37:16) picture New Testament believers who have been made "partakers of the divine nature" (2 Pet. 1:4). The dishes held on the table of showbread (Num. 4:7) reveal that "we being many are one bread" (1 Cor. 10:17). Judas Iscariot, who dipped into the Lord's dish (Mt. 26:23), had his hand, not his heart, on the table (Jn. 21:20). Believers reach out to others with the joy of the Lord, for "a merry heart doeth good like a medicine..." (Prov. 17:22). Waters out of our sanctuary (Ezek. 47:12; see also Jn. 7:38) are like medicine "...for the healing of the nations" (Rev. 22:2). Equipped by the Spirit to serve others, Jesus' disciples have been given "...power and authority over all devils, and to cure diseases" (Lk. 9:1; see also Mk. 16:17-18; Lk. 10:19).

Go Deeper

See Ex. 25:29; 37:16; Num. 7:13; Judg. 7:20; Ruth 3:15; 2 Kings 21:13; Neh. 4:16-21; Ps. 150:2; Prov. 8:6; 22:20; Song 7:5; Is. 1:6; 4:2; 12:5; Jer. 8:22; 33:6;

Dan. 5:12-14; 6:3; Mt. 17:18; Mk. 7:3; 14:20; Rom. 2:18; Phil. 1:10; 1 Tim. 1:19; 3:9; 2 Pet. 1:17; Rev. 6:9.

∾   ∾   ∾

𝕯𝔬𝔢𝔤

Betrayal; fleshly anxiety

Key Scriptures: 1 Sam. 21:7; 22:9,18-22; Ps. 52;
Mt. 6:25-34; Mk. 4:19; Gal. 5:17-21.

Foundational Information

Doeg the Edomite (a descendant of Esau), the chief of King Saul's herdsmen, be-trayed David and, on Saul's orders, killed 85 priests of Nob. "Doeg" is transliterated from the Hebrew *Do'eg* (Strong's #1673), which means "anxious." Its root *da'ag* is translated in the King James Version as "be afraid (careful, sorry), sorrow, take thought." The Greek word for "careful" means "to be anxious about, to have a distracting care." "Doeg" has also been translated as "fearful, timid." The Hebrew root for "betray" (Strong's #7411) means "to hurl; specifically, to shoot; figuratively, to delude or betray (as if causing to fall)." The Greek word *paradidomi* means "to surrender, yield up, intrust, transmit"—"to give over."

The title of Psalm 52 reads, "To the chief Musician, Maschil [which means "instruc-tion"], A Psalm of David, when Doeg the Edomite came and told Saul, and said unto him, 'David is come to the house of Ahimelech.' " David described this murderer as a "deceit-ful tongue," a man "that made not God his strength" (Ps. 52:4,7). The man who betrayed the king was judged and sentenced, "God shall likewise destroy thee for ever, He shall take thee away, and pluck thee out of thy dwelling place, and root thee out of the land of the living" (Ps. 52:5).

Fulfilled in Christ

Jesus Christ, the greatest son of David (Mt. 1:1), was betrayed by evil men (Mt. 17:22; 26:21-25). The King taught His subjects to "take no thought" for the lower realms, but to seek first His Kingdom (Mt. 6:25-34). The devil is the cowardly lion (1 Pet. 5:8); Jesus is the fearless "…lion of the tribe of Juda…" (Rev. 5:5). He personifies the perfect love that casts out all fear (1 Jn. 4:18). Jesus conquered the flesh; Paul taught, "For what the law could not do, in that it was weak through the flesh, God sending His own Son in the likeness of sinful flesh, and for sin, condemned sin in the flesh" (Rom. 8:3; see also Heb. 4:15; 1 Pet. 2:24; 4:1-2). Jesus said that "the cares of this world" would choke the

Word of God and bring about unfruitfulness (Mk. 4:19). He admonished fretful Martha, "...thou art careful and troubled about many things" (Lk. 10:41).

Applied to the Christian ⚖

Doeg came from the seed of Esau, who typifies the flesh (Rom. 8:1-6; Gal. 5:17). Fleshly, religious men who sought the life of the heavenly David also seek the life of His followers (1 Sam. 22:23; see also Lk. 22:2; Jn. 5:18; 7:1). Such men revolt from the dominion of "Judah" ("praise") to make themselves a king (2 Chron. 21:8,10). John explained, "Whoso hateth his brother is a murderer..." (1 Jn. 3:15; see also Jn. 8:44; Acts 3:14). The old order (pictured by Saul) despises the priesthood of all believers (1 Pet. 2:9) and the vital truths of body life and ministry (Rom. 12; 1 Cor. 12). Paul warned, "Be careful for nothing; but in every thing by prayer and supplication with thanksgiving let your requests be made known unto God" (Phil. 4:6). Doeg's name means "anxious," revealing him to be full of fear; Paul assured us that "...God hath not given us the spirit of fear..." (2 Tim. 1:7). Worry is sin.

Go Deeper 📖

See Gen. 36:9,43; 1 Kings 1:11; 1 Chron. 12:17; Jer. 17:8; Mt. 10:4,19; 20:18; 24:10; 26:2,16,45-48; 27:3-4; Mk. 13:12; 14:11; Lk. 8:14; 10:41; 12:11,22-26; 21:26, 34; Jn. 6:64; Rom. 8:15; 1 Cor. 7:32-34; 11:23; 12:25; Phil. 2:20; Heb. 2:15.

∞ ∞ ∞

Dog

Contempt; savage greed

Key Scriptures: Prov. 18:3; Is. 56:10-11; Mt. 7:6; Phil. 3:2; 2 Pet. 2:22.

Foundational Information ✎

In ancient Israel, the dog was not "man's best friend." To be called a dog was most offensive and insulting. "Dog" is from the Hebrew *keleb* (Strong's #3611), which means "to yelp, or else to attack; a dog; hence (by euphemism) a male prostitute." Interestingly, the name "Caleb" is derived from this same root. *Kaleb* (Strong's #3612) means "forcible," and has also been translated as "bold, fearless, ferocious to enemies, impetuous." The Greek word for "dog" is *kuon* and means "a dog (hound)." Dogs in Palestine were more treacherous and wild than tame, often banding together in packs, living off trash as they roamed the back streets of the city. The dog was an unclean animal, cowardly and lazy, eating garbage, even human flesh and blood. However, some shepherds made use of dogs in herding.

Fulfilled in Christ ☀

When Jesus Christ, the unselfish Passover Lamb was killed at the cross, the dogs stopped barking (Ex. 11:7; see also Jn. 1:29; 1 Cor. 5:7)! Caleb said, "Now therefore give me this mountain..." (Josh. 14:12); Jesus conquered every foe and obtained His inheritance (Ps. 2:7-8; Phil. 2:9-11; Heb. 1:4). Like the giant Goliath, the devil is a dog (1 Sam. 17:43), a dog on a divine leash (Job 1:6-12). Messiah prophetically spoke through the psalmist in "the Psalm of the Cross" (Ps. 22), "For dogs have compassed me: the assembly of the wicked have enclosed me: they pierced my hands and my feet" (Ps. 22:16). Jesus taught, "Give not that which is holy unto the dogs..." (Mt. 7:6).

Applied to the Christian ⚖

Solomon said, "When the wicked cometh, then cometh also contempt..." (Prov. 18:3). The apostle Paul warned, "Beware of dogs..." (Phil. 3:2). Many "dogs" are wandering through the city (the Church), peddling their spiritual junk food. Some in high positions are watchmen who are spiritually blind and ignorant; "...they are all dumb dogs, they cannot bark; sleeping, lying down, loving to slumber. Yea, they are greedy dogs which can never have enough, and they are shepherds that cannot understand: they all look to their own way, every one for his gain, from his quarter" (Is. 56:10-11). These backslidden preachers have prostituted their ministries for the love of money (Deut. 23:18; see also Tit. 1:11), and have turned to their own vomit again (Prov. 26:11; 2 Pet. 2:22).

The prophet Elijah declared that Jezebel (a picture of proud, whorish religious systems) was destined to be eaten by dogs (1 Kings 21:19-23; 2 Kings 9:10,36; see also Prov. 7; Rev. 17–18). Isaiah foretold the days of her demise, "The Lord of hosts hath purposed it, to stain the pride of all glory, and to bring into contempt all the honourable of the earth" (Is. 23:9; see also Job 12:21; 1 Cor. 1:26-29; 3:11-15).

Go Deeper 📖

See Judg. 7:5; 1 Sam. 24:14; 2 Sam. 9:8; 16:9; 1 Kings 14:11; 16:4; 22:38; 2 Kings 8:13; Job 30:1; Ps. 59:6,14; 68:23; 107:40; 119:22; 123:3-4; Prov. 26:17; Eccles. 5:10; 9:4; Is. 1:23; Jer. 15:3; Dan. 12:2; Mic. 3:11; 7:3-4; Mt. 13:14-15; 15:26-27; Mk. 7:27-28; Lk. 16:21; Jn. 8:43; 2 Pet. 2:15-16; Rev. 22:15.

∞ ∞ ∞

𝔇oor

Entrance, access

Key Scriptures: Ex. 12:22-23; Hos. 2:15; Jn. 10:1-2,7,9;
Rom. 5:2; Eph. 2:18; 3:12; 2 Pet. 1:11.

Foundational Information ✐

A door is the covering over an entrance into a tent, a permanent house, or a public building. The doors of Bible times were made of a wide variety of material, ranging from animal hides to wood and metal. "Door" or "entrance" is from the Hebrew *pethach* (Strong's #6607), which means "an opening (literally), door (gate) or entrance way." Its root *pathach* (Strong's #6605) means to "open wide (literally or figuratively); specifically, to loosen, begin, plough, carve." The Greek word for "door" is *thura*, which means "a portal or entrance (the opening or the closure, literally or figuratively)."

The Greek word for "access" is *prosagoge* (Strong's #4318), meaning "admission." It is derived from *prosago* (Strong's #4317), which means "to lead towards, to conduct near (summon, present), or to approach." The word *prosagoge*, taken from *pros* ("to, toward") and *ago* ("to lead"), indicates that men are led or brought into the presence of God. This access is a freedom to enter through the assistance of the favor of another. The Greek word for "entrance" is *eisodos*, from *eis* ("into") and *hodos* ("road, way").

Fulfilled in Christ ✝

Jesus Christ announced to all men, "Verily, verily, I say unto you, I am the door of the sheep...I am the door: by Me if any man enter in, he shall be saved, and shall go in and out, and find pasture" (Jn. 10:7,9). In the "pattern" of Moses' tabernacle (Ex. 25:40; see also Ex. 25:8; Jn. 1:14), the gate into the Outer Court, the door into the Holy Place, and the veil into the Most Holy Place reveal a threefold entrance into the things of God (the word "excellent" in Proverbs 22:20 means "threefold"). These three entrances parallel the three major feasts of Jehovah—Passover, Pentecost, and Tabernacles (Deut. 16:16)— Jesus Christ is respectively revealed as Savior, Baptizer (with the Holy Spirit), and Lord (Lk. 2:11; Acts 2:36). Jesus, the bloody Door, was hanged for us (Ex. 12:22-23; see also Ex. 40:5; Gal. 3:13-14). Jesus Christ is the only valid entry, man's only "door of hope" (Hos. 2:15), into the realm of supernatural Spirit; all else is counterfeit (Jn. 14:6). This glorious access which He has provided is appropriated by grace and faith (Rom. 5:2). Jesus stands at the door and knocks (Rev. 3:20).

Applied to the Christian ⚖

We have been given access with confidence unto God the Father through the blood of His Son by the operation of the Spirit (Eph. 2:18; 3:12; Heb. 10:19-22). Divine wisdom is ever crying at "the openings" of our ear-gates and eye-gates (Prov. 1:21; 8:3,34). We must enter the Kingdom now (Jn. 3:5), before the door is shut (Mt. 25:10). Some doors were left open all day long as an invitation to hospitality (Rev. 3:8). At the right season, the Lord will raise us up and teach us how to walk at the door or gate called "Beautiful" (Acts 3:2,10; see also Ps. 48:2). Through Christ, the "door of faith" has been opened to all nations (Acts 14:27). As with Paul, the Lord will open effectual and abundant doors of ministry and utterance, that the gospel of Christ might be proclaimed (see 1 Cor. 16:9; 2 Cor. 2:12; Col. 4:3; 2 Pet. 1:11). Some must enter into His sabbath rest (Heb. 4:9). The psalmist declared, "The entrance of Thy words giveth light..." (Ps. 119:130). As "doors," believers give fresh access to the Lord (Ps. 24:7,9; see also 1 Kings 6:31-34; 2 Chron. 28:24; 29:3).

Go Deeper 📖

See Gen. 4:7; 18:1; Ex. 29:4,11; 36:37; Deut. 31:15; 1 Kings 6:8; 7:5; 14:27; 1 Chron. 9:21; 2 Chron. 4:22; Ps. 100:4; Song 7:13; Is. 26:20; Jer. 36:10; Ezek. 8:3,8; 46:3; 47:1; Mt. 5:20; 6:6; 7:13; Mk. 1:33; 11:4; Lk. 11:7; 13:25; Jn. 10:1-2; Acts 5:19; 14:22; 1 Thess. 1:9; 2:1; Jas. 5:9; 4:1; 21:27; 22:14.

∞ ∞ ∞

𝕯orcas

The beauty of compassion

Key Scriptures: Song 4:5; 7:3; Mt. 9:36; Lk. 10:33; Acts 9:36-43.

Foundational Information ✏

Dorcas was a Christian woman from Joppa known for befriending and helping the poor; also called Tabitha, she was raised from the dead by the apostle Peter. "Dorcas" is transliterated from the Greek *Dorkas* (Strong's #1393), which means "gazelle." The word "gazelle" is Arabic for "affectionate." "Tabitha" is of Aramaic origin; compare the Hebrew *tsebiyah* (Strong's #6646), which means "a female gazelle." It is translated as "roe" in Song of Solomon 4:5; 7:3. It is derived from *tsebiy* (Strong's #6643), which means "prominence; splendor (as conspicuous); also a gazelle (as beautiful)."

The Greek word for "almsdeeds" is *eleemosune* (Strong's #1654), which means "compassionateness, (as exercised towards the poor) beneficence, or (concretely) a benefaction." Its root is *eleos* (Strong's #1656), meaning "compassion (human or divine, especially active)." *Eleos* is the New Testament word for "mercy," and it is the outward manifestation of pity. It assumes need on the part of him who receives it, as well as resources adequate to meet the need on the part of him who shows it! The Greek word for "compassion" means "to have the bowels yearn, (figuratively) feel sympathy, to pity."

Fulfilled in Christ ☀

Just as Peter raised Dorcas, so Jesus Christ has raised us from the death of trespasses and sins (Eph. 2:1). Our beloved is Heaven's Roe (Song 2:9,17; 8:14), the Husband of the Church (Eph. 5:22-33). Jesus, our "propitiation" or "mercy-seat," is our merciful and faithful High Priest (Rom 3:25; see also Heb. 2:17). The Good Shepherd (Jn. 10:11,14) is also the Good Samaritan who has shown "compassion" to broken humanity (Lk. 10:33; see also Mt. 9:36). The psalmist declared, "But thou, O Lord, art a God full of compassion, and gracious, longsuffering, and plenteous in mercy and truth...He hath made his wonderful works to be remembered: the Lord is gracious and full of compassion" (Ps. 86:15; 111:4).

Applied to the Christian ⚖

Dorcas is a picture of the end-time Church, reaching out from within the rent veil as she sits with Christ in His mercy-seat, the throne of grace (Heb. 4:14-16; Rev. 3:21). Dorcas' ministry was marked by faith and love (see Gal. 5:6; 1 Thess. 5:8; 1 Tim. 1:14; 2 Tim. 1:13)! When Dorcas saw Peter, she sat up (Acts 9:40); when the Church beholds and experiences real apostolic ministry (Eph. 3:1-5; 4:11), she too will rise from her sleep! This can only happen after the weeping "widows" who are living on past memories—local churches who have no Husband—are put out of the room (Acts 9:39-40; compare Eph. 5:23; Rev. 21:2). Then we can receive His "hand" (Acts 9:41)—the fivefold ascension gifts of Ephesians 4:11. We will be "presented" or "exhibited" alive to Him and to the world (2 Cor. 11:2; Eph. 5:27; Col. 1:22). Just as Peter turned toward the body of Dorcas, the Lord "...will turn again, He will have compassion upon us..." (Mic. 7:19).

Go Deeper 📖

See Ex. 2:6; Deut. 13:17; 30:3; 1 Sam. 23:21; 1 Kings 8:50; 2 Kings 13:23; 2 Chron. 30:9; 36:15,17; Ps. 78:38; 112:4; 145:8; Is. 49:15; Jer. 12:15; Lam. 3:32; Mt. 6:1-4; 14:14; 15:32; 18:27; Mk. 5:19; Lk. 12:33; 15:20; Acts 3:2-3; 10:2-4; Rom. 9:15; Heb. 5:2; 10:34; 1 Pet. 3:8; 1 Jn. 3:17.

∞ ∞ ∞

Dothan

Double-mindedness; two visions, two feasts; mixture; an open heaven

Key Scriptures: Gen. 37:17; 2 Kings 6:13; Mt. 6:22; Jn. 1:45-51; Jas. 1:8; 4:8.

Foundational Information ✎

Dothan was a city of the tribe of Manasseh west of the Jordan River and northeast of Samaria near Mount Gilboa. "Dothan" is transliterated from the Hebrew *Dothayin* (Strong's #1886), which means "dual." "Dothan" has also been translated to mean "two wells, double cistern; double feasts; double sickness, double decree; edicts, decrees, laws, customs." The Greek word for "double minded" is *dipsuchos* (Strong's #1374), which means "two-spirited, vacillating (in opinion or purpose)"—two minds. At Dothan, Joseph found his brethren, who put him in a pit and sold him into slavery. It was also here that the Syrians were blinded by God in the time of the prophet Elisha, then released by grace and sent home.

Fulfilled in Christ ⚓

Jesus Christ is the heavenly Joseph, destined for the throne, envied by his brethren, plotted against, stripped, and sold for silver (Gen. 37:17-36; compare Rev. 3:21). He is also like Elisha, who walked in an open heaven (2 Kings 6:16-17), and who ministered grace to the invading Syrians (2 Kings 6:22-23; see also Jn. 1:16-17). Jesus taught, "The light of the body is the eye: if therefore thine eye be single, thy whole body shall be full of light" (Mt. 6:22). The Pattern Son was unmixed in His devotion to the Father's will (Jn. 5:30; 8:29). Heaven—the realm of the Spirit—was opened over the Messiah at His baptism (Lk. 3:21), and stayed open (Jn. 3:13).

Applied to the Christian ⚖

James declared, "A doubleminded man is unstable in all his ways" (Jas. 1:8; see also Jas. 4:8). Christians must not be of "double heart" (1 Chron. 12:33; Ps. 12:2), beguiled away from the "simplicity" or "singleness" that is in Christ (2 Cor. 11:3). We must choose between the old order and the new; we cannot focus on two feasts, two visions. Our eye must be kept on King Jesus, our vision riveted on spiritual things (Heb. 12:2). Dothan is the place of the open heaven (Jn. 1:51), pictured by Joseph's supernatural dreams about the throne (Gen. 37:5-11), and Elisha's opening the eyes of his servant to see into the realm of Spirit (2 Kings 6:16-17). Jesus is interceding for every believer (Rom. 8:34; Heb. 7:25), saying, "...Lord, I pray Thee, open his eyes, that he may see..." (2 Kings 6:17). The psalmist prayed, "Open Thou mine eyes, that I may behold wondrous things out of Thy law" (Ps. 119:18).

Go Deeper 📖

See Gen. 7:11; 21:19; Ex. 12:38; Deut. 28:12; 2 Kings 4:35; 2 Chron. 7:15; Neh. 13:3; Ps. 34:15; 78:23; Prov. 20:13; 23:30; Is. 42:7; Jer. 25:20,24; 50:37; Ezek. 30:5; Hos. 7:8; Zech. 12:4; Mal. 3:10; Jn. 10:21; Acts 9:8,40; 10:11; 26:18; Rev. 4:1; 11:19; 15:5; 19:11.

∾ ∾ ∾

Dove (Pigeon)

The Holy Spirit; gentleness

Key Scriptures: Mt. 3:16; Mk. 1:10; Lk. 3:22;
Jn. 1:32; Gal. 5:22-23; Eph. 5:17-18.

Foundational Information ✐

"Dove" is from the Hebrew *yownah* (Strong's #3123), which means "a dove (apparently from the warmth of their mating)." Its root is *yayin* (Strong's #3196), which means "to effervesce; wine (as fermented); by implication, intoxication." "Pigeon" is from the Hebrew *gowzal* (Strong's #1469, which means "a nestling (as being comparatively nude of feathers)." The Greek word *peristera* (Strong's # 4058) is translated in the King James Version as "dove, pigeon." The dove is a symbol for the Holy Spirit, as well as for peace, love, and forgiveness. Note the characteristics of the dove (pigeon):

1. Doves come in several colors.
2. Doves have a single eye.
3. Doves can travel long distances and find their way home.
4. Doves were used to carry messages.
5. Doves were used as sacrifices.
6. Doves express affection (coo) and stroke each other.
7. Doves mate for life.
8. Doves are gentle and will not retaliate.
9. Doves mourn.
10. Doves make their nests in the clefts of the rocks.

Fulfilled in Christ ✝

Jesus Christ was given the promise of the Father and poured out the Holy Spirit (Acts 2:33-40; Rom. 5:5). The Holy Spirit is the Spirit of the Father and the Son who make their "abode" in us (Jn. 14:23)—"Christ in you, the hope of glory" (Col. 1:27). Luke records that when Jesus was baptized, "...the Holy Ghost descended in a bodily shape like a dove upon Him" (Lk. 3:22; see also Mt. 3:16; Mk. 1:10; Jn. 1:32). The eyes of the Bridegroom in the Song of Solomon were "...as the eyes of doves by the rivers of waters, washed with milk, and fitly set" (Song 5:12). Jesus walked in an open heaven and saw everything with the eyes of the Spirit (Jn. 1:45-51; 3:13).

Applied to the Christian ⚖

It is the will of God for us to be "filled" with the Holy Spirit (Eph. 5:17-18), symbolized by new wine (Is. 65:8; Joel 3:18; Acts 2:12-18). Spirit-filled Christians are always singing, always thankful, and always submitted to one another in the fear of God (Eph. 5:19-21)—characteristics of the Pattern Son (Gal. 4:6). The Shulamite, a type of the Bride of Christ, had "dove's eyes" (Song 1:15; 4:1). Just as the dove lives "in the clefts of the rock," the believer is "in Christ" (Song 2:14; compare Eph. 1:1,3,10,12,20). Note the parallel characteristics of the dove listed above and consider these personal realities of the Holy Spirit in the life of the believer:

1. The diversity of the Spirit (1 Cor. 12:8-20).
2. The vision of the Spirit (Mt. 6:22-23).
3. The leading of the Spirit (Rom. 8:14).
4. The word of the Spirit (Rev. 3:22).
5. The love of the Spirit (Rom. 5:5).
6. The expression of the Spirit (Rom. 12:3-8).
7. The loyalty of the Spirit (Heb. 9:14).
8. The gentleness of the Spirit (Gal. 5:22-23).
9. The intercession of the Spirit (Rom. 8:26-27).
10. The abode of the Spirit (Jn 14:23).

Go Deeper 📖

See Gen. 8:8-12; Lev. 1:14; 5:7; 12:6-8; Num. 6:10; 2 Kings 6:25; Ps. 55:6; 68:13; Song 5:2; 6:9; Is. 38:14; 59:11; 60:8; Jer. 48:28; Ezek. 7:16; Hos. 7:11; 11:11; Nahum 2:7; Mt. 5:6; 10:16; 21:12; Mk. 11:15; Lk. 1:15,41,67; 11:13; Jn. 2:14-16; Acts 2:1-4; 4:8,31; 6:3; 7:55; 9:17; 11:24; 13:9,52; Eph. 3:19.

∞ ∞ ∞

𝔇own

Humiliation; the curse; death

Key Scriptures: Prov. 15:33; Lk. 10:33; Acts 8:32-33; Phil. 2:5-8; 1 Tim. 3:16.

Foundational Information ❐

"Down" is from the Hebrew root *yarad* (Strong's #3381), which means "to descend (literally, to go downwards; or conventionally to a lower region, as the shore, a boundary, the enemy; or figuratively, to fall); causatively, to bring down (in all the above applications)." Basically, this verb connotes "movement" from a higher to a lower location. *Yarad* is used frequently of "dying"—one "goes down" to his grave. The Greek word for "down" is *katabaino* and means "to descend."

"Humiliation" is the Greek word *tapeinosis* (Strong's #5014), which means "depression (in rank or feeling)." It can also mean "abasement, low estate." It is taken from *tapeinos* which means "lowly, low-lying, of no degree; that which does not rise far from the ground."

Fulfilled in Christ 🜔

Jesus Christ came "down" from Heaven in His incarnation and humiliation (Phil. 2:5-8). The Lord of glory "descended" (Eph. 4:9-10) that He might "...condescend to men of low estate" (Rom. 12:16). In His humiliation, Jesus answered Agur's question (Prov. 30:4; see also Acts 8:33). He was the Bread of life who came down from Heaven to do the Father's will, ever "...meek and lowly in heart..." (Mt. 11:29; compare Jn. 6:33,38). From a child, Jesus knew the meaning of true humility (Lk. 2:51). The Good Shepherd of John 10 is the Good Samaritan of Luke 10. The man who went "down from Jerusalem to Jericho" (Lk. 10:30) is a picture of broken humanity falling from the presence of God ("Jerusalem" means "habitation of peace") to the place of the curse (Josh. 6:26). When the Word made flesh (Jn. 1:14) died on the cross for our sins (Mt. 27:50-51), He answered Isaiah's cry, "Oh that Thou wouldest rend the heavens, that Thou wouldest come down, that the mountains might flow down at thy presence" (Is. 64:1).

Applied to the Christian ⚖

Solomon wisely observed that "...before honour is humility" (Prov. 15:33; 18:12). God has to come "down" to see the best efforts of men (Gen. 11:5; see also Ps. 39:5). Believers must not go "down into Egypt," a type of sin and bondage (see Gen. 12:10; 26:2; Num. 20:15; Is. 31:1). It's the "third day" since Jesus walked the earth (Hos. 6:1-3; see also 2 Pet. 3:8); God is ready to come down in the sight of all the people (Ex. 19:11). Naomi's counsel to Ruth is good for us, "Wash thyself therefore, and anoint thee, and put thy raiment upon thee, and get thee down to the floor..." (Ruth 3:3). The anointing flows down from the Head (Ps. 133:2-3).

With regard to the work of the Lord, let us say with Nehemiah, "...I am doing a great work, so that I cannot come down: why should the work cease, whilst I leave it, and come down to you" (Neh. 6:3; see also Mt. 27:40; Mk. 15:30)? Reluctant sons will always go "down" (Jn. 1:3,5; 2:6). God resists the proud but gives grace to the humble (Jas. 4:7). Solomon declared, "By humility and the fear of the Lord are riches, and honour, and life" (Prov. 22:4).

Go Deeper 📖

See Gen. 24:16; 39:1; Ex. 3:8; 32:6; 33:9; 1 Sam. 2:6; 10:5; 2 Chron. 7:1; Ps. 18:9; 28:1; 115:17; Prov. 5:5; 7:27; Song 6:2,11; Is. 14:11; Lam. 2:10; Ezek. 34:26; 47:1; Joel 2:23; 3:13; Obad. 3-4; Hag. 2:22; Mt. 17:9; Lk. 1:48-52; 19:5; Jn. 3:13; Acts 10:11; 20:19; 2 Cor. 7:6; 10:1; Jas. 1:9,17; 1 Pet. 5:5; Rev. 3:12; 10:1; 21:2.

∾ ∾ ∾

𝔇𝔬𝔴𝔯𝔶 (𝔓𝔩𝔢𝔡𝔤𝔢)

The earnest of our inheritance; the firstfruits of the Spirit

Key Scriptures: Gen. 38:17-20; Rom. 8:23; 2 Cor. 1:22; 5:5; Eph. 1:13-14.

Foundational Information ✐

A dowry was a gift given to the father of one's bride. This was not considered a payment or a purchase price for a wife, but compensation to the father for the loss of her help as a daughter. "Earnest" is the Greek word *arrhabon* (Strong's #728), which means " a pledge, part of the purchase-money or property given in advance as security for the rest." It came to denote "a pledge" of any sort.

"Pledge" is from the Hebrew *'arabown* (Strong's #6162), which means "(in the sense of exchange); a pawn (given as security)." Its root *'arab* (Strong's #6148) means "to braid, intermix; technically, to traffic (as if by barter); also or give to be security (as a kind of exchange)." The dowry could be money or goods, service to make up for the loss, or the performance of some assigned task.

Fulfilled in Christ ☀

Jesus Christ is the Husband of His Church, whom He has purchased with His own blood (Acts 20:28; see also Eph. 5:23; 1 Pet. 1:18-19). As Hosea bought back Gomer, Christ has redeemed His people (Gal. 3:13-14), saying, "And I will betroth thee unto Me for ever; yea, I will betroth thee unto Me in righteousness, and in judgment, and in lovingkindness, and in mercies. I will even betroth thee unto Me in faithfulness..." (Hos. 2:19-20). Jesus is the "one husband" to whom the virgin Church is espoused (2 Cor. 11:2). He has purchased Naomi (the Jew) and Ruth (the Greek), "...reconciling both unto God in one body by the cross" (Eph. 2:16; see also Ruth 4:5; Gal. 3:13-14).

Applied to the Christian ⚖

Believers who are Christ's purchased possession have been sealed with the Holy Spirit of promise, the earnest of our inheritance (Eph. 1:13-14). The Holy Ghost Baptism is God's engagement ring for every Christian. The Pentecostal experience of Acts 2 is not the fullness of the Spirit, but rather "...the firstfruits of the Spirit..." (Rom. 8:23). Paul preached that God has "...sealed us, and given the earnest of the Spirit in our hearts" (2 Cor. 1:22; see also 2 Cor. 5:5; Gal. 4:6). In Genesis 38:17-20, the word used for "pledge" in the Septuagint, the Greek translation of the Old Testament, is *arrhabon*—it refers to Judah's signet, bracelets, and staff, and reveals the power of the Holy Spirit in our lives:

1. Signet (power of attorney)—the Spirit's authority.
2. Bracelets (power of adornment)—the Spirit's beauty.
3. Staff (power of alignment)—the Spirit's government.

Go Deeper 📖

See Gen. 24:1-5; 43:9; 44:32; Ex. 22:26; Deut. 24:6,17; 1 Sam. 17:18; 2 Kings 18:23; Ezra 9:2; Neh. 5:3; Job 17:3; 22:6; 24:3,9; Ps. 45:10-11; 74:2; 78:54; 119:122; Prov. 22:26; Is. 36:8; 54:5; Jer. 32:11-16; Ezek. 18:7,12; 16:11-13; 33:15; Amos 2:8; Rev. 5:9; 14:3-4.

∞ ∞ ∞

𝔇ragon

The devil

Key Scriptures: Ps. 74:13; 91:13; Is. 27:1-2; 51:9; Rev. 12:9.

Foundational Information ✎

"Dragon" is from the Hebrew *tanniyn* (Strong's #8577), which means "a marine or land monster, sea-serpent or jackal." It comes from an unused root probably meaning "to elongate; a monster (as preternaturally formed), a sea-serpent (or other huge marine animal); also a jackal (or other hideous land animal)." The Greek word for "dragon" is *drakon* (Strong's #1404), which means "a fabulous kind of serpent (perhaps as supposed to fascinate)." Its root *derk* ("to see") indicates a keen power of sight.

Fulfilled in Christ ☥

Jesus slew the dragon, the "old" or "ancient" serpent (Rev. 12:9)! Isaiah prophesied, "In that day the Lord with his sore and great and strong sword shall punish leviathan the piercing serpent, even leviathan that crooked serpent; and He shall slay the dragon that is in the sea" (Is. 27:1; see also Is. 57:20; Heb. 4:12). Jesus defeated the devil and broke the power of his demonic "heads" (Ps. 74:13; see also Eph. 6:12; Col. 2:15). The dragon is often connected with the term "leviathan," which is linked with Egypt (Ezek. 29:3). Pharaoh, the king and god of Egypt, typifies satan, the "prince" and "god" of this world system (Jn. 12:31; 2 Cor. 4:4), the "...king over all the children of pride" (Job 41:34). Isaiah prophesied of Him who cut Rahab (Egypt) and wounded the dragon (Is. 51:9; see also Gen. 3:15).

Applied to the Christian ⚖

The serpent of Genesis 3 becomes the dragon of Revelation 12 because men have made him what he is, by giving "place" or "opportunity" to the devil (Eph. 4:27). Originally, the serpent was cursed to go on his belly. Men have ignorantly magnified and worshiped him with their words, giving him mobility—arms and legs (Job 1:7; 2:2)—weapons of unrighteousness (Rom. 6:18-20). Babylon, the spirit of religious confusion has become "...a dwellingplace for dragons..." (Jer. 51:37; see also Rev. 18:2). But the promise is sure to God's people, "Thou shalt tread upon the lion and adder: the young lion and the dragon shalt thou trample under feet" (Ps. 91:13; see also Lk. 10:19; Rom. 16:20). Isaiah foretold a day of restoration for the nations when "the habitation of dragons" would become a lush garden (Is. 35:7).

Go Deeper 📖

See Deut. 32:33; Neh. 2:13; Job 30:29; 41:1; Ps. 24:8; 41:11; 44:19; 98:1; 104:26; 148:7; Is. 13:22; 34:13; 43:20; Jer. 9:11; 10:22; 14:6; 49:33; 51:34; Mic. 1:8; Mal. 1:3; Lk. 10:18; Jn. 16:11; Heb. 2:14-18; 1 Jn. 3:8; Rev. 12:3-4,7,13,16-17; 13:2,4,11; 16:13; 20:2.

∞ ∞ ∞

𝔇rink 𝔒ffering

The blood of Jesus; the sacrifices of joy

Key Scriptures: Lev. 17:11; Ps. 27:6; Mt. 26:28; 2 Cor. 12:15; Phil. 2:17.

Foundational Information ✐

Under the Levitical economy, a drink offering was a libation, an outpouring of wine that normally accompanied the burnt offering and meal offering. The quantity of wine (in proportion to the nature of the sacrifice) was poured out like the blood at the foot of the altar of burnt offerings. "Drink offering" is from the Hebrew *necek* (Strong's #5262), which means "a libation; also a cast idol." Its root *nacak* (Strong's #5258) means "to pour out, especially a libation, or to cast (metal); by analogy, to anoint a king." The Greek word *spendo* (Strong's #4689) means "to pour out as a libation, (figuratively) to devote (one's life or blood, as a sacrifice)." Compare the English word *spend*.

Fulfilled in Christ ✝

Jesus Christ was Heaven's "drink offering" whose blood was poured out at the cross for our sins. At the last supper, the Savior declared, "For this is My blood of the new testament, which is shed for many for the remission of sins" (Mt. 26:28; see also Mk. 14:24; Lk. 22:20). From everlasting, Jesus is the anointed King set in Zion, the Prince who made reconciliation for the people of God (See Ps. 2:6; Prov. 8:23; Is. 9:6; Ezek. 45:17; Acts 5:31). In the "Psalm of the Cross," Messiah prophesied, "I am poured out like water..." (Ps. 22:14; see also Is. 53:12). Doctor Luke vividly described the beginnings of Jesus' "drink offering" in the Garden of Gethsemane, "And being in an agony He prayed more earnestly: and His sweat was as it were great drops of blood falling down to the ground" (Lk. 22:44).

Applied to the Christian ⚖

"...The life of the flesh is in the blood..." (Lev. 17:11). Jesus completely shed His life's blood for us; so "...we ought to lay down our lives for the brethren" (1 Jn. 3:16). True New Testament apostolic ministry is pictured by the drink offering. Paul declared, "And I will very gladly spend and be spent for you; though the more abundantly I love you, the less I be loved" (2 Cor. 12:15). With reference to his life's work and impending martyrdom, the apostle added, "Yea, and if I be offered upon the sacrifice and service of your faith, I joy, and rejoice with you all...For I am now ready to be offered, and the time of my departure is at hand" (Phil. 2:17; 2 Tim. 4:6). The lack of such dedication should make us weep and pray (Joel 1:13). The Body of Christ is a holy priesthood of believers, called to "...offer up spiritual sacrifices, acceptable to God by Jesus Christ" (1 Pet. 2:5). The psalmist declared that he would offer "sacrifices of joy" and "sing praises" in the house of the Lord (Ps. 27:6).

Go Deeper 📖

See Gen. 35:14; Ex. 29:40-41; Lev. 4:34; 23:37; Num. 6:17; 15:5; 28:7-10; 29:6; 1 Sam. 1:15; 2 Kings 16:13-15; 1 Chron. 29:21; 2 Chron. 29:35; Ezra 7:17; Job 30:16; Is. 57:6; Hos. 9:4; Joel 2:14; Acts 20:24; 2 Cor. 8:2; 1 Thess. 1:6; Heb. 12:2; 1 Pet. 4:13.

∞   ∞   ∞

𝔇𝔯𝔬𝔰𝔰

Impurities, imperfections; apostasy, backsliding

Key Scriptures: Ps. 119:119; Prov. 17:3; 25:4; Is. 1:21-28; 2 Tim. 2:20-22; Heb. 10:38-39.

Foundational Information ✐

Dross is the residue left at the end of the smelting process after precious metal has been separated from its impurities. "Dross" is from the Hebrew *ciyg* (Strong's #5509), which means "refuse; scoria." Its root is *cuwg* (Strong's #5472), which means "to flinch, (by implication) to go back, literally (to retreat) or figuratively (to apostatize)." The latter is translated in the King James Version as "backslider, drive, go back, turn (away, back)."

The Hebrew word for "backsliding" is *meshuwbah* (Strong's #4878), which means "apostasy." Its root means "to turn back, retreat." Compare the Greek word *apostasia* (Strong's #646), which means "defection from truth (properly, the state) [apostasy]," and is translated in the King James Version as "falling away, forsake." Similar Greek words mean "divorce" and "revolt, desist, desert, defect."

Fulfilled in Christ ☀

Jesus Christ was perfect, without dross, without sin (2 Cor. 5:21; Heb. 7:26; 1 Pet. 2:22). John declared, "And ye know that He was manifested to take away our sins; and in Him is no sin" (1 Jn. 3:5). Jesus, "the perfect man" (Ps. 37:37), was the Word made flesh (Jn. 1:14); the psalmist declared of Him, "The words of the Lord are pure words: as silver tried in a furnace of earth, purified seven times" (Ps. 12:6; see also Ps. 119:140; Prov. 30:5). Jesus was also "the wisdom from above" that was "first pure..." (Jas. 3:17; see also 1 Cor. 1:30). The King taught, "Blessed are the pure in heart: for they shall see God...Be ye therefore perfect, even as your Father which is in heaven is perfect" (Mt. 5:8,48).

Applied to the Christian ⚖

Solomon said, "The fining pot is for silver, and the furnace for gold: but the Lord trieth the hearts…Take away the dross from the silver, and there shall come forth a vessel for the finer" (Prov. 17:3; 25:4; see also Mal. 3:3; 2 Tim. 2:20-22). Isaiah warned that those who dared to forsake the Lord would be "consumed" in the fire (Is. 1:28). Isaiah's description of Israel (Is. 1:22-23) could apply to God's people today, but His promise is sure, "And I will turn My hand upon thee, and purely purge away thy dross, and take away all thy tin" (Is. 1:25; see also Ezek. 22:18-20). The psalmist described the "wicked of the earth" to be like dross (Ps. 119:119). We can say with the patriarch Job, "But He knoweth the way that I take: when He hath tried me, I shall come forth as gold" (Job 23:10; see also 1 Pet. 1:7; 4:12-13). Let us not "draw back" from present truth (Heb. 10:38-39). God has given us hope, "I will heal their backsliding…" (Hos. 14:4).

Go Deeper 📖

See Deut. 12:19; Josh. 24:16; 2 Sam. 22:27; 2 Chron. 7:19; 15:2; Ps. 19:8; 24:4; 119:53; Prov. 1:8; 14:14; 26:23; 28:4; Jer. 3:6-22; Hos. 4:16; 11:7; Mal. 1:11; Phil. 4:8; Col. 1:28; 1 Tim. 1:5; 3:9; 5:22; 2 Tim. 1:3,5; Tit. 1:15; Jas. 1:4; 1 Pet. 5:10; 1 Jn. 3:3; Rev. 3:2,18.

∾ ∾ ∾

𝔇rought

Lack of the Word; rebellion; thirst

Key Scriptures: Josh. 1:18; Ps. 68:6; Is. 44:3; Amos 8:11; Jn. 7:37; 19:28.

Foundational Information ✎

Drought is the lack of a supply of water. "Drought" is from the Hebrew *choreb* (Strong's #2721), which means "drought or desolation." Its root *charab* (Strong's #2717) means "to parch (through drought)(by analogy), to desolate, destroy, kill." Compare *batstsoreth* (Strong's #1226), which means "restraint (of rain), drought." Its root means "to be isolated."

"Dry" is from the Hebrew *yabbashah* (Strong's #3004), which means "dry ground." Its root *yabesh* (Strong's #3001) means "to be ashamed, confused or disappointed; also (as failing) to dry up (as water) or wither (as herbage)." The Greek word for "dry" is *anudros* (Strong's #504), which means "waterless, dry." The Hebrew word for "rebel" is *marah* (Strong's #4784), which means "to be (causatively, make) bitter (or unpleasant); (figuratively) to rebel (or resist; causatively, to provoke)."

Fulfilled in Christ ☩

Jesus Christ was the Water of the Word from Heaven who broke the drought of man's sin (Jn. 1:1; Eph. 5:26). He still stands in the time of the Feast of Tabernacles and cries, "If any man thirst, let him come to Me…" (Jn. 7:37). Our Lord is "a shadow from the heat" of famine (Is. 25:4; see also Heb. 6:18). As God thirsting for man, and as man thirsting for God, the Savior cried, "…I thirst" (Jn. 19:28; see also Ps. 69:21). The side of the Rock was opened up at Calvary (Ps. 105:41), and the waters ran in the dry places like a river (Jn. 19:34; see also 1 Cor. 10:4). Jesus ascended on high, led captivity captive and gave gifts for the rebellious (Ps. 68:18; compare Eph. 4:8-15). Isaiah prophesied of Jesus' relationship with the Father, "For He shall grow up before Him as a tender plant, and as a root out of a dry ground…" (Is. 53:2). Those who live without Jesus "rebel against the light" (Job 24:13; see also Jn. 8:12).

Applied to the Christian ⚖

Amos predicted the spiritual famine of our day, "…not a famine of bread, nor a thirst for water, but of hearing the words of the Lord" (Amos 8:11). Isaiah described the Church as "…a tabernacle for a shadow in the daytime from the heat, and for a place of refuge, and for a covert from storm and from rain" (Is. 4:6). God has led His people through the wilderness and the place of "…drought, where there was no water…" (Deut. 8:15). God's promise is sure, "And the Lord shall…satisfy thy soul in drought…and thou shalt be like a watered garden, and like a spring of water, whose waters fail not" (Is. 58:11; see also Jer. 2:6). God has promised to send revival, "For I will pour water upon him that is thirsty, and floods upon the dry ground…" (Is. 44:3). The day will come when we will thirst no more (Rev. 7:16).

There is a drought upon the waters of Babylon, the idolatrous spirit of religious confusion (Jer. 50:38; 51:43). Men without the Word are wells and clouds "without water" (2 Pet. 2:17; Jude 12) who have vexed the Holy Spirit (Is. 63:10). Like the Gibeonites who deceived Joshua, the bread (word) of these preachers is "dry and mouldy" (Josh. 9:5); men who are void of His Spirit can never cover God's people (Is. 30:1). The rebellious who have isolated themselves from the family and government of God dwell in a dry land (Ps. 68:6; see also Ezek. 37:1-4; Jon. 2:10). Unclean spirits inhabit and walk through "dry places" (Mt. 12:43; Lk. 11:24). The wages of rebellion is death (Josh. 1:18; Rom. 6:23).

Go Deeper 📖

See Gen. 31:40; Ex. 17:3; Num. 20:10; Deut. 9:7; Judg. 6:36-40; 1 Sam. 12:14-15; 15:23; Job 12:15; 30:30; Ps. 32:4; 63:1; 78:8; 107:11; Is. 1:2,20,23; 41:17-18; 65:2; Jer. 14:1; 17:8; Ezek. 2:3-8; 20:38; Dan. 9:9; Hos. 2:3; 9:14; 13:5; Nahum 1:10; Zeph. 2:13; Hag. 1:11; 2:6; Mt. 5:6; Jn. 4:13-15; 6:35.

∞ ∞ ∞

𝔇runkard (𝔊lutton)

Excess; the abuse of God's gifts

Key Scriptures: Deut. 21:20; Prov. 23:20-21; Rom. 13:13;
1 Cor. 5:11; 6:10; Gal. 5:21,23; Eph. 5:18.

Foundational Information ✐

A drunkard is one who suffers from a drugged or deranged condition that results from drinking intoxicating beverages. "Drunkard" is from the Hebrew *cobe'* (Strong's #5435), which means "potation, concretely (wine), or abstractly (carousal)." Its root is *caba'* (Strong's #5433), which means "to quaff to satiety, become tipsy." Compare *shikkowr* (Strong's #7910), which means "intoxicated, as a state or a habit." Its root means "to satiate with a stimulating drink or influence." The Greek word for "drunkard" is *methusos* (Strong's #3183), which means "tipsy, (as noun) a sot." Drunkenness and gluttony go hand in hand.

A glutton is a person who is debased and excessive in his eating habits. "Glutton" or "riotous eater" is from the Hebrew *zalal* (Strong's #2151), which means "to shake (as in the wind), to quake; figuratively, to be loose morally, worthless or prodigal." Its root *zuwl* (Strong's #2107) means "to shake out, (by implication) to scatter profusely; figuratively, to treat lightly." Different Greek words for "excess" mean "the lack of self-restraint; un-savedness; an overflow or surplus of wine; license."

Fulfilled in Christ ☦

Jesus Christ is our sober Savior, the One who knew that the Father's will was serious business (Lk. 2:49). The fruit of the Spirit—the divine nature of Jesus—is "temperance" or "self-control" (Gal. 5:23). The "Master" mastered His appetites (see Mt. 9:11; Jn. 13:13; Eph. 6:9; Col. 4:1). Our King, the Son of nobility, ate and drank for strength, not for drunkenness (Eccles. 10:17). Jesus' food and drink was to do the will of the Father, and to finish His work (Jn. 4:34; 17:4). He warned His followers, "And take heed to yourselves, lest at any time your hearts be overcharged with surfeiting, and drunkenness, and cares of this life, and so that day come upon you unawares" (Lk. 21:34). Because Jesus befriended and loved publicans and sinners, He was accused by religious men of being a glutton and a winebibber (Mt. 11:19; Lk. 7:34).

Applied to the Christian ⚖

The whole of Scripture teaches temperance, not total abstinence; however, it would be wise for kings (leaders) to abstain from wine (Prov. 31:4-6; see also 1 Tim. 3:2,11; 5:23; Tit. 1:8; 2:2-4). God has a word for every bartender, "Woe unto him that giveth his neighbour drink, that puttest thy bottle to him, and makest him drunken..." (Hab. 2:15). Let us heed Paul's advice, "And be not drunk with wine, wherein is excess; but be filled with the Spirit" (Eph. 5:18). The Holy Spirit, the Restrainer, lives within (Gal. 4:6;

Col. 1:27). Drunkards and gluttons are stubborn and rebellious, refusing to hear the voice of God (Deut. 21:20). Solomon warned, "Be not among winebibbers; among riotous eaters of flesh: For the drunkard and the glutton shall come to poverty: and drowsiness shall clothe a man with rags" (Prov. 23:20-21; see also Rom. 13:13).

Isaiah prophesied of those in the old order, "whose glorious beauty is a fading flower,"—men who play with the gifts of the Holy Spirit (symbolized by wine)— as "the drunkards of Ephraim" (Is. 28:1-3). Religious Babylon has made all the nations drunk (Jer. 51:7; see also Rev. 17:6; 18:1-4). Believers are not to keep company with "drunkards" who will not inherit the Kingdom (1 Cor. 5:11; 6:10; Gal. 5:21). Paul admonished, "And every man that striveth for the mastery is temperate in all things..." (1 Cor. 9:25).

Go Deeper 📖

See Gen. 9:20-21; 1 Sam. 25:36; Job 12:25; Ps. 69:12; 107:27; Prov. 26:9; 28:7; Is. 19:14; 24:20; Jer. 23:9; 25:27; 48:26; Ezek. 23:33; Joel 1:5; Nahum 1:10; Mt. 24:49; Lk. 12:45; Acts 2:15; Rom. 14:17,21; 1 Cor. 11:21; 1 Thess. 5:6-8; Tit. 2:6; 1 Pet. 1:13; 4:7; 5:8.

∽ ∽ ∽

𝔇umbness

No prophetic voice, no word from God; silence; contentment

Key Scriptures: Amos 3:7; Mk. 7:32-37; 9:17-29; Acts 8:32-33;
1 Cor. 12:1-3; 1 Tim. 6:6-8; Rev. 19:10.

Foundational Information ✐

Dumbness or being mute is the inability to speak. "Dumb" is from the Hebrew *'illem* (Strong's #483), which means "speechless." Its root is *'alam* (Strong's #481), which means "to tie fast; hence (of the mouth) to be tongue-tied." The Greek word for "dumb" is *siapao* (Strong's #4623), which means "silence, a hush; properly, muteness, involuntary stillness, or inability to speak." Compare *kophos* (Strong's #2974), which means "blunted, (figuratively) of hearing (deaf) or speech (dumb)." This word signifies "blunted, dull," as of a weapon; hence, "blunted in tongue." Compare *aphonos* (Strong's #880), which means "voiceless; mute (by nature or choice); figuratively, unmeaning."

Fulfilled in Christ ✝

Jesus Christ is the sum of the Father's "Word" to man—the Logos, the divine Discourse (Jn. 1:1). The words that He speaks "...are spirit, and they are life" (Jn. 6:63).

Redemption's ropes "tied" Jesus to the cross (Ps. 118:27). The testimony of Jesus is the spirit of prophecy (Rev. 19:10). Jesus healed the boy with a dumb spirit (Mk. 9:17-29; see also Mt. 9:32-33; 12:22; 15:30-31). Mark testified, "...He maketh botl. the deaf to hear, and the dumb to speak" (Mk. 7:37). Ever content to rest in the will of His Father, the Lamb of God was led to the cross without one sound of complaint (Is. 53:7-8; Mt. 26:63; Acts 8:32-33). The psalmist declared, "Our God shall come, and shall not keep silence..." (Ps. 50:3). The inscription over Psalm 56 describes our King's earthly ministry: *Jonath-elem-rechokim* means "the silent dove among the strangers; the mute dove among them that are afar off."

Applied to the Christian ⚖

Amos declared, "Surely the Lord God will do nothing, but He revealeth His secret unto His servants the prophets" (Amos 3:7). Watchmen without the Holy Spirit "cannot bark" (Is. 56:10; see also Hab. 2:18-19; 1 Cor. 12:1-3); they cannot order their speech because of darkness (ignorance) (Job 37:19). As the Lord restores His Church, He makes the "...tongue of the dumb sing" (Is. 35:6). The Pentecostal experience releases the prophetic dynamic; Jesus promised His disciples that they would "speak with new tongues" in His name (Mk. 16:17; see also Acts 2:1-4; 10:46-47; 19:6). The end-time Church shall go forth like cherubim, "as the voice of the Almighty, the voice of speech, as the noise of an host..." (Ezek. 1:24). Believers must learn to be "content" in all things (Phil. 4:11; Heb. 13:5), for "...godliness with contentment is great gain" (1 Tim. 6:6).

Go Deeper 📖

See Gen. 11:7; Ex. 4:10-11; Job 12:20; Ps. 19:1-3; 38:13; 83:1; Prov. 31:8; Song 4:3; Is. 33:19; 62:6; Jer. 1:6-7; Ezek. 3:26; 24:27; 33:22; Dan. 10:15; Hab. 2:20; Mt. 26:73; Lk. 1:20-22,64; 11:14; 1 Cor. 2:4; 14:10; 2 Cor. 10:10; 11:6; 1 Pet. 2:15; 2 Pet. 2:16; Rev. 8:1.

∞ ∞ ∞

𝕯𝖚𝖓𝖌

Refuse, rubbish, garbage; that which is useless,
rejected, despised; the sins of the past

Key Scriptures: 1 Sam. 2:8; 2 Kings 9:37; Job 20:7; Mal. 2:3; Phil. 3:8.

Foundational Information ✐

Dung is waste produced by humans and animals as a part of the process of digesting food. "Dung" is from the Hebrew *peresh* (Strong's #6569), which means "excrement (as eliminated)." Its root is *parash* (Strong's #6567), meaning "to separate, literally (to disperse) or figuratively (to specify); also (by implication) to wound." The Greek word for "dung" is *skubalon* (Strong's #4657), which means "what is thrown to the dogs, refuse (ordure)"; it also denotes "the leavings of a feast," that which is thrown away from the table.

Dung was used as fertilizer, and dried dung was used as fuel. A dunghill was a heap or pit of human and animal wastes. "Dunghill" is from the Hebrew *'ashpoth* (Strong's #830), which means "a heap of rubbish or filth." Compare *nevaluw* (Strong's #5122), which means "to be foul; a sink."

Fulfilled in Christ

Jesus, the divine Bullock, took away the dung (the sin) of the world, and buried it "without the camp" (Lev. 16:27; compare Jn. 1:29; Heb. 13:11-12). He who was rich became poor (2 Cor. 8:9) that He might raise up the poor out of the dust and lift "...the needy out of the dunghill" (Ps. 113:7; see also Is. 53:3). Dung can represent the sins of the past; Jesus was set forth by the Father "...to be a propitiation through faith in His blood, to declare His righteousness for the remission of sins that are past, through the forbearance of God" (Rom. 3:25). In the sacrifices of the Old Testament, there was "...a remembrance again made of sins every year" (Heb. 10:3). Our sins are past (like dung) in Christ; the better blood of the New Testament has this promise, "...and their sins and their iniquities will I remember no more" (Heb. 8:12; 10:17). Messiah knew how "...to refuse the evil, and choose the good" (Is. 7:15).

Applied to the Christian

Satan is "beelzebub," the "lord of the flies," the god of the dunghill. Our victorious Lord has raised us up "from the dunghill" that we might inherit the throne of glory (1 Sam 2:8; see also Eph. 2:6; Rev. 3:21). The apostle Paul testified, "...I count all things but loss for the excellency of the knowledge of Christ Jesus my Lord...and do count them but dung, that I may win Christ" (Phil. 3:8; see also Ps. 45:10; Lk. 9:62). So may we not be content to eat yesterday's leftovers, the table scraps of a previous order or feast (see Deut. 16:16; Mal. 2:3; Lk. 15:16; Phil. 3:12-14). "Dove's dung" (2 Kings 6:25)—the residue of a previous move of the Spirit of God (Mt. 3:16)—is what is left of the dove after the dove has flown away! The carcass of dead religious systems are as dung to the Lord (2 Kings 9:37; see also Rev. 2:20). The wicked man and the hypocrite "...shall perish for ever like his own dung" (Job 20:7).

Go Deeper

See Ex. 29:14; Lev. 4:11; 8:17; Num. 19:5; 1 Kings 14:10; 2 Kings 18:27; Neh. 2:13; 3:13-14; 4:2,10; 12:31; Ps. 83:10; Song 2:11; Jer. 8:2; 9:22; 16:4; 25:33; Lam. 4:5; Ezek. 4:12,15; Zeph. 1:17; Lk. 13:8; 1 Cor. 1:28; Gal. 1:13; Eph. 2:1-3,11; 1 Tim. 4:7; 1 Pet. 2:10.

∞ ∞ ∞

𝕯ust

The lowness and frailty of the Adamic nature;
death; the carnal mind; sorrow, mourning; Abraham's seed

Key Scriptures: Gen. 2:7; 3:14; 13:16; 28:14; Is. 65:25; 1 Cor. 15:44-49.

Foundational Information

Dust is loose earth. "Dust" is from the Hebrew *'aphar* (Strong's #6083), which means "dust (as powdered or gray); hence, clay, earth, mud." This word can also mean "clods, plaster, ashes, rubbish." The Greek word for "dust" is *koniortos* (Strong's #2868), which means "(to rouse); pulverulence (as blown about)." Compare *choos* (Strong's #5522), which means "a heap (as poured out), rubbish; loose dirt."

God fashioned Adam from the dust of the earth. The serpent was cursed to eat dust as he crawled on his belly. Dust was poured upon the head as a sign of mourning. To rise from the dust meant to rise from the place of mourning, not to sit down again in the dust. To throw dust at a person expressed anger and contempt. The scribes taught that the dust of heathen lands was defiling; to shake the dust from one's feet indicated that that house was heathen, impure, and profane.

Fulfilled in Christ

The first Adam was made a living soul, a man of dust; Jesus Christ, the Last Adam, was made a quickening or life-giving spirit. Paul added, "The first man is of the earth, earthy: the second man is the Lord from heaven" (1 Cor. 15:47). Through the power of His resurrection, Jesus has "raised" us up from the dust (1 Sam. 2:8; Rom. 6:4-5; Eph. 2:1-6). He was the fiery Light who came from Heaven and consumed the dust, swallowing up death in victory (1 Kings 18:38; Is. 25:8; 1 Cor. 15:54). Jesus made every enemy to "lick the dust" (Ps. 72:9)! The Psalm of the Cross prophesied the agony of the Messiah's sorrow, "My strength is dried up like a potsherd; and My tongue cleaveth to my jaws; and thou hast brought Me into the dust of death" (Ps. 22:15).

Applied to the Christian

Moses wrote, "And the Lord God formed man of the dust of the ground..." (Gen. 2:7; see also Prov. 8:26). Paul declared, "And as we have borne the image of the earthy, we shall also bear the image of the heavenly" (1 Cor. 15:49; see also Rom. 8:29; 2 Cor. 3:18). As new creatures, we are no longer living loose, blown, and "tossed about" (Eph. 4:14; see also Jas. 1:6). The only thing that the serpent can feed upon is dust (Gen. 3:14; Is. 65:25); the carnal mind of man is where the devil lives, and moves, and operates (Rom. 8:1-6). The Church is Abraham's seed through Jesus Christ (see Gen. 13:16; 28:14; Mt. 1:1; Gal. 3:29). Isaiah exhorted us, "Shake thyself from the dust; arise, and sit down, O Jerusalem: loose thyself from the bands of thy neck, O captive daughter of Zion" (Is. 52:2).

Go Deeper 📖

See Gen. 3:19; 18:27; Deut. 32:24; Josh. 7:6; 2 Sam. 16:13; 1 Kings 16:2; Job 4:19; 7:5; 17:16; 21:26; 22:24; 34:15; 42:6; Ps. 7:5; 18:42; 30:9; 102:14; 103:14; 113:7; Eccles. 3:20; 12:7; Is. 5:24; 40:12,15; Lam. 2:10; Ezek. 27:30; Dan. 12:2; Mic. 1:10; 7:17; Zeph. 1:17; Mt. 10:14; Mk. 6:11; Lk. 9:5; 10:11; Acts 13:51; 22:23.

∾ ∾ ∾

𝔇𝔴𝔞𝔯𝔣

Immaturity; that which is small

Key Scriptures: Lev. 21:18-20; Lk. 2:52; Eph. 3:17-18; 4:13-15.

Foundational Information ✑

A dwarf is a person, animal, or plant significantly below normal size. "Dwarf" is from the Hebrew *daqaq* (Strong's #1854), which means "to crush (or intransitively) crumble." Its root *hadak* (Strong's #1915) means "to crush with the foot," and it is translated in the King James Version as "tread down."

The Greek word for "stature" is *helikia* (Strong's #2244), which means "maturity (in years or size)." Its root *helikos* means "comrade, one of the same age; as big as." The Greek word for "height" is *hupsos* (Strong's #5311), which means "elevation, (abstractly) altitude, (specifically) the sky, or (figuratively) dignity." *Hupsos* can also mean "summit, top"; its root is the preposition *huper* which means "over, above."

Fulfilled in Christ ⵙ

Almighty God dwarfed Himself in the incarnation, reducing Himself down to eight pounds of love to be laid in a manger (see Lk. 2:11-12; Col. 1:19; 2:9; 1 Tim. 3:16)! Jesus Christ was crushed and bruised by the Father at the cross (Is. 53:5). Just as the incense in Moses' tabernacle was beaten very small, so Jesus was "scourged" for us (Mt. 27:26; Mk. 15:15; see also Ex. 30:36; Lev. 16:12), and with His "stripes" we were healed (1 Pet. 2:24). The manna that appeared on the ground as a "small round thing" (Ex. 16:14) prefigured the Bread from heaven who was that "holy thing" in the virgin's womb (Lk. 1:35; see also Jn. 6:48). Yet "Jesus increased in wisdom and stature, and in favour with God and man" (Lk. 2:52). By His incarnation Jesus was made a "little lower" than the angels

(Heb. 2:7-9), but His exaltation and ascension catapulted the King to the top of the mountain as the Head of the Church (Eph. 1:20-23). The "still small voice" (1 Kings 19:12) is the voice of the Lord from within (Gal. 4:6; Col. 1:27). We have a fully qualified High Priest "over" the Church, the House of God (Heb. 3:6; 10:21).

Applied to the Christian   ⚖

Under the Levitical economy, a dwarf was disqualified from the priesthood; the New Testament "royal priesthood" is called to be a mature Church (1 Pet. 2:9). Believers cannot by anxiety add one cubit to their spiritual stature (Mt. 6:27; Lk. 12:25); we must "grow in grace" (2 Pet. 3:18). Jesus, the Seed of the woman, had a small beginning (Lk. 2:16), but greatly increased and multiplied through His people (see Acts 2:41; 4:4; 5:14; Rev. 7:9; 19:6). The full "height" or "dignity" of our Lord (Eph. 3:17-18) will be realized in a many-membered, corporate Man who grows unto the fullness of His "stature" (Eph. 4:13; see also Song 7:7). This "glorious Church" (Eph. 5:27), the "city" of the living God (Mt. 5:14; Heb. 11:10; 12:22-23), will reach its maximum "height" (Rev. 21:16). Daniel saw this people and Kingdom as a great Stone who "...became a great mountain, and filled the whole earth" (Dan. 2:35; see also Rev. 11:15).

Go Deeper   📖

See Gen. 41:3-7,23-24; Ex. 12:4; Deut. 9:21; 1 Sam. 14:43; 1 Kings 3:7; 17:12-13; Eccles. 5:12; Song 2:15; 8:8; Is 40:15; Mal. 4:2; Mt. 6:30; 8:26; 10:42; 14:31; 15:34; 16:8; Mk. 4:36; Lk. 5:3; 19:3; Acts 5:24; Rom. 8:39; Gal. 4:19; Eph. 2:21; 4:15; 2 Thess. 1:3; 1 Pet. 2:2; 1 Jn. 2:1,12-13,18,28; 3:7,18; 4:4; 5:21.

𝕰agle

The overcomer; resurrection; heavenly things

Key Scriptures: Deut. 32:11-12; Ps. 103:5; Is. 40:31;
Ezek. 1:10,14; Eph. 1:3; 2:6; Rev. 3:21.

Foundational Information ✐

The eagle is the king of the birds. "Eagle" is from the Hebrew *nesher* (Strong's #5404), which is taken from an unused root meaning "to lacerate; the eagle (or other large bird of prey)." The Greek word for "eagle" is *aetos* (Strong's #105). It means "an eagle (from its wind-like flight)," and is taken from *aer*, the word for "air."

The majestic golden eagle (so named for its golden crown which becomes more evident with maturity), or imperial eagle, has a wingspan of six to ten feet and builds its up to two-ton nest in lofty, virtually inaccessible, rocky places (6,000 to 10,000 feet high). The courting behavior and eventual locking of talons in "marriage" takes place high in the heavens (eagles mate for life). The female lays from one to three eggs and will not raise more than two eaglets. Both parents sit on the eggs, guard the nest, and bring food to the young. As the eaglet matures, it is taught how to stand before it is taught how to fly. Later, the parent eagle carries its eaglet on its back until the youngster masters the art of flying. This great bird has keen eyesight (eight times more powerful than man's) and swift flight enabling it to seize the prey. These skills allow the eagle to pick its diet, finding whatever it wants. The eagle can see a storm coming from a distance; therefore, the eagle can rise above the wind and rain. The primary enemy of the eagle is the serpent. An eagle can stay aloft for hours, rarely moving his wings and riding wind currents. An eagle renews its strength and youthful appearance yearly after shedding its feathers. Eagles tend to do have a long lifespan, living 20 to 30 years in the wild, and longer in captivity.

Fulfilled in Christ ☦

Jesus Christ is the majestic Son of God, the high-flying golden Eagle (so revealed in the Gospel of John) (Ps. 93:1-5). He is the resurrected, enthroned King of the air (Rev. 19:16). Jesus is the imperial Eagle, the Overcomer, the One who even conquered and subdued death (see Lk. 11:22; Jn. 16:33; 1 Cor. 15:55-58; Rev. 3:21). All authority has been given Him to rule Heaven and earth (Mt. 28:18). Having soared far above all principalities and powers, He is forever seated in the heavens, having made His "nest as high as the eagle" (Jer. 49:16; see also Eph. 1:20-23). The good Shepherd who carries His young (Is. 40:11; Jn. 10:11), like the parent eagle (Deut. 32:11-12), is the God who leads and feeds His people.

Applied to the Christian ⚖

Golden eagle Christians, partakers of the divine nature and the heavenly calling, have been raised up to sit with Christ in "heavenly places" (Eph. 1:3,20; 2:6; 3:10; see also Heb. 3:1; 2 Pet. 1:4). "Imperial" means "having supreme authority," and it reveals the authority of the believer in Jesus' name (Mk. 16:15-20). We have been raised from the death of trespasses and sins (Eph. 2:1-3). Isaiah declared, "But they that wait upon the Lord shall renew their strength; they shall mount up with wings as eagles; they shall run, and not be weary; and they shall walk, and not faint" (Is. 40:31; see also Job 39:27). The ninety-first Psalm describes the "nest" of eagle Christians. The psalmist further affirmed the faithfulness of God, "Who satisfieth thy mouth with good things; so that thy youth is renewed like the eagle's" (Ps. 103:5). Eagle Christians have learned the ways of the wind of God's Spirit (Jn. 3:8; Rom. 8:14). Like the eagle, our primary enemy is the serpent; yet we need not fear him (Lk. 10:19; 1 Pet. 5:8-10). The eagle nature, our new nature in Christ, is greater than he that is in the world (1 Jn. 4:4; 5:4).

Go Deeper 📖

See Ex. 19:4; Lev. 11:13,18; Num. 13:30; Deut. 14:12,17; 28:49; 2 Sam. 1:23; Job 9:26; Prov. 23:5; 30:17,19; Jer. 4:13; 48:40; 49:22; Lam. 4:19; Ezek. 17:3,7; Dan. 4:33; Hos. 8:1; Obad. 4; Mic. 1:16; Hab. 1:8; Mt. 24:28; Lk. 17:37; Rom. 3:4; 12:21; 1 Jn. 2:13-14; Rev. 2:7,11,17,26; 3:5,12; 4:7; 12:11,14.

∞ ∞ ∞

𝔈ar

Hearing; understanding; channel to receive faith

Key Scriptures: Prov. 20:12; Is. 11:3; 50:4-5; Mt. 11:5; Rom. 10:17; Heb. 5:7-9.

Foundational Information ✐

The ear is the organ of hearing. "Ear" is from the Hebrew *'ozen* (Strong's #241), which means "broadness, (concrete) the ear (from its form in man)." Compare *shama* (Strong's #8085), which means "to hear intelligently (often with implication of attention, obedience…)." To give ear means to pay careful attention. Stopping the ears means refusing to listen. To incline, or turn the ear toward, is to desire to understand. The ears of the Lord reveal that He hears and understands our prayers (in contrast to idols which cannot hear).

Fulfilled in Christ ✝

Jesus Christ, completely obedient to do the will of the Father without complaining, had perfect hearing (Heb. 5:7-8). The ear of the Messiah, the servant of Jehovah, was pierced or "opened" (Is. 50:5; see also Ex. 21:1-6; Deut. 15:16-17; Ps. 40:6). Jesus the

Word is the Creator of all things (Jn. 1:1-3). This includes "the hearing ear, and the seeing eye" (Prov. 20:12). Jesus healed the deaf (see Mt. 11:5; Mk. 7:32-37; 9:25; Lk. 7:22), and He can also restore our ear (Lk. 22:49-51). The psalmist declared of Him, "The eyes of the Lord are upon the righteous, and His ears are open unto their cry" (Ps. 34:15). Jesus the Messiah, the righteous Judge (Jn. 5:22; 7:24; 2 Tim. 4:8), did not "reprove after the hearing of His ears" (Is. 11:3). The Messiah admonished, "Who hath ears to hear, let him hear" (Mt. 13:9; see also verses 15-16,43).

Applied to the Christian ⚖

We are to give our ears to God, ever ready to hear His voice (Eccles. 5:1). Those who have the tongue of the learned have the ear of the learned (Is. 50:4-5), but the wicked "...are like the deaf adder that stoppeth her ear" (Ps. 58:4). Men with partial hearing have what Amos described as "a piece of an ear" (Amos 3:12). But the priestly ears of the believer have been consecrated by the blood of the Lamb (Ex. 29:20; Rev. 1:5-6). The prophet Isaiah admonished, "Incline your ear, and come unto Me: hear, and your soul shall live..." (Is. 55:3). God hears us when we pray; we can say with the psalmist, "Because He hath inclined His ear unto me, therefore will I call upon him as long as I live" (Ps. 116:2). The believer is to experience all three feasts (Deut. 16:16): Passover (the new birth), Pentecost (filled with the Spirit), and Tabernacles (maturity)—we thus receive the "ear" of the Spirit so that we might fully understand the "corn" of His Word (Mk. 4:28; see also Prov. 1:22-23; Jn. 16:13). "He that hath an ear, let him hear..." (Rev. 2:17; 3:22).

Go Deeper 📖

See Ex. 15:26; Lev. 8:23-24; 1 Sam. 9:15; Job 42:5; Ps. 5:1; 10:17; 17:6; 18:6; 49:1; 86:1; 94:9; 115:6; Prov. 2:2; 5:1; 15:31; 28:9; Eccles. 1:8; Is. 33:15; 35:5; 42:20; Jer. 5:21; Ezek. 3:10; 44:5; Mt. 10:27; 11:15; 13:15-16; Mk. 4:28; 7:35; Acts 7:51,57; 28:27; 1 Cor. 2:9; 12:16; 2 Tim. 4:3-4; 1 Pet. 3:12.

∞ ∞ ∞

Early Rain (Former Rain)

The Pentecostal outpouring; the firstfruits of the Spirit

Key Scriptures: Deut. 11:14; Ps. 84:6; Jer. 5:24;
Hos. 6:3; Joel 2:23; Rom. 8:23; Jas. 5:7.

Foundational Information ✎

The "early" or "former" or "first" rain is to be differentiated from the "latter" rain. The "early" rains were the first autumn showers (October) and the "latter" rains were the last spring showers (May). No rain fell in the land from May until September. The "early" rains signaled the farmer to begin his plowing, to prepare the soil for the seed; the "latter" rains matured the barley and wheat crops for harvest.

"Early" in James 5:7 is from the Greek *proimos* (Strong's #4406), which means "dawning, (by analogy) autumnal (showering, the first of the rainy season)." "First" in Deuteronomy 11:14 and "former" in Jeremiah 5:24 and Hosea 6:3 are from the Hebrew *yowreh* (Strong's #3138), which means "sprinkling; hence, a sprinkling (or autumnal showers)." Derived from the primitive root *yarah* (Strong's #3384), it means "to flow as water (to rain); transitively, to lay or throw (especially an arrow, to shoot); figuratively, to point out (as if by aiming the finger), to teach." This is the same root for the Hebrew *mowreh* (Strong's #4175), meaning "an archer; also teacher or teaching; also the early rain," translated in the King James Version as "former" in Joel 2:23 and "rain" in Psalm 84:6.

Fulfilled in Christ

Hosea prophesied of the Lord Jesus, "...and He shall come unto us as the rain, as the latter and former rain unto the earth" (Hos. 6:3; see also Ps. 72:6). The rain is a Person! Paul explained, "And because ye are sons, God hath sent forth the Spirit of His Son into your hearts..." (Gal. 4:6). The apostle also described this experience as "Christ [the anointed One] in you" (Col. 1:27). The early rain is the "teaching rain" (Joel 2:23; see also Deut. 32:2): Jesus sent the Teacher, the Holy Ghost, to guide His Church into all truth (Jn. 14:26; 15:26; 16:13). Jesus is the One who baptizes the believer with the Holy Ghost and with fire (Acts 1:5). He sent this former rain in the appointed season of the Feast of Pentecost (Lev. 23:15-21; Jer. 5:24; Acts 2:1). The Father, the Husbandman (Jn. 15:1), waits for the precious fruit—the divine nature of His Son, the true Vine—revealed in a people, "...and hath long patience for it, until He receive the early and latter rain" (Jas. 5:7).

Applied to the Christian

The "early" rain was the Pentecostal outpouring of the Spirit at the beginning of this age (Acts 2). The "latter" rain is the present outpouring of the Spirit at the end of this age. The "first rain" (Deut. 11:14) is the "firstfruits of the Spirit" (Rom. 8:23). The purpose of the Holy Ghost, our Teacher, is to reveal Jesus (Jn. 14:26; 15:26; 16:13). The early rain prepares our hearts for the seed of God's Word (Prov. 1:22-23); the latter rain brings that harvest of His nature within His people to maturity (Eph. 4:13; 1 Jn. 4:17). This former rain is sent "moderately" or "righteously" (Joel 2:23). His righteous Kingdom is in the Holy Ghost (Rom. 14:17; see also Hos. 10:12). The power of His Spirit turns our places of weeping into pools of life-giving water (Ps. 84:6; Jn. 4:13-14).

Go Deeper

See Lev. 26:4; Deut. 28:12; Ezra 10:9; Job 28:26; 29:23; 36:27; 37:6; Ps. 46:5; 57:8; 63:1; 68:9; 78:34; 90:14; 108:2; Prov. 8:17; Song 7:12; Is. 26:9; 30:23; 55:10; Ezek. 1:28;

Hos. 5:15; Mt. 5:45; Lk. 21:38; Jn. 8:2; Acts 2:4; 5:21; 10:46; 14:17; 19:6; 2 Cor. 1:22; 5:5; Eph. 1:13-14; Heb. 6:7.

∾ ∾ ∾

𝕰arring

Covenant; man's ear married to God's voice

Key Scriptures: Gen. 24:22; Ex. 32:1-3; Ps. 29; Song 2:8; 5:2; Ezek. 16:12; Heb. 3:15.

Foundational Information

Earrings were pieces of jewelry, generally fashioned from silver or gold, used to adorn the ear lobe in Bible times. Although these were generally worn only by Hebrew women, Ishmaelite men also wore earrings. "Earring" is from the Hebrew *nexem* (Strong's #5141), which means "a nose-ring," translated as "earring, jewel" in the King James Version. Earrings were loops worn alone or with pendants attached. They were made from various metals (such as silver and gold) or stones and were sometimes decorated with jewels. These earrings were signs of luxury, and as personal possessions, they were sometimes offered to God.

Fulfilled in Christ

Jesus Christ was the divine Earring, "an offering of gold" unto the Father (Ex. 35:22). He was the the One who was offered "...to make an atonement for our souls before the Lord" (Num. 31:50). Long before His incarnation, He agreed to the everlasting, intertheistic covenant between the Father and the Son (see Ps. 2:7; 110:4; Heb. 10:5-10; 13:20). Gold speaks of the divine nature. Jesus' human ear was attuned to His Father's voice; He was perfectly obedient— sinless (Jn. 8:29; Heb. 4:15; 7:26). The Savior declared, "...as I hear, I judge: and My judgment is just; because I seek not Mine own will, but the will of the Father which hath sent Me" (Jn. 5:30). The sweetest sound of all is the voice of Jesus (Song 2:8; 5:2).

Applied to the Christian

Adam heard the voice of His Creator walking in the Garden in the "cool" or "spirit" of the day (Gen. 3:8; compare Rev. 1:10). The Christian's greatest priority is to learn to hear the voice of his God. Our ears must be pierced with divine things (symbolized by the gold). We must be "willing hearted" (Ex. 35:22), offering our ears to God. As with Isaac and his bride Rebekah, Jesus has sent the Holy Spirit (typified by Eliezer) to the Church with a golden earring (Gen. 24:22,30,47; see also Eph. 5:22-33). We are warned by the poor example of the faithless Israelites who broke off (divorced) the covenant between their ears and God's voice in the day of provocation (Ex. 32:1-3; Heb. 3:7-15; 4:7). In Christ, we have been given the following items (Ezek. 16:12):

1. A jewel for our forehead—the mind of Christ.
2. Earrings for our ears—the ability to hear His voice.
3. A beautiful crown upon our head—the full assurance of His finished work.

Go Deeper 📖

See Gen. 22:18; 35:4; Ex. 19:5; Deut. 5:22-28; Judg. 8:24-26; 1 Sam. 15:22; 2 Sam. 22:14; 1 Kings 19:12; Job 42:11; Ps. 46:6; 68:33; 95:7; Prov. 8:1; 11:12; 25:12; Is. 3:20-21; 6:4-6; 40:3; Jer. 33:11; Ezek. 1:24-28; 43:2; Dan. 10:6; Hos. 2:13; Joel 2:11; 3:16; Hab. 3:16; Hag. 1:12; Jn. 3:29; 5:25; 10:4; Acts 9:7; Heb. 12:26; Rev. 18:23.

∞ ∞ ∞

Earth (Earthy)

Man; Adamic realm

Key Scriptures: Ex. 20:24; Ps. 24:1; Mt. 6:10; Jn. 17:4; 1 Cor. 15:47-49.

Foundational Information ✐

Earth is the planet upon which mankind lives. After the fall of man, the earth was cursed. Throughout the ages, the earth is the Lord's, subject to His rule. "Earth" is from the Hebrew *'erets* (Strong's #776), which means "to be firm; the earth (at large, or partitively a land)." It speaks of the scene of human activity, experience, and history.

The Greek word for "earthy" is *epigeios* (Strong's #1919) and means "worldly (physically or morally)"; it is translated in the King James Version as "earthly, in earth, terrestrial." Compare *choikos* (Strong's #5517), which means "dusty or dirty (soil-like), terrene." The Greek word for "earth" is *ge* (Strong's #1093), meaning "soil; by extension a region, or the solid part or the whole of the terrene globe (including the occupants in each application)."

Fulfilled in Christ ✝

Jesus is the Creator God, the One who fashioned the heavens and the earth (Gen. 1:1; Jn. 1:1-3; Col. 1:16). The first man Adam was of the earth, earthy; Jesus Christ, "the second man," was the Lord from Heaven (1 Cor. 15:47; see also Jn. 3:31). Our King became a partaker of the human nature, totally identifying with our frailty, "yet without sin" (Heb. 4:15; see also Jn. 1:14; Heb. 2:14-18). Jesus was the heavenly Ezekiel (Ezek. 2–3), the "son of man" (Ps. 8:4; Mt. 12:40; Acts 7:56). His consecrated life was an "altar of earth" (Ex. 20:24; see also Jn. 17:4; Heb. 13:10). During Gethsemane's passion, the suffering Savior became like "a furnace of earth, purified seven times" (Ps. 12:6; see also Lk. 22:39-44). Contrary to earthly wisdom (Jas. 3:15), Jesus is the Wisdom from above (Jas. 3:17; see also 1 Cor. 1:30). He declared to the Pharisees, "Ye are from beneath; I am from above..." (Jn. 8:23). The earth is the Lord's (Ex. 9:29; Ps. 24:1); all authority in earth is His (Mt. 28:18).

Applied to the Christian ⚖

Our old nature prior to regeneration was "of the earth, earthy" (1 Cor. 15:47). Before we knew Jesus as Savior, we minded earthly things (Phil. 3:19). Our lives were "without form, and void," filled with darkness and spiritual death (Gen. 1:2; see also Eph. 2:1-3; 5:8). As believers, our lives are to be vessels of honor, not vessels of wood and earth (2 Tim. 2:20). His Kingdom is to come and His will is to be done "in earth [man]" as it is in Heaven (Mt. 6:10). Apostle Paul declared God's promise, "And as we have borne the image of the earthy, we shall also bear the image of the heavenly" (1 Cor. 15:49). He added, "For we know that if our earthly house of this tabernacle were dissolved, we have a building of God, an house not made with hands, eternal in the heavens" (2 Cor. 5:1).

Go Deeper 📖

See Gen. 1:12; 6:6,11-13; 11:1; 28:12; Ex. 19:5; Lev. 15:12; 1 Kings 8:27; 1 Chron. 29:15; Ps. 104:32; Song 2:12; Is. 18:3; Lk. 12:49; 18:8; Jn. 3:12; Eph. 6:3; Phil. 2:10; Col. 3:2; Jas. 5:5; 1 Jn. 5:8; Rev. 5:3; 6:10; 7:1; 11:10; 13:14; 17:8.

∞ ∞ ∞

𝔈arthquakes

Shakings and movings, divine disturbances; God's power and judgment shaking all things, causing men to shake with fear

Key Scriptures: Ezek. 37:7-10; Mt. 27:51-54; 28:1-4;
Acts 16:26; Heb. 12:25-29.

Foundational Information ✐

An earthquake is a great trembling or powerful convulsion of the earth, often accompanied by volcanic eruptions. "Earthquake" is from the Hebrew *ra'ash* (Strong's #7494), which means "vibration, bounding, uproar," and is translated in the King James Version as "commotion, confused noise, earthquake, fierceness, quaking, rattling, rushing, shaking." Its root means to "undulate or vibrate, particularly through fear."

The Greek word for "earthquake" is *seismon* (Strong's #4578), which means "a commotion, (of the air) a gale, (of the ground) an earthquake." Its root verb is *seio* (Strong's #4579), meaning "to rock (vibrate, properly, sideways or to and fro), (generally) to agitate (in any direction; cause to tremble); figuratively, to throw into a tremor (of fear or concern)." *Seismos* can also mean "shock" (compare the English *seismic, seismology*).

Fulfilled in Christ ☥

The very visible presence of Jesus Christ, the living Word, shook the earth (Mt. 10:34; Jn. 1:1; Heb. 4:12). When He came into Jerusalem before the week of His Passion, all the city was "moved" (Mt. 21:10). At His crucifixion and resurrection, there were earthquakes (Mt. 27:51-54; 28:1-4). The foundations of every human bondage were destroyed by His finished work (Acts 16:26). Nothing can shake the life or ministry that is founded upon the Rock (Lk. 6:48; see also Col. 1:23; 1 Thess. 3:3). When our great High Priest moves to answer our prayer, things of earth will shake and tremble (2 Sam. 22:8; Ps. 68:8). The prophet Nahum described the Day of the Lord, "The mountains quake at Him, and the hills melt, and the earth is burned at His presence, yea, the world, and all that dwell therein" (Nahum 1:5; see also Is. 2:19-21; Joel 3:16).

Applied to the Christian ⚖

God's voice, His Word, will shake our earth, our lives, ministering the fear of the Lord (Heb. 12:25-29). In Ezekiel's vision, the bones (typifying the members of the Body of Christ) experienced the noise of His voice, then shook before they came together (Ezek. 37:7; see also Job 4:14). The end-time Church, the army of the Lord, will shake the nations (Joel 2:10; see also Acts 21:30). Divinely ordained personal "earthquakes" disturb our comfort zones, loosing us into His purposes (Is. 52:2; Jer. 23:9). As with the judge Samson, the Spirit of the Lord will "move" us at times (Judg. 13:25; see also Acts 17:28; 2 Pet. 1:21). Like the personal experience of Isaiah in his prophetic calling, our hearts are "moved" at the sound of God's voice (Is. 6:4).

Go Deeper 📖

See 2 Sam. 7:10; 1 Kings 19:11-12; Ps. 46:1-6; 72:16; 77:18; 99:1; Song 5:4; Is. 13:13; 19:16; 29:6; 30:32; Ezek. 12:18; 38:19; Dan. 10:7; Amos 1:1; Hag. 2:6-7,21; Zech. 14:5; Mt. 24:7; Mk. 13:8; Lk. 21:9-11; Acts 20:24; Heb. 12:21; Rev. 6:12-14; 8:5; 11:13,19; 16:18.

∞ ∞ ∞

𝔈ast

The dawning of a new day, the rising of the sun;
resurrection life and light

Key Scriptures: Num. 2:3; Ezek. 43:1-4; Lk. 1:78-79; Jn. 11:25; 2 Pet. 1:19.

Foundational Information ✎

East was the basic direction for the Hebrews—the direction of the rising sun. The east was the front, sometimes called the "place of dawning." All other directions received their designations relative to the east as the front. Thus, west was the "rear," north was on the left, and south was on the right.

"East" is from the Hebrew *qedem* (Strong's #6924), which means "the front, of place (absolutely, the fore part, relatively the East) or time (antiquity); often used adverbially (before, anciently, eastward)." Compare *mizrach* (Strong's #4217), meaning "sunrise, the east." Its root *zarach* (Strong's #2224) means "to irradiate (or shoot forth beams), to rise (as the sun)." The Greek word for "east" is *anatole* (Strong's #395), which means "a rising of light, dawn (figuratively); by implication, the east"; it can also be rendered as "a rising up."

Fulfilled in Christ ☥

Jesus is the "dayspring" or "dawn" from on high (Lk. 1:78; see also Job 38:12), the bright "morning star" (Rev. 2:28; 22:16). He is the Sun of righteousness, the Light of the world who has arisen with healing in His rays (Mal. 4:2; Jn. 8:12). Our Savior who declared Himself to be "the resurrection, and the life" (Jn. 11:25) is "the eternal God," literally, "the God of the east" (Deut. 33:27; see also Jn. 17:3; 1 Tim. 1:17; 1 Jn. 5:20). Isaiah prophesied that the Messiah would be "the righteous man from the east" to whom would be given power over the nations (Is. 41:2; see also Mt. 28:18). Jesus is the declared Son of God who arose on resurrection morning "...with power, according to the spirit of holiness..." (Rom. 1:4). His eternal priesthood after the order of Melchisedec is made "...after the power of an endless life" (Heb. 7:16).

Applied to the Christian ⚖

Peter declared, "We have also a more sure word of prophecy; whereunto ye do well that ye take heed, as unto a light that shineth in a dark place, until the day dawn, and the day star arise in your hearts" (2 Pet. 1:19). This Daystar is "Christ in you" (Col. 1:27), the "spirit of His Son" sent into our hearts (Gal. 4:6). In the days of the corporate Messiah (when Christ's anointing is fully formed in a people), wise worshipers will come from the "east" in the dawning of a new day (Mt. 2:1-12; see also Gal. 4:19)! The Bible reveals these worshipers from the "east" to be:

1. From the tribe of Judah, which means "praise" (Num. 2:3).
2. Priestly singers and trumpeters (2 Chron. 5:12).

3. Those who open the doors to the House of the Lord (2 Chron. 29:3-4).
4. Righteous rulers (Is. 41:2).
5. A people who experience God's glory (Ezek. 43:1-4).
6. A people who experience the living waters (Ezek. 47:1,9).
7. The bright shining of God's light (Mt. 24:27).

Go Deeper 📖

See Gen. 2:8; 3:24; Lev. 1:16; Josh. 6:15; Judg. 19:26; Neh. 3:29; Job 3:9; 7:4; Ps. 50:1; 113:3; 119:130,147; Prov. 4:18; Song 2:17; 4:6; Is. 9:2; 41:25; 43:5; 45:6; 46:11; 59:19; 60:1-5; Mal. 1:11; Mt. 8:11; 28:1; Lk. 13:29; Jn. 1:7-9; 2 Cor. 4:4-6; Rev. 7:2; 16:12; 21:13.

∞ ∞ ∞

East Wind (Euroclydon)

The operation of God's Spirit in trials, tribulations, and testings

Key Scriptures: Job 1:19; Lk. 4:1-14; Acts 27:14; 1 Pet. 1:7; 4:12.

Foundational Information ✍

The east wind is the wind of the wilderness. The wind most often mentioned in the Bible, this violent, desert wind scorched the grain, brought the locusts, withered the vine, parched the fruit, and dried up the springs of water. "East wind" is from the Hebrew *qadiym* (Strong's #6921), which means "the fore or front part; hence (by orientation) the East (often adverbially, eastward, for brevity the east wind)." The Arabs call the east wind a *khamsin.* It leaves people irritable and feeling like doing nothing because of the oppressive heat.

In the New Testament, "Euroclydon" is transliterated from *Eurokludon* (Strong's #2148), which means "a storm from the East (or Southeast), (in modern phrase) a Levanter." A "levanter" is a strong easterly wind in the Levant (the eastern Mediterranean and its shores). "Euroclydon" is taken from *Euros* ("the east wind") and *kludon* ("to billow or dash over; a surge of the sea").

Fulfilled in Christ ✴

Jesus Christ, the Pattern Son, was totally directed by the Spirit of God (Rom. 8:14,29). He was led by that Spirit into the wilderness to be thoroughly tested in the areas of the lust of the flesh, the lust of the eyes, and the pride of life (Lk. 4:1-14; 1 Jn. 2:15-17). Throughout the Scriptures, the moving of the Spirit of God is pictured as wind on water (Gen. 1:2). Jesus walked on the stormy waters, having overcome all things, passing every test (see Mt. 14:22-27; Jn. 6:19; 16:33; Rev. 3:21). He is the "tried stone" in Zion (Is. 28:16). Our King commanded the winds and the water, and they obeyed Him (Lk. 8:22-25). The Apostle Christ Jesus (Heb. 3:1) is our Elder Brother and as John described himself, our constant "companion in tribulation" (Rev. 1:9; see also Deut. 31:6; Is. 41:10; Heb. 13:5).

Applied to the Christian ⚖

Every house—life, family, ministry, or nation—is tested by the wind of the Spirit (Lk. 6:46-49). Each must face his own personal "Euroclydon" and be brought to the end of mere human wisdom and strength (Acts 27:14-15). This "great wind from the wilderness" smote Job's house (Job 1:19). The east wind will break us, but it will also deliver us (Ps. 48:7; Ezek. 27:26). As with ancient Israel, when our backs are against the wall in rough times (Is. 27:8), the Lord will make a way through the waters (Ex. 14:21; see also Rev. 7:14). The prophet Jonah learned that God will deal with comfort zones and biased attitudes by the power of the east wind (Jon. 4:8). Peter encouraged every believer concerning the "trial" of his faith (1 Pet. 1:7; 4:12). Paul knew that such tribulation produces patience, or endurance (Rom. 5:3; 12:12).

Go Deeper 📖

See Gen. 41:6,23,27; Ex. 10:13; Deut. 4:30; 1 Sam. 10:19; Job 15:2; 27:21; 38:24; Ps. 12:6; 78:26; Jer. 13:24; 18:17; Ezek. 17:9-10; 19:12; Hos. 12:1; 13:15; Hab. 1:9; Mt. 13:21; Acts 14:22; Rom. 8:35; 1 Cor. 3:13; 2 Cor. 1:4; 7:4; 8:2; Eph. 3:13; 1 Thess. 3:4; 2 Thess. 1:4-6; Heb. 11:36; Jas. 1:12; Rev. 2:10; 3:10.

𝔈ating

Enjoyment; appetite, assimilation

Key Scriptures: Lev. 21:22; Neh. 7:65; Ps. 34:8;
Jer. 15:16; Jn. 4:32-34; Heb. 2:9.

Foundational Information ✐

Eating is taking, chewing, and swallowing food. "Eating" is from the Hebrew *'okel* (Strong's #400), which means "food," and is also translated in the King James Version as "meal [-time], meat, prey, victuals." The Greek word *esthio* (Strong's #2068) means "to eat." It is also translated as "devour, live."

Fulfilled in Christ ✝

Christ fully delighted to digest the will of the Father contained in the volume of the Book (Heb. 10:5-10). The Messiah declared, "My meat [food] is to do the will of Him that sent Me, and to finish His work" (Jn. 4:34; see also Is. 7:15). He shared this truth of covenantal obedience at the Last Supper when He took bread and gave it to His disciples, saying, "Take, eat; this is My body" (Mt. 26:26; see also Mk. 14:14; Lk. 22:15; 1 Cor. 11:24-28). Our heavenly High Priest and His royal priesthood eat "the bread of his God" (Lev. 21:22; see also 1 Pet. 2:9). By the grace of God, Jesus tasted death for every man (Heb. 2:9), swallowing death in victory (1 Cor. 15:54). He is the Priest who stood up in resurrection, enabling men to partake of "the most holy things" of the Most Holy Place (Neh. 7:65; see also Heb. 10:19-22). In the Song of Solomon, the King enjoyed His bride as His garden, partaking of His own nature and Spirit within her (Song 4:16; 5:1).

Applied to the Christian ⚖

The believer is to enjoy the reality of God's Word (Jer. 15:16; Ezek. 3:1-3), which is described in the Scriptures as:

1. Bread (Deut. 8:3).
2. Milk (1 Pet. 2:2).
3. Meat (Heb. 5:12-14).
4. Honey (Ps. 119:103).
5. Corn (Ps. 65:9; 78:24).
6. Lamb (Ex. 12:4,7-11).

The Old Testament saints ate the daily manna "according to his eating" (Ex. 16:16, 18); today we partake of Christ, the living bread (Jn. 6:31,48-53). We have tasted the heavenly gift, the good Word of God (Heb. 6:4-5). As the Christian matures, his spiritual diet changes (Josh. 5:11-12; Heb. 5:12–6:3). Those who are willing and obedient will eat the good of the land (Is. 1:19). The Psalmist declared, "O taste and see that the Lord is good..." (Ps. 34:8). In the early Church, if a man would not work, he would not eat (2 Thess. 3:10-12).

Go Deeper 📖

See Gen. 2:16-17; 3:1-6; Num. 11:18; Ruth 3:3; 1 Sam. 1:18; 9:13; 2 Sam. 9:7-13; 1 Kings 2:7; 4:20; 2 Kings 4:40; 1 Chron. 12:39; 2 Chron. 30:22; 31:10; Neh. 8:10; Ps. 22:26; 78:24-25; 128:2; Prov. 13:2; 18:21; 24:13; Is. 55:1-2; 61:6; 66:17; Mt. 6:25; 11:18-19; 24:38; Lk. 10:7; Acts 2:46; 1 Cor. 8:4; 11:21; Gal. 5:15; Rev. 2:7,17.

∞ ∞ ∞

𝔈bal

The curse of the law

Key Scriptures: Deut. 28; Josh. 8:30-35; Rom. 8:1-2;
Gal. 3:13-14; Heb. 12:18-24.

Foundational Information ✐

Ebal, a mountain north of Shechem and opposite Mount Gerizim, is the location where Moses instructed that stones be set up and an altar erected to the Lord. Joshua obeyed Moses' command and renewed the covenant there, reading the curses of the law. The people responded by saying "amen," and Ebal became known as the mount of cursing. "Ebal" is transliterated from the Hebrew *Eybal* (Strong's #5858), which means "to be bald; bare." It has also been translated to mean "stripped of all covering; naked, barren, stone."

The Hebrew word for "curse" is *arar* (Strong's #779), which means "to execrate." To "execrate" is to "utterly detest; treat as abominable." The Hebrew word for "cursing" is *qelalah* (Strong's #7045), meaning "vilification." The Greek word for "curse" is *katara* and means "to curse (down)." This denotes an imprecation uttered out of malevolence or pronounced by God in His righteous judgments.

Fulfilled in Christ ✝

Jesus Christ reversed the curse by stripping Himself of deity and being shamefully crucified (Phil. 2:6-11). Paul declared that our Savior "redeemed us from the curse of the law, being made a curse for us…" (Gal. 3:13a). Just as the Ark of the Covenant stood between two mountains, Ebal (the mount of cursing) and Gerizim (the mount of blessing), Jesus, the Word made flesh, came and stood between two covenants. He is the Mediator of the New Covenant who fulfilled the law (Mt. 5:17; 1 Tim. 2:5). The Father paid the penalty of the curse to lay the foundation of His City with the death of His firstborn Son (Josh. 6:26; see also Mt. 5:14; 16:18; Jn. 3:16; 1 Cor. 3:9-11; Heb. 11:10). Because of Jesus' finished work, there is "…no more curse" (Rev. 22:3).

Applied to the Christian ⚖

The law of the Spirit of life in Christ Jesus has made us free from the law of sin and death (Rom. 8:1-2). Freed from condemnation and sin's penalty, the Church, the Body of Christ, has become "an altar of whole stones" on whom is written the law of the Lord (Josh. 8:31; see also 2 Cor. 3:1-6). Ebal represents the Old Covenant of the law, Mount Sinai; Gerizim represents the New Covenant of grace and truth, Mount Zion (Heb. 12:18-24; see also Jn. 1:17; Gal. 4:21-31). Believers now walk in a better priesthood and confession (Heb. 3:1; 1 Pet. 2:9-10). To obey Him is to be blessed; to disobey is to be cursed (Deut. 28). The Lord declared through Moses, "…I have set before you life and death, blessing and cursing…" (Deut. 30:19).

Go Deeper 📖

See Gen. 3:14,17; 12:3; 36:23; Lev. 21:5; Deut. 11:29; 27:4-5,13; Josh. 6:18; 2 Kings 2:23; 1 Chron. 1:22,40; Ps. 109:18; Prov. 3:33; 26:2; 28:27; 29:24; Is. 3:24; Jer. 11:3; Dan. 9:11; Mal. 3:9; 4:6; Mt. 5:44; 25:41; Jn. 7:49; Acts 23:12-14; Rom. 3:14; 5:21; 7:21-24; 12:14; Gal. 3:10; Heb. 6:8; Jas. 3:10; 2 Pet. 2:14.

∞ ∞ ∞

𝔈𝔟𝔢𝔫𝔢𝔷𝔢𝔯

God's help

Key Scriptures: 1 Sam. 4:1; 5:1; 7:1-12; Ps. 33:20; 44:26; 124:8; Heb. 4:16.

Foundational Information ✏️

Ebenezer is the name of a place where Israel was defeated by the Philistines, who captured the Ark of the Covenant. It was also a stone monument later erected to commemorate Israel's victory over the Philistines. "Ebenezer" is transliterated from the Hebrew *'Eben ha-'ezer* (Strong's #72), which means "stone of the help." It has also been translated as "precious stone of succor, gem of help." Compare the root *'azar,* which means "to surround, protect or aid." The Greek word for "help" is *hoetheo* (Strong's #997), and it means "to aid or relieve." Its root means to "shout or call for help."

Fulfilled in Christ ✝

Jesus Christ, the "chief corner stone" (Eph. 2:20; 1 Pet. 2:6), is our Ebenezer, our set "stone of help." He was the Help sent from Heaven, the strength of the Father out of Zion (Ps. 20:2). Jesus was the greatest son of David upon whom help was laid, anointed by the Holy Ghost (Ps. 89:19-20; Acts 10:38). Our Lord is typified by the "sucking lamb" that Samuel offered (1 Sam. 7:9; see also Jn. 1:29): When the real Lamb was sacrificed on the cross, the Father "thundered with a great thunder" and slew the enemy (1 Sam. 7:10; see also Mt. 27:45-53)! Trust Him for every need, for "...Hitherto ['up till now, heretofore, thus far, certainly'] hath the Lord helped us" (1 Sam. 7:12).

Applied to the Christian ⚖️

God is "our help" (Ps. 33:20; 44:26; 124:8). Jesus is our Comforter and Advocate (Jn. 14:16; 1 Jn. 2:1). The Lord is our Helper, and we need not fear (Heb. 13:6; see also Rom. 8:31). When Jesus ascended back to Heaven, He sent the fivefold ministries, His "hand" to help us (Ps. 119:173; see also Eph. 4:8-13). The prophet Isaiah confirmed that promise, "Fear thou not; for I am with thee: be not dismayed; for I am thy God: I will strengthen thee; yea, I will help thee; yea, I will uphold thee with the right hand of my righteousness" (Is. 41:10). True worshipers come boldly to His throne, finding grace to help in time of need, saying, "Lord, help me" (Mt. 15:25; see also Heb. 4:16).

Go Deeper 📖

See Gen. 2:18; 49:25; Ex. 18:4; Deut. 33:26,29; 1 Chron. 12:18; 2 Chron. 14:11; 32:8; Ps. 10:14; 46:5; 54:4; 70:5; 115:9-11; 121:1-2; 146:5; Is. 41:13-14; 44:2; 46:3-4; Hos. 13:9; Mk. 9:22-24; Lk. 5:7; Acts 16:9; 18:27; 26:22; Rom. 16:3,9; 2 Cor. 1:10,24; 8:23; 3 Jn. 8.

∞ ∞ ∞

𝔈𝔠𝔠𝔩𝔢𝔰𝔦𝔞𝔰𝔱𝔢𝔰

Natural man at his best; the vanity of human reasoning

Key Scriptures: Eccles. 1:1,2,12; 7:27-29; 12:8-10; Ps. 39:5;
Mt. 12:42; Rom. 8:1-6; 1 Cor. 1:18-31; Eph. 4:17-19.

Foundational Information ✐

Ecclesiastes is a wisdom book of the Old Testament that wrestles with the question of the meaning of life. It takes its name from the Greek word *ekklesiastes*, meaning "convener of an assembly." This has also been translated as "leader of a convocation, speaker before the congregation." The book is often referred to by its Hebrew name, *qoheleth* (Strong's #6953), which means "a (female) assembler (lecturer); abstractly, preaching." Its root *qahal* (Strong's #6950) means "to convoke" and is translated in the King James Version as "assemble (selves) (together), gather (selves) (together)." It is found seven times in the Book of Ecclesiastes, revealing the complete vanity of man living apart from the life of God. It's feminine gender references the soul of man, his mind.

Fulfilled in Christ ☀

Jesus Christ, the greatest Preacher of them all, declared, "Behold, a greater than Solomon is here" (Mt. 12:42; Lk. 11:31; see also Mt. 7:28-29; Jn. 7:46). He is "...the son of David, king in Jerusalem" (Eccles. 1:1; see also Mt. 1:1; Heb. 7:1-2). Jesus is the "sun of righteousness" (Mal. 4:2). Life without Him is living "under the sun"—the land of darkness and spiritual ignorance—"...to be carnally minded is death" (Eccles. 1:14;

Rom. 8:6a). Paul declared of Him, "We preach Christ crucified...Christ the power of God, and the wisdom of God" (1 Cor. 1:23-24; see also verse 30).

Applied to the Christian ⚖

The psalmist revealed that "...man at his best state is altogether vanity" (Ps. 39:5). There is none righteous (Rom. 3:10,23). Life without Jesus Christ is merely existing "under the sun," where "all is vanity and vexation of spirit" (Eccles. 1:14). Christians have been raised from the death of trespasses and sins (Eph. 2:1; see also Prov. 15:24) to live "in the Son" (Jn. 14:13; 1 Jn. 2:24). Those who walk after the flesh of their own minds live in the world of "time and chance" (Eccles. 9:11), but Christians who walk after the Spirit live in the purposes of God (Rom. 8:28; Eph. 1:1-11; 2 Tim. 1:9). Unsaved men go forth in the vanity of their minds, "...alienated from the life of God through the ignorance that is in them..." (Eph. 4:18). The conclusion of the wayward king who knew it all, had it all, and did it all (under the sun) was this admonition: "Fear God, and keep His commandments: for this is the whole duty of man" (Eccles. 12:13).

Go Deeper 📖

See Ps. 39:11; 62:9; 92:6; 94:8-11; 144:4; Prov. 12:1; Eccles. 1:3,9; 2:11,17-22; 3:16; 4:1-7; Is. 5:13; 6:1,12; 8:9,15-17; 9:3; 10:5; 40:17; Jer. 10:8,14,21; Dan. 5:20; Mt. 11:6; Jn. 6:56; 11:25-26; 14:1; 15:1-9; 16:33; 17:21-24; Acts 14:15; Rom. 1:21-23; Eph. 2:11-12; 2 Thess. 2:3-8; 1 Tim. 4:2; 1 Jn. 1:7; 5:13-16.

∞ ∞ ∞

𝕰𝖉𝖊𝖓

Paradise; the Kingdom of God on earth; beauty or fruitfulness

Key Scriptures: Gen. 2–3; Ezek. 36:35; Joel 2:3; Lk. 23:43; 2 Cor. 12:4; Rev. 2:7.

Foundational Information ✐

Eden was the first garden home of Adam and Eve, the first man and woman. "Eden" is derived from the Hebrew masculine *'Eden* (Strong's #5731) and the Hebrew feminine *'eden* (Strong's #5730), both meaning "pleasure." The latter is also translated in the King James Version as "delicate, delight." Their root *'adan* (Strong's #5727) means "to be soft or pleasant."

The Hebrew word for "garden" means "a garden that is fenced or hedged about (for protection)." The Greek word for "paradise" is *paradeisos* (Strong's #3857). It means "a park, (specifically) an Eden." This is an Oriental word, first used by historians to denote the parks of kings and nobles. It is akin to the Greek *peri* ("around") and *teichos* ("a wall").

Fulfilled in Christ ☀

Jesus Christ is the "…tree of life, which is in the midst of the paradise of God" (Rev. 2:7; see also Jn. 15:1-5). The Pattern Son went through two gardens—the Garden of Gethsemane (Mt. 26:36,39) and the garden of the cross and tomb (Mt. 27:57-60; Jn. 19:41)—to open up the third garden (of which Eden, the first garden, is a type). The apostle Paul referred to being caught up into this "third heaven," which he also called "paradise" (2 Cor. 12:2,4). This third dimension is also typified by the Most Holy Place in the divine "pattern" of Moses' tabernacle (Ex. 25:40); it, like the City of God, was in the shape of a cube (Rev. 21:16). As He did with the repentant thief (Lk. 23:43), Jesus restored man to the first garden. This is also pictured by the Old Testament land of Canaan (Deut. 11:11-12).

Applied to the Christian ⚖

The Garden of Eden, a prototype of the Kingdom of God on earth, was marked by certain fundamental ingredients. Consider the following elements:

1. Relationships—worship, union and communion.
2. Productivity and creativity—subjugation of the earth.
3. Discipline—two trees.
4. Priesthood ministry—the river out of Eden.

There is a tremendous parallel between Eden (Gen. 2–3) and the City of God (Rev. 21). In Eden there was a serpent, and through the cunning of that serpent, man was cast out. In the City of God there is no serpent, for through the dominion of the Christ nature, the serpent is cast out. In Eden there were two trees: the tree of life and the tree of the knowledge of good and evil. In God's City, there is only the former. Eden is man on trial. The City of God is man purified and perfected.

Eden is first and foremost a state of being. (Man was **in** a garden, but man also **was** a garden, as in Song of Solomon 4:12-16; 5:1; 6:2,11.) This state is man in the presence of God with the incorruptible life of God available to him, as master and lord over all things, and living above sin, sickness, pain, or death. Eden is a "pleasant" land indeed, revealing God's nature and intent toward His creation: He desires to "delight" us with Himself. The Garden of God is the Kingdom of Heaven come to earth—His pleasure and will (Mt. 6:10)—the fullness of righteousness, peace, and joy in the Holy Ghost (Rom. 14:17). We have been delivered from sin's desolation to "…become like the garden of Eden" (Ezek. 36:35; see also Jn. 1:12). God's army is headed back to Eden (Joel 2:3).

Go Deeper 📖

See Gen. 4:16; 13:10; Num. 24:6; Neh. 3:15; Ps. 51:18; 102:14; 103:21; 111:2; 149:4; Eccles. 2:5; Is. 1:30; 51:3; 53:10; 58:11; 61:11; Jer. 29:5; 31:12; 39:4; Lam. 2:6;

Ezek. 28:13; 31:8-9,16,18; Mt. 3:17; 17:5; Lk. 12:32; 13:19; Jn. 18:1,26; Eph. 1:5,9; Phil. 2:13; 2 Thess. 1:11; Rev. 4:11.

∞ ∞ ∞

𝔈𝔡𝔬𝔪

The flesh

Key Scriptures: Gen. 25:29-34; 32:3; 36:1-43; 1 Chron. 1:34-54;
Obad. 1-21; Rom. 8:1-6; Gal. 5:13-24.

Foundational Information

Edom was the name given to Esau after he forfeited the birthright to his brother Jacob; it also was the name of the land inhabited by the descendants of Edom, or Esau. Other Bible designations for Edom are Mount Seir or Idumea. "Edom" is derived from the Hebrew *'Edom* (Strong's #123), which means "red; Edom, the elder twin-brother of Jacob; hence the region (Idumea) occupied by him." Its root *'adam* (Strong's #119) means "to show blood (in the face), flush or turn rosy."

Fulfilled in Christ

Jesus Christ completely subdued the appetites of the flesh, overcoming all things (see Jn. 8:29; 16:33; Heb. 4:15; 1 Jn. 2:15-17). He is the greatest son of David who caused the flesh to become His servant (2 Sam. 8:14; Mt. 1:1). Jesus is the One who came from Edom (Adam) with garments dyed red in His own blood, glorious in apparel and great in strength—our mighty Savior, who tread Gethsemane's winepress alone, has become our righteousness (Is. 63:1-3; see also Lk. 22:44; 2 Cor. 5:17-21). On that day when Jesus died on Calvary's cross, He destroyed the wisdom and understanding of the flesh (Obad. 8; see also 1 Cor. 1:18-31).

Applied to the Christian

Edom typifies Adam, the natural man. Paul declared, "For they that are after the flesh do mind the things of the flesh..." (Rom. 8:5a). The believer is to crucify the flesh with the affections and lusts (Gal. 5:24). The flesh wants to be king instead of the Lord (2 Kings 8:20). The works of the flesh were the kings who reigned before Jesus became our Lord (1 Chron. 1:43-54; Gal. 5:19-21); their uncircumcised purpose is to tear down the people of God (Ps. 137:7; Jer. 9:26). The end-time, glorious Church, the rebuilt and restored Tabernacle of David, will possess "the remnant of Edom" (Amos 9:12), the "residue of men" who will seek after the Lord (Acts 15:16-17). In that day "saviours ['deliverers'] shall come up on Mount Zion to judge the mount of Esau; and the kingdom shall be the Lord's" (Obad. 21; see also Rev. 14:1-5).

Go Deeper 📖

See Gen. 32:3; Ex. 15:15; Num. 20:18-21; 21:4; 24:18; Judg. 5:4; 11:17-18; 1 Sam. 14:47; 1 Kings 9:26; 11:14-16; 2 Kings 14:7-10; 1 Chron. 18:11-13; 2 Chron. 25:20; Ps. 60:8-9; 83:6; Jer. 49:7,17; Lam. 4:21-22; Ezek. 25:12-14; Joel 3:19; Amos 1:6-11; Rom. 13:14; 2 Cor. 7:1; 10:3; Gal. 3:3; Eph. 2:3,11; Phil. 3:3; Col. 2:11-13; 1 Pet. 1:24.

∞ ∞ ∞

𝕰𝖌𝖌

Foreordained destiny; relationships

Key Scriptures: Ps. 31:15; 37:18; Lk. 11:12; Acts 1:7;
4:28; Eph. 1:5,11; 1 Pet. 1:20.

Foundational Information ✍

An egg, or ovum, is a round or oval body laid by birds, reptiles, and fishes from which the young are hatched. "Egg" is from the Hebrew *beytsah* (Strong's #1000), which means "an egg (from its whiteness)." Its root *buwts* (Strong's #948) means "to bleach; be white; probably cotton (of some sort)," and it is translated in the King James Version as "fine (white) linen." The Greek word for "egg" is *oon* (Strong's #5609); compare the Latin *ovum.*

The Greek word for "predestinate" is *proorizo* (Strong's #4309), which means "to limit in advance, (figuratively) predetermine." It is rendered in the King James Version as "determine before, ordain, predestinate." It is taken from *pro* which means "before; in front of, prior (figuratively, superior) to; beforehand"; and *horizo,* which means "to mark out or bound ('horizon'), (figuratively) to appoint, decree, specify."

Fulfilled in Christ ☀

Jesus Christ was the foreordained Pattern Son, the Firstborn among His predestinated brethren (Rom. 8:29-30), "the Lamb slain from the foundation of the world" (Rev. 13:8). The apostle Peter declared of Him "who verily was foreordained before the foundation of the world, but was manifest in these last times for you" (1 Pet. 1:20). The Son knew the predetermined times of the Father's will (Jn. 13:1; 17:1).

The Lord Jesus specializes in healing relationships that are impotent and crippled, bringing new life and hope (Jn. 5:1-9; Acts 14:8). The Lord, like a great hen, is gathering His people unto His purposes (Mt. 23:37; Eph. 1:9-10).

Applied to the Christian ⚖️

An egg, like a relationship, is fragile in its beginnings, and can be dropped (2 Sam. 4:4). The Hebrew root for "egg" is the same word used for "fine linen," a symbol of righteousness (Rev. 19:8). God is honest and just in His relationship with us; when His sons ask for an egg, He will not give them a scorpion (Lk. 11:12). Wicked relationships hatch rotten, deadly plans (Is. 59:4-5). But the righteous need not fear, for our predetermined "times" are in His hand (Ps. 31:15; see also Acts 1:7). We have been predestinated and purposed unto the adoption of sons by the will of God (Eph. 1:5,11). The Psalmist declared, "The Lord knoweth the days of the upright: and their inheritance shall be for ever" (Ps. 37:18).

Go Deeper 📖

See Ex. 33:12; Deut. 22:6; Job 6:6; 24:1; 39:14; Ps. 1:6; Eccles. 3:1-8; Is. 10:14; Jer. 1:5; 17:11; Lk. 9:51; 13:34; Jn. 7:6,30; 12:27; Acts 2:23; 17:26; 23:11; 26:5; Rom. 11:2; 1 Cor. 2:7; Phil. 2:13; 2 Thess. 1:11; 2 Tim. 2:19; 4:6; 2 Pet. 1:14.

∞ ∞ ∞

𝕰𝖌𝖑𝖔𝖓 (𝕰𝖍𝖚𝖉)

The complete defeat of satan

Key Scriptures: Judg. 3:12-30; Ps. 103:12; 108:13; Col. 2:15; Heb. 4:12; 1 Jn. 3:8.

Foundational Information ✎

Eglon was an evil, obese Moabite king who was slain by Ehud during the period of the judges. "Eglon" is transliterated from the Hebrew *'Eglown* (Strong's #5700), and it means "vituline (pertaining to a calf)." Compare *'egel* (Strong's #5695), which means "a (male) calf (as frisking round)." Their root *'agol* (Strong's #5696) means "to revolve, circular." *Eglon* has also been rendered as "a bull calf, young bullock, round, rolling, a threshing drag, an oxcart, a war chariot."

Ehud is from the Hebrew *'Echuwd* (Strong's #261), which means "united." Its root *'achad* (Strong's #258) means "to unify, (figuratively) collect (one's thoughts). "Ehud" has also been translated as "joined together, undivided, union, strong."

Fulfilled in Christ ☥

Judge Jesus (Jn. 5:22), our heavenly Ehud, completely defeated the devil, pictured by the evil Eglon. Ehud was a Benjamite, which means "the son of the right hand" (Judg. 3:15); our victorious King has been exalted to the right hand of the Father, "...angels and authorities and powers being made subject to Him" (1 Pet. 3:22b). Jesus, the living Word, is also revealed by the "dagger" that slew the evil king; this word means "a cutting instrument (from its destructive effect), as a knife, sword or other sharp implement" (Judg. 3:16; compare Jn. 1:1; Heb. 4:12). The dagger "under his raiment" reveals the Word in humility (Phil. 2:5-11). Jesus was the Father's "present" to the devil (Judg. 3:15-18); this is the Old Testament word for "meat (cereal) offering," also translated in the King James Version as "gift, oblation, sacrifice." Just as Eglon could not remove Ehud's dagger (Judg. 3:22), so satan was completely vanquished by our Savior on the cross (Col. 2:15). Ehud locked Eglon in the place of His own death (Judg. 3:23)—Jesus bound the strong man and threw away the key (Mt. 12:29; Lk. 11:21-22; Rev. 20:1-3).

Applied to the Christian ⚖

Until Jesus defeated the evil one, we served the devil for "eighteen years," the Bible number denoting bondage (Judg. 3:14; see also Lk. 13:11,16; Eph. 2:1-3). When Ehud slew Eglon, "the dirt came out" (Judg. 3:22); when Jesus defeated the devil for us, our sin was removed (Ps. 103:12; Jn. 1:29)! We can sing with the psalmist, "Through God we shall do valiantly: for He it is that shall tread down our enemies" (Ps. 108:13). Because of Jesus' victory over satan, believers have been given the same authority in His name (Mt. 18:20; Mk. 16:15-20). We have heard the sound of the trumpet to follow Him in faith (Judg. 3:27-28; see also Rom. 10:17; 1 Jn. 5:4)!

Go Deeper 📖

See Gen. 3:15; 18:25; Neh. 2:20; Ps. 20:3; 40:6; 68:5; 75:7; 94:2; 98:1; 118:15-16; Is. 25:8; 26:13-14; 49:24-26; 53:10; Dan. 9:27; Mt. 12:20; Lk. 10:18; Jn. 12:31; 14:13-14; 15:16; 16:11,23-26; Acts 10:42; 17:31; 1 Cor. 15:54-57; 2 Tim. 4:1; Heb. 2:14-18; Rev. 12:7-10; 15:2; 19:11; 20:10.

∞ ∞ ∞

𝔈𝔤𝔶𝔭𝔱 (𝔐𝔦𝔷𝔯𝔞𝔦𝔪)

The world; the bondage of sin

Key Scriptures: Gen. 10:6,13; 37–50; Ex. 1–12; 1 Chron. 1:8,11; Jn. 1:29;
1 Cor. 5:5-8; Eph. 2:1-3; 1 Jn. 2:15-17.

Foundational Information ✏

Egypt is the country in the northeast corner of Africa where the Israelites spent 430 years in servitude. "Egypt" is from the Hebrew *Mitsrayim* (Strong's #4714); compare *matsowr* (Strong's #4692), which means "a limit; something hemming in, (objectively) a mound (of besiegers), (abstractly) a siege, (figuratively) distress; or (subjectively) fastness." Its root *tsuwr* (Strong's #6696) means "to cramp, confine."

Fulfilled in Christ ☀

The Lord Jesus Christ was the Word made flesh who came to deliver all men from the bondage of sin (Heb. 2:14-18). In the story of the Exodus, Pharaoh is a type of satan, the prince and god of this world (Jn. 12:31; 2 Cor. 4:4). Jesus fulfilled the type of the Passover Lamb (Ex. 12; see also Jn. 1:29; 1 Pet. 1:18-19; Rev. 13:8). Paul declared that "...Christ our passover is sacrificed for us" (1 Cor. 5:7b). The primary figures of Moses and Aaron point to the dual offices of Him who is both King and High Priest (Heb. 5–7). Jesus announced the good news, "...be of good cheer; I have overcome the world" (Jn. 16:33c; see also 1 Jn. 2:15-17). Our Lord fulfilled the prophecy of Hosea (Hos. 11:1) as explained by Matthew, "Out of Egypt have I called My son" (Mt. 2:15).

Applied to the Christian ⚖

The blood of the Passover Lamb Christ Jesus has delivered us from the tyranny of satan and the "house of bondage" (Ex. 13:14; see also Rom. 6:1-14; Eph. 2:1-14). That blood covenant includes the healing of our bodies; the Lord promised, "...I will put none of these diseases upon thee, which I have brought upon the Egyptians: for I am the Lord that healeth thee" (Ex. 15:26). We have been purchased and purposed—God brought us out that He might bring us in (Deut. 6:21-23)! Worldly folks despise spiritual authority and the local church, "...for every shepherd is an abomination unto the Egyptians" (Gen. 46:34; see also Rom. 13:1-7; Eph. 4:11; Heb. 13:7,17). The beds of religious systems are decked with the "fine linen of Egypt" (Prov. 7:16), where seducing spirits rest in their own righteousness (Is. 64:6 with Rev. 19:8). Whoever is a friend of the world is the enemy of God (Jas. 4:4).

Go Deeper 📖

See Gen. 12:10; 13:1; 37:28; Ex. 3:7; 12:12; 14:30; 32:11; Lev. 11:45; 25:38; Num. 3:13; 14:4; Deut. 4:34; Josh. 24:5; Ps. 68:31; 78:12,43,51; 80:8; 81:5,10; 105:23,38;

106:21; Is. 7:18; 10:24-26; 11:11-16; 19:1; 30:2; Amos 2:10; 3:1,9; 4:10; 8:8; 9:5-7; Mic. 6:4; 7:15; Hag. 2:5; Zech. 10:10-11; 14:18-19; Acts 7:22; Rom. 5:12-21; 6:23; Gal. 6:14; Col. 2:20; Heb. 9:26; 11:29; Jas. 1:15.

∞ ∞ ∞

Elam

Things which are hidden or veiled; secret things

Key Scriptures: Gen. 10:22; Deut. 29:29; Ezra 4:9; Ps. 25:14; Mt. 27:51; Acts 2:9; 1 Cor. 2:7; 2 Cor. 3:1–4:7.

Foundational Information

Elam was the son of Shem and grandson of Noah, the ancestor of the Elamites. *Elam* is transliterated from the Hebrew *'Eylam* (Strong's #5867), and means "hidden, distant." Its root *'alam* (Strong's #5956) means "to veil from sight, conceal (literally or figuratively)." "Elam" has also been translated as "remote time, eternal, everlasting, fully developed, a young man, puberty." It is rendered as "secret, or secret thing" in the King James Version.

Fulfilled in Christ

The tearing of Jesus' flesh on the cross rent the veil of the Old Covenant from top to bottom (Mt. 27:51; see also Heb. 10:19-22). The Living Word came out of the hiding place of the Father's bosom (Jn. 1:18) like a swift arrow out of the quiver (Is. 22:6). Moses declared, "The secret things belong unto the Lord our God..." (Deut. 29:29a). The psalmist affirmed, "The secret of the Lord is with them that fear Him; and He will shew them His covenant" (Ps. 25:14; see also Prov. 3:32). God reveals the deep and secret things (Dan. 2:22,47). The prophet Amos declared, "Surely the Lord God will do nothing, but He revealeth His secret unto His servants the prophets" (Amos 3:7).

Applied to the Christian

New Testament Elamites dwell in the secret place of the Most High (Ps. 91:1; see also Is. 45:3; Col. 3:1-3). Those who are in Christ are His "hidden ones" (Ps. 83:3). Everything that had been hidden from ages and generations is now made manifest to His saints, in particular, the mystery of "Christ in you, the hope of glory" (Col. 1:26-27). This reality was experienced by the Elamites on the Day of Pentecost (Acts 2:9). Paul declared that believers "speak the wisdom of God in a mystery, even the hidden wisdom..."

(1 Cor. 2:7; see also Rev. 22:17). With an unveiled face, Christians are transformed by worshiping the true and living God (2 Cor. 3:18).

Go Deeper 📖

See Gen. 14:1,9; 1 Sam. 19:2; 1 Chron. 1:17; 8:24; 26:3; Ezra 2:7,31; 8:7; 10:2,26; Neh. 7:12,34; 10:14; 12:42; Ps. 18:11; 27:5; 31:20; 51:6; Song 2:14; Is. 11:11; 21:2; 45:3; 48:6; Jer. 25:25; 32:24; 49:34-39; Dan. 8:2; Acts 26:26; Rom. 16:25; Heb. 6:19; 1 Pet. 3:4.

∾ ∾ ∾

𝔈leazar

Jesus, our great High Priest

Key Scriptures: Ex. 6:23-25; Lev. 10:1-7; Num. 4:16; 20:25-28; Josh. 14:1; Heb. 5:1–8:6; 13:6.

Foundational Information ✐

Eleazer, the father of Phineas, was Aaron's third son by his wife Elisheba. "Eleazer", transliterated from the Hebrew *'El'azar* (Strong's #499), means "God is helper." It is taken from *'El* ("strength, mighty; the Almighty") and *'azar* ("to surround, protect, or aid"). "Eleazar" has also been translated as "whom God aids; God has surrounded; God succors; help of God." After his brothers Nadab and Abihu were killed for offering strange fire, Eleazar became high priest, serving during the remainder of Moses' life and throughout Joshua's leadership (whom he helped to allot the land of Canaan).

Fulfilled in Christ ⵣ

Jesus Christ is our great high priest after the order (manner, similitude) of Melchisedec (Heb. 5:1–8:6). He is the God-man, wholly sympathetic to every human need, "touched with the feeling of our infirmities" (Heb. 4:15). The writer to the Hebrews adds that our priestly Savior "…became us, who is holy, harmless, undefiled, separate from sinners, and made higher than the heavens" (Heb. 7:26). Jesus Christ is our Advocate, the One who ever lives to make intercession for us (Rom. 8:34; Heb. 7:25; 1 Jn. 2:1). As did Moses and Aaron, Joshua and Eleazar represent Jesus as King and High Priest, respectively. As Joshua and Eleazar crossed the Jordan river, our King-Priest rent the veil and entered into the New Testament land as a Forerunner for us, causing us to inherit that which God had promised (see Eph. 1:11,14,18; Col. 1:12; Heb. 6:12,19-20; 1 Pet. 1:4;

Rev. 21:7). Our heavenly Eleazar is the Head of the Church, the One who has "oversight of all the tabernacle" (Num. 4:16; see also Eph. 1:20-23; Heb. 3:6).

Applied to the Christian ⚖

As with his father Aaron, Eleazar's priesthood points to the New Testament "royal priesthood" of the Church, the Body of Christ (1 Pet. 2:5,9-10). In Christ, every believer has been given kingly authority mingled with priestly mercy and compassion (Rev. 1:6; 5:10; 20:6). Aaron was stripped, and his garments placed upon Eleazar (Num. 20:25-28). Likewise the anointing of the incarnate Word has been placed upon His sons (see Ps. 133; Jn. 14:12; Gal. 4:6; 1 Jn. 4:17). "Eleazar" means "God is helper"—because of the blood of the Lamb, we can now "...come boldly unto the throne of grace, that we may obtain mercy, and find grace to help in time of need" (Heb. 4:16; see also Ps. 30:10; Heb. 13:6).

Go Deeper 📖

See Ex. 28:1; 40:15; Num. 3:1-4,32; 16:10,37; 18:1; 19:1-4; 25:11-13; 26:63; 27:21; 31:51-54; 34:17; Deut. 10:6; Josh. 17:4; 18:7; 19:51; 21:1; 24:33; Judg. 20:28; 1 Chron. 6:3-4; 9:20; 24:1-6; Ezra 2:62; Neh. 7:64; 13:29; Heb. 2:17; 3:1; 9:7,11,25; 10:21; 13:11.

∞ ∞ ∞

𝔈lect 𝔏ady

The Church, the Bride of Christ

Key Scriptures: Is. 42:1; Lk. 23:35; 1 Pet. 2:9; 2 Jn. 1,5.

Foundational Information ✐

The "elect lady" is the person or the church to which the Epistle of Second John is addressed. "Elect" is from the Greek *eklektos* (Strong's #1588), which means "select, by implication, favorite." It signifies "picked out, chosen," taken from *ek* ("out of, from") and *lego* ("to gather, pick out"). The verb *eklego* ("to pick out, select") in the middle voice means "to choose for oneself," revealing God's kindness, favor, and love.

"Lady" is from the Greek *Kuria* (Strong's #2959) and could mean "Cyria, a Christian woman." It is the feminine of *kurios* (Strong's #2962), which means "supreme in authority, (as noun) controller; by implication, Mr. (as a respectful title)." It is translated in the King James Version as "God, Lord, master, Sir."

Fulfilled in Christ ✝

Jesus Christ is the Messiah, "the chosen of God" (Lk. 23:35). He is the living, Chief Corner Stone, elect and precious (1 Pet. 2:4,6). The prophet Isaiah declared Him to be the Servant of Jehovah, the elected Son who was His Father's delight (Is. 42:1 with Mt. 3:17). The Father chose to make covenant with the greatest Son of David (Ps. 89:3; Mt. 1:1). The elect Lady is the Bride of Christ; as the husband is the head of the wife, so Christ is the Head of the Church (Eph. 5:23). Paul declared, "For I am jealous over you with godly jealousy: for I have espoused you to one husband, that I may present you as a chaste virgin to Christ" (2 Cor. 11:2).

Applied to the Christian ⚖

The "elect lady" can speak of the Church, the Bride of Christ. We are the "chosen generation" (1 Pet. 2:9), "elect according to the foreknowledge of God the Father, through sanctification of the Spirit, unto obedience and sprinkling of the blood of Jesus Christ" (1 Pet. 1:2). Believers were chosen in Christ before the foundation of the world (Eph. 1:4) unto:

1. Conformity to His divine image (Rom. 8:29).
2. The glory of God (Rom. 9:23).
3. The adoption of sons (Eph. 1:4-5).
4. Good works (Eph. 2:10).
5. Salvation through His Spirit and Word (2 Thess. 2:13).

The source of our "election" is the grace of God (Rom. 9:11; 11:5). We are admonished by the apostle Paul to "put on therefore, as the elect of God, holy and beloved, bowels of mercies, kindness, humbleness of mind, meekness, longsuffering" (Col. 3:12).

Go Deeper 📖

See 1 Chron. 16:13; Ps. 105:6,43; 106:5,23; Is. 43:20; 45:4; 61:10; 65:9,15,22; Jer. 33:11; Mt. 20:16; 22:14; 24:31; Lk. 18:7; Rom. 8:33; 11:7,28; 1 Thess. 1:4; 1 Tim. 5:21; 2 Tim. 2:10; Tit. 1:1; 1 Pet. 5:13; 2 Pet. 1:10; 2 Jn. 13; Rev. 17:14; 21:2,9; 22:17.

∞ ∞ ∞

𝕰𝖑-𝕰𝖑𝖞𝖔𝖓

The Most High God of the Most Holy Place

Key Scriptures: Gen. 14:18-22; Dan. 7:18; Lk. 1:32-35;
Acts 7:48; Heb. 5:1–8:6.

Foundational Information

El-Elyon, a Hebrew name for God, is translated into English as "God Most High."
Melchizedek, king of Salem, was the priest of the most high God. "El" is derived from
the Hebrew *'el* (Strong's #410), and means "strength; mighty; especially the Almighty."
"Elyon," transliterated from the Hebrew *'elyown* (Strong's #5945), means "an elevation,
(adj.) lofty; as title, the Supreme." Its root *'alah* means "to go up, to ascend, offer up."
'Olah, the Hebrew word for "burnt offering," means "a step or (collectively, stairs, as ascending; usually a holocaust (as going up in smoke)." Compare *hupsistos,* the Greek superlative that means "most high, highest, the Supreme (God)."

Fulfilled in Christ

Abraham was a priest of El-Shaddai, and Moses, a priest of Yahweh. But Jesus, "the
Son of the most high God" (Mk. 5:7; compare Lk. 1:32-35), is a Priest of El-Elyon. His
high priestly ministry is after the order (manner, similitude) of Melchizedek—in Jesus are
mingled the offices of Prophet, Priest, and King (Acts 3:22-23; Heb. 7:26; Rev. 17:14).
"El-Elyon" is the God who possesses heaven and earth, the God of fullness within the
veil. Jesus Christ has received the full authority of that name or nature (Mt. 28:18). His
sinless life of pure worship constantly ascended to the Father (Jn. 8:29). On Calvary's
cross, the divine Lamb was the supreme whole burnt offering who put away sin by the
sacrifice of Himself (Heb. 9:26).

Applied to the Christian

Jesus Christ, the anchor of our soul, entered within the veil as our Forerunner (Heb.
6:19-20). The Mosaic tabernacle is a divine "pattern" (Ex. 25:40): In the Outer Court, Jesus is our Savior; in the Holy Place, He is the One who baptizes the believer with the
Holy Ghost (Acts 1:5; 4:12). But within the Most Holy Place, He is King and Lord (Rev.
19:16). As members of the Body of Christ in particular, we are "the tabernacles of the
most High" (Ps. 46:4; compare Acts 7:48). The psalmist declared, "He that dwelleth in
the secret place of the most High shall abide under the shadow of the Almighty" (Ps.
91:1). The prophet Daniel foresaw the day when "the saints of the most High," or the
most high saints who had experienced the reality of the Most Holy Place, would possess
the Kingdom (Dan. 7:18).

Go Deeper 📖

See Num. 24:16; Deut. 32:8; 2 Sam. 22:14; Ps. 7:17; 9:2; 21:6-7; 47:2; 50:14; 56:2; 57:2; 73:11; 77:10; 78:17,56; 82:6; 83:18; 91:9; 92:1,8; 107:11; Is. 14:14; Lam. 3:35,38; Dan. 3:26; 4:17,24-25,32,34; 5:18,21; 7:22,25,27; Hos. 7:16; 11:7; Lk. 8:28; Acts 16:17.

∞   ∞   ∞

𝔈𝔩𝔦

Corrupt priestly ministry

Key Scriptures: 1 Sam. 1:1–4:22; 14:3; 1 Kings 2:27; Mal. 2:7; 2 Cor. 2:17.

Foundational Information ✎

Eli was a a judge and high priest with whom the prophet Samuel lived during his childhood. He failed to discipline his sons, Hophni and Phineas; consequently, his fleshly priesthood was judged. "Eli" is transliterated from the Hebrew *'Eliy* (Strong's #5941) and means "lofty." Its root *'alah* means "to ascend."

Fulfilled in Christ ☨

Jesus Christ is the genuine Vine (Jn. 15:1). He is the true Priest who is "holy, harmless, undefiled, separate from sinners, and made higher than the heavens" (Heb. 7:26). As the Word of the Lord through Samuel brought Eli's demise, Jesus Christ will reckon with the religious systems of men. He will judge "the great whore, which did corrupt the earth with her fornication" (Rev. 19:2). His disciples declared of Him, "Master, we know that thou art true, and teachest the way of God in truth, neither carest thou for any man: for thou regardest not the person of men" (Mt. 22:16). Malachi prophesied of the Messiah's priestly role, "For the priest's lips should keep knowledge, and they should seek the law at his mouth: for he is the messenger of the Lord of hosts" (Mal. 2:7).

Applied to the Christian ⚖

Every generation of Christian ministry is contaminated by its share of Elis who "corrupt" or "peddle, huckster" the Word of God (2 Cor. 2:17). They can be characterized by the following attributes:

1. Failure to discern genuine intercession (1 Sam. 1:12-13).
2. Raising worthless sons (1 Sam. 2:12,22).

3. Blind with no vision (1 Sam. 3:1-3; 4:15).
4. Heavy of flesh (1 Sam. 4:18).
5. Destined to be toppled from their thrones (1 Sam. 4:18).

Like the boy Samuel, we must learn to distinguish between the voice of God and the voice of man (1 Sam. 2:4-10). There is an existing Eli and a growing Samuel. One order of ministry is passing from the scene as an end-time prophetic Church arises to turn the nation back to God!

Go Deeper 📖

See Gen. 6:11-12; Deut. 4:16,25; 31:29; Job 17:1; Ps. 14:1; 38:5; 53:1; 73:8; Prov. 25:26; Ezek. 20:44; 23:11; Dan. 2:9; 11:32; Mal. 1:14; 2:3; Mt. 6:19-20; 7:17-18; 12:33; Lk. 6:43; 1 Cor. 15:33; 2 Cor. 4:2; Eph. 4:22,29; 1 Tim. 6:5; 2 Tim. 3:8; Jude 10.

∞   ∞   ∞

𝔈liezer

The Comforter, the Holy Spirit; the fivefold ministries, especially the apostles and prophets

Key Scriptures: Gen. 15:2; 24:1-67; Jn. 14:16,26; 15:26; 16:13; Eph. 4:11-13.

Foundational Information ✐

Eliezer of Damascus was Abraham's chief servant (steward) and possible heir (if Abraham had not conceived a son). He was instrumental in bringing Rebekah to be the bride of Isaac. "Eliezer" is transliterated from the Hebrew *'Eliy'ezer* (Strong's #461), which means "God of help." It is a compound of *'el* ("strength, mighty, the Almighty") and *'ezer* ("aid; surround, protect"). The Hebrew word for "steward" (unique to Genesis 15:2) means "son of my holdings, possessions."

Fulfilled in Christ ✝

Jesus is the Comforter; the Holy Spirit, "another Comforter" (Jn. 14:16), is His Spirit, the Spirit of the Son (Jn. 14:26; Gal. 4:6). Just as Eliezer steered the way for Rebekah, so the Spirit of the Son has come to guide the Bride of Christ into all truth (Jn. 16:13). On the way to meet Isaac, Eliezer told Rebekah all about her new husband; even so the Holy Spirit testifies of Jesus, constantly revealing the Son (Jn. 16:7). As a picture of the Spirit of the Son, Eliezer served in the following ways:

1. He knew Abraham's (the father's) instruction (Gen. 24:4-9).
2. He was perceptive through prayer (Gen. 24:10-20).
3. He understood worship (Gen. 24:26,52).
4. He honestly spoke the truth in love (Gen. 24:34-49).
5. He was not moved by human sentiments (Gen. 24:56).

Applied to the Christian ⚖

Eliezer brought Rebekah to Isaac. The fivefold ministries, especially the apostles and prophets, anointed by the Holy Spirit, are bringing the Church to the spiritual stature of Jesus, the Son of the Father (Eph. 4:11-13). They have been empowered by the nine supernatural gifts of the Spirit (1 Cor. 12:8-10), typified by Eliezer's camels (Gen. 24:10)—one for Eliezer and nine loaded with gifts for Rebekah! These ministries have been given stewardship of the mysteries of God (Eph. 3:1-5; see also Lk. 11:49; 1 Cor. 12:28). Paul affirmed, "I have espoused you to one husband, that I may present you as a chaste virgin to Christ" (2 Cor. 11:2b). The Greek word for "present" is *parastemi* and means "to stand beside, to exhibit; to place beside." It was also used by the apostle in Ephesians 5:27, "That He might present it to Himself a glorious church, not having spot, or wrinkle, or any such thing...."

Go Deeper 📖

See Lev. 14:11; 16:7; 21:13-15; Num. 3:6; Deut. 31:14; Ps. 45:10-15; Eccles. 4:1; Song 2:10; Is. 54:5; Jer. 3:15; 31:32; Lam. 1:9,16; Ezek. 44:22; Hos. 2:19-20; Lk. 2:22; Jn. 16:7; Rom. 10:14-15; 12:1-2; 2 Cor. 4:14; Gal. 4:1-2; Eph. 2:20; Col. 1:22,28; 1 Pet. 5:1-4; 2 Pet. 3:2; Jude 24; Rev. 18:20.

∞ ∞ ∞

𝔈𝔩𝔦𝔥𝔲

Presumption, supposition

Key Scriptures: Job 32:1-6; 34:1-2; 35–36; 1 Cor. 8:2; 1 Jn. 2:12-14.

Foundational Information ✎

Elihu, the youngest of Job's "comforters," spoke to the patriarch after his three friends—Eliphaz, Bildad, and Zophar—failed to give convincing answers to Job's questions. Elihu was the son of Barachel the Buzite of the family of Ram. "Elihu" is transliterated from the Hebrew *'Eliyhuw* (Strong's #453), which means "God of him." It is taken from *'el* ("strength, mighty, the Almighty") and *huw'* ("he"). "Elihu" has also been translated as "God is Lord, my God is that which is, whose God is he, my God is He, or God is He (Jehovah)."

Fulfilled in Christ ⳨

Jesus Christ is the Word, and the Word is truth (Jn. 1:1; 14:6; 17:17). Some say that Elihu was the "daysman" of Job 9:33; in that view, he would typify the New Testament Mediator (1 Tim. 2:5; compare Job 31:35-37). Isaiah foretold the coming King to be the wonderful Counsellor (Is. 9:6). Jesus admonished the religious spirits of His day, "Search the scriptures; for in them ye think ['suppose'] ye have eternal life: and they are they which testify of Me" (Jn. 5:39). It is not enough to know the letter of the Word; we must have an experience with the Word Himself (2 Cor. 3:1-6)! The apostle Paul said it simplest and best, "...the truth is in Jesus" (Eph. 4:21).

Applied to the Christian ⚖

Elihu, the self-assertive youth with a far more spiritual conception of dealing with Job's problem, gives only half the truth, which is marred by his own manner. Revelation gave way to speculation, and the mouthy, immature preacher committed the common mistake of extending himself beyond the anointing (Job 32:6). Ready to burst if he could not speak, Elihu rushed in over his head, demonstrating the "young men" realm of spiritual adolescence (1 Jn. 2:12-14; see also Job 23:18-22; 1 Cor. 14:32). The Greek word for "suppose" is *dokeo* and means "to be of opinion" (compare Job 32:17). The psalmist prayed, "Lord, my heart is not haughty, nor mine eyes lofty: neither do I exercise myself in great matters, or in things too high for me" (Ps. 131:1). Paul added, "And if any man think that he knoweth any thing, he knoweth nothing yet as he ought to know" (1 Cor. 8:2).

Go Deeper 📖

See Gen. 18:14; Num. 14:44; Deut. 18:20; 2 Sam. 13:32; Esther 7:5; Ps. 12:6; 19:7; 118:23; 119:9; Prov. 24:7; Zech. 8:6; Mt. 3:9; Mk. 6:49; Lk. 7:43; 12:51; 13:2; 19:11; 24:37; Jn. 11:13; 16:2; 20:15; 21:25; Acts 2:15; 27:13; 1 Cor. 3:18; 10:12; Gal. 2:6; 6:3; Jas. 1:26.

∾ ∾ ∾

Elijah (Elisha)

The end-time prophetic Church; restoration; resurrection; repentance

Key Scriptures: 1 Kings 17–21; 2 Kings 1–8; Mal. 4:5-6; Mt. 17:1-13; Lk. 1:17; Jas. 5:17.

Foundational Information

Elijah the Tishbite was an influential prophet who lived during the ninth century B.C. during the reigns of Ahab and Ahaziah in the northern kingdom of Israel. "Elijah" is transliterated from the Hebrew *'Eliyah* (Strong's #452), which means "God of Jehovah." It is taken from *'el* ("strength, mighty, the Almighty") and *Yahh* ("the self-existent or Eternal"). "Tishbite" means "carrying off, capturing, making a prisoner, leading captive." "Elijah" has also been translated as "Jehovah is God, my God is Jah, Jehovah God." Elijah ("Elias") is mentioned a total of 30 times in the New Testament—this is the Bible number denoting priesthood, the throne of God, authority, and maturity.

Elisha was the Hebrew prophet who succeeded the prophet Elijah, receiving a double portion of his spirit. Elisha ministered for about 50 years in the northern kingdom of Israel, serving God during the reigns of Jehoram, Jehu, Jehoahaz, and Joash. "Elisha" is transliterated from the Hebrew *'Eliysha'* (Strong's #477), which means "the God of supplication (or of riches)." "Elisha" has also been translated as "my God is salvation, God is a Savior, to whom God gives victory, God of deliverance, God is rich."

Fulfilled in Christ

Jesus Christ is that "prophet" foretold by Moses (Deut. 18:15-18; Acts 3:18-24). Just as Elijah was a man subject to like passions as our own, so Jesus was the Word manifested in mortal flesh (Jn. 1:14; Jas. 5:17). In a similar, supernatural public ministry of three-and-one-half years, Jesus performed many of the same miracles as Elijah (see 1 Kings 17:1,14,22; 18:38,45; 2 Kings 1:10,12; 2:8). Elijah ascended and bestowed his mantle (anointing)—the "double portion" or the "portion of the firstborn"—upon Elisha (2 Kings 2:9-15). So Jesus resurrected, ascended and poured out His Holy Spirit as well as the fivefold ministry gifts upon the New Testament "church of the firstborn" (Heb. 12:23). As revealed in the name "Tishbite," Jesus overcame the kingdom of darkness and led captivity captive (Acts 2:33-36; Eph. 4:8-15). John the Baptist came preaching repentance in the spirit and power of Elijah as the preparatory, prophetic forerunner for his divine Cousin (Mt. 17:10-13; Lk. 1:17). Elijah (along with Moses) actually appeared to Jesus on the Mount of Transfiguration (Mt. 17:1-3; Mk. 9:2-4; Lk. 9:28-30). Moses taught Jesus how to die (the word for "decease" in Luke 9:31 is *exodos* and means "exit, departure; death"); Elijah came to show Jesus how to live!

Applied to the Christian   ⚖

The Elijah-Elisha ministry, which reveals the sovereignty of God, is primarily one of repentance and restoration, especially with regard to the home and family (Mal. 4:5-6). Jesus made two distinct statements in Matthew 17:11-12: 1) that Elias (Elijah) "is come already" (John the Baptist), and 2) that Elias "shall first come" (the end-time prophetic Church). Jesus predicted that His Church would do even "greater works" (Jn. 14:12); Elisha did 16 miracles—exactly double that of Elijah (see 2 Kings 2:14,21,24; 3:20; 4:6,16,35,41,43; 5:10,27; 6:6,17-20; 7:1; 8:15; 13:21)! Moreover, just as John the Baptist preceded the Pattern Son in His first Advent, there will be an end-time prophetic Church, an Elijah-Elisha ministry, who will spearhead the spiritual, corporate manifestation of the Son in His sons. Then Jesus' literal return will occur. Elijah's contest with the prophets of Baal on Mount Carmel (1 Kings 18) is a prophetic panorama of end-time spiritual warfare. Elijah's arch-enemies were Ahab and Jezebel, who prefigure political and religious Babylon (Rev. 17–18).

Go Deeper   📖

See 2 Kings 9:1,36; 10:10,17; 13:14-21; 2 Chron. 21:12; Mt. 11:14; 16:14; 27:47-49; Mk. 6:15; 8:28; 15:35-36; Lk. 4:25-27; 9:8,19,54; Jn. 1:21,25; Acts 10:43; 13:27; 24:14; 26:22; 28:23; Rom. 1:2; 3:21; 11:2-3; 12:6; 16:26; 1 Cor. 12:10; 1 Thess. 5:20; Heb. 1:1; 11:32; Jas. 5:10; 1 Pet. 1:10; 2 Pet. 1:21; 3:2; Rev. 19:10.

∞   ∞   ∞

Elim

Strength and refreshing

Key Scriptures: Ex. 15:27; Num. 33:9-10; Neh. 8:10;
Ps. 84:7; Is. 40:31; Acts 3:19.

Foundational Information   ✐

Elim was an encampment of the Israelites after they crossed the Red Sea, famous for its 12 wells of springs of water and 70 palm trees. "Elim" is transliterated from the Hebrew *'Eylim* (Strong's #362), and means "palm-trees." Compare *'ayil* (Strong's #352), which means "strength; hence, anything strong; specifically a chief (politically); also a ram (from his strength); a pilaster (as a strong support); an oak or other strong tree."

Its root *'uwl* means "to be strong or powerful." "Elim" has also been translated as "oaks, mighty ones, terebinths."

The Hebrew word for "refreshing" is *marge'ah* (Strong's #4774) and means "rest." Its root means "to settle, to be quiet." The New Testament word for "refreshing" is *anapsuxis* (Strong's #403) and means "a recovery of breath, (figuratively) revival." Compare *anapsucho*, which means "to cool off, (figuratively) relieve."

Fulfilled in Christ 🕆

Nehemiah declared, "...for the joy of the Lord is your strength" (Neh. 8:10). Jesus Christ, mankind's oasis and refreshing, is represented in the following four-fold Hebrew definition of "Elim":

1. The "chief" Singer, Corner Stone, and Shepherd (Hab. 3:19; 1 Pet. 2:6; 5:4).
2. The "Ram" of substitution and priestly consecration (Gen. 22:13; Ex. 29:15-32).
3. The "Pillar," the Overcomer (Rev. 3:12,21).
4. The True Vine, the "Tree" of life (Jn. 15:1-5; Rev. 2:7; 22:14).

Jesus came to refresh mankind. He is the great Rock in a weary land (Is. 32:2). The King anointed and sent out His 12 and 70 disciples, which were prefigured by the 12 wells of water and 70 palm trees of Elim (Ex. 15:27). Likewise, these apostles were anointed to bring healing and strength to others (Mt. 10:1; Lk. 10:1). Twelve is the Bible number for government and 70 represents the nations of the earth (Gen. 10).

Applied to the Christian ⚖

Those who wait upon the Lord "renew," or "exchange," their strength (Is. 40:31). Believers grow in grace from strength to strength (Ps. 84:7; compare Rom. 1:17; 2 Cor. 3:18). Just as the Israelites removed from Marah (the place of bitterness) and came unto Elim (the place of refreshing), so the believer has passed from death unto life (Num. 33:9; see also Jn. 5:24; 1 Jn. 3:14). Peter prophesied that "times of refreshing" would come from the presence of the Lord (Acts 3:19). The sabbath (the seventh day) was to be a season of refreshing (Ex. 23:12; 31:17); even so, there remains a rest to the people of God (Heb. 4:9).

Go Deeper 📖

See Ex. 23:12; Deut. 25:18; 1 Sam. 16:23; 2 Sam. 16:14; 1 Kings 13:7; Job 10:1; 32:20; Ps. 6:6; 68:9; 69:3; 92:12; Song 7:7-8; Is. 5:27; 40:28; 50:4; Jer. 4:31; Jn. 4:6; Acts 27:3; Rom. 15:32; 1 Cor. 16:18; 2 Cor. 7:13; Gal. 6:9; 2 Thess. 3:13; 2 Tim. 1:16; Philem. 7,20; Heb. 12:3.

∾ ∾ ∾

𝔈𝔩𝔦𝔭𝔥𝔞𝔷

Religious theology based upon human experience

Key Scriptures: Job 2:11; 4:12-16; 1 Cor. 15:44-49; 2 Cor. 4:18; 5:7; Col. 2:3.

Foundational Information

Eliphaz the Temanite was the chief and oldest of Job's three friends or "comforters." A very religious man, Eliphaz sought to uphold the holiness, purity, and justice of God. "Eliphaz" is transliterated from the Hebrew *'Eliyphaz* (Strong's #464), which means "God of gold." It is taken from *'el* ("strength, mighty, the Almighty") and *paz* ("pure gold"). "Eliphaz" has also been translated as "my God has refined, God is purification, God is dispenser, God of strength." "Teman" means "south" and refers to the land of Teman or Edom.

Fulfilled in Christ

Jesus Christ is the Author and Finisher of real faith (Heb. 12:2). He is the personification of the wisdom from above (1 Cor. 1:24,30; Jas. 3:17). From a child, the Messiah was filled with the wisdom of God (Lk. 2:40,52). Jesus walked in an open Heaven (Jn. 3:13)—the realm of the Holy Spirit was ever open to Him. He is the "last Adam," the Lord from Heaven who came to bring a lasting end to the earthy, first man Adam (1 Cor. 15:45). Out of His own mouth, Jesus announced that "a greater than Solomon is here" (Mt. 12:42). All the treasures of wisdom and knowledge are hidden in Him (Col. 2:3).

Applied to the Christian

Believers are to walk by faith, not by sight (2 Cor. 5:7). Faith, which alone pleases God, is contrary to reason (Heb. 11:6). In the Book of Job, the patriarch's three "comforters" illustrate the three components of man's "psyche" or soul:

1. Man's emotions—Eliphaz the theologian based his arguments upon his religious experiences.
2. Man's intellect—Bildad based his view on the time-honored wisdom of the fathers.
3. Man's will—Zophar based his opinions upon his own stubbornness.

Man's soul or mind is insufficient with regard to new creation realities (1 Cor. 2:9–16). That he was a "Temanite" reveals Eliphaz to have been a man of fleshly wisdom, like Adam or Esau. Eliphaz had one experience and seemed to understand it all (Job 4:12-16). His cry was based on, "I have seen..." (Job 4:8; 5:3; 15:17). Paul made it clear, "While we look not at the things which are seen, but at the things which are not seen: for the things which are seen are temporal; but the things which are not seen are eternal" (2 Cor. 4:18).

Go Deeper

See Gen. 3:6-7; Job 4:1; 15:1; 22:1; 42:7-9; Prov. 3:7; 16:25; 18:1; 21:30; Eccles. 1:17-18; Is. 33:17; Jer. 9:23-24; 49:7; Lk. 10:21; 16:8; 21:15; Acts 6:10; Rom. 8:24-25;

1 Cor. 2:1-5; Gal. 5:17; Eph. 1:8; Phil. 3:20; Col. 2:8; 3:1-3; 1 Tim. 6:20-21; Heb. 11:1,25-27; 1 Jn. 2:15-17.

∾ ∾ ∾

𝔈𝔩𝔦𝔰𝔞𝔟𝔢𝔱𝔥

Covenantal faithfulness; agreement

Key Scriptures: Ps. 2:7; 40:7-8; 110:4; Lam. 3:23; Amos 3:3; Mt. 18:19; Lk. 1.

Foundational Information ✑

Elisabeth, of the priestly line of Aaron, was the wife of Zacharias and the mother of John the Baptist. Visited by her cousin Mary, she confirmed and acknowledged the Messiah before He had been born. "Elisabeth" is derived from the Hebrew *'Eliysheba* (Strong's #472), and it means "God of the oath." It is taken from *'el* ("strength, mighty, the Almighty") and *sheba* ("seven; oath"). "Elisabeth" has also been translated as "my God is my oath (a worshiper), God of the seven."

The Hebrew word for "faith" or "faithfulness" is *'aman* (Strong's #539), and means "to build up or support; to foster as a parent or nurse; figuratively to render (or be) firm or faithful, to trust or believe, to be permanent or quiet; morally to be true or certain." The New Testament word *pistis* carries much of the same idea. The Greek word for "agree" is *sumphoneo* (Strong's #4856). It means "to be harmonious, (figuratively) to accord (be suitable, concur) or stipulate (by compact); to sound together, to be in accord, primarily of musical instruments." The noun *sumphonos* (English, *symphony*) means "sounding together (alike), accordant (agreement)."

Fulfilled in Christ ⵣ

Jesus Christ, the Pattern Son, intertheistically entered into the "everlasting covenant" (Heb. 13:20) with His Father before the world began. The Father decreed, "Thou art My Son" and "Thou art a Priest" (Ps. 2:7; 110:4). Jesus agreed, "Lo, I come: in the volume of the book it is written of Me; I delight to do Thy will, O my God; yea, Thy law is within My heart" (Ps. 40:7-8; compare Heb. 10:6-10). Their symphony of redemption introduced "the faith of God" into the creation (Mk. 11:22-23; compare Heb. 12:2). Jesus walked in perfect covenantal obedience (Jn. 8:29; Heb. 4:15). Isaiah prophesied of the coming Messiah, "And righteousness shall be the girdle of His loins, and faithfulness the girdle of His reins" (Is. 11:5). Great is His faithfulness (Lam. 3:23).

Applied to the Christian   ⚖

Amos prophesied, "Can two walk together, except they be agreed?" (Amos 3:3) Though old and barren, Elisabeth believed the supernatural words of Gabriel conveyed through her husband (Lk. 1:5-7,13,24,36). When later visited by Mary, the mother of the Baptist prophesied, "And blessed is she that believed: for there shall be a performance of those things which were told her from the Lord" (Lk. 1:45). The keynote of Psalm 89 is faithfulness. The psalmist declared, "I will sing of the mercies of the Lord for ever: with my mouth will I make known thy faithfulness to all generations" (Ps. 89:1). Jesus taught His disciples, "...if two of you shall agree on earth as touching any thing that they shall ask, it shall be done for them of my Father which is in heaven" (Mt. 18:19).

Go Deeper   📖

See 1 Sam. 26:23; 2 Kings 18:31; Ps. 5:9; 36:5; 40:10; 88:11; 89:2,5,8,24,33; 92:2; 119:75; 143:1; Is. 25:1; 28:15-18; Dan. 11:6; Hos. 2:20; Mt. 5:25; 20:2,13; 14:59; Mk. 14:56; Lk. 5:36; Jn. 9:22; Acts 5:9,40; 15:15; 23:20; 28:25; 2 Cor. 6:16; 1 Jn. 5:8; Rev. 17:17.

∾   ∾   ∾

𝔈𝔩𝔬𝔥𝔦𝔪

The Creator God; the Creator's family

Key Scriptures: Gen. 1–5; Is. 40:28; Jn. 1:1-3; 10:34;
Eph. 2:10; 3:9; Col. 1:16-17; 1 Pet. 4:19.

Foundational Information   ✐

Elohim is the plural form of El, but it is usually translated in the singular. Some believe it describes the supreme God and His heavenly court of created beings. Still others hold that the plural form refers to the triune God who worked through Word and Spirit in the creation of the world. "Elohim" is transliterated from the Hebrew *'elohiym* (Strong's #430), which means "gods in the ordinary sense; but specifically used (in the plural thus, especially with the article) of the supreme God; occasionally applied by way of deference to magistrates; and sometimes as a superlative." It is the plural of *'elowahh* ("the Deity") and the shortened form of *'el* or *'ayil* which means "strength, mighty, the Almighty."

Fulfilled in Christ   ✝

Jesus Christ, the Word, is the Creator (Is. 40:28; 1 Pet. 4:19). John exclaimed, "All things were made by Him; and without Him was not any thing made that was made...He was in the world, and the world was made by Him, and the world knew Him not" (Jn. 1:3,10). The Psalmist prophesied of Messiah, "Thy throne, O God [*Elohim*], is for ever and ever: the sceptre of Thy kingdom is a right sceptre" (Ps. 45:6; Heb. 1:8). God created all things by Christ Jesus (Eph. 3:9). Paul explained, "For by Him were all things created...And He is before all things, and by Him all things consist" (Col. 1:16-17). All things were created for His pleasure (Rev. 4:11).

Applied to the Christian ⚖️

God created man in His own image and likeness (Gen. 1:26). In regeneration, we are recreated or born again by the work of His Word and Spirit (Jn. 3:1-8). We are His workmanship, created in Christ Jesus (Eph. 2:10). "Elohim" can also refer to the Creator's family. Moses was made a "god" unto Pharoah (Ex. 7:1). "Elohim" is translated as "judges" ("magistrates") (Ex. 21:6; 22:8-9) and "angels" (Ps. 8:5; compare Heb. 2:7) in the King James Version. Jesus quoted the psalmist, "...Ye are gods [*elohim*]; and all of you are the children of the most High" (Ps. 82:6; Jn. 10:34; compare Dan. 2:47; Rev. 19:16). Isaiah declared that believers are "...Priests of the Lord; men shall call you the Ministers of our God [*Elohim*]" (Is. 61:6a). Could Jesus also have been calling out to His family from the cross? He cried, "Eloi, Eloi...why hast thou forsaken Me?" (Mk. 15:34b)

Go Deeper 📖

See Gen. 1:1; 2:4,7,21-22; Ex. 3:6; 24:10; Deut. 6:4; Ruth 1:16; 1 Sam. 3:3; Ps. 20:5; 47:1; 95:6; 102:25; Prov. 3:19; 25:2; Eccles. 12:1; Is. 37:16; 40:3; 44:24; 45:7,12,18; 52:7; 65:17-18; Jer. 10:12; Ezek. 1:1; Mal. 2:10; 3:8; Rom. 1:25; 1 Cor. 8:6; 2 Cor. 5:17; Gal. 6:15; Eph. 4:24; Col. 3:10; Heb. 1:2-3,10-12; 3:3-4; 1 Pet. 1:23.

∞ ∞ ∞

𝔈𝔩-𝔖𝔥𝔞𝔡𝔡𝔞𝔦

Nurture, nursing, intimacy; sucklings

Key Scriptures: Gen. 17:1; Mt. 21:16; Jn. 1:18; 21:20;
1 Thess. 2:7,11; Rev. 15:3.

Foundational Information ✏️

El-Shaddai is the name for God that reveals Him as the source of all blessing, the One who is intimate with His children. "El-Shaddai" is a compound of *'El* ("strength, mighty") and *Shadday* (Strong's #7706), which means "the Almighty" (used 48 times in the Old Testament, 31 of which are in the Book of Job). The latter's root is *shadad* (Strong's #7703), which means "to be burly, (figuratively) powerful (passively, impregnable); by implication, to ravage." Some scholars have attempted to understand the word relating it to the Akkadian *shadu* ("mountain"). Compare *shad* (Strong's #7699), the Hebrew word for "breast." Accordingly, "El-Shaddai" is sometimes referred to as "the breasted One," revealing the intimate, mother-side of God's love.

The Greek word for "almighty" is *pantokrator* (Strong's #3841), and it means "the all-ruling God (as absolute and universal sovereign)." It is taken from *pas* ("all") and *krateo* ("to hold or have strength; to rule"). It is mentioned nine times in the New Testament, once in First Corinthians 6:18 and nine times in the Book of Revelation.

Fulfilled in Christ ✝

Jesus Christ, the personification of the love of God, came forth from the "bosom" of the Father (Jn. 1:18). He is the Lamb of whom Moses sang, "Great and marvellous are Thy works, Lord God Almighty..." (Rev. 15:3b). The Book of Job declares, "The Spirit of God hath made me, and the breath of the Almighty hath given me life" (Job 33:4; compare Jn. 1:3). Jesus is the Rock from which we "suck honey" (Deut. 32:13; see also 1 Cor. 10:4). He is the offered "sucking lamb" who constantly drew from the life of the Father (1 Sam. 7:9; compare Jn. 1:29). At the last supper, it was John the beloved who "leaned on His breast" (Jn. 21:20).

Applied to the Christian ⚖

A man and a woman rightly related reveal the image of God (Gen. 1:26). God is love, fully expressed through "mother's love" (unconditional love) and "father's love" (a firm respect) (1 Jn. 4:8). The apostle Paul manifested both to the church at Thessalonica, "But we were gentle among you, even as a nurse cherisheth her children ...we exhorted and comforted and charged every one of you, as a father doth his children" (1 Thess. 2:7,11). The first revelation of "El-Shaddai" was to the patriarch Abraham (Gen. 17:1; see also Gal. 3:29). Men may drop you (2 Sam. 4:4) but El-Shaddai will sustain you; "He that dwelleth in the secret place of the most High shall abide under the shadow of the Almighty" (Ps. 91:1). Out of the mouths of sucklings has God ordained strength and perfected praise (Ps. 8:2; Mt. 21:16).

Go Deeper 📖

See Gen. 28:3; 35:11; 48:3; 49:25; Ex. 2:7-9; Num. 11:12; Deut. 33:19; Ruth 4:16; Job 11:7; 22:25; 29:5; 31:35; 32:8; 33:4; Ps. 22:9; 68:14; Is. 11:8; 13:6; 49:15; 60:4,16; 66:11-12; Ezek. 1:24; 10:5; Joel 1:15; 2:16; Lk. 11:27; Eph. 1:3; Rev. 1:8; 4:8; 11:17; 16:7,14; 19:6,15; 21:22.

∞ ∞ ∞

𝕰𝖒𝖇𝖗𝖔𝖎𝖉𝖊𝖗𝖞 (𝕹𝖊𝖊𝖉𝖑𝖊𝖜𝖔𝖗𝖐)

The daily workings of the Holy Spirit

Key Scriptures: Ex. 26:36-37; 28:39; 35:35; Ps. 45:14; 1 Cor. 12:1-26; Phil. 2:13; Eph. 2:10.

Foundational Information 🖎

Embroidery or needlework are decorations on cloth sewn in with needle and thread. Embroidered work was valuable; it gave evidence of wealth, the prized spoils of war, and commercial goods. "Embroider" is from the Hebrew *shabats* (Strong's #7660), which means "to interweave (colored) threads in squares; by implication (of reticulation) to inchase gems in gold." Its root *raqam* (Strong's #7551) means "to variegate color, embroider; by implication, to fabricate," and is translated as "embroiderer, needlework, curiously work" in the King James Version.

Fulfilled in Christ 🕆

The Father was the Designer of the Pattern (Ex. 25:40); Jesus the Son was the Pattern, "the express image" of the Father's person (Heb. 3:1), and the Holy Spirit did the work (Acts 10:38). Jesus was the "door" and the "hanging" wrought with needlework (Ex. 26:36-37; see also Jn. 10:7-9; Gal. 3:13-14). The Pattern Son was ever "led" by the Holy Spirit (Mt. 4:1; Lk. 4:1; Rom. 8:14). Like the showbread ("pierced cakes") in the Mosaic tabernacle, Jesus the bread of life was "pierced" when He died to put away sin (see Ps. 22:16; Zech. 12:10; Jn. 19:34,37; Rev. 1:7). God instructed Moses, "And thou shalt embroider the coat of fine linen, and thou shalt make the mitre of fine linen, and thou shalt make the girdle of needlework" (Ex. 28:39). Jesus is our righteousness, our victor's crown, and our strength. Aaron, who wore the Levitical "curious girdle," prefigures Him who is our merciful and faithful High Priest (Lev. 8:7; see also Heb. 2:17).

Applied to the Christian ⚖

Believers are His workmanship, created in Christ Jesus (Eph. 2:10). The Church is the Bride of Christ (Eph. 5:22-24; Rev. 21:9); the psalmist declared of her, "She shall be brought unto the king in raiment of needlework: the virgins her companions that follow her shall be brought unto thee" (Ps. 45:14). God anointed certain embroiders to distinctly fashion the Old Testament tabernacle (Ex. 35:35); so "there are diversities of operations [of the Holy Spirit], but it is the same God which worketh all in all" (1 Cor. 12:6). God works in and through us according to His own pleasure and will (Eph. 2:10; Phil. 2:13). These daily workings of the Holy Spirit:

1. Are the fulfillment of the law (Rom. 13:10).
2. Produce the life of God (2 Cor. 4:12).

3. Bring the glory of God (2 Cor. 4:17-18).

4. Abundantly surpass our every expectation (Eph. 3:20).

Go Deeper 📖

See Ex. 27:16; 28:8,27-28; 29:5; 35:32; 38:18,23; 39:5,20-21,29; Judg. 5:26,30; Job 30:17; Ps. 139:15; Song 1:4; Zech. 4:6; Lk. 2:35; Jn. 16:13; Acts 1:8; Rom. 5:3; 1 Cor. 2:4-5; 16:10; 2 Cor. 7:10; Gal. 5:6; Col. 1:27-29; 1 Thess. 2:13; 1 Tim. 6:10; Jas. 1:3,20; Rev. 21:27.

∞   ∞   ∞

𝔈merald

Sonship; the firstborn; covenantal authority

Key Scriptures: Ex. 28:18; 39:11; Ezek. 27:16; 28:13; Mt. 3:17; 17:5; Rev. 4:3; 21:19.

Foundational Information ✍

Emerald, one of the rarest gems, is a deep green variety of beryl. "Emerald" is from the Hebrew *nophek* (Strong's #5306), which means "to glisten; shining; a gem, probably the garnet." Compare the Greek word *smaragdos* (Strong's #4665), which means "the emerald or green gem so called." The emerald was the first stone in the second row of Aaron's breastplate—on this fourth stone was engraven the name of the tribe of Reuben. The emerald, used to describe the rainbow around the throne, was also included in the foundation of the New Jerusalem.

Fulfilled in Christ ☀

"Reuben," the firstborn of Jacob, means "behold a son" or "vision of a son." Jesus Christ is the Pattern Son of whom the Father declared, "This is My beloved Son" (Mt. 3:17; 17:5). Paul declared Him to be the firstborn among many brethren (Rom. 8:29), and the psalmist prophesied of the Messiah, "Also I will make Him my firstborn, higher than the kings of the earth" (Ps. 89:27). Jesus has been given all executive authority in Heaven and in earth (Mt. 28:18). The writer to the Hebrews declared that Jesus was "made like unto His brethren, that He might be a merciful and faithful high priest" (Heb. 2:17). John the revelator described our enthroned Lord and King, and testified that "there was a rainbow round about [His] throne, in sight like unto an emerald" (Rev. 4:3).

Applied to the Christian ⚖

As Christians, we are the "brethren" of Jesus Christ, our elder Brother (Heb. 2:11-12). Green is the Bible color that represents life, and we are alive in Christ (Rom. 6:11-13; Gal. 2:20). The rainbow signifies covenant, and to those who are in union with Him, Jesus declared through John, "To him that overcometh will I grant to sit with Me in My throne…I will be his God, and he shall be My son" (Rev. 3:21; 21:7). True believers belong to the "church of the firstborn" (Heb. 12:23), and are called to rule and reign with Christ (Rom. 5:17-21). The redeemed have been destined to receive "the adoption of sons" (Gal. 4:5). We have inherited the authority of His name (Mk. 16:15-20; Jn. 14:13-14).

Go Deeper 📖

See Gen. 9:13-16; 29:31-32; 49:3-4; Ex. 4:22; Deut. 21:17; 33:6; Ps. 2:7; Jer. 31:9; Hos. 11:1; Mic. 6:7; Zech. 12:10; Mt. 1:25; 21:37; Lk. 1:31-33; 2:7; Jn. 1:12; 3:1-8; Acts 13:33; Rom. 8:15,23; 9:4; 1 Cor. 15:25; Eph. 1:5; Col. 1:15-18; 2 Tim. 2:12; Heb. 1:5; 12:5-11; Rev. 5:10; 6:2; 10:1; 11:15; 20:6; 22:5.

∞ ∞ ∞

𝔈mmanuel (𝔍mmanuel)

The incarnation of Jesus Christ, the Word made flesh; the abiding presence of the Lord

Key Scriptures: Is. 7:14; 8:8; Mt. 1:23; Jn. 1:14; 1 Tim. 3:16.

Foundational Information ✐

Emmanuel is a symbolic name given by the prophet Isaiah for the coming Messiah. "Immanuel" is transliterated from the Hebrew *'Immanuw'el* (Strong's #6005). It means "with us (is) God." "Emmanuel," or "God with us," is a compound of three Hebrew words: *'im* ("with"), *'amam* ("to associate; to overshadow by huddling together"), and *'el* ("strength, mighty, the Almighty").

The Greek word for "abide" is *meno* (Strong's #3306) and means "to stay (in a given place, state, relation or expectancy)." It is translated in the King James Version as "abide, continue, dwell, endure, be present, remain, stand, tarry (for)."

Fulfilled in Christ

Jesus Christ is Emmanuel, the Word made flesh (Jn. 1:14). Isaiah prophesied His virgin birth, "Therefore the Lord Himself shall give you a sign; Behold, a virgin shall conceive, and bear a son, and shall call his name Immanuel" (Is. 7:14; see also Mt. 1:23). The apostle Paul affirmed, "And without controversy great is the mystery of godliness: God was manifested in the flesh" (1 Tim. 3:16). Jesus emptied Himself and was tempted in every way, yet without sin (Phil. 2:5-8; Heb. 4:15). Luke recorded "how God anointed Jesus of Nazareth with the Holy Ghost and with power: who went about doing good, and healing all that were oppressed of the devil; for God was with Him" (Acts 10:38).

Applied to the Christian

Because of Jesus' incarnation, believers have been blessed with the abiding presence of the Lord Himself, who pledged, "...lo, I am with you alway, even unto the end of the world" (Mt. 28:20). He has promised never to leave us or forsake us (Heb. 13:5). Through the power of His indwelling Holy Spirit, the Church has become His ongoing incarnation (Jn. 14:16,26; 15:26; 16:13). John declared God's never-failing presence to be sure, "Behold, the tabernacle of God is with men, and He will dwell with them, and they shall be His people, and God Himself shall be with them, and be their God" (Rev. 21:3). Jesus admonished, "If ye abide in me, and my words abide in you, ye shall ask what ye will, and it shall be done unto you" (Jn. 15:7).

Go Deeper

See Gen. 3:15; 35:3; Deut. 5:2,24; 1 Kings 8:56-57; 2 Chron. 13:12; 32:8; Ps. 40:7; 46:7,11; Is. 8:10; 9:6; Ezek. 3:15; 48:35; Mic. 5:2; Mk. 16:20; Lk. 19:5; 24:39; Jn. 15:1-10; Acts 2:30; Rom. 1:3-4; 8:3; 9:5; Gal. 4:4; Heb. 1:3; 2:14-18; 1 Jn. 1:2; 2:24-28; 4:1-3; 2 Jn. 7; Rev. 22:16.

∞ ∞ ∞

Emptiness

Void, vanity; idolatry

Key Scriptures: Gen. 1:2; 1 Sam. 15:23; Ps. 39:5-6; Eccles. 1–2; Eph. 2:1-3.

Foundational Information

"Void" is from the Hebrew *bohuw* (Strong's #922). It means "(to be empty); a vacuity, (superficially) an undistinguishable ruin." "Vanity" is from the Hebrew *hebel*

(Strong's #1892), meaning "emptiness or vanity; figuratively, something transitory and unsatisfactory." It has also been rendered as "breath" or "idol."

Fulfilled in Christ

Jesus Christ, who was all the fullness of the Godhead bodily (Col. 2:9), came to fill the void in every man. He was the Word who went forth from the Father who did not return void. He accomplished the Father's divine plan (Is. 55:11; see also Jn. 1:1). The purpose of Christ's present reign is "that He might fill all things" (Eph. 4:10; compare Num. 14:21; Hab. 2:14; Lk. 3:5-6). Because of Jesus' finished work, men can be "filled" with the following qualities:

1. His righteousness (Mt. 5:6).
2. His Holy Spirit (Acts 2:4; Eph. 5:18).
3. His joy (Acts 13:52).
4. His fullness (Eph. 3:19).
5. His wisdom and understanding (Col. 1:9).
6. His glory (Rev. 15:8).

Applied to the Christian

Life without Jesus is empty. Man at his best state is altogether vanity (Ps. 39:5-6). Solomon, the man who knew it all, had it all, and did it all, observed that life "under the sun" (natural life apart from the life of God) was altogether "vanity" (Eccles. 1:2,14). In the unregenerated state (before the power of God's Spirit transforms his sinful life), man is like the pristine earth—"without form, and void; and darkness was upon the face of the deep" (Gen. 1:2; compare Eph. 2:1-3). We were idolaters, worshiping other gods, living by the "doctrine of vanities" and "doctrines of devils" (Jer. 10:8; 1 Tim. 4:1; see also 1 Sam. 15:23). May we say with the psalmist, "I have hated them that regard lying vanities: but I trust in the Lord" (Ps. 31:6).

Go Deeper

See Deut. 32:21,28; 1 Kings 16:13,26; 2 Kings 17:15; Ps. 39:11; 62:9; 94:11; 119:126; Prov. 7:7; 10:13; 11:12; 12:11; 17:18; 31:30; Eccles. 12:8; Is. 34:11; Jer. 2:5; 4:23; 51:18; Jon. 2:8; Nahum 2:10; Zech. 10:2; Mt. 12:44; Lk. 1:53; Acts 4:25; 17:23; 1 Cor. 10:14; 15:10-14; Gal. 2:2; 5:20; Eph. 5:6; Col. 2:8; 3:5; Jas. 2:20.

𝕰𝖓𝖈𝖆𝖒𝖕𝖒𝖊𝖓𝖙

Providential placement; the angelic host

Key Scriptures: Gen. 32:1-2; Num. 1–4; Ps. 2:6-7;
16:6; 34:7; 110:4; 1 Cor. 12:18,28.

Foundational Information ✑

The sites where the Hebrew people stopped on their wilderness journey to the prom-ised land were temporary dwelling places. Their encampments were to be set up in a spe-cific manner. The tabernacle of meeting was erected in the center, surrounded by the Levites and the 12 tribes. "Encamp" is from the Hebrew *chanah* (Strong's #2583), which means "to incline; by implication, to decline (of the slanting rays of evening); specifi-cally, to pitch a tent; to encamp (for abode or siege)."

"Camp" is from the Hebrew *machaneh* (Strong's #4264), and it means "an encamp-ment (of travellers or troops); hence, an army, whether literal (of soldiers) or figurative (of dancers, angels, cattle, locusts, stars; or even the sacred courts)." It is translated as "army, band, battle, camp, company, drove, host, tents" in the King James Version.

Fulfilled in Christ ☥

The entire earthly life and ministry of Jesus Christ was providentially predestined, especially the "place" called Gethsemane and Calvary (Mt. 26:36; 27:33). Jesus was the Son "set" in Zion (Ps. 2:6-7), the Word forever "settled" in Heaven (Ps. 119:89) whose immutable priesthood was declared beforehand (Ps. 110:4). Jesus is the One to whom we gather (Gen. 49:10). He is the true Tabernacle, the center of our lives, who promised, "For where two or three are gathered together in My name, there am I in the midst of them" (Mt. 18:20). Our Lord is the fiery bright cloud who has gone before us to search out a place for our tents (Deut. 1:33; compare Jn. 8:11-12; 14:6). God has blessed us with all spiritual blessings in heavenly "places" in Christ Jesus (Eph. 1:3,20; 2:6; 3:10). Jesus was the Father's house; in Him, in the world of worship, there's a "place" for you (Jn. 14:2).

Applied to the Christian ⚖

Each of us has our unique place in the Body of Christ, the army of God. The Lord has "set" the leadership in His Church, and then the members according to His will and pleasure (1 Cor. 12:18,28). He distributes the *charismata*, the gifts of the Holy Spirit, among us "severally as He will" (1 Cor. 12:11). The boundary lines of His desire have fallen unto us in "pleasant places" (Ps. 16:6). For example, Jacob experienced the protec-tion of God's angelic host (Gen. 32:1-2). The psalmist assured every believer that "the an-gel of the Lord encampeth round about them that fear Him, and delivereth them" (Ps. 34:7). Because of God's protection and direction, His people are admonished, "the Lord thy God walketh in the midst of thy camp, to deliver thee, and to give up thine enemies before thee; therefore shall thy camp be holy" (Deut. 23:14).

Go Deeper 📖

See Gen. 28:15; 32:2; Ex. 14:2,19; 33:21; Num. 10:31; Deut. 12:11; 23:12; Josh. 3:3; 2 Sam. 7:10; 1 Chron. 15:1; 17:9; Ps. 18:33; 27:3; 84:1-4; Prov. 14:26; Song 2:14; Is. 4:6; 33:21; 56:5; 65:10; Ezek. 1:24; Joel 2:11; Zech. 3:7; 9:8; Mk. 11:4; Jn. 20:7; Heb. 1:14; 11:8; Rev. 12:6.

∞ ∞ ∞

𝕰𝖓𝖌𝖊𝖉𝖎

Springs of joyous refreshing; spiritual renewal

Key Scriptures: Josh. 15:62; 1 Sam. 23:29; 24:1; 2 Chron. 20:2; Song 1:14; Ezek. 47:10.

Foundational Information ✏

Engedi was an oasis on the barren western shore of the Dead Sea. Its ancient name was *Hazeazon-tamar* which means "pruning of palms." "Engedi" is transliterated from the Hebrew *'Eyn Gediy* (Strong's #5872), which means "fountain of a kid." "Engedi" has also been translated as "spring of the kid, God's fountain, fountain of fortune." It was there that David refreshed himself when running from King Saul.

The Hebrew word for "renew" is *chadash* (Strong's #2318). It means "to be new; causatively, to rebuild," and is translated in the King James Version as "renew, repair." The noun *chodesh* means "new moon; month." The Greek word for "renewing" is *anakainosis* (Strong's #342), and it means "renovation." Also translated as "to make new," it is taken from *ana* ("back, again") and *kainos* ("new, not recent but different").

Fulfilled in Christ ✝

Jesus Christ, "God's fountain," sprang up out of death in His resurrection! He revealed Himself as the source of "living water" to the woman of Samaria (Jn. 4:10-11). He is our stronghold (1 Sam. 23:29), for the joy of the Lord is our strength (Neh. 8:10). The Shulamite, a type of the Bride of Christ, declared of Him, "My beloved is unto me as a cluster of camphire in the vineyards of Engedi" (Song 1:14). Jesus' finished work has given birth to a new creation (2 Cor. 5:17; Gal. 6:15) which is expressed in the following:

1. New song (Ps. 40:3).
2. New wine or new joy (Prov. 3:10).
3. New covenant (Jer. 31:31; Heb. 8:8).

4. New spirit (Ezek. 11:19).
5. New heart (Ezek. 36:26).
6. New treasure (Mt. 13:52).
7. New tongues (Mk. 16:17).
8. New commandment (Jn. 13:34).
9. New name or new nature (Rev. 2:17).

Applied to the Christian ⚖

Believers who have drunk from Jesus' fountain have been filled with the Holy Spirit, the leaping fountain—"rivers of living water" (Jn. 7:37-39). From these times of spiritual refreshing, we can go forth to evangelize the nations, to spread forth our nets (Ezek. 47:10). Believers have experienced His mercy in the washing of regeneration and the renewing of the Holy Ghost (Tit. 3:5). So Paul admonishes us, "And be not conformed to this world: but be ye transformed by the renewing ['renovating'] of your mind" (Rom. 12:2). In these places of spiritual refreshing (Acts 3:19), a prophetic Church destined to share His Davidic throne moves ever forward into new phases (like the moon) of God's will and purpose.

Go Deeper 📖

See Lev. 23:16; 1 Sam. 11:14; 20:5; 2 Kings 2:20; 1 Chron. 23:31; 2 Chron. 15:8; 24:4,12; Neh. 10:39; Job 29:20; Ps. 33:3; 51:10; 81:3; 103:5; 104:30; 144:9; Song 7:13; Is. 28:12; 41:5; 42:9; 43:19; 61:4; 65:17; Lam. 5:21; Zech. 9:17; Mt. 9:16-17; 1 Cor. 5:7; 2 Cor. 4:16; Eph. 4:23-24; Col. 3:10; Philem. 20; Heb. 10:20.

∾ ∾ ∾

𝔈ngine (𝔍nvention)

Human wisdom; the destructive plans of men

Key Scriptures: Ps. 106:39; Prov. 8:12; 14:12; Ezek. 26:9;
1 Cor. 1:18-31; 2 Cor. 10:3-6; Jas. 3:13-16.

Foundational Information ✐

The engine of war, or battering ram, was a long, pointed pole on wheels driven with great, destructive force against fortified city walls. "Engine" is taken from the Hebrew *chishshabown* (Strong's #2810), which means "a contrivance, actual (a warlike machine) or mental (a machination)." It is translated as "engine, invention" in the King James Version. Its root *chashab* (Strong's #2803) means "to plait or interpenetrate, (literally) to weave or to fabricate; figuratively, to plot or contrive (usually in a malicious sense); hence (from the mental effort) to think, regard, value, compute." The word for "engines" is *mechiy* (Strong's #4239) and means "a stroke, battering-ram."

There are other Hebrew words translated in the King James Version as "inventions"— *'aliylah* (Strong's #5949) means "a performance (of man, often in a bad sense); by implication, an opportunity." Its root means "to overdo, maltreat, impose." *Mezimmah* (Strong's #4209) means "a plan, usually evil (machination)." It is also rendered as "purpose; evil device; evil thoughts; discretion."

Fulfilled in Christ

Wisdom is personified in the Book of Proverbs, declaring, "I wisdom dwell with prudence, and find out knowledge of witty inventions" (Prov. 8:12). In the New Testament, Christ is the wisdom of God (1 Cor. 1:24,30; Jas. 3:17). The faith that He authored (Heb. 12:2) does not stand in the wisdom of men, but in the power of God (1 Cor. 2:5). All the treasures of wisdom and knowledge are hidden in Christ (Col. 2:3). Jesus' incarnation answered Job's questions (Job 28:12). Isaiah prophesied that the "spirit of wisdom and understanding" would rest upon the Messiah (Is. 11:2). The apostle Paul declared, "Let this mind be in you, which was also in Christ Jesus" (Phil. 2:5).

Applied to the Christian

Apart from Christ, man's wisdom is earthly, sensual, and demonic (Jas. 3:13-16). Old Testament Israel provoked Jehovah in the wilderness when "they defiled with their own works, and went a whoring with their own inventions" (Ps. 106:39). Real apostles and prophets, to whom have been stewarded the mysteries of the gospel (Eph. 2:20; 3:1-5; 4:11), are Jesus' "engines of war" set against the walls and towers of Babylonish, religious traditions (Ezek. 26:9; compare Jer. 51:11). The weapons of the believer's warfare are not carnal, but they are mighty through God to pull down these strongholds and lofty imaginations (2 Cor. 10:3-6). The Lord has warned man, "Behold, I know your thoughts, and the devices which ye wrongfully imagine against Me" (Job 21:27).

Go Deeper

See 2 Chron. 26:15; Job 42:2; Ps. 10:1-4; 14:1; 21:11; 37:7; 99:8; 106:29; 139:20; 141:4; Prov. 1:4; 2:11; 3:21; 5:2; 12:2; 14:17; 24:8; Eccles. 7:29; Jer. 11:15; 23:20; 30:24; Ezek. 20:43-44; 21:24; 24:14; 36:17-19; Zeph. 3:7,11; 1 Cor. 1:17,19; 2:1-4,9-16; 3:19; 2 Cor. 1:12; Col. 2:23; Jas. 1:5.

∞   ∞   ∞

𝔈ngraver

The Holy Spirit in His creative workings

Key Scriptures: Ex. 31:18; Mt. 13:55; Mk. 6:3; 1 Cor. 2:10; 2 Cor. 3:1-18.

Foundational Information

"Engraver" is from the Hebrew *charash* (Strong's #2796) and means "a fabricator or any material." The verb is "to plow, work in metals." *Charash* is translated in the King James Version as "artificer, carpenter, craftsman, engraver, maker, mason, smith, worker, workman." Its root means "to scratch, (by implication) to engrave, plough; hence (from the use of tools) to fabricate (of any material)." Compare the word *pittuwach* (Strong's #6603), which means "sculpture."

The Greek word *charagma* (Strong's #5480) means "a scratch or etching, stamp (as a badge of servitude), or sculptured figure (statue)," and is translated as "graven, mark" in the King James Version. It is taken from *charasso* ("to sharpen to a point") and is akin to *grapho* (Strong's #1125), which means "to 'grave', especially to write; figuratively, to describe."

Fulfilled in Christ

The Holy Spirit is the Spirit of the Son (Gal. 4:6). Jesus was a carpenter (Mt. 13:55; Mk. 6:3). The two onyx stones on the shoulders of Aaron, "the work of an engraver" (Ex. 28:11), bear witness to the One of whom Isaiah prophesied, "and the government shall be upon His shoulder" (Is. 9:6). Jesus is the one stone with seven eyes (representing all understanding) who has removed the iniquity of the land (Zech. 3:9). The writer to the Hebrews repeated the words of the Messiah, "Then said I, Lo, I come (in the volume of the book it is written of me) to do thy will, O God" (Heb. 10:7). John said that Jesus' "eyes were as a flame of fire, and on His head were many crowns; and He had a name written, that no man knew, but He Himself" (Rev. 19:12). The work of the Spirit was perfect in His life.

Applied to the Christian

Every man bears one of two "marks"—the "mark" of the beast (the Adamic nature) or the "mark" of the Lord (Rev. 13:16-17; 14:1-5). The wisdom of the Holy Spirit carved into the life of the Christian is pictured by the "wisdom of heart" given to those who fashioned Moses' tabernacle (Ex. 35:35). Each of the twelve stones on Aaron's breastplate, "like the engravings of a signet" (Ex. 28:21), reveal a different facet of Christ's nature in those who have been sealed by the Holy Spirit of promise (Eph. 1:13-14). The carved ornamentation of Solomon's temple (1 Kings 6:29) reveal the deep workings of the Holy Spirit (1 Cor. 2:10) in the life of the believer:

1. Cherubim—mercy.
2. Palm trees—victory.
3. Open flowers—resurrection life.

Just as God wrote the law on tables with His own finger, so Paul declared that we are living epistles "written not with ink, but with the Spirit of the living God; not in tables of stone, but in fleshy tables of the heart" (Ex. 31:18; 2 Cor. 3:2-3).

Go Deeper 📖

See Ex. 32:15; 38:23; 39:14,30; 2 Chron. 2:7,14; Ps. 139:16; 149:9; Prov. 3:3; Hab. 2:2; Acts 17:29; Rom. 2:15; 1 Cor. 6:11; 12:1-13; 2 Cor. 3:7,18; Gal. 3:1-5; Eph. 3:16; Phil. 2:13; Col. 1:29; Heb. 9:4; Rev. 1:11; 2:17; 3:12; 5:1; 13:8; 14:9-11; 15:2; 16:2; 19:20; 20:4; 21:5.

∞ ∞ ∞

Enoch

Translation, transformation

Key Scriptures: Gen. 5:18-24; 1 Chron. 1:3; Jn. 11:25; Rom. 8:11; 1 Cor. 15; Phil. 3:10; Heb. 11:5; Jude 14.

Foundational Information ✍

Enoch, the son of Jared and the father of Methuselah, was translated—taken directly into God's presence without experiencing physical death. "Enoch," from the Hebrew *Chanowk* (Strong's #2585), means "initiated." It is taken from the root *chanak* (Strong's #2596), which means "to narrow to initiate or discipline." The latter is translated in the King James Version as "dedicate, train up." "Enoch" has also been translated as "experienced, founder, centralizer, teacher, instructor, initiator, fixer."

The Greek word for "translated" in Hebrews 11:5 is *metatithemi* (Strong's #3346), which means "to transfer, (literally) transport, (by implication) exchange (reflexively) change sides." Taken from *meta* ("to change") and *tithemi* ("to put or place"), it means "to transfer to another place." The Greek word for "pleased" is *euaresteo* (Strong's #2100). It means "to gratify entirely." Compare *euarestos* which means "fully agreeable."

Fulfilled in Christ ☦

"By faith Enoch was translated that he should not see death; and was not found, because God had translated him: for before his translation he had this testimony, that he pleased God" (Heb. 11:5). Jesus Christ is the resurrection and the life (Jn. 11:25), the One who has given us the victory over death (1 Cor. 15:55-58). In Him is life; He that hath the Son hath life (Jn. 1:4; 1 Jn. 5:12). Like Enoch, Jesus fully agreed to the Father's will (Mt. 3:17; 17:5), declaring, "I do always those things that please Him" (Jn. 8:29). Jude rehearsed Enoch's prophecy concerning the Lord: "And Enoch also, the seventh from Adam, prophesied of these, saying, Behold, the Lord cometh with ten thousands of his saints" (Jude 14).

Applied to the Christian ⚖

Believers have been filled with the Holy Ghost, the Spirit that raised Jesus from the dead. Paul affirmed that "He that raised up Christ from the dead shall also quicken your mortal bodies by His Spirit that dwelleth in you" (Rom. 8:11). The apostle longed to know Jesus in the power of His resurrection (Phil. 3:10-11). "Can two walk together, except they be agreed?" (Amos 3:3) Enoch was a man who loved to "walk" or "go" with God (Gen. 5:22,24). Initially, believers are "translated" or "transferred" out of the kingdom of darkness and into the Kingdom of light and life (Col. 1:9-13). Ultimately, there will be a remnant people like Enoch who will not experience physical death (1 Cor. 15:51).

Go Deeper 📖

See Gen. 6:9; 2 Sam. 7:7; 2 Kings 2:11; Job 31:5; Ps. 26:1-3; 55:14; 81:13; Mal. 2:6; Mk. 16:12; Lk. 3:37; Jn. 3:15-16; 5:28-29; 6:54,68; 8:51; 17:2; Acts 13:35; Rom. 1:4; 2:7; 5:21; 6:5,23; 2 Cor. 12:18; Col. 3:1-3; 1 Tim. 1:5; 6:12,19; Tit. 1:2; 3:7; Heb. 6:2; 7:12; 11:35; 13:16; 1 Pet. 1:3; 3:21; 1 Jn. 1:2; 2:6; 5:11,20; Rev. 20:5-6.

∞ ∞ ∞

Ensign (Standard)

Deliverance, victory, conquest

Key Scriptures: Is. 11:10-12; 59:19; Jn. 3:14; 12:32;
Rom. 8:37; 1 Cor. 15:54-57.

Foundational Information ✐

An ensign was a symbol carried on a pole and raised high in the air, much like a flag, to rally a tribe or a group of warriors in battle. These standards were usually set on a hill and often accompanied by the sound of a trumpet. "Ensign" is from the Hebrew *'owth* (Strong's #226), which means "a signal (literally or figuratively), as a flag, beacon, monument, omen, prodigy, evidence, mark." Compare *nec* (Strong's #5251), which means "a flag; also a sail; by implication, a flagstaff; generally a signal; figuratively, a token."

"Standard" is from the Hebrew *degel* (Strong's #1714), which means "a flag." It is translated as "banner, standard" in the King James Version. Its primitive root *dagal* means "to flaunt, raise a flag; figuratively, to be conspicuous."

Fulfilled in Christ

Jesus Christ is Heaven's Ensign. He is the Deliverer, the Victor, the Conqueror who overcame sin, sickness, poverty, and death (1 Cor. 15:54-57; Rev. 3:21). On Golgotha's hill, the rallying point of all creation, the sinless Son of God was raised high upon the cross to take away our sin (Jn. 3:14-16). He Himself prophesied, "And I, if I be lifted up from the earth, will draw all men unto Me" (Jn. 12:32). The blood of the lamb was a standard that first Passover night in Goshen (Ex. 12:13); Paul declared that Christ our Passover is sacrificed for us (1 Cor. 5:7). Jesus is the Banner who was displayed because of the truth (Ps. 60:4; Jn. 14:6; 18:37). Isaiah prophesied, "And in that day there shall be a root of Jesse, which shall stand for an ensign of the people; to it shall the Gentiles seek: and his rest shall be glorious" (Is. 11:10).

Applied to the Christian

Believers are to proudly uphold the conspicuous blood-stained banner of our Lord. "...We are more than conquerors through Him that loved us" (Rom. 8:37). The prophet assured us that when the enemy shall come in, like a flood the Spirit of the Lord shall lift up a standard against him (Is. 59:19). Zechariah prophesied about the end-time Church, "And the Lord their God shall save them in that day as the flock of His people: for they shall be as the stones of a crown, lifted up as an ensign upon His land" (Zech. 9:16). The apostle Paul affirmed the eternal victory of our glorious Head, "Now thanks be unto God, which always causeth us to triumph in Christ" (2 Cor. 2:14). We offer our devotion and love to to Him alone!

Go Deeper

See Gen. 9:13,17; 17:11; Ex. 3:12; Num. 1:52; 2:2; Ps. 18:2; 32:7; 98:1; 144:2; Is. 5:26; 10:18; 13:2; 18:3; 25:8; 30:17; 31:9; 49:22; 62:10; Jer. 4:6,21; 51:12,27; Mt. 12:20; Lk. 4:18; Rom. 7:6; 8:21; 11:26; 2 Cor. 1:10; Col. 2:15; 1 Thess. 1:10; 1 Jn. 5:4; Rev. 6:2.

∞ ∞ ∞

𝔈𝔭𝔥𝔞𝔥

The measure of Christ; the balanced integrity of God's Word

Key Scriptures: Deut. 25:14-15; Ezek. 45:10-11;
Mt. 7:2; Eph. 4:13; 2 Tim. 2:15.

Foundational Information ✏

The ephah was the equivalent in dry measure as the bath in liquid measure. It was equal to one-tenth of a homer, the standard unit for dry measure (about 6 1/4 bushels or a normal donkey load). "Ephah" is transliterated from the Hebrew *'eyphah* (Strong's #374), which means "an ephah or measure for grain; hence, a measure in general."

Fulfilled in Christ ✝

Jesus Christ, who created and measured all things (Is. 40:12; Jn. 1:3), is the "perfect and just weight," the divine Measure for all things (Deut. 25:15). He is the "just Ephah," the righteous Word of the Father's integrity (Ezek. 45:10; compare Jn. 1:1,14). Jesus was the "ephah of fine flour for a sin offering" (Lev. 5:11). In Him there was "no fault" (Lk. 23:4,14; Jn. 18:38; 19:4-6). Then and now, Jesus is coming to "measure" His people and their worship (Zech. 2:2; Mk. 11:11; Rev. 11:1). Our King is anointed with the fullness of the Word and Spirit without measure (Jn. 3:34). All things are judged according to "the measure of [the] man" Christ Jesus, the incarnate Angel of Jehovah (Rev. 21:17).

Applied to the Christian ⚖

Each believer is to come to the stature of Christ's full measure (Eph. 4:13). The key to our maturation, our growth in grace, is to feed on the whole of Scripture, "all the counsel of God" (Acts 20:27). We are to be diligent, "rightly dividing the word of truth" (2 Tim. 2:15; compare Ruth 2:17). Believers, especially those who handle the Word of God, are admonished, "Ye shall do no unrighteousness in judgment, in meteyard, in weight, or in measure" (Lev. 19:35). Righteous judgment is based upon righteous measure (Mt. 7:2; Lk. 6:38; Jn. 5:24). To every believer has been justly apportioned "the measure of faith" (Rom. 12:3). The Church is to receive the balance of God's Word in "three measures" (Mt. 13:33; Lk. 13:21; see also Deut. 16:16; 1 Thess. 5:23).

Go Deeper 📖

See Ex. 16:36; 26:2; Lev. 6:20; 19:36; Num. 5:15; 28:5; Judg. 6:19; 1 Sam. 1:24; 17:17; 1 Kings 6:25; 7:37; Job 28:25; Ps. 39:4; Prov. 20:10; Is. 40:12; Ezek. 45:24; 46:5-14; Amos 8:5; Mic. 6:10; Hab. 3:6; Zech. 5:6-10; Mt. 23:32; 2 Cor. 1:8; 2 Cor. 10:13-15; 11:23; 12:7; Gal. 1:13; Eph. 4:7,16; Rev. 21:15.

∞ ∞ ∞

Ephesdammim

Protection through Jesus' blood

Key Scriptures: Ex. 12:13; Lev. 17:11; 1 Sam. 17:1;
Eph. 1:6-7; Heb. 9:22; 1 Jn. 1:7; Rev. 12:11.

Foundational Information

Ephesdammim was the place where the Philistines camped at the time when David killed Goliath. "Ephesdammim" is transliterated from the Hebrew *'Ephec Dammiym* (Strong's #658), which means "boundary of blood-drops." It is taken from *'ephec* ("an end, no further") and the plural of *dam* ("blood"). The primitive root *'aphec* means "to disappear, cease." *Ephesdammim* has also been translated as "limit of bloods, end of bloodshed."

Fulfilled in Christ

David killed Goliath; King Jesus slew the devil at the cross (Col. 2:15; 1 Jn. 3:8)! The Lamb of God did more than atone for or cover sin—He made it disappear (Jn. 1:29)! Jesus was manifested at the end of the Mosaic era to put away sin by the sacrifice of Himself (Heb. 9:26). The drops of Lamb's blood stretched from Gethsemane to the cross (Lk. 22:44; Jn. 19:34). Jesus poured out His life for all men; without the shedding of blood, there is no remission (Lev. 17:11; Heb. 9:22). Our God is a protecting wall around us and the glory in the midst of us (Zech. 2:5)! Paul taught, "The cup of blessing which we bless, is it not the communion of the blood of Christ?" (1 Cor. 10:16) Through Jesus Christ "we have redemption through His blood, the forgiveness of sins" (Eph. 1:7).

Applied to the Christian

In David's day, the two armies were camped between two mountains, representing two kingdoms. But God's people are protected by the "boundary of blood"! The enemy cannot get past this divine "hedge" (Job 1:10). Jehovah's promise is sure: "and when I see the blood, I will pass over you, and the plague [of sin] shall not be upon you to destroy you" (Ex. 12:13). John affirmed, "But if we walk in the light, as he is in the light, we have fellowship one with another, and the blood of Jesus Christ his Son cleanseth us from all sin" (1 Jn. 1:7). The blood of Jesus has kept us "by the power of God through faith unto [a full] salvation ready to be revealed" (1 Pet. 1:5). We overcome the enemy by the blood of the Lamb (Rev. 12:11).

Go Deeper

See Gen. 15:1; 37:31; 49:11; Ex. 8:22; 9:4; 12:23; 29:20-21; Deut. 33:27; Josh. 2:12-21; 1 Sam. 25:16; Ps. 5:12; 91:7; Is. 5:2; Ezek. 9:4; Zech. 9:11; Eph. 2:13; Col. 1:20;

1 Thess. 1:10; Heb. 9:12-20; 10:4,19,29; 11:28; 12:24; 13:20; 1 Pet. 1:2; 1 Jn. 5:8; Rev. 7:3,14.

∞ ∞ ∞

𝔈phesus

The place of apostolic confrontation and conflict

Key Scriptures: Acts 18–20; 1 Cor. 15:32; Eph. 1–6; 1 Tim. 1; Rev. 2:1-11.

Foundational Information ✐

Ephesus was a large city on the west coast of Asia Minor where the apostle Paul founded a church. The temple of Artemis (or Diana, according to her Roman name) at Ephesus ranked as one of the Seven Wonders of the Ancient World. It was there that Paul wrote First Corinthians and where his teaching caused a riot. Paul left Timothy to care for the church there. "Ephesus" is transliterated from the Greek *Ephesos* (Strong's #2181). Of a probable foreign origin, this word has been variously translated as "full purposed; a throwing at; desirable, appealing."

The Greek word for "conflict" is *agon* (Strong's #73), which means "a place of assembly (as if led), (by implication) a contest (held there); figuratively, an effort or anxiety." *Agon* is translated in the King James Version as "conflict, contention, fight, race." Also rendered as "a contest of athletes," its root is *ago,* which means "to lead, bring, or drive." Compare the verb *agonizomai* (Strong's #75), which means "to struggle, (literally) to compete for a prize, figuratively (to contend with an adversary), or (to endeavor to accomplish something)." This latter word is translated in the King James Version as "fight, labor fervently, strive."

Fulfilled in Christ ✝

Jesus is the chief Apostle (Heb. 3:1) who experienced the conflict of the ages at the cross. In the six chapters of Ephesians, He is revealed as the Head of the Church, the Temple, the Family, the Body, the Wife, and the Army, respectively. Jesus is to be our "first love" (Rev. 2:4; compare Mt. 6:33; 22:37-38). The divine Lamb was ever led by the Spirit (Lk. 4:1; Rom. 8:14); in particular, He was led as a sheep to the place of agony and slaughter, Gethsemane and Calvary (Acts 8:32-33). The contest was to the death and Jesus prevailed (Acts 2:24)! Of Him it is written, "For the Lord your God is He that goeth with you, to fight for you against your enemies, to save you" (Deut. 20:4).

Applied to the Christian   ⚖

Paul admonished us to put on the whole armor of God to be able to stand and to withstand the enemy (Eph. 6:11,13): "for we wrestle not against flesh and blood, but against principalities, against powers, against the rulers of the darkness of this world, against spiritual wickedness in high places" (Eph. 6:12). At Ephesus, the apostle reasoned with the Jews, daily disputing the things of the Kingdom (Acts 18:19; 19:8-9). He wrought special miracles and cast out demons (Acts 19:11-12). There was a revival among those in the occult, including the magicians (Acts 19:17-20). Commenting on the city-wide riot that consequently ensued (Acts 19:23-41), the apostle reflected, "I have fought with beasts at Ephesus" (1 Cor. 15:32).

Go Deeper   📖

See Ex. 14:14; Deut. 1:30,41; 3:22; Josh. 10:25; 2 Chron. 20:17; Neh. 4:20; Ps. 35:1; 56:2; 144:1; Zech. 14:3; Acts 5:39; 23:9; 1 Cor. 9:24-26; 16:8; Phil. 1:30; Col. 1:29; 2:1; 4:12; 1 Thess. 2:2; 1 Tim. 1:3; 6:12; 2 Tim. 1:18; 4:7,12; Heb. 10:32; 11:34; 12:1; Rev. 1:11.

∞   ∞   ∞

𝔈𝔭𝔥𝔬𝔡

Mature priestly ministry

Key Scriptures: Ex. 19:1-6; 28:1-43; Is. 61:6; Heb. 3:1; 4:14-16; 5:1–8:6; 1 Pet. 2:5,9-10; Rev. 1:6; 5:10.

Foundational Information   ✐

The ephod or vest of the high priest, worn over the blue robe, was made of fine linen interwoven with threads of pure gold, blue, purple, and scarlet. It consisted of two pieces joined at the shoulders and bound together at the bottom by a woven band of the same material as the ephod. Two onyx stones engraven with the names of the 12 tribes and set in gold rested upon the shoulders of the ephod. The front of the vest, or the breastplate, was fastened to the shoulder straps by two golden chains and a blue cord.

"Ephod" is transliterated from the Hebrew *'ephowd* (Strong's #646), and it means "a girdle; specifically the ephod or high-priest's shoulderpiece." This word occurs 49 times in the biblical Hebrew.

Fulfilled in Christ ⚑

The ephod was worn by Aaron the priest, Samuel the prophet (1 Sam. 2:18), and David the king (2 Sam. 6:14). All three offices meet in Jesus Christ, our great High Priest after the order (manner, similitude) of Melchisedec (Heb. 5:1–8:6)—He is Prophet, Priest, and King! Like the Ark of the Covenant, the ephod is mentioned first among Aaron's garments. Typologically, it pertains to the Most Holy Place, the realm of maturity in Christ. The typology of the ephod is fulfilled in Him in the following ways:

1. The white linen demonstrates His righteousness.
2. The gold reveals His divine nature.
3. The blue speaks of His heavenly origin.
4. The purple signifies His royalty.
5. The scarlet represents His blood sacrifice.
6. The two pieces stand for His resurrection and judgment.
7. The onyx stones commemorate His government.
8. The breastplate represents His faith and love.

Applied to the Christian ⚖

From the beginning, God has wanted a kingdom of priests, not just the tribe of Levi (Ex. 19:1-6). The Spirit of the Son is "Christ in you" (Col. 1:29). "Christ" means "the anointed one"—in the Old Testament, God anointed prophets, priests, and kings. In Christ, the Church constitutes a "royal priesthood," a people who were not a people (1 Pet. 2:9-10). John declared that God "hath made us kings and priests" and that "we shall reign on the earth" (Rev. 1:6; 5:10). Isaiah prophesied, "But ye shall be named the Priests of the Lord: men shall call you the Ministers of our God" (Is. 61:6). The Body of Christ is a holy priesthood called to be worshipers, ordained by the Spirit "to offer up spiritual sacrifices" (1 Pet. 2:5).

Go Deeper 📖

See Gen. 14:18-20; Ex. 25:7; 29:5; 35:27; 40:15; Lev. 8:7; Num. 16:10; 25:13; Deut. 17:9-12; Josh. 3:3; 6:4-8; 18:7; Judg. 8:27; 17:5; 18:14; 1 Sam. 2:28,35-36; 14:3; 21:9; 22:18; 23:6-9; 30:7; 1 Chron. 15:14,27; Ezra 2:62; Neh. 7:64; 13:29; Ps. 99:6; 110:4; 132:9,16; Is. 66:21; Hos. 3:4; Joel 1:9,13, 2:17; Mic. 3:11; Zeph. 3:4; Zech. 6:13; Mal. 1:6; 2:1-7; Acts 6:7; Rev. 20:6.

∾ ∾ ∾

𝔈phraim

Fruitfulness

Key Scriptures: Gen. 41:52; Jer. 31:6; Zech. 10:7; Jn. 15:1-5; Gal. 5:22-24.

Foundational Information ✏

Ephraim was the second son of Joseph by Asenath and founder of one of the 12 tribes of the nation of Israel. "Ephraim" is transliterated from the Hebrew *'Ephrayim* (Strong's #669), which means "double fruit." Its root *parah* is translated in the King James Version as "bear, bring forth (fruit), (be, cause to be, make) fruitful, grow, increase." "Ephraim" has also been translated as "doubly fruitful, very fruitful, productive."

Fulfilled in Christ ✝

The *charismata*, the gifts or manifestations of the Spirit (1 Cor. 12:8-10), are the supernatural ministry of Jesus Christ. The fruit of the Spirit reveals the divine nature of our risen King (Gal. 5:22-24)! He must increase; we decrease (Jn. 3:30). Jesus Christ is the son or seed of Abraham (Mt. 1:1; Gal. 3:16); to Him was made this promise, "And I will make thee exceeding fruitful, and I will make nations of thee, and kings shall come out of thee" (Gen. 17:6). Jesus has been crowned King in Zion, a very fruitful hill (Ps. 2:6; Is. 5:1). Jesus, the genuine Vine, admonished us to bear fruit, more fruit, and then much fruit (Jn. 15:2,8).

Applied to the Christian ⚖

Joseph named his son "Ephraim" because God had caused him to be "fruitful" (Gen. 41:52). Through the reality of His Word, we have become "partakers of the divine nature" (2 Pet. 1:4). Paul explained, "But the fruit of the Spirit is love, joy, peace, long-suffering, gentleness, goodness, faith, meekness, temperance" (Gal. 5:22-23). Jeremiah prophesied, "For there shall be a day, that the watchmen upon the mount Ephraim shall cry, Arise ye, and let us go up to Zion unto the Lord our God" (Jer. 31:6). Zechariah predicted the outpouring of the joy of Holy Spirit upon the Church, "And they of Ephraim shall be like a mighty man, and their heart shall rejoice as through wine: yea, their children shall see it, and be glad; their heart shall rejoice in the Lord" (Zech. 10:7).

Go Deeper 📖

See Gen. 1:22,28; 9:1; 35:11; 46:20; 48:20; 49:22; Ex. 1:7; Num. 1:10,33; 2:18; 13:8; Deut. 33:17; Josh. 16:1-9; 1 Chron. 12:30; Neh. 8:16; Ps. 60:7; 128:3; Is. 28:1; 32:15-16; Jer. 31:9,20; 23:3; Ezek. 37:16-19; Hos. 4:17; 7:8,11; 8:9; 11:3; 14:8; Zech. 9:10-13; Jn. 11:54; Acts 14:17; Eph. 5:9; Phil. 4:17; Col. 1:10; Heb. 13:15; Jas. 3:18; 5:7; Rev. 22:2.

∾ ∾ ∾

𝔈sau

The flesh

Key Scriptures: Gen. 25:19-34; Obad. 1-21; Rom. 8:1-13;
Gal. 5:1-21; 1 Jn. 2:15-17.

Foundational Information ✐

Esau was the son of Isaac and Rebekah and the twin brother of Jacob. Esau was the ancestor of the Edomites. "Esau" is the transliteration of the Hebrew *'Esav* (Strong's #6215), which means "rough (sensibly felt)." "Esau" has also been translated as "shaggy, hairy, his doings."

"Edom" is transliterated from the Hebrew *'Edom* (Strong's #123), which means "red; Edom, the elder twin-brother of Jacob; hence the region (Idumea) occupied by him." Its root *'adam* (Strong's #119) means "to show blood (in the face), flush or turn rosy."

Fulfilled in Christ ⚊

Jesus Christ completely subdued the appetites of the flesh, conquering every obstacle (see Jn. 8:29; 16:33; Heb. 4:15; 1 Jn. 2:15-17). Esau—the old man of the flesh—despised his birthright (Gen. 25:34); Jesus, the new Man of the Spirit, loved His birthright (Ps. 40:6-8; Heb. 10:6-10). Jesus warned His disciples, "Watch and pray, that ye enter not into temptation: the spirit indeed is willing, but the flesh is weak" (Mt. 26:41). He knew that it is the Spirit that makes alive; the flesh profits nothing (Jn. 6:63). God sent His own Son in the likeness of sinful flesh and condemned sin in the flesh "that the righteousness of the law might be fulfilled in us, who walk not after the flesh, but after the Spirit" (Rom. 8:3-4).

Applied to the Christian ⚖

Esau typifies Adam, the natural man. Paul declared, "For they that are after the flesh do mind the things of the flesh…" (Rom. 8:5a). Esau was a man of the "field" (Gen. 25:27) which Jesus likened to the "world" (Mt. 13:38). Esau was worldly (1 Jn. 2:15-17), a man of wild and lawless habits (Eph. 2:3). He was "faint" or "languished" because the world will not satisfy (Gen. 25:29). Like many immature believers, Esau loved the blessing but despised the responsibility of the birthright (Gen. 27:34-42). Fleshly people will marry the unsaved (Gen. 28:6-9; 2 Cor. 6:14-18). The Lord has purposed to bring an end to all fleshly wisdom and understanding (Obad. 8; 1 Cor. 1:18-31). The victory is secure, for "saviours ['deliverers'] shall come up on mount Zion to judge the mount of Esau; and the kingdom shall be the Lord's" (Obad. 21).

Go Deeper 📖

See Gen. 26:34; 27:1-42; 32:1-19; 33:1-16; 35:29; 36:1-43; Deut. 2:1-8,12,22,29; Josh. 24:4; 1 Chron. 1:34-35; Jer. 49:8-10; Mal. 1:2-3; Jn. 8:15; Rom. 7:5,25; 9:13; 13:14; 1 Cor. 1:26; 2 Cor. 7:1; 10:3; Gal. 3:3; 6:8; Phil. 3:3; Col. 2:11,23; Heb. 11:20; 12:16; 1 Pet. 4:2; 2 Pet. 2:10,18; Jude 8,23; Rev. 19:18.

∾ ∾ ∾

𝔈𝔰𝔥𝔠𝔬𝔩

The unified togetherness of the Body of Christ

Key Scriptures: Num. 13:23-24; 32:9; Deut. 1:24; Ps. 133;
Song 1:14; Is. 65:8; Mic. 7:1; Jn. 17; Eph. 4:1-16.

Foundational Information ✏️

Eshcol was a valley north of Hebron, famous for its grapes. The 12 Hebrew spies cut down one cluster of grapes from Eshcol to show the fertility of the land. "Eshcol" is transliterated from *'eshkowl* (Strong's #811), which means "a bunch of grapes or other fruit." Translated as "cluster (of grapes)" in the King James Version, it comes from an un-used root meaning "to bunch together; a testicle (as a lump)."

Fulfilled in Christ 🔆

All unity in the Body of Christ essentially flows from the intertheistic union be-tween the Father and the Son. This is pictured by the cluster of grapes (the Church) being carried "between two" on a covenantal staff (Num. 13:23)! Jesus prayed, "That they all might be one; as thou, Father, art in Me, and I in Thee, that they also may be one in Us...even as We are one" (Jn. 17:21-22). In the Song of Solomon, the Shulamite, a type of the Bride of Christ, declared, "My beloved is unto me as a cluster of camphire in the vineyards of Engedi" (Song 1:14). This pictures the "manifold" or many-sided wisdom and grace of Jesus Christ (Eph. 3:10; 1 Pet. 4:10). This glorious assortment is manifested through the varied, unique expressions of the members of His Body (Rom. 12; 1 Cor. 12).

Applied to the Christian ⚖️

Real unity cannot be created; it can only be kept (Eph. 4:1-3,13), based upon seven absolutes (Eph. 4:4-7). The challenge is before us—will we see big giants (disunity) or big grapes (Num. 13:26-33)? Don't be discouraged (Num. 32:9; Deut. 1:24). Eshcol was by a "brook" or "stream" (Num. 13:24)—only the life-sustaining power of the Holy Spirit, the River of God, can bring us together (Jn. 7:37-39). Strife-ridden homes and local churches are but a stinking witness (Gen. 34:30)—grapes of gall, bitter clusters (Deut. 32:32). Yet the psalmist exclaimed, "Behold, how good and pleasant it is for brethren to dwell together in unity" (Ps. 133:1)! The new wine, the joy of the Lord, is found in the "cluster" (Is. 65:8).

Go Deeper 📖

See Gen. 40:10; Lev. 21:20; Song 7:7-8; Mt. 18:20; 19:6; 24:31; Lk. 6:38; Jn. 4:36; Acts 1:15; 2:44; 4:31-32; 12:12; 13:44; 14:27; 15:6; 20:7-8; Rom. 6:5; 8:17,28; 1 Cor. 1:10; 3:9; 5:4; 12:24; 14:23; 2 Cor. 2:11; 6:1; Eph. 1:10; 2:5-6,21-22; 4:16; Phil. 1:27; 3:17; Col. 2:2; 1 Thess. 4:17; Heb. 10:25; 1 Pet. 3:7; 5:13; Jude 13.

∾ ∾ ∾

𝔈spousal (𝔈arnest)

The Holy Ghost Baptism; the earnest of our inheritance

Key Scriptures: Gen. 38:17-30; Hos. 2:19-20; Lk. 1:27; Acts 1:5;
2 Cor. 1:22; 5:5; 11:2; Eph. 1:13-14; 5:18.

Foundational Information ✐

Espousal or betrothal was a mutual promise or contract for a future marriage. This was undertaken by a friend representing the bridegroom and the parents representing the bride. It was confirmed by oaths, accompanied with presents and celebrated by a feast. There are different words for "espousal." *Chathunnah* (Strong's #2861) means "a wedding." Its root *chathan* means "to give (a daughter) away in marriage; hence (generally) to contract affinity by marriage." Compare *keluwlah* (Strong's #3623), which means "bridehood." Its root *kalal* means "to complete, make perfect." Another root *'aras* (Strong's #781) means "to engage for matrimony."

The Greek verb for "espouse" is *mnesteuo* (Strong's #3423), and it means "to give a souvenier (engagement present), betroth." It can also mean "to woo a woman and ask for her in marriage." Compare *harmozo*, which means "to fit, join." Its derivative *harma* signifies "a chariot (as raised or fitted together)." The Greek word for "earnest" is *arrahbon* and means "a pledge, part of the purchase-money given in advance as security." Used in the Septuagint (the Greek Old Testament) to translate the word "pledge" in Genesis 38:17-20, *arrahbon* has its origin in the Hebrew word *arabown* (Strong's #6162), which means "a pawn (given as security)."

Fulfilled in Christ ☀

Jesus Christ is the Head and Husband of the Church (Eph. 5:22-33). Matthew records His birth: "...His mother Mary was espoused to Joseph, before they came together, [and] she was found with child of the Holy Ghost" (Mt. 1:18; compare Lk. 1:27; 2:5). The Old Testament "pledge" (the signet, bracelet, and staff) given by Judah to Tamar reveals respectively (Gen. 38:17-18):

1. The authority of Jesus, for government.
2. The adornment of Jesus, for grace.
3. The alignment of Jesus, for guidance.

All these things are by and through the Holy Spirit, whose purpose is to reveal Jesus (Jn. 14:26; 15:26). The Lord affirmed His love for His bride, "And I will betroth thee unto Me for ever; yea, I will betroth thee unto Me in righteousness, and in judgment, and in lovingkindness, and in mercies. I will even betroth thee unto Me in faithfulness: and thou shalt know the Lord" (Hos. 2:19-20). Jesus said it this way in the New Testament, "For John truly baptized with water; ye shall be baptized with the Holy Ghost" (Acts 1:5).

Applied to the Christian ⚖

The Church is the Bride of Christ, "espoused" to one Husband (2 Cor. 11:2). Paul declared that believers have been "sealed with that holy Spirit of promise, which is the earnest of our inheritance until the redemption of the purchased possession, unto the praise of His glory" (Eph. 1:13-14; see also 2 Cor. 1:22; 5:5). Paul admonished, "be filled with the Spirit" (Eph. 5:18). The Church is the "heavenly Jerusalem" (Heb. 12:22-23), "prepared as a bride adorned for her husband"—she is the "Lamb's wife" (Rev. 21:2,9).

Go Deeper 📖

See Ex. 21:8-9; 22:16,23-30; Lev. 19:20; Deut. 20:7; 2 Sam. 3:14; Ps. 19:5; Song 3:11; Is. 49:18; 61:10; Jer. 2:2,32; 3:14; 7:34; 16:9; 33:11; Joel 2:16; Mt. 9:15; 22:1-14; 25:1-6; Jn. 2:1-9; 3:29; Heb. 13:4; Rev. 18:23; 19:7-9; 22:17.

∞ ∞ ∞

Esther (Hadassah)

The Bride of Christ

Key Scriptures: Esther 1–10; Ps. 45:9-15; Eph. 5:22-33; Rev. 21:1-10.

Foundational Information

Esther or Hadassah was the Jewish queen of Persia's King Xerxes who saved her people, the Jews, from extinction. "Esther," from the Hebrew *'Ecter* (Strong's #635), is of Persian derivation and has been translated as "star, the planet Venus, happiness, good fortune; secret, hidden, I will be hidden."

"Hadassah" is taken from the Hebrew *Hadaccah* (Strong's #1919), the feminine of *hadac* (Strong's #1918), which means "the myrtle (tree)." "Hadassah" has also been translated as "leaping, springing up, joy, gladness."

Fulfilled in Christ

Jesus Christ is the heavenly Bridegroom, the Sun of righteousness (Ps. 19:5; Mal. 4:2). In the Book of Esther, Jesus is seen as the king for whom the Church is prepared to be married by the ministry of the Word (Mordecai) and the Holy Spirit (Hegai). He is also pictured in the following:

1. The "golden sceptre" (Esther 4:11), for Jesus has been given all authority (Mt. 28:18-20; Eph. 1:20-23).
2. The "gallows" upon which Haman was hung (Esther 5:14; 7:9-10), for this word means "tree" and points to His cross (see Acts 5:30; 10:39; 13:29; 1 Pet. 2:24).
3. The "crown royal" (Esther 6:8), for Jesus is the King of kings (Heb. 2:9; Rev. 19:16).
4. The "seed of the Jews" (Esther 6:13), for Jesus is the Seed of Abraham (Mt. 1:1; Gal. 3:16).
5. The "king's ring" (Esther 8:8), for Jesus is the Pattern Son (see Hag. 2:20-23; Lk. 3:22; 9:35; 15:22).
6. The heavenly "Pur" ("lot or portion") (Esther 9:24-26), for Jesus is Heaven's portion, the Word made flesh (Jn. 1:14; Col. 1).

Applied to the Christian

The Church is the "heavenly Jerusalem" (Heb. 12:22-23), "prepared as a bride adorned for her husband"—she is the "Lamb's wife" (Rev. 21:2,9). Esther was a "star." She was a light placed by Jehovah in a dark place, causing all to gaze toward the heavens. The Church is the light of the world (Mt. 5:14; compare Lk. 12:35; Phil. 2:15; Jas. 1:17). The myrtle tree, noted for its fragrance and beauty, emphasizes the principle of purification (Is. 55:13). The myrtle was used in making booths for the Feast of Tabernacles (Neh. 8:15-16); the Bride of Christ is a habitation of the Spirit (Eph. 2:21-22). The myrtle is one of the seven trees of Isaiah 41:19; the Church is to experience the "seven spirits of God" (Rev. 1–5), the fullness of the Spirit. The Man among the myrtles is Jesus (Zech. 1:8-11); Jesus walks in our midst (Mt. 18:20; Rev. 1:13,20).

Go Deeper 📖

See Esther 2:7-11,15-17,20-22; 4:5,8-10,13-17; 5:1-7,12; 6:14; 7:1-8; 8:1-7; 9:12-13, 25,29-32; Is. 49:18; 61:10; Jer. 2:32; 3:14; 7:34; 16:9; 25:10; 33:11; Joel 2:16; Mt. 22:1-14; Jn. 2:1-2; 3:29; Heb. 13:4; Rev. 19:17-19; 22:17.

∞   ∞   ∞

𝔈𝔱𝔥𝔦𝔬𝔭𝔦𝔞

Greatness

Key Scriptures: Gen. 2:13; 1 Chron. 29:11; Ps. 68:31; 145:3;
Is. 11:11; Lk. 1:32; Acts 8:26-40.

Foundational Information ✎

Ethiopia is the ancient African nation south of Egypt. Ham was the father of Cush (Ethiopia) and Mizaim (Egypt). "Ethiopia" is from the Hebrew *Kuwsh* (Strong's #3568). It has been translated as "burned faces, country of the burning; black." "Cush" means "firelike, burned, blackened, combustible." Compare the Greek *Aithiops* (Strong's #128), which is taken from *aitho* ("to scorch") and *ops* ("the face").

Fulfilled in Christ ✝

Jesus Christ is the greatest Son of Abraham and David (Mt. 1:1). Of Him it was prophesied (Acts 3:13; compare Rom. 15:8), "And I will make of thee a great nation, and I will bless thee, and make thy name great; and thou shalt be a blessing" (Gen. 12:2). Gabriel declared, "He shall be great, and shall be called the Son of the Highest" (Lk. 1:32; see also Lk. 8:39). Jesus is our:

1. Great Light (Mt. 4:16; Jn. 8:12).
2. Great King (Mt. 5:35).
3. Great calm (Mt. 8:26; Eph. 2:14).
4. Great power and glory (Mk. 13:26).
5. Great grace (Acts 4:33).
6. Great Door (Jn. 10:7-9; 1 Cor. 16:9).
7. Great love (Eph. 2:4).

8. Great High Priest (Heb. 4:14; 7:3-4).
9. Great Shepherd of the sheep (Heb. 13:20).
10. Great God (Rev. 19:17).

Applied to the Christian ⚖

In Genesis 9, God blessed Noah and his sons, including Ham. Drunken Noah cursed Canaan, not Ham, for violating his grandmother (Lev. 18:7-8; 20:11); that curse was fulfilled when Canaan was subjugated (Josh. 9). Greatness is attributed to Ethiopia throughout the Scriptures, but such greatness is only found in Christ. The Gihon River, out of Eden, the place of dominion (Gen. 1:28), encompassed Ethiopia (Gen. 2:13). The empire-builder Nimrod was "a mighty one in the earth" (Gen. 10:8). The great leader Moses married Zipporah, a great wife (Num. 12:1). Ethiopia was famous for its jewels (Job 28:19). The men of Ethiopia were "men of stature" (Is. 45:14). Ebedmelech saved the life of a great prophet (Jer. 38:6-13). Zephaniah was the son of Cushi (Zeph. 1:1). The eunuch was a man "of great authority" (Acts 8:27). The psalmist prophesied, "Princes shall come out of Egypt; Ethiopia shall soon stretch out her hands unto God" (Ps. 68:31). The end-time remnant includes Cush (Is. 11:11).

Go Deeper 📖

See Gen. 10:6-7; Ex. 15:7,16; Deut. 3:24; 5:24; 1 Sam. 12:24; 1 Chron. 1:8-10; 2 Chron. 12:3; 14:9; 16:8; Esther 10:2; Ps. 31:19; 79:11; 87:4; 92:5; Is. 40:26; 43:3; Jer. 13:23; 46:9; Dan. 4:3; 7:27; 11:43; Amos 9:7; Zeph. 3:10; Mk. 5:19-20; Eph. 1:19.

∞ ∞ ∞

Eunuch

Complete consecration

Key Scriptures: 1 Chron. 29:5; Ps. 9:1; Is. 56:1-5; Mt. 19:12; Acts 8:26-40.

Foundational Information ✎

A eunuch was a male servant of a royal household, often emasculated by castration as a precautionary measure, especially if he served among the wives in a ruler's harem. "Eunuch" is from the Hebrew *cariyc* (Strong's #5631), which means "to castrate; a eunuch; by implication, valet (especially of the female apartments), and thus, a minister of state." It is also translated in the King James Version as "chamberlain, officer."

The Greek word for "eunuch" is *eunouchos* (Strong's #2135), which means "a castrated person (such being employed in Oriental bed-chambers); by extension an impotent or unmarried man; by implication, a chamberlain (state-officer)." Literally, the word means "bed-guard," taken from *eune* ("bed") and *ekhein* ("have charge of, keep").

Fulfilled in Christ

Jesus Christ, who fulfilled the meaning of the whole burnt offering (Ps. 51:19; Mk. 12:33), declared His complete consecration to do the will of the Father, "I have glorified thee on the earth: I have finished the work which thou gavest Me to do" (Jn. 17:4). Jesus, the Prince of Peace (Is. 9:6), is also "the prince of eunuchs" (Dan. 1:7-11,18). The great Teacher revealed that there are three kinds of eunuchs (Mt. 19:12):

1. Some were born eunuchs. Spiritually, these are those persons who will never reproduce the Kingdom of God.
2. Some were made eunuchs. Some persons are emasculated by the religious systems of men, and therefore can no longer reproduce the Kingdom of God.
3. Some have made themselves eunuchs. We see this in those who reproduce nothing *but* the Kingdom of God!

Applied to the Christian

To the eunuchs—who keep His sabbaths (rest), choose the things that please Him, and take hold of His covenant—the Lord has promised "an everlasting name, that shall not be cut off" (Is. 56:4-5). The eunuch's anointing throws down the manipulative spirit of Jezebel (2 Kings 9:30-33). The psalmist boldly declared, "I will praise thee, O Lord, with my whole heart" (Ps. 9:1). The phrase "whole heart" is mentioned six times in the longest chapter of the Bible (Ps. 119:2,10,34,58,69,145). David asked, "And who then is willing to consecrate his service this day unto the Lord?" (1 Chron. 29:5).

Go Deeper

See Ex. 29:22-31; Lev. 8:22,29,33; 21:10; Num. 3:3; 6:7-9; Deut. 27:6; 33:10; Josh. 6:19; 2 Kings 20:18; 2 Chron. 26:18; 29:31-33; 31:6; Ezra 3:5; Ps. 111:1; Is. 39:7; Jer. 29:2; 34:19; 38:7; 41:16; 52:25; Dan. 1:3; Heb. 7:28; 10:20.

∞ ∞ ∞

𝔈𝔲𝔭𝔥𝔯𝔞𝔱𝔢𝔰

The flow of the Holy Ghost; spiritual breakthroughs

Key Scriptures: Gen. 2:14; Is. 35:6; Mic. 2:13;
Jn. 7:37-39; Acts 2:1-4; Eph. 2:14.

Foundational Information ✑

The Euphrates is the longest river of Western Asia (about 1,780 miles). It is referred to in the Bible as "the River Euphrates," "the great river," or only "the River." "Euphrates" is from the Hebrew *Perath* (Strong's #6578), which means "to break forth; rushing." Compare *parah*, a primitive root that means "to bear fruit." "Euphrates" has also been rendered as "fertile river, fruitfulness, bursting forth, breaking out."

Fulfilled in Christ ☦

Jesus Christ the Messiah was "the breaker" (Mic. 2:13), the One who rent the veil and led captivity captive (Mt. 27:51-52; Eph. 4:8). Paul affirmed, "For He is our peace, who...hath broken down the middle wall of partition between us" (Eph. 2:14). The Euphrates flowed out of Eden, the place of dominion (Gen. 2:14); the Holy Ghost flows from the exalted King who sits on the throne of His father David (Acts 2:33-36). Daniel heralded His Messianic Kingdom, "And in the days of these kings shall the God of heaven set up a kingdom, which shall never be destroyed: and the kingdom shall not be left to other people, but it shall break in pieces and consume all these kingdoms, and it shall stand for ever" (Dan. 2:44).

Applied to the Christian ⚖

In the Upper Room on the Day of Pentecost, there suddenly came from Heaven a sound like "a rushing mighty wind...and they were all filled with the Holy Ghost..." (Acts 2:2,4). Isaiah saw an end-time revival, "Then shall the lame man leap as an hart, and the tongue of the dumb shall sing: for in the wilderness shall waters break out, and streams in the desert" (Is. 35:6). Christians everywhere are experiencing spiritual breakthroughs. Many are tasting the reality of the Feast of Pentecost for the first time (Eph. 5:18-19). Others are pressing their way into the third dimension of the Most Holy Place and the Feast of Tabernacles, the realm of His full stature (Deut. 16:16; Eph. 4:13).

Go Deeper 📖

See Gen. 15:18; Deut. 1:7; 11:24; Josh. 1:4; 2 Sam. 8:3; 2 Kings 23:29; 24:7; 1 Chron. 5:9; 18:3; 2 Chron. 35:20; Ps. 2:9; 10:15; 58:6; Prov. 3:10; Eccles. 3:3; Is. 14:25; 45:2; 52:9; 54:1-5; 55:12; 58:6-8; Jer. 13:1-7; 46:2,6,10; 51:63; Hos. 2:18; Gal. 4:27; Rev. 9:14; 16:12.

∞ ∞ ∞

𝕰𝖚𝖊

The Church; the New Jerusalem, the mother of us all

Key Scriptures: Gen. 1:1–4:1; 2 Cor. 11:3; Gal. 4:21-31;
1 Tim. 2:13-15; Heb. 12:22-24; Rev. 21:1-14.

Foundational Information

Eve was the first woman, created from Adam's side to be his helper and co-regent of the earth. "Eve" is from the Hebrew *Chavvah* (Strong's #2332), and it means "life-giver." Its root *chavah* (Strong's #2331) means "to live; to declare or show." "Eve" has also been translated as "life-spring." The word "Eve" is mentioned four times in the Bible, emphasizing the number for creation.

Fulfilled in Christ

The apostle declared, "The first man Adam was made a living soul; the last Adam was made a quickening [life-giving] spirit...The first man is of the earth, earthy: the second man is the Lord from heaven" (1 Cor. 15:45,47). Jesus Christ, the "last Adam," came to bring a lasting end to the first Adam. Adam was first formed; then Eve was formed from his rib (1 Tim. 2:13). Similarly, the Church was created from the side of our Lord through the means of blood and water (Jn. 19:34). Adam was created first; so Jesus "is the head of the body, the church...that in all things He might have the preeminence" (Col. 1:18). Jesus Christ, like Melchisedec, is King of Salem (Jerusalem) or King of Peace (Heb. 7:1-2).

Applied to the Christian

Adam named his wife Eve "because she was the mother of all living" (Gen. 3:20). Paul explained the antitype, "But Jerusalem which is above is free, which is the mother of us all" (Gal. 4:26). The writer to the Hebrews adds, "But ye are to come unto mount Sion, and unto the city of the living God, the heavenly Jerusalem...to the general assembly and church of the firstborn..." (Heb. 12:22-23). The serpent "beguiled" or "seduced," Eve; and he still attempts to deceive Christians away from the simplicity or singleness that is in Christ (2 Cor. 11:3). The revelator exclaimed, "And I John saw the holy city, new Jerusalem, coming down from God out of heaven, prepared as a bride adorned for her husband" (Rev. 21:2).

Go Deeper

See Ps. 87:3-6; Prov. 10:11; 18:4; Song 4:15; 8:1-2; Is. 2:2-3; 50:1; 52:9; 58:11; 62:1-2; 65:18; 66:10; Ezek. 47:1-12; Hos. 2:1-5; 4:5; Joel 3:17; Mic. 4:1-2; Zech. 14:8; Jn. 4:14; 7:37-39; 8:36; Rom. 6:14,18; Gal. 5:1; Phil. 3:20; 1 Pet. 2:16; Rev. 3:12; 17:5.

∞ ∞ ∞

Evening Sacrifice

The finished work of Jesus Christ

Key Scriptures: Gen. 1; Ex. 40:33; Dan. 9:20-24; Jn. 4:34; 17:4; 19:30.

Foundational Information

Evening was the period of time between sunset and bedtime, the early part of the night. For the Hebrew people, the old day ended and the new day began at evening, or sunset. The evening sacrifice was offered at the ninth hour (three o'clock in the afternoon), the hour of prayer.

"Even, evening" is from the Hebrew *'ereb* (Strong's #6153), and means "dusk." Its root *'arab* means "(covering with a texture); to grow dusky at sundown." The Greek word for "evening" is *opsios* (Strong's #3798) and means "late; afternoon (early eve) or nightfall (later eve)." It is taken from *opse* which means "(through the idea of backwardness) late in the day; after the close of the day."

Fulfilled in Christ

The hanging of the last curtain at the court gate was the finishing touch to Moses' tabernacle (Ex. 40:33)—Jesus Christ was the evening Sacrifice; He hung from the cross, crying out at the ninth hour, "It is finished" (Jn. 19:30; compare Dan. 9:20-24; Jn. 4:34; 5:36; 17:4)! As the ashes of the Levitical sacrifices were carried aside "unto a clean place" (Ex. 27:3; Lev. 6:10-11), so His body was laid aside in the tomb of Joseph of Arimathaea (Mt. 27:57-60; Mk. 15:43-46). The Sun of righteousness (Mal. 4:2) went "down" into death and burial that He might ascend in resurrection and ascension to fill all things (Eph. 4:8). Mark recorded the time of Jesus crucifixion, "And when the sixth hour was come, there was darkness over the whole land until the ninth hour" (Mk. 15:34).

Applied to the Christian

God's day begins in the evening and ends in the morning (Gen. 1). Every aspect of the Father's dealings in our lives is from the posture of the finished work of His only begotten Son (Jn. 3:16; Heb. 4:3). At the time of the evening sacrifice (Jesus' finished work):

1. Judgment for sin is complete (Gen. 8:11).
2. Women (churches) go out to draw water (Gen. 24:11).
3. The Passover lamb is killed (Ex. 12:6).
4. God supernaturally sustains His prophets (1 Kings 17:6).
5. God shuts the mouths of false prophets (1 Kings 18:29).
6. God opens the mouths of true prophets (Ezek. 33:22).
7. Men cease from their labors (Ps. 104:23).

8. Hands are lifted up (Ps. 141:2).
9. God opens His hand (Eccles. 11:6).
10. It shall be light (Zech. 14:7).

Go Deeper 📖

See Gen. 2:1; Josh. 4:10; Ruth 3:18; 1 Kings 6:14; 18:36; 1 Chron. 28:20; 2 Chron. 2:4; 13:11; 31:3; Ezra 6:15; 9:4-5; Neh. 6:15; Ps. 55:17; Dan. 9:21; Zech. 4:9; Mt. 14:15,23; 16:2; Mk. 14:17; Lk. 24:29; Jn. 20:19; Acts 20:24; 28:23; Rom. 9:28; 2 Tim. 4:7; Rev. 16:17; 21:6.

∞ ∞ ∞

𝔈𝔳𝔦𝔩 𝔈𝔶𝔢

Selfishness, doublemindedness

Key Scriptures: Prov. 23:6; 28:22; Mt. 6:22-24; Mk. 7:22; Jas. 1:5-8,22-25.

Foundational Information ✐

"Evil eye" is a symbolic phrase that refers to the will of a grudging, selfish person. The opposite of an evil or double eye is the single eye. The Hebrew word for "evil" is *ra'* (Strong's #7451), and means "bad or (as noun) evil (natural or moral)." Its root *ra'a'* (Strong's #7489), means "to spoil (literally, by breaking to pieces); figuratively, to make (or be) good for nothing, bad (physically, socially or morally)."

The Greek word for "evil" is *poneros* (Strong's #4190), and it means "hurtful, evil (properly, in effect or influence); figuratively, calamitous; also (passively) ill, diseased; but especially (morally) culpable, derelict, vicious; mischief, malice, guilt." It is derived from *ponos* (English, *pain*), which means "toil, anguish;" and *penes* which means "to toil for daily subsistence; starving, indigent, poor."

The Greek word for "double minded" is *dipsuchos* (Strong's #1374), and means "two-spirited, vacillating (in opinion or purpose)." It literally means, "double-souled." The word for "simplicity" or "singleness" is *haplotes* (Strong's #572). It means "single-ness, (subjectively) sincerity (without dissimulation or self-seeking), or (objectively) generosity (copious bestowal)." *Haplous* means "single," and *diplous* means "double."

Fulfilled in Christ ⚚

Jesus explained, "The light of the body is the eye: if therefore thine eye be single, thy whole body shall be full of light. But if thine eye be evil, thy whole body shall be full of darkness. ...No man can serve two masters..." (Mt. 6:22-24; compare Lk. 11:34).

The Lamb of God was completely unselfish, laying down His life for us all (Jn. 10:15; 15:13). Jesus was totally focused on doing the will of the Father (Jn. 4:34; Jn. 17:4). Paul therefore admonished, "Let this mind be in you, which was also in Christ Jesus" (Phil. 2:5). God promised through Paul, "But the Lord is faithful, who shall stablish you, and keep you from evil" (2 Thess. 3:3). Simplicity (the single eye) is in Christ (2 Cor. 11:3).

Applied to the Christian

John declared, "Hereby perceive we the love of God, because He laid down His life for us: and we ought to lay down our lives [souls] for the brethren" (1 Jn 3:16). To be double-minded is to be double-souled (Jas 1:8)—always having to think twice about serving God and His people. Duality is idolatry. "Di-vision" is having two visions. We cannot be focused on God and the devil, the new man and the old man, at the same time. Don't just make up your mind; take on His mind! Christians are to have a single eye, to stay focused on the Lord. The Man in the mirror of His Word is the New Man, and He only has one eye (Jas. 1:22-25)! Solomon warned about the dangers of an evil eye (Prov. 23:6; 28:22).

Go Deeper

See Deut. 15:9; 28:54; Prov. 1:16; 2:12; 4:14; 6:24; 8:13; 11:19; 12:20; 16:6; 17:11; 24:1; 31:12; Mt. 20:15; Rom. 12:8-9; 2 Cor. 1:12; Gal. 1:4; Eph. 5:16; 6:5,13; 1 Thess. 5:22; 1 Tim. 6:4; 2 Tim. 3:13; 4:18; Heb. 3:12; 10:22; Jas. 2:4; 4:8; 1 Jn. 3:12.

∾ ∾ ∾

Exodus

Deliverance from bondage; death

Key Scriptures: Ex. 1–17; Josh. 24:17; Lk. 9:31; Jn. 14:6; 1 Cor. 10:1-11; Heb. 2:15.

Foundational Information

The Exodus was the departure of the Israelites from captivity in Egypt under the leadership of Moses. The word "Exodus" is transliterated from the Greek *exodos* (Strong's #1841), which means "an exit, (figuratively) death." Translated as "decease, departing" in the King James Version, it is taken from two words: *ek* ("out of") and *hodos* ("a road or way; a progress [the route, act or distance]; a mode or means"). An *exodus* is a "way out."

"Bondage" is taken from the Hebrew *'abodah* (Strong's #5656), and it means "work of any kind." Its root *'abad* means "to work; to serve, till, enslave." Compare the

Greek *douleuo* (Strong's #1398), which means "to be a slave to (literal or figurative, involuntary or voluntary)." It is derived from *doulos* ("a slave") and *deo* ("to bind").

Fulfilled in Christ ⚚

Jesus Christ, the personification of the Passover Lamb, delivered the human family from the tyranny of sin and satan (see Jn. 1:29; 1 Cor. 5:7-8; 1 Pet. 1:18-19; Rev. 13:8). The "firstborn among many brethren" (Rom. 8:29) followed the same path as did ancient Israel, fulfilling prophecy—"Out of Egypt have I called my son" (Mt. 2:15; compare Hos. 11:1). On the Mount of Transfiguration, Moses "appeared in glory, and spake of His [Jesus'] decease [*exodos*] which He should accomplish at Jerusalem" on the cross (Lk. 9:31). Our Savior is the only "way" or "road" out of sin and unto God (Jn. 14:6). He came to deliver men "who through fear of death were all their lifetime subject to bondage" (Heb. 2:15).

Applied to the Christian ⚖

As our fathers in the Exodus (1 Cor. 10:1-4,11), believers have been delivered by the blood, the water, and the Spirit (1 Jn. 5:8):

1. Jesus' blood—the Passover Lamb (Ex. 12).
2. Water baptism—the Red Sea (Ex. 14–15).
3. The Holy Ghost Baptism—the glory cloud (Ex. 13).

Before the Lamb became our Way out of sin's bondage (Jn. 14:6), satan (typified by Pharaoh) had made our lives bitter with hard bondage, making us serve with "rigour" or "severity, cruelty" (Ex. 1:13; compare Eph. 2:1-3). We can rejoice with Joshua, Moses' successor, "For the Lord our God, He it is that brought us up and our fathers out of the land of Egypt, from the house of bondage, and which did those great signs in our sight, and preserved us in all the way wherein we went..." (Josh. 24:17).

Go Deeper 📖

See Ex. 2:23; 3:10; 6:5-9,27; 13:3,14; 23:15; 34:18; Num. 14:19; 22:5; Deut. 5:6; 26:6; Judg. 6:8,13-16; 1 Sam. 15:2; 2 Sam. 7:23; Ezra 9:8-9; Neh. 5:18; Ps. 68:31; 80:8; 114:1; Is. 11:11; 14:3; Hos. 12:13; Acts 7:6-7; Rom. 8:15,21; Gal. 2:4; 4:3,9,24-25; 5:1; Heb. 11:22; 2 Pet. 1:15; 2:19.

∞   ∞   ∞

Eye (Eyes)

Understanding; the seven spirits of God; prophetic ministry

Key Scriptures: Gen. 6:8; 2 Chron. 16:9; Ps. 34:15; Is. 11:1-2;
Zech. 3:9; 1 Cor. 12:16-21; Eph. 1:18; Rev. 5:6.

Foundational Information

The eye is the light-sensitive organ of vision in animals and humans. "Eye" is from
the Hebrew *'ayin* (Strong's #5869), which means "an eye (literally or figuratively); by
analogy, a fountain (as the eye of the landscape)." *'Ayin* has also been translated as "well,
surface, appearance, spring." The Greek word for "eye" is *ophthalmos* (Strong's #3788),
which means "the eye (literally or figuratively); by implication, vision; figuratively, envy
(from the jealous side-glance)." It is akin to *opsis* ("sight"), probably from a root signifying "penetration, sharpness."

Fulfilled in Christ

To see is to understand. Jesus Christ is the "one stone" with seven eyes, the One
with complete understanding (Zech. 3:9). Those "seven eyes" are the "seven Spirits of
God" (Rev. 1:4; 3:1; 4:5; 5:6) expressed in Isaiah 11:1-2, denoting the fullness of the
Spirit's anointing that rested upon Messiah (Jn. 3:34), including "all wisdom and spiritual
understanding" (Col. 1:9; see also Mk. 12:33; Lk. 1:3; 2:47; 2 Tim. 2:7). Solomon understood that "the hearing ear, and the seeing eye, the Lord hath made even both of them"
(Prov. 20:12 with Jn. 1:1-3). Daniel said that the Lord had eyes like "lamps of fire" (Dan.
10:6; compare Rev. 1:14; 2:18). The eyes of the Lord Jesus:

1. Are the source of grace (Gen. 6:8).
2. Are always upon His land of promise (Deut. 11:12).
3. Run to and fro throughout the earth (2 Chron. 16:9).
4. Are upon the righteous (Ps. 34:15).
5. Are in every place, beholding all things (Prov. 15:3).
6. Preserve knowledge (Prov. 22:12).

Applied to the Christian

Paul declared, "The eyes of your understanding [literally, 'the eyes of your heart']
being enlightened; that ye may know…" (Eph. 1:18; compare 1 Sam. 14:27). The psalmist prayed, "Open thou mine eyes, that I may behold wondrous things out of thy law" (Ps.
119:18). The Bride of Christ has been given "doves' eyes" (Song 1:15; 4:1)—Holy Spirit
understanding. The prophetic ministries (or seers) are the "eyes" of the Body of Christ
(1 Cor. 12:16-21; see also 1 Sam. 9:9,19). Amos declared, "Surely the Lord God will do
nothing, but He revealeth His secret unto His servants the prophets" (Amos 3:7; see also
1 Cor. 12:28; Eph. 2:20; 4:5,11; Heb. 1:1).

Go Deeper 📖

See Gen. 3:5-8; 49:12; Ex. 13:9; Num. 22:31; Ruth 2:9; 1 Sam. 3:2; Ps. 11:4; 19:8; 32:8; 66:7; 94:9; 139:16; Prov. 15:30; Song 4:9; Is. 6:10; 29:18; 32:3; 33:7,20; 42:7; 52:8; Zech. 4:10; Lk. 24:45; Jn. 9:6,30; Acts 16:4; 2 Cor. 4:4; Eph. 5:8; Heb. 4:13; 10:32; 1 Pet. 3:12; 1 Jn. 2:11; Rev. 1:7; 3:18; 4:6.

∞ ∞ ∞

𝔈𝔶𝔢 𝔬𝔣 𝔞 𝔑𝔢𝔢𝔡𝔩𝔢

Reduction; humility

Key Scriptures: Num. 22:26; Prov. 28:11; Jer. 9:23; Mt. 7:14; 19:24; Mk. 10:25; Lk. 18:25; Jn. 3:30; Phil. 2:6-8.

Foundational Information ✐

The "eye of a needle" was a figure of speech used by Jesus to illustrate the extreme difficulty of one who is self-sufficient to enter the Kingdom of God. Some say that the "Needle's Eye" was a particularly narrow gate adjacent to one of the main gates of Jerusalem. A camel could pass through this gate, but only with great difficulty. It had to be stripped of the burden it carried and then bow to its knees to get through. Others suggest that "camel" (*kamelos*) should be translated "rope" (*kamilos*).

"Needle" is from the Greek *rhaphis* (Strong's #4476), and means "to sew (through the idea of puncturing); a needle." It is akin to *rhapizo* (Strong's #4474), which means "(to let fall, 'rap'); to slap," translated in the King James Version as "smite (with the palm of the hand)." The Greek word for "camel" is *kamelos* (Strong's #2574) and has a Hebrew origin, *gamal*, which means "a bearer, carrier."

Fulfilled in Christ ☀

Jesus Christ is the divine Camel who willingly came to walk through the dust of this earth to bear our griefs and carry our sorrows (Is. 53:4). He humbly bowed down and emptied Himself of the weight of glory and became obedient unto the death of the cross (Phil. 2:6-8). Jesus declared, "It is easier for a camel to go through the eye of a needle, than for a rich man to enter into the kingdom of God" (Mt. 19:24; Mk. 10:25; Lk. 18:25). In Jesus' teaching, the "rich man" is the self-sufficient man (depending on his wealth); the "poor man" is the man who sees His need of God. Our King explained, "And whosoever shall exalt himself shall be abased; and he that shall humble himself shall be exalted" (Mt. 23:12). This path, this gate, this way is "narrow" (Mt. 7:14).

Applied to the Christian ⚖️

Solomon understood that "the rich man is wise in his own conceit" (Prov. 28:11). Jeremiah warned against men trusting in their own resources (Jer. 9:23). John the Baptist announced, "He must increase, but I must decrease" (Jn. 3:30). If the word "camel" is indeed the word for "rope," we can begin to understand how God humbles us, unravelling our pride, taking us through the "narrow place" (Num. 22:26), and then putting us back together on the other side! Luke knew that "we must through much tribulation ['pressure'] enter into the kingdom of God" (Acts 14:22). Solomon revealed a great truth: "The fear of the Lord is the instruction of wisdom; and before honour is humility" (Prov. 15:33). Worship, bow down, and kneel before the Lord your Maker (Ps. 95:6).

Go Deeper 📖

See Ex. 10:3; Deut. 8:2,16; 2 Chron. 7:14; 34:27; Ps. 9:12; 10:12,17; 34:2; 69:32; Prov. 6:3; 16:19; 18:12; 22:4; 29:23; Is. 57:15; Mt. 7:21; 18:4,9; Acts 20:19; 2 Cor. 12:21; Col. 2:18,23; Jas. 4:6,10; 5:1; 1 Pet. 5:5-6.

∞ ∞ ∞

Ezekiel

Strength through glorious vision; the Son of man

Key Scriptures: Is. 40:31; Ezek. 1–48; Jn. 1:14-18; Acts 26:18; 2 Cor. 12:9.

Foundational Information ✎

Ezekiel was a prophet of a priestly family carried captive to Babylon in 597 B.C.; his call to the prophetic ministry came five years later. Ezekiel ministered to the captives who dwelt by the River Chebar at Tel Abib, and is the author of the Book of Ezekiel. The phrase "the son of man" is used over 90 times in the Book of Ezekiel to describe the prophet.

"Ezekiel" is taken from the Hebrew *Yechezqe'l* (Strong's #3168), and it means "God will strengthen." It is a compound of *'el* ("strength, mighty, the Almighty") and *chazaq* ("to seize, be strong, courageous, or obstinate; cure, help, repair, fortify, bind, restrain, conquer"). "Ezekiel" has also been translated as "God is strong, God is powerful, whom God makes strong." He is the prophet who saw the glory of the Lord.

Fulfilled in Christ ✝

Ezekiel was a priest who became a prophet; Jesus is our Prophet, Priest, and King. The Book of Ezekiel opens, "Now it came to pass in the ['my' in Hebrew] thirtieth year...that the heavens were opened, and I saw visions of God" (Ezek. 1:1). The heavens opened and the glory of the Spirit descended upon Jesus when He was the same age (Lk. 3:21-23)! Ezekiel saw four living creatures (with faces like a man, a lion, an ox, and an eagle) who had "the likeness of a man" (Ezek. 1:5). Thus is revealed the Man Christ Jesus: His first 30 obscure years were as the man. His next three-and-a-half years were as the conquering lion. Then Jesus laid down His life like the ox in sacrifice, yet rose from the dead as the high-flying eagle! These four faces also reveal the four Gospels: Matthew (the lion, the King), Mark (the ox, the Servant), Luke (the Son of Man), and John (the eagle, the Son of God).

Jesus was the full expression of the "glory" of His Father (see Jn. 1:14; 2:11; 11:40; Heb. 1:3). Over 80 times in the four Gospels, Jesus is called "the son of man." This emphasizes His identification with humanity as our great and merciful High Priest (Heb. 4:14-16). In the Book of Ezekiel, Jesus is seen in the following ways:

1. The voice of the Almighty (Ezek. 1:24).
2. The One who bears the iniquity (Ezek. 4:5).
3. The Man with the writer's inkhorn (Ezek. 9:2).
4. The One whose right it is (Ezek. 21:27).
5. The one Shepherd (Ezek. 34:23).
6. The Man with the measuring reed (Ezek. 40:3).
7. The Prince of the temple (Ezek. 44:3).
8. The One who is there (Ezek. 48:35).

Applied to the Christian ⚖

Believers can either look around at their circumstances or look up to see visions of God (Ps. 137 with Ezek. 1:1). The glory of the Lord is returning to a new temple and holy nation, the Church (see Ezek. 43:1-5; Mt. 21:42-43; Eph. 2:19-22; 1 Pet. 2:9-10). The Book of Ezekiel shows us five reoccurring themes:

1. The otherness (holiness) of God.
2. The sinfulness of men.
3. The fact of judgment.
4. The importance of individual responsibility.
5. The promise of restoration.

In spite of captivity, God has promised to strengthen His people and restore His glory (Joel 2:25). This magnificent promise is seen in the restoration of Judah following the Babylonian Captivity, the restoration of the Church following the Dark Ages (Ezek. 37:1-14; 47:1-12; Acts 3:19-21), and the ultimate restoration of the creation (Rom. 8:19-23).

Go Deeper   📖

See Ex. 13:14-16; 15:2; 1 Chron. 16:11; Ps. 18:1-2; 19:14; 27:1,14; 31:24; 93:1; Is. 12:2; 33:6; 40:31; Joel 3:16; Hab. 3:19; Mt. 17:9; Lk. 1:22; 24:23; Acts 2:17; 9:10-12; 10:3,17,19; 11:5; 12:9; 16:9-10; 18:9; 26:19; Rom. 5:6; 2 Cor. 12:1; Rev. 1:16; 5:12; 12:10.

∞ ∞ ∞

𝔈zra

The restoration of God's law; God's help

Key Scriptures: Ezra 1–10; Neh. 8; 12; Ps. 46:1; Jn. 3:2.

Foundational Information   ✑

Ezra, a descendant of Aaron through Eleazar, was a scribe and priest commissioned by the king of Persia to lead the returned captives in Jerusalem toward a new commitment to God's Law. "Ezra," the transliteration of the Hebrew *'ezrah* (Strong's #5833), means "aid." It is translated in the King James Version as "help." Its root *'azar* (Strong's #5826) means "to surround, protect, or aid." "Ezra" has also been rendered as "God is a help."

Fulfilled in Christ   ☨

Jesus Christ, the greatest Teacher who ever lived (Jn. 3:2), is our "helper" and Friend (Ps. 30:10; 54:4). Our Savior came from Heaven "ready" to do His Father's will (Ezra 7:6); He was granted His every request because God was with Him (Acts 10:38). Ezra wept in prayer and a great congregation assembled (Ezra 10:1)—Jesus prayed in the Garden of Gethsemane and was lifted at Calvary so that all men might gather unto Him (Lk. 22:44; Jn. 3:14; 12:32).

Jesus is seen in the Book of Ezra in the following ways:

1. The heavenly Zerubbabel, our Governor.
2. Our heavenly Ezra, our Priest and Scribe.
3. The One who restores order to society.
4. The heavenly Cyrus, King of all (Ezra 1:1-4).
5. The heavenly Jeshua (Ezra 3:2).
6. The Foundation of the temple (Ezra 3:6).
7. The Intercessor and Advocate (Ezra 9:1-15).

Applied to the Christian ⚖️

The Psalmist affirmed, "God is our refuge and strength, a very present help in trouble" (Ps. 46:1). The Helper lives within (Job 6:13; Col. 1:27; 1 Jn. 4:4)! In every generation, God brings a remnant back into the center of His purposes—"And now for a little space grace hath been shewed from the Lord our God, to leave us a remnant to escape, and to give us a nail in His holy place, that our God may lighten our eyes, and give us a little reviving in our bondage" (Ezra 9:8). We must prepare our hearts to be hearers and doers of the Word (Ezra 7:10; Jas. 1:22). On the first day of the seventh month (the Feast of Trumpets), Ezra gathered the nation as "one man" to hear and understand the Word at the water gate (Neh. 8:1-5)—the present end-time revival will bring God's people back to the Bible!

Go Deeper 📖

See Gen. 26:5; Ex. 18:16; Josh. 24:26; Neh. 8:8; 10:28; Ps. 27:9; 40:13,17; 51:12; 60:11; 63:7; 94:17; 105:45; Prov. 6:31; Is. 1:26; 31:1-2; 42:22; 49:6; Jer. 30:17; Lam. 4:17; Ezek. 44:24; Dan. 9:10; Mt. 17:11; Lk. 19:8; Rom. 7:22; 8:7; Gal. 6:1; Heb. 4:16; 8:10.

𝕱𝖆𝖈𝖊

The mirror of the heart; God's presence and glory

Key Scriptures: Gen. 32:30; Ex. 25:30; Ezek. 1:10;
1 Cor. 13:12; 2 Cor. 3:18; 4:6.

Foundational Information

The face is that part of the human body that contains a person's unique, identifying characteristics; a term used in a symbolic way in the Bible to express the presence of God. "Face" is from the Hebrew *paniym* (Strong's #6440), a plural word that means "the face (as the part that turns)." The Greek word is *prosopon* (Strong's #4383) and means "the front (as being towards view), the countenance, aspect, appearance, surface; by implication, presence, person." The latter is taken from *pros* ("towards") and *ops* ("the eye").

Fulfilled in Christ

Paul declared that the light of the knowledge of the glory of God was revealed "in the face of Jesus Christ" (2 Cor. 4:6). Jesus, the Son, was the full expression of the Father's glorious heart, coming forth from His eternal bosom (Jn. 1:18; Heb. 1:3). Jesus put a "face" on the invisible God (Col. 1:15). The "showbread" in Moses' tabernacle, a type of Jesus as the Bread of life (Ex. 25:30 with Jn. 6:48), was literally, "the bread of faces" or "presence bread." Both Ezekiel and John saw the four faces of the Messiah (Ezek. 1:10; Rev. 4:7):

1. The face of a man—revealing Jesus as the Son of Man, set forth in the Gospel of Luke.
2. The face of a lion—revealing Jesus as the King of kings, set forth in the Gospel of Matthew.
3. The face of an ox or calf—revealing Jesus as the Servant of Jehovah, the divine burden-bearer, set forth in the Gospel of Mark.
4. The face of an eagle—revealing Jesus as the resurrected Son of God, set forth in the Gospel of John.

In His glorious transfiguration, Jesus' face "did shine as the sun, and His raiment was white as the light" (Mt. 17:2). Men spat on the face of the Savior (Mt. 26:67), but the Word admonishes, "The face of the Lord is against them that do evil" (Ps. 34:16; 1 Pet. 3:12).

Applied to the Christian

When we were sinners, darkness was upon our hearts, "the face of the deep" (Gen. 1:2; compare Jn. 11:44). Now that we are saved, we look into the Scriptures to behold our "natural face," literally, "the face of our birth": The Man in the mirror is the new man, the new creation (2 Cor. 5:17, Jas. 1:18-23)! As we gaze upon the Lord with an "open" or "unveiled" face, we are changed into the same image (2 Cor. 3:18). Like the patriarch Jacob, we can now commune with God "face to face," heart to heart (Gen. 32:30; 1 Cor. 13:12). John the Baptist exemplifies an end-time prophetic ministry sent forth before the face of the Lord to prepare His way (Mt. 11:10; see also Mal. 4:5-6; Mt. 17:10-13; Lk. 1:76). Let us say with David, "I foresaw the Lord always before my face, for He is on my right hand, that I should not be moved" (Acts 2:25).

Go Deeper 📖

See Gen. 3:8; Ex. 14:25; 33:14-15; 34:35; Deut. 1:17; 1 Kings 13:6; 1 Chron. 16:27; Job 26:9; Ps. 16:11; 31:20; 68:8; 100:2; 104:30; Is. 25:7; 27:6; Mt. 6:17; 16:3; 18:10; Lk. 9:51; 10:1; Acts 6:15; 20:38; 2 Cor. 3:7; Gal. 2:11; 2 Jn. 12; Jude 24; Rev. 6:16; 10:1; 20:11; 22:4.

∾ ∾ ∾

𝔉allo𝔴 𝔊round

The hardened heart; idle things; that which is weak, feeble, or barren

Key Scriptures: Job 41:24; Jer. 4:3; Dan. 5:20; Hos. 10:12; Mt. 12:36; Mk. 6:52; 8:17.

Foundational Information ✐

Fallow ground is farm land left idle during a growing season to allow the fertility of the soil to be restored. "Fallow ground" is from the Hebrew *niyr* (Strong's #5215), which means "plowing, (concretely) freshly plowed land." It's root means "the gleam of a fresh furrow; to till the soil; to glisten; a lamp (the burner) or light."

The Hebrew word for "weak" is *rapheh* (Strong's #7504), which means "slack (in body or mind)." The Greek word for "idle" or "barren" is *argos* (Strong's #692), which means "inactive, unemployed; (by implication) lazy, useless"; it is a compound of *a* (the negative particle) and *ergon* ("work, toil"). Compare *steiros* (Strong's #4723), taken from the root *ster,* meaning "hard, firm" (hence the English *sterile*); it signifies "barren, not bearing children."

Fulfilled in Christ ✝

Jesus Christ is heaven's Candle, Lamp, and Light (Jn. 8:12). He is the living Word, the sharp Plow sent into the earth to break up hardened hearts that men might become productive in the divine purpose (Jn. 1:1; Heb. 4:12). The apostle Paul declared, "For what the law could not do, in that it was weak through the flesh, God sending His own Son in the likeness of sinful flesh, and for sin, condemned sin in the flesh" (Rom. 8:3). Jesus was the Salt of Heaven who healed the deadly waters and the barren land (2 Kings 2:21). The Lord warned His disciples, "Watch and pray, that ye enter not into temptation: the spirit indeed is willing, but the flesh is weak" (Mt. 26:41). He also taught that men will give account of "every idle word" (Mt. 12:36).

Applied to the Christian ⚖

The prophet Jeremiah called out to God's people, "…Break up your fallow ground, and sow not among thorns" (Jer. 4:3). Hosea added, "Sow to yourselves in righteousness, reap in mercy; break up your fallow ground: for it is time to seek the Lord, till He come and rain righteousness upon you" (Hos. 10:12). The heart (ground) of sinful king Zedekiah was as firm as a stone (2 Chron. 36:13; Job 41:24). As with Adam in the Garden of Eden, mighty King Nebuchadnezzar's mind was hardened in pride, and he lost his throne and his glory (Dan. 5:20). Even Jesus' twelve disciples had hearts like fallow ground (Mk. 6:52; 8:17). But the day has come when the Lord encourages His Church, the New Testament Zion, "Fear thou not…let not thine hands be slack" (Zeph. 3:16).

Go Deeper 📖

See Ex. 5:8,17; 7:13; Deut. 2:30; 2 Sam. 3:39; 2 Chron. 15:7; Ps. 6:2; 105:37; 113:9; Prov. 13:23; 19:5; 24:10; 30:16; 31:27; Song 4:2; Is. 35:3; 54:1; 63:17; Ezek. 7:17; Joel 3:10; Mt. 20:3-6; Lk. 24:25; Jn. 12:40; Acts 20:35; Rom. 4:19; 15:1; 1 Cor. 11:30; Gal. 4:9; 1 Thess. 5:14; 1 Tim. 5:13; Tit. 1:12; Heb. 12:12; 2 Pet. 1:8.

∞ ∞ ∞

𝔉amiliar 𝔖pirits

Contact with the dead; spiritual necromancy

Key Scriptures: Lev. 19:31; 20:6,27; Num. 19:11; Deut. 18:10-11;
1 Sam. 28:3-9; Is. 8:19; Rom. 6:1-14; Gal. 2:19-21.

Foundational Information ✎

Familiar spirits have to do with spiritism and necromancy, or the calling up of the dead, practices which are forbidden in the Bible. "Familiar spirit" is from the Hebrew *'owb* (Strong's #178), which means "(the idea of prattling a father's name); properly, a mumble, a water skin (from its hollow sound); hence a necromancer (ventriloquist, as from a jar)." It can also mean "pit," referring to a place out of which a departed spirit may be summoned.

"Necromancer" is taken from two Hebrew words: *darash* (Strong's #1875), which means "to follow or frequent (for pursuit or search), to seek or ask, specifically to worship"; and *muwth* (Strong's #4191), which means "to kill; dead." Necromancy is seeking after the dead.

Fulfilled in Christ

Jesus Christ is "the resurrection and the life" (Jn. 11:25), the One who came that men might have life more abundantly (Jn. 10:10). The true Passover Lamb is the heavenly Josiah who put away sin, including "the workers with familiar spirits, and the wizards, and the images, and the idols, and all the abominations" in the midst of God's people (2 Kings 23:24). Jesus described the religious Pharisees as whited sepulchres full of dead men's bones (Mt. 23:27). He taught His disciples, "Follow me; and let the dead bury their dead" (Mt. 8:22). Jesus is Lord of both the dead and the living (Rom. 14:9). His blood has purged our conscience from dead works to serve the living God (Heb. 9:14).

Applied to the Christian

God's people are admonished, "Regard not them that have familiar spirits, neither seek after wizards, to be defiled by them" (Lev. 19:31). In the Old Testament, those who sought after familiar spirits were to be cut off and even put to death (Lev. 20:6,27). In our day, men follow after psychics or mediums who exercise witchcraft. When Israel was tempted with these false advisers in his day, Isaiah asked, "Should not a people seek unto their God?" (Is. 8:19) God's people were defiled by touching things that were dead (Lev. 11:24,31; Num. 19:11). Believers practice spiritual necromancy whenever they try to stay in contact with the old Adamic man, who was killed at the cross (Rom. 6:1-14; Gal. 2:20)! Christians are dead to their past, having been freed from sin (Rom. 6:7). There are not two natures in the believer; there is but one—the new nature. We are fighting a memory. The old man is dead.

Go Deeper

See Lev. 5:2; 11:39; Deut. 14:8; Num. 19:13-16; 2 Kings 21:6; 1 Chron. 10:13; 2 Chron. 33:6; Is. 19:3; 29:4; Hag. 2:13; Lk. 9:60; 10:30; 15:24,32; Jn. 11:39,41; Rom. 7:1-8; 8:10-11; 10:7; 11:15; 1 Cor. 7:39; Eph. 2:1-6; Col. 2:11-13,20; 3:3; 2 Tim. 2:11; Heb. 6:1; 1 Pet. 2:24; Jude 12; Rev. 3:1.

∞ ∞ ∞

𝔉amily

The Body of Christ, the household of faith

Key Scriptures: Ps. 68:6; Mt. 12:47-50; Gal. 6:10;
Eph. 2:19; 3:14-15; 1 Tim. 5:1-2.

Foundational Information ✐

A family is a group of persons related by marriage and blood ties, generally living together in the same household. "Family" is from the Hebrew *mishpachah* (Strong's #4940), meaning "a family, circle of relatives; figuratively, a class (of persons), a species (of animals) or sort (of things); by extension, a tribe or people." This word could also mean "kindred, clan." The Greek word for "family" is *patria* (Strong's #3965), and means "paternal descent, (concretely) a group of families or a whole race (nation)." It can also mean "ancestry, lineage." Compare *oikos* ("a dwelling, house").

Fulfilled in Christ ☦

Jesus Christ is the Head of the Church, the Body of Christ. Paul proclaimed, "I bow my knees unto the Father of our Lord Jesus Christ, of whom the whole family in heaven and earth is named" (Eph. 3:14-15). Jesus Christ is our Jubilee (Lk. 4:18). It is He who liberated us from sin that mankind might return to his rightful, original, creative purpose (Lev. 25:10,41). King Jesus belonged to the house and lineage of David after the flesh (Lk. 2:4; see also Mt. 1:1; Rom. 1:3). As the seed of Abraham, our Savior's finished work has blessed "all the kindreds of the earth" (Gen. 12:1-3; Acts 3:25). His blood has redeemed men "out of every kindred, and tongue, and people, and nation" (Rev. 5:9). He is the Passover Lamb who was killed for every family (Ex. 12:21).

Applied to the Christian ⚖

The Church is the corporate Body of Christ, and each Christian is a vital member of "the household of faith" and "the household of God" (Gal. 6:10; Eph. 2:19). Other Christians are our spiritual fathers, mothers, brothers, and sisters (Mt. 12:47-50; 1 Tim. 5:1-2). Jeremiah prophesied, "Turn, O backsliding children, saith the Lord; for I am married unto you: and I will take you one of a city, and two of a family, and I will bring you to Zion" (Jer. 3:14). "The virtuous woman," a type of the Church, is fearless, providing meat for her family (Prov. 31:10,15,21): "She looketh well to the ways of her household, and eateth not the bread of idleness" (Prov. 31:27). The psalmist declared, "God setteth the solitary in families" (Ps. 68:6).

Go Deeper 📖

See Gen. 10:5,32; 24:4; 31:3; Num. 10:30; Josh. 7:14; Ruth 2:1-3; 3:2; 1 Chron. 13:14; Esther 2:10,20; 8:6; 9:28; Ps. 107:41; Jer. 31:1; Amos 3:1-2; Zech. 12:14; 14:17;

Mt. 24:45; Lk. 12:42; Acts 7:14; 16:15; Rom. 16:10-11; 1 Cor. 1:16; Phil. 4:22; 2 Tim. 4:19; Rev. 14:6.

∞ ∞ ∞

Famine

The lack of hearing God's Word and Spirit

Key Scriptures: Ezek. 36:29-30; Amos 8:11; Mt. 4:4; 5:6; Jn. 6:35; Rom. 8:35.

Foundational Information

Famine is the prolonged lack of food or water. In biblical times, the line between famine and plenty depended mainly on the rains coming at the right time and in the proper amount. The most famous famine recorded in the Bible is the seven-year famine in Egypt, which was foretold by Joseph through his interpretation of Pharaoh's dream. "Famine" is from the Hebrew *ra'ab* (Strong's #7458), which means "hunger." It is also translated as "dearth" in the King James Version. The Greek word *limos* (Strong's #3042) means "(destitution); a scarcity of food." The Greek word for "hunger" is *peinao* (Strong's #3983), and it means "('pine'); to famish: to crave."

Fulfilled in Christ

Jesus Christ is the living Word, the Bread from heaven (Jn. 1:1; 6:48). The voice of the Spirit is the voice of the Son of God, for "the testimony of Jesus is the spirit of prophecy" (Rev. 19:10). Paul declared that famine could not separate us from the love of Christ (Rom. 8:35). Our Lord experienced hunger—as God, He hungered for man, and as man He hungered for God (Mk. 11:12)! Jesus taught that those who hunger and thirst after righteousness shall be filled (Mt. 5:6). He said, "He that cometh to Me shall never hunger; and he that believeth on Me shall never thirst" (Jn. 6:35; compare Rev. 7:16). Jesus mentioned the famine in the days of Elijah (1 Kings 17:1; 18:1-2; Lk. 4:25).

Applied to the Christian

Jesus declared that man cannot live by natural bread alone, "but by every word that proceedeth out of the mouth of God" (Mt. 4:4). The prophet Amos foresaw our day, "Behold, the days come, saith the Lord God, that I will send a famine in the land, not a famine of bread, nor a thirst for water, but of hearing the words of the Lord" (Amos 8:11). Famine can be so severe that men will feed on "ass's head" (human wisdom without God) and

"dove's dung" (all that is left after the dove has flown away) (2 Kings 6:25)! The patriarch Job knew that God would redeem him from the death of famine (Job 5:20-22). God
has promised His people, "I will call for the corn, and will increase it, and lay no famine
upon you...that ye shall receive no more reproach of famine among the heathen" (Ezek.
36:29-30). But spiritual Babylon shall be strongly judged with famine (Rev. 18:8).

Go Deeper 📖

See Gen. 12:10; 26:1; 41:27-36,56-57; 45:11; 47:4,20; Ruth 1:1; 2 Sam. 21:1;
24:13; 1 Kings 8:37; 18:2; 2 Kings 8:1; 25:3; Ps. 33:19; 37:19; 105:16; Is. 51:19; Jer.
11:22; 14:12-18; 15:2; 52:6; Lam. 5:10; Ezek. 5:16-17; Lk. 1:53; 15:14,17; 1 Cor. 4:11;
2 Cor. 11:27; Phil. 4:12; Rev. 6:8.

∞ ∞ ∞

Fan (Fork)

Sifting, separation

Key Scriptures: Ruth 3:2; Is. 30:24; Jer. 15:7; Mt. 3:12; Lk. 3:17.

Foundational Information ✍

The fan was a type of long-handled winnowing fork used to toss the threshed grain
into the air. The wind blew the chaff away, allowing the heavier grain to fall into a separate pile. "Fan" is from the Hebrew *mizreh* (Strong's #4214), which means "a winnowing
shovel (as scattering the chaff)." Compare the verb *zarah* (Strong's #2219), which means
"to toss about; by implication, to diffuse, winnow." The Greek word for "fan" is *ptuon*
(Strong's #4425), which means "a winnowing-fork (as scattering like spittle)."

Fulfilled in Christ ✝

Jesus Christ, the heavenly Boaz, is our kinsman-redeemer (Gal. 3:13-14). "Behold,
he winnoweth barley to night in the threshingfloor" (Ruth 3:2). Jesus, the Lord of the harvest, is sifting and cleansing His Church, separating the sheep from the goats (Mt. 9:38;
25:32; Lk. 10:2). He was the answer to the psalmist's prayer, the One who purged away
our sins (Ps. 79:9; compare Heb. 1:3). John the Baptist prophesied about His divine
Cousin, "Whose fan is in His hand, and He will throughly purge His floor, and gather His
wheat into the garner" (Mt. 3:12). Malachi predicted that Messiah would "purify the sons
of Levi, and purge them..." (Mal. 3:3).

Applied to the Christian ⚖

Believers are like wheat, separated from the tares of this world (Mt. 13:25-30). Jesus explained that "the good seed are the children of the kingdom, but the tares are the children of the wicked one" (Mt. 13:38). Like King Josiah of Judah, believers are to rid their lives of every man-made idol (2 Chron. 34:3). The Lord promised through Isaiah that His people would thresh their enemies: "Thou shalt fan them, and the wind shall carry them away" (Is. 41:16). Religious Babylon shall be sifted and judged (Jer. 51:2). Let us cry with David, "Purge me with hyssop, and I shall be clean; wash me, and I shall be whiter than snow" (Ps. 51:7).

Go Deeper 📖

See Gen. 49:26; Ex. 32:20; Lev. 15:31; 22:2; 2 Chron. 34:8; Ps. 1:4; 35:5; Prov. 16:6; Is. 1:25; 4:4; 6:7; 27:9; 30:28; Jer. 4:11; 15:7; 49:36; Ezek. 20:38; 43:20,26; Dan. 11:35; Amos 9:9; Mal. 2:3; Lk. 22:31; Jn. 15:2; Acts 13:2; 1 Cor. 5:7; 2 Cor. 6:17; 2 Tim. 2:21; Heb. 9:14,22; 2 Pet. 1:9.

∞ ∞ ∞

𝔉asting

Self-denial; distress, grief, repentance, humility

Key Scriptures: Ps. 35:13; Is. 58:6; Jer. 36:6; Joel 1:14; Mt. 4:2; Acts 27:9.

Foundational Information ✐

Fasting is abstaining from food or water for a period of time, usually for religious purposes. Fasting could be described as intensified prayer. The Day of Atonement, the tenth day of the seventh month, when the nation of Israel repented of sin, was also called "The Fast." "Fasting" is from the Hebrew root *tsuwm* (Strong's #6684), which means "to cover over (the mouth), to fast." The Greek verb is *nesteuo* (Strong's #3522), which means "to abstain from food." The noun *nesteia* is taken from two words: *a* (the negative particle) and *esthio* ("to eat").

Fulfilled in Christ ☦

Jesus Christ, the supreme example of self-denial, humbled Himself and became obedient to the death of the cross (Phil. 2:5-11). On the Day of Atonement, or "The Fast," two goats were chosen. Jesus fulfilled both types, as the Lord's goat, our sin offering, and the "scapegoat" (Lev. 16:8; compare Is. 53:6; Heb. 9:26). Jehovah declared His purpose for fasting through Isaiah, "Is not this the fast that I have chosen? To loose the bands of wickedness, to undo the heavy burdens, and to let the oppressed go free, and that ye break every yoke?" (Is. 58:6) Joel added, "Therefore also now, saith the Lord, turn ye even to Me with all your heart, and with fasting, and with weeping, and with mourning" (Joel 2:12). Jesus fasted for 40 days and 40 nights (Mt. 4:2).

Applied to the Christian

The Christian life is governed by the principle of the cross (Gal. 2:20). The apostle John explained, "Hereby perceive we the love of God, because He laid down His life for us: and we ought to lay down our lives for the brethren" (1 Jn. 3:16). The psalmist declared, "I humbled my soul with fasting" (Ps. 35:13). There are four different kinds of fast for the believer:

1. The personal fast (Ps. 109:24).
2. The proclaimed fast (2 Chron. 20:3; Joel 1:14; 2:15).
3. The purposed fast (Is. 58:6; Mt. 17:21).
4. The prophet's fast (see Ex. 34:28; 1 Kings 19:8; Dan. 9:13; Mt. 4:2).

Go Deeper

See 1 Sam. 7:6; 31:13; 2 Sam. 1:12; 12:16; 1 Kings 21:9-12; Ezra 8:21-23; Neh. 1:4; 9:1; Esther 4:3,16; 9:31; Ps. 69:10; Is. 58:3,5; Dan. 9:3; Jon. 3:5; Zech. 7:5; 8:19; Mt. 6:16-18; Mk. 2:18-20; Lk. 2:37; 18:12; Acts 10:30; 13:1-3; 14:23; 27:33; 1 Cor. 7:5; 2 Cor. 6:5; 11:27.

∞ ∞ ∞

𝔉at

The best or richest part; God's portion; obedience

Key Scriptures: Gen. 4:4; Lev. 6:12; Num. 18:12,29-30; 1 Sam. 15:22; Neh. 8:10; Rom. 5:19; Phil. 2:8.

Foundational Information

The fat was the richest part of an animal eaten as food or used as a sacrifice. This best part belonged only to the Lord. "Fat" is from the Hebrew *cheleb* (Strong's #2459), which means "to be fat; fat, whether literally or figuratively; hence, the richest or choice part."

Fulfilled in Christ ☦

Jesus was the chosen portion of the Godhead, the best part of the Father. As the Firstborn Son, He personified the "double portion" or the "worthy portion" (Deut. 21:17; 1 Sam. 1:5; see also Rom. 8:29). In His earthly life and vicarious death, Jesus withheld nothing, always pleasing the Father (Jn. 8:29). He was completely dedicated, thus totally victorious over sin and the devil. Jesus explained, "…And he [satan] has no claim on Me. [He has nothing in common with Me; there is nothing in Me that belongs to him, and he has no power over Me]" (Jn. 14:30 AMP). Our Savior "became obedient unto death, even the death of the cross" (Phil. 2:8). Now exalted above all things, His throne "of ivory" (the pain of Gethsemane and Calvary) is overlaid with "the best gold" (the fullness of the divine nature) (1 Kings 10:18)!

Applied to the Christian ⚖

Like Abel, Christians are to give the "best" of their time, talent, and treasure to the Lord (Gen. 4:4; see also Num. 18:12; 29-30,32). "The fat that covereth the inwards" (the best of our motives) must be offered to God (Lev. 3:3). The fat of the Old Testament offerings pictures New Testament obedience, the "better" fat of a "better" covenant (1 Sam. 15:22; Heb. 8:6; 9:23)! Let us not be as King Saul, who kept the "best" for himself (1 Sam. 15:9,15). Like as with Esther who overcame, the Lord has provided the "best place" for us (Esther 2:9; compare Rev. 3:21). Joseph's choice, covenantal birthright coat (Gen 37:3), foreshadows the "best robe" of the believer (Lk. 15:22), our inheritance because of Jesus' "obedience" and ultimate sacrifice (Rom. 5:19).

Go Deeper 📖

See Gen. 43:11; 45:18; 47:6; 49:11; Ex. 22:5; 29:13,22; 10:15; Deut. 32:14; 1 Sam. 2:15-16; 2 Sam. 10:9; 1 Kings 8:64; 2 Chron. 29:35; 35:14; Ps. 39:5; 63:5; 81:16; 147:14; Song 7:9; Is. 43:24; Ezek. 24:5; 31:16; 34:3; 44:15; Acts 15:7; Rom. 1:5; 6:16; 1 Cor. 12:31; 2 Cor. 10:5-6; Heb. 5:8; 1 Pet. 1:2.

∾   ∾   ∾

Fathers

Apostolic ministry; spiritual maturity; divine provision

Key Scriptures: Prov. 13:22; Is. 1:26; 9:6; Mt. 6:9; 1 Cor. 4:15; 12:28; Gal. 4:6; Eph. 2:20; 3:5; 4:11; Heb. 3:1.

Foundational Information ✐

The father was the male parent of a household in Bible times, charged with the responsibility of providing for the family and giving religious instruction to the children. "Father" is from the Hebrew *'ab* (Strong's #1), and it is translated in the King James Version as "chief, forefather, father." It can also mean "grandfather, ancestor." The Greek word *pater* comes from a root signifying "a nourisher, protector, upholder."

Fulfilled in Christ ✟

Within the Godhead, Jesus and the Father are one (Jn. 17:22). Jesus said, "He that hath seen Me hath seen the Father..." (Jn. 14:9b; see also Col. 2:9; Heb. 1:3). Isaiah prophesied that one of Messiah's designations would be "The everlasting Father" (Is. 9:6). Jesus Christ is "the Apostle and High Priest of our profession" (Heb. 3:1). Our King has been given "all power [authority] ...in Heaven and in earth" (Mt. 28:18). The name of God "Jehovah-jireh" ("the Lord will see and provide") has been fulfilled in Him (Phil. 4:19), and all things are upheld by Him (Col. 1:17). Jesus is the master "teacher come from God" (Jn. 3:2). The psalmist declared, "A father of the fatherless, and a judge of the widows, is God in His holy habitation...Like as a father pitieth his children, so the Lord pitieth them that fear Him" (Ps. 68:5; 103:13).

Applied to the Christian ⚖

A good father provides an inheritance for his children and grandchildren (Prov. 13:22). In the Church, "fathers" are apostles, fully authorized to represent the name of Him who sent them (Eph. 2:19-20; 3:5). Paul declared, "For though ye have ten thousand instructors in Christ, yet have ye not many fathers..." (1 Cor. 4:15). Joseph was made a father to Pharaoh and a ruler in Egypt (Gen. 45:8). The ministry of the Old Testament judge parallels the ministry of the New Testament apostle—the prophet Isaiah prophesied, "And I will restore thy judges as at the first..." (Is. 1:26; compare Joel 2:25-26; Acts 3:19-21). There are three levels of apostolic ministry:

1. Jesus, the Chief Apostle (Heb. 3:1).
2. The twelve apostles of the Lamb (Mt. 10:2; Rev. 21:14).
3. The many apostles of the Spirit (1 Cor. 12:28; Eph. 4:11).

Go Deeper   📖

See Gen. 17:4-5; 44:19-20; Job 29:16; 38:28; Prov. 3:12; 4:1; Is. 22:21; Jer. 31:9; Mal. 1:6; Mk. 6:30; Lk. 11:11,49; 22:14; Acts 1:2; 2:42-43; 4:33; 5:12; 8:1; 16:4; Rom. 1:1; 4:17; 11:13; 1 Cor. 4:9; 9:1-2; 15:7-9; 2 Cor. 6:18; 11:13; 12:12; 1 Thess. 2:11; 1 Tim. 5:1; Heb. 1:5; Rev. 2:2; 18:20.

∾ ∾ ∾

𝕱𝖆𝖙𝖍𝖊𝖗'𝖘 𝕳𝖔𝖚𝖘𝖊

Jesus, the Pattern Son; the household of faith, the Body of Christ

Key Scriptures: Lk. 6:48; Jn. 14:2,23; 2 Cor. 5:1; Gal. 6:10;
Eph. 2:19-22; Col. 1:19; 2:9; 1 Tim. 3:15.

Foundational Information   ✐

The "father's house" is the house that the father lives in. "House" is from the Greek *oikia* (Strong's #3614), which means "residence (abstractly), but usually (concretely) an abode (literally or figuratively); by implication a family (especially domestics)." Compare *oikos,* translated in the King James Version as "home, house, household, temple." Note also the word *mone* (Strong's #3438), which means "a staying, residence (the act or the place)." It is translated in John 14:2,23 of the King James Version as "mansions" and "abode." Vine's Dictionary adds that there is nothing in the word *mone* to indicate separate compartments in Heaven.

Fulfilled in Christ   ✝

Jesus, the Pattern Son, the Word made flesh, was the "house" in which the Father lived. Our Savior declared, "In My Father's house are many mansions ['dwelling-places']…"; in Him there is a place for us (Jn. 14:2). Paul explained that "it pleased the Father that in Him [Jesus, the Son] should all fulness dwell…For in Him dwelleth all the fulness of the Godhead bodily" (Col. 1:19; 2:9). Moses' tabernacle (Ex. 25–40) and Solomon's glorious temple (1 Kings 5–8) prefigure Him who is the "true tabernacle, which the Lord pitched, and not man" (Heb. 8:2). The archangel declared to the virgin Mary, "The Holy Ghost shall come upon thee, and the power of the Highest shall overshadow thee: therefore also that holy thing that shall be born of thee shall be called the Son of God" (Lk. 1:35).

Applied to the Christian ⚖

When Jesus spoke the words of John 14:2, He wasn't on His way to Heaven, but to Calvary! Through His finished work, we didn't receive a "mansion"; we **became** His "mansion," His temple, the habitation of God through the Spirit (1 Cor. 3:16; Eph. 2:19-22)—the "abode" for the Father and the Son through the Person of the Holy Spirit (Jn. 14:23). The "house of God" is the Church (1 Tim. 3:15; Heb. 3:5-6). We are to build our "house" (life, family, ministry) upon the Rock, Christ Jesus (Lk. 6:48-49). Paul declared this mystery, "For we know that if our earthly house of this tabernacle were dissolved, we have a building of God, an house not made with hands, eternal in the heavens" (2 Cor. 5:1). The apostle admonished, "As we have therefore opportunity, let us do good unto all men, especially unto them who are of the household of faith" (Gal. 6:10).

Go Deeper 📖

See Mt. 5:15; 7:25-27; 10:12-14,25,36; 12:25,29; 24:45; Mk. 3:25-27; Lk. 12:42; 22:11; Acts 10:7; 16:15; Rom. 16:10-11; 1 Cor. 1:16; 6:19; 2 Cor. 6:16; Phil. 4:22; 1 Tim. 3:16; 2 Tim. 2:20; 4:19; Heb. 2:14-17; 10:5,21; 1 Pet. 2:5; 4:17; 1 Jn. 4:1-3; 2 Jn. 10.

∞ ∞ ∞

𝔉𝔞𝔱𝔥𝔢𝔯𝔩𝔢𝔰𝔰

Spiritual orphans; the needy

Key Scriptures: Deut. 10:18; Ps. 68:5; Lam. 5:3; Jn. 14:18; Jas. 1:27.

Foundational Information ✐

An orphan is a child deprived by death of one or both parents. "Fatherless" is from the Hebrew "yathowm" (Strong's #3490), which means "to be lonely; a bereaved person." The Greek word *orphanos* means "bereaved ('orphan'), parentless." The latter was also used in the general sense of being "friendless or desolate."

Fulfilled in Christ ✝

Jesus promised to send the Holy Spirit to serve as the believer's teacher, guide, guardian, and protector, "I will not leave you comfortless [orphans]: I will come to you" (Jn. 14:18). The Lord will "execute the judgment of the fatherless and widow, and loveth the stranger, in giving him food and raiment" (Deut. 10:18). Jesus has delivered those who had no one else to help them (Job 29:12; Ps. 10:14). The psalmist declared, "A father of the fatherless, and a judge of the widows, is God in His holy habitation" (Ps. 68:5). Jesus is the "friend" who sticks closer than a brother (Prov. 18:24). Messiah defends the poor and the fatherless, executing justice for the afflicted and needy (Ps. 82:3).

Applied to the Christian

Before we knew Jesus Christ as our personal Savior, we were "fatherless"— spiritual orphans. Jesus alone is the "way" back to the Father (Jn. 14:6; compare Acts 4:12). Believers have received the "spirit of adoption," the spirit of sonship whereby we now cry, "Abba, Father" (see Rom. 8:15,23; 9:4; Gal. 4:5; Eph. 1:5). In the days of calamity and judgment, Jeremiah cried out, "We are orphans and fatherless, our mothers are as widows" (Lam. 5:3). Paul referred to his apostolic function as the ministry of a "father" (1 Cor. 4:15). God is restoring the apostolic ministry to the Church (Eph. 2:20; 3:5; 4:11). There is a spirit of adoption in the land; men are weary of being "fatherless," void of the wise influence of seasoned ministry. James revealed that "pure religion and undefiled before God and the Father is this, to visit the fatherless and widows in their affliction, and to keep [oneself] unspotted from the world" (Jas. 1:27).

Go Deeper   📖

See Ex. 22:22-24; Deut. 14:29; 16:11-14; 24:17-21; 26:12-13; 27:19; Job 6:27; 22:9; Ps. 10:18; 25:9; 32:8; 146:9; Prov. 17:17; 22:11; 23:10; Song 5:16; Is. 1:17; 41:8; Jer. 7:6; 22:3; 49:11; Zech. 7:10; Mal. 3:5; Mt. 11:19; Lk. 1:79; Jn. 15:13-15; 16:13; Acts 8:31; Rom. 11:3; Phil. 4:19; 1 Thess. 3:1; 3 Jn. 14.

∾ ∾ ∾

𝔉ear

The absence of love; reverence

Key Scriptures: Prov. 1:7; 9:10; Eccles. 12:13; Is. 11:2; 2 Tim. 1:7; 1 Jn. 4:18.

Foundational Information   ✐

Fear is an unpleasant emotion caused by a sense of danger. It is also a feeling of reverence, awe, and respect. Fear may be directed toward God or man, and it is either healthy or harmful. "Fear" is from the Hebrew *yare* (Strong's #3372), which means "to fear;

morally, to revere; causatively, to frighten." It can also mean "to stand in awe." The Greek verb *phobeo* (Strong's #5399) means "to frighten, (passively) to be alarmed; by analogy, to be in awe of, revere." It can also mean "to put to flight."

Fulfilled in Christ ☦

Jesus Christ is the Lion of the tribe of Judah; He is the love of God and fears nothing (Prov. 28:1)! In Gethsemane and on Calvary, our Savior put the devil to flight (Jn. 16:11; Col. 2:15)! Jesus the Messiah was anointed with the spirit of "the fear of the Lord" (Is. 11:2). The opposite of love (light) is fear (darkness). There is no fear in love; but "perfect love" (Jesus) casts out fear (1 Jn. 4:18). John declared, "God is light, and in Him is no darkness at all" (1 Jn. 1:5; compare Jn. 8:12). Moses articulated the cry of the Lord, "O that there were such an heart in them, that they would fear Me, and keep all My commandments..." (Deut. 5:29).

Applied to the Christian ⚖

Paul affirmed, "For God hath not given us the spirit of fear; but of power, and of love, and of a sound mind" (2 Tim. 1:7). We only fear God, knowing that the "fear of the Lord" is the beginning of all knowledge and wisdom (Prov. 1:7; 9:10). The devil is afraid of Spirit-filled Christians (Acts 19:15; 1 Jn. 4:4). The psalmist cried out, "The Lord is my light and my salvation; whom shall I fear? The Lord is the strength of my life; of whom shall I be afraid?" (Ps. 27:1) Solomon concluded, "Fear God, and keep His commandments: for this is the whole duty of man" (Eccles. 12:13). The admonition of the ages is simple: "Fear ye not, stand still, and see the salvation of the Lord..." (Ex. 14:13)!

Go Deeper 📖

See Gen. 3:10; 15:1; Ex. 1:21; 15:11; Lev. 19:30; Num. 14:9; Deut. 6:2; Josh. 4:14; 24:14; 1 Sam. 12:18; Ps. 23:4; 40:3; 56:4; 91:5; 111:9; 119:63; Prov. 3:7; 24:21; 31:21; Is. 35:4; 54:4; Jer. 23:4; Ezek. 2:6; Amos 3:8; Mal. 3:16; Mt. 10:28; Lk. 1:50; 12:32; Acts 10:35; Col. 3:22; Heb. 4:1; 13:6; 1 Pet. 2:17; Rev. 15:4.

∞ ∞ ∞

𝔉east

Celebration, harvest

Key Scriptures: Lev. 16; 23; Deut. 16; Neh. 8; Jn. 7.

Foundational Information ✐

The feasts of Jehovah were scheduled at specific times in the annual calendar. They were both civil and religious in nature. "Feast" is from the Hebrew *chag* (Strong's #2282), which means "a festival, or a victim therefor." It is translated in the King James Version as "(solemn) feast (day), sacrifice, solemnity." Its root *chagag* (Strong's #2287) means "to move in a circle, (specifically) to march in a sacred procession, to observe a festival; by implication, to be giddy." The Greek word *heorte* means "a feast or festival." Compare *deipnon*, (also translated as "supper") meaning "dinner, the chief meal (usually in the evening) and prepared at great expense." The seven Feasts of Jehovah were the following:

1. Passover (Ex. 12:1-30; Lev. 23:4-5; Deut. 16:1-3).
2. Unleavened bread (Ex. 12:15-20; Lev. 23:6-8; Deut. 16:3-4).
3. Firstfruits (Lev. 23:9-14).
4. Pentecost (Lev. 23:15-22; Deut. 16:9-12; Acts 2).
5. Trumpets (Lev. 23:23-25; Num. 10:1-10; 29:1-6).
6. Day of Atonement (Lev. 16:1-34; 23:26-32).
7. Tabernacles (Lev. 23:33-44; Deut. 16:13-15; Neh. 8).

Fulfilled in Christ ✝

Jesus Christ is revealed in each of the seven feasts of Jehovah:

1. Passover: He is our Savior, whose sacrificial blood was shed at Calvary (Jn. 1:29; 1 Cor. 5:6-8).
2. Unleavened bread: He is the Bread of life, the One who removed the leaven of sin from mankind (Jn. 6:48).
3. Firstfruits: He is the resurrected Messiah, the firstfruits of them that slept (1 Cor. 15:20).
4. Pentecost: He fulfilled the law and is the Anointed One who baptizes with the Holy Ghost (Lk. 4:16-21; Acts 1:5).
5. Trumpets: He is the clear-sounding, living Word who introduced the message of perfection (maturity), the One who was the beginning of it (Jn. 6:63; Rev. 3:14).
6. Day of Atonement: He is the High Priest who atoned for man, the Scapegoat and Lord's goat who put away sin, sickness, poverty, and death (Is. 53; Gal. 3:13-14).
7. Tabernacles: He is all the fullness of the Godhead bodily, the Lord of this feast, the Booth in whom the Father lived and moved and had His being (Jn. 17).

Applied to the Christian ⚖️

Each of the seven Feasts of Jehovah reveal our progressive walk in Christ in the following ways:

1. Passover: We are redeemed by His blood and saved from the destroyer (Rom. 5:9-10; 1 Pet. 1:18-19).
2. Unleavened bread: We forsake Egypt and begin to walk with God in holiness, sincerity, and truth (1 Cor. 5:5-8).
3. Firstfruits: We arise to walk in newness of life, knowing Him in the power of His resurrection (Rom. 6:1-14; Phil. 3:10-11).
4. Pentecost: We are filled with the Holy Spirit and endued with power from on high (Acts 2:1-4; Eph. 1:13-14).
5. Trumpets: We hear the call to come to maturity within the rent veil (Joel 2:1,14-18; Rev. 1:10; 4:1-2).
6. Day of Atonement: We experience the baptism of fire as we afflict our soul, humbling ourselves (Jas. 4:10; 1 Pet. 5:6).
7. Tabernacles: We will receive the full adoption and the redemption of our bodies, becoming a tabernacle for all the fullness of God (see Rom. 8:14-23; 1 Cor. 13:8-13; Eph. 3:19; 4:13).

Go Deeper 📖

See Ex. 5:1; 12:14,17; 23:14; 1 Kings 8:2; 2 Chron. 7:8; 35:17; Ezra 3:4; 6:22; Ps. 42:4; 81:3; 118:27; Ezek. 45:17; Hos. 9:5; Nahum 1:15; Zech. 14:16-19; Mt. 23:6; 26:5; Mk. 15:6; Lk. 2:41-42; 14:12-24; 22:1; Jn. 2:23; 4:45; 5:1; 6:4; 12:12,20; 13:1; 21:20; Acts 18:21; Col. 2:16; Rev. 19:9,17.

∽ ∽ ∽

Feeble Knees

Exhaustion, weakness

Key Scriptures: Job 4:4; Ps. 105:37; Is. 35:3; Heb. 12:12.

Foundational Information ✎

Feeble knees are weak knees. This describes persons who are unstable or exhausted. "Feeble" is from the Hebrew root *kashal* (Strong's #3782), which means "to totter or waver (through weakness of the legs, especially the ankle); by implication, to falter, stumble, faint or fall." Compare *kara'* (Strong's #3766), which means "to bend the knee; by implication, to sink, to prostrate." The Greek word *paraluo* (Strong's #3886) means "to loosen beside, relax (perfect passive participle, paralyzed or enfeebled)."

Fulfilled in Christ 🕆

Jesus Christ took upon Himself all the sinful weaknesses, infirmities, and frailties of the human race (Mt. 8:17). The shed blood of the Passover Lamb is the ground of our justification, restoring our right standing with God (Rom. 5:9). When Jehovah brought the children of Israel out of Egypt by the strength of His mighty hand (a picture of our deliverance from sin), "there was not one feeble person among their tribes" (Ps. 105:37). Jesus is the living Word who has upheld us from falling, strengthening the "feeble knees" (Job 4:4; see also Jn. 1:1). He declared, "Come unto Me, all ye that labour [to the point of exhaustion] and are heavy laden, and I will give you rest" (Mt. 11:28).

Applied to the Christian ⚖

Adam's transgression caused the human race to stumble and fall (Rom. 5:12-21), ultimately to be exhausted by sin (Rom. 6:23). The old man was sown in weakness; the new creation man has been raised in power (1 Cor. 15:43; compare Rom. 8:3; 2 Cor. 13:4)! Christ has redeemed us from the curse and weakness of the law (Rom. 8:3; Gal. 3:13-14; Heb. 7:18). The strong water of His Word has touched and healed our "ankles" (Ezek. 47:3; compare Acts 3:1-10). Isaiah encourages us to share His great love with others, "Strengthen ye the weak hands, and confirm the feeble knees" (Is. 35:3). The writer to the Hebrews confirms this: "Wherefore lift up the hands which hang down, and the feeble knees" (Heb. 12:12). Paul admonished, "Him that is weak in the faith receive ye..." (Rom. 14:1; compare Rom. 15:1; 1 Cor. 9:22).

Go Deeper 📖

See Gen. 30:42; Deut. 25:18; 1 Sam. 2:5; 2 Sam. 3:39; 2 Chron. 28:15; Neh. 4:2; Job 4:3; Ps. 6:2; 38:8; Prov. 30:26; Is. 16:14; Ezek. 21:7; Joel 3:10; Zech. 12:8; Mt. 26:41; Lk. 5:18-24; Acts 8:7; 9:33; 20:35; 1 Cor. 1:25-27; 12:22; 2 Cor. 12:9-10; Gal. 4:9; 1 Thess. 5:14; Heb. 11:34.

∾ ∾ ∾

𝕱𝖊𝖓𝖈𝖊 (𝕱𝖊𝖓𝖈𝖊𝖉 𝕮𝖎𝖙𝖞)

Protection, isolation; a hardened heart or mind

Key Scriptures: Josh. 14:12; Jer. 19:15; Mic. 4:8; Zech. 9:12; 2 Cor. 10:3-6.

Foundational Information ✐

A fenced city is a fortified city, a walled city. "Fenced" is from the Hebrew *mibtsar* (Strong's #4013), which means "a fortification, castle, or fortified city; figuratively, a defender." It is also translated in the King James Version as "fortress, stronghold." Its root is *batsar* (Strong's #1219), which means "to be isolated (inaccessible by height or fortification)."

Fulfilled in Christ ☦

Jesus Christ is the strong Rock of Ages, mankind's only protection from death, the penalty of sin. He alone is our defense and Defender (Nahum 1:7; Zech. 9:12). Our King has been exalted "far above" all principalities and powers, inaccessible to the evil one (Eph. 1:20-23). From another perspective, the Lord is against every proud, independent spirit that refuses to submit to His rightful jurisdiction. He sternly warns us through His weeping prophet, "Behold, I will bring upon this city and upon all her towns all the evil that I have pronounced against it, because they have hardened their necks, that they might not hear my words" (Jer. 19:15; compare Rev. 18:2).

Applied to the Christian ⚖

Believers are safe and secure, protected and preserved by Christ and His finished work. The Church is the City of God, the stronghold of Zion (2 Sam. 5:7: Mt. 5:14; compare Heb. 12:22-24). Micah prophesied, "And thou, O tower of the flock, the strong hold of the daughter of Zion, unto thee shall it come, even the first dominion; the kingdom shall come..." (Mic. 4:8; see also Dan. 7:27; Mt. 6:33; Lk. 12:32).

In another application, we, like Caleb, are to possess the fenced cities of every giant (Josh. 14:12). Paul explained, "(For the weapons of our warfare are not carnal, but mighty through God to the pulling down of strong holds;) casting down imaginations, and every high thing that exalteth itself against the knowledge of God..." (2 Cor. 10:4-5). Man's haughty, hardened attitudes toward the Lord are but "a bowing wall" and "a tottering fence" (Ps. 62:3).

Go Deeper 📖

See Ex. 14:8; Num. 32:17,36; Deut. 2:30; 3:5; 9:1; 15:7; 28:52; 2 Sam. 20:6; 2 Kings 3:19; 17:9,14; 18:13; 2 Chron. 8:5; 19:5; 33:14; 36:13; Neh. 9:16-17; Job 9:4;

10:11; 19:8; Ps. 95:8; Is. 2:15; 5:2; Jer. 5:17; 7:26; 15:20; Ezek. 36:35; Dan. 5:20; Hos. 8:14; Zeph. 1:16; Mk. 6:52; 8:17; Jn. 12:40; Acts 19:9; Heb. 3:8,13,15; 4:7.

∾   ∾   ∾

Fetters

Bondages; complete obedience

Key Scriptures: Job 36:8; Ps. 105:18; 149:8; Is. 42:7; Mk. 5:4; Eph. 4:1; Phil. 2:8.

Foundational Information

Usually made of iron or bronze, fetters were shackles or chains attached to the ankles of prisoners to restrain movement. "Fetter" is from the Hebrew *nechosheth* (Strong's #5178), meaning "copper, hence, something made of that metal; coin, a fetter." It can also mean "bronze chains." Compare *kebel* (Strong's #3525), which means "to twine or braid together; a fetter." The Greek word is *pede* (Strong's #3976). It means "a shackle for the feet."

Fulfilled in Christ

At Calvary, Jesus Christ was shackled by mankind's sin. (Brass or bronze is a symbol of judgment.) Nails fixed Christ's hands and feet to the cross (Lk. 24:39-40; Jn. 20:25). Jesus, a prisoner of His Father's will, "became obedient unto death, even the death of the cross" (Phil. 2:8). He was the heavenly Joseph, "whose feet they [evil men] hurt with fetters: he was laid in iron" (Ps. 105:18). The prophet Isaiah described the mission of Messiah, the servant of Jehovah: "To open the blind eyes, to bring out the prisoners from the prison, and them that sit in darkness out of the prison house" (Is. 42:7; compare Lk. 4:17-21; Col. 1:12-13; 1 Pet. 2:9-10). The New Covenant in His blood has brought the prisoners out of the pit (Zech. 9:11).

Applied to the Christian

All our sins, judged in Christ at Calvary, bound Him to the cross. We once were wild and untamed (Mk. 5:4), bound by the fetters of sin and "cords of affliction" (Job 36:8). Now we are bound to obey His will, as was Paul, "the prisoner of the Lord" (Eph. 4:1). The waters of life have liberated our "ancles" to walk in His paths (Ezek. 47:3; compare Acts 3:7). Our captivity has been turned (Ps. 126:1). Now through spiritual warfare, we can bind kings with chains, and nobles with fetters of iron (Ps. 149:8; Eph. 6:12). Now we are "prisoners of hope," sons of God who have been promised the double portion (Zech. 9:12). It is important that we obey God in every circumstance by praying and singing His praises, even in times of great testing and difficulty, because the "prisoners" are listening (Acts 16:25)!

Go Deeper 📖

See Gen. 39:20-22; Num. 21:1; Judg. 16:21; 2 Sam. 3:34; 2 Kings 25:7; 2 Chron. 33:11; 36:6; Job 3:18; Ps. 69:33; 79:11; 102:20; 146:7; Is. 10:4; 20:4; 24:22; 38:17-18; 49:9; 51:1,14; Mt. 12:11; 27:15-16; Lk. 8:29; Acts 23:18; 27:1; 28:17; Eph. 3:1; 2 Tim. 1:8; Philem. 1,9.

∾ ∾ ∾

Fever

The infection of sin; lust; covetousness

Key Scriptures: Lev. 26:16; Deut. 28:22; Lk. 4:38-39;
Jn. 4:46-54; Acts 28:8; Rom. 7:7; Gal. 5:19-21.

Foundational Information ✎

The King James Version uses the word "fever" to describe a burning fever, the most common of which were malaria and typhoid. "Fever" is from the Hebrew *qaddachath* (Strong's #6920), which means "inflammation, febrile disease." The King James Version also renders it as "burning ague." Its primitive root *qadach* means "to inflame."

The Greek word *puresso* (Strong's #4445) means "to be on fire, (specifically) to have a fever." Its root *pur* is the word for "fire." Compare *puroo* (Strong's #4448), which means "to kindle, to be ignited, glow, be refined, or (figuratively) to be inflamed (with anger, grief, lust)." The New Testament word for "lust" is *epithumia* (Strong's #1939). It means "a longing (especially for what is forbidden)." It is also translated in the King James Version as "concupiscence, desire." The verb *epithumeo*, the word for "covet," means "to set the heart upon, long for (rightfully or otherwise)." Compare *thumos* ("passion, as if breathing hard") and *thuo* ("to rush, breathe hard").

Fulfilled in Christ ✝

Jesus Christ, the fountain of the water of life (Rev. 21:6), came to earth to put out the fire of the spiritual fever of man's sin. He healed Simon Peter's mother-in-law, rebuking her physical fever (Lk. 4:38-39). The nobleman of Capernaum had a son whose fever was healed by the Lord at the seventh hour (Jn. 4:52).

Our Savior was sinless. He never succumbed to the fever of lust (Heb. 4:15; 7:26). He constantly walked and lived in the Spirit, never fulfilling the heated desires of the flesh (Gal. 5:16). Jesus warned His disciples about the cares of this world "and the lusts of other things entering in" that choke the Word (Mk. 4:19). He also warned, "Beware of covetousness: for a man's life consisteth not in the abundance of the things which he possesseth" (Lk. 12:15).

Applied to the Christian   ⚖

Included in the curse of the law described in Deuteronomy 28 was consumption, fever, inflammation, and "an extreme burning" (Deut. 28:22; compare Gal. 3:13-14). The fevered longing for sin and the things of the world used to infect our members (Eph. 2:3; 4:22), but we have been delivered by Jesus' death, burial and resurrection (Rom. 6:1-14). Paul explained, "I had not known sin, but by the law: for I had not known lust, except the law had said, Thou shalt not covet" (Rom. 7:7). Those who belong to Jesus have crucified the flesh with all its fevers and desires (Gal. 5:24). Believers have been given authority over disease in the name of Jesus (Mk. 16:18). Paul knew this when he found Publius' father laying sick of a fever—he "prayed, and laid his hands on him, and healed him" (Acts 28:8).

Go Deeper   📖

See Ex. 15:9; 20:17; Josh. 7:21; Ps. 78:18,30; 81:12; Prov. 6:25; Mt. 5:28; Mk. 1:30-31; Jn. 8:44; Acts 20:33; Rom. 1:24,27; 6:12; 13:14; 1 Cor. 10:6; 12:31; 14:39; 1 Thess. 4:5; 1 Tim. 6:9-10; 2 Tim. 2:22; 3:6; 4:3; Tit. 2:12; 3:3; Jas. 1:14-15; 4:1-3; 1 Pet. 1:14; 2:11; 4:2-3; 2 Pet. 1:4; 2:10,18; 3:3; 1 Jn. 2:15-17; Jude 16-18.

∞ ∞ ∞

𝕱𝖎𝖊𝖑𝖉

The world

Key Scriptures: Mt. 4:8; 13:38; Jn. 1:29; 3:16-19; 4:42; 8:12; Rom. 12:2; 1 Jn. 2:15-17.

Foundational Information   ✎

A field is a plot of open ground that might be used for many different purposes. In contrast to an enclosed land, such as a vineyard, a field was not generally closed in.

"Field" is from the Hebrew *sadeh* (Strong's #7704), which means "to spread out; a field (as flat)." This word often represents the "open field" where animals roam wild. The Greek word is *agros* (Strong's #68), which means "a field (as a drive for cattle); the country; specially, a farm, hamlet."

The Greek word for "world" is *kosmos* (Strong's #2889), which means "orderly arrangement, decoration; by implication, the world." It denotes an order, a system, an arrangement of things, a mindset. There is a difference between the "earth" and the "world."

Fulfilled in Christ

Jesus is the Christ, the Savior and Light of the world (Jn. 4:42; 8:12). He taught, "The field is the world; the good seed are the children of the kingdom; but the tares are the children of the wicked one" (Mt. 13:38). The part of the field covenantally belonging to our heavenly Boaz is the local church. All churches are to be under the jurisdiction of our Redeemer and King (Ruth 2:3). In His temptation, the devil took Jesus up into a high mountain, and showed Him "all the kingdoms of the world" (Mt. 4:8). Jesus was the Lamb of God who took away the sin of the world (Jn. 1:29; see also Jn. 3:16-19). God was in Christ, reconciling the world unto Himself (2 Cor. 5:19). John declared, "The kingdoms of this world are become the kingdoms of our Lord, and of his Christ" (Rev. 11:15).

Applied to the Christian

John explained, "Love not the world, neither the things that are in the world…the lust of the flesh, and the lust of the eyes, and the pride of life…And the world passeth away, and the lust thereof: but he that doeth the will of God abideth for ever" (1 Jn. 2:15-17). The psalmist added, "As for man, his days are as grass: as a flower of the field, so he flourisheth" (Ps. 103:15). Worldly Esau was a cunning hunter, "a man of the field" (Gen. 25:27; compare Heb. 12:16-17). Jesus warned, "For what is a man profited, if he shall gain the whole world, and lose his own soul?" (Mt. 16:26a) Satan is the prince and god of this world (see Jn. 12:31; 14:30; 16:11; 2 Cor. 4:4). Paul declared, "Now we have received, not the spirit of the world, but the spirit which is of God" (1 Cor. 2:12a). The apostle would only boast in the cross of Christ, saying, "by whom the world is crucified unto me, and I unto the world" (Gal. 6:14). Friendship with the world is enmity with God (Jas. 4:4).

Go Deeper

See Ps. 50:11; 78:12,43; 80:13; Jn. 1:10; 4:35; 6:33; 18:36; Acts 1:18-19; Rom. 12:2; 1 Cor. 1:21,27; 3:19; 2 Cor. 7:10; Gal. 4:3; Eph. 2:2,12; 6:12; Phil. 2:15; Col. 2:8,20; 1 Tim. 1:15; 6:7; Heb. 11:7,38; Jas. 1:27; 2 Pet. 1:4; 2:20; 1 Jn. 3:1; 3:13; 4:5; 5:4.

∞ ∞ ∞

Field of Blood

The world redeemed by Jesus' blood; betrayal

Key Scriptures: Zech. 11:12; Mt. 13:38; 27:6-10; Jn. 17:12; Acts 1:18-19; 2 Thess. 2:3-4.

Foundational Information ✐

Aceldama, or "the field of blood," previously known as the "potter's field," was purchased by the chief priests as a burial place for strangers. It was the place where Judas, the disciple who betrayed Jesus, died. "Blood" is from the Greek *haima* (Strong's #129), which means "blood, literally (of men or animals), figuratively (the juice of grapes) or specially (the atoning blood of Christ); by implication bloodshed, also kindred."

The Greek word for "redeem" is *agorazo* (Strong's #59), which means "to go to market, by implication) to purchase; specially, to redeem." It can also mean "to buy or sell." "Betray" is from the Hebrew *ramah* (Strong's #7411), which means "to hurl; specifically, to shoot; figuratively, to delude or betray (as if causing to fall)." The Greek word *paradidomi* means "to surrender, yield up, intrust, transmit." It also means "to hand over."

Fulfilled in Christ ☨

Judas Iscariot betrayed our Lord for 30 pieces of silver (Zech. 11:12; compare Mt. 10:4; 26:21-25; 27:3-4). The chief priests took that silver (a symbol for redemption) and "bought the potter's field, to bury strangers in" (Mt. 27:7). Jesus Christ died for the sins of the whole world, buying the field with His "own blood" (Mt. 13:38; see also Acts 20:28; Heb. 9:12; 13:12; Rev. 1:5). Cracked and discarded pottery vessels are a picture of broken humanity redeemed by grace and faith. His finished work provided the means whereby men might be made "again" through the new birth (Jer. 18:4; Jn. 3:3,7). Jesus joyfully gave His all to buy the whole field that He might obtain the hidden treasure He had found in it—His Church (Mt. 13:44)!

Applied to the Christian ⚖

All men were estranged from God by Adam's transgression (Rom. 3:10,23; 5:12-21). The field of blood is where the "stranger," the old Adamic man, fractured by sin, is buried! Said another way, it was the place where Judas died—Judas' "reward of iniquity" for betraying innocent blood was death (Acts 1:18; see also Rom. 6:23). Matthew's Gospel adds that he "hanged himself" there (Mt. 27:5). The old man has been crucified (Gal. 5:24; compare Esther 7:10). Judas, also called "the son of perdition ['destruction']" (Jn. 17:12), is a picture of the carnal mind. This "son of perdition" opposes and exalts himself above all that is called God (the Word), so that he "as God" (the spirit of antichrist) sits in the "temple" (*naos,* the spiritual temple), ever trying to upsurp the place of God with his own ideas, customs, and traditions (2 Thess. 2:3-4). The son of perdition is buried in the field of Jesus' blood!

Go Deeper 📖

See Gen. 25:10; 49:32; Ex. 15:16; 21:32; Lev. 25:33; 27:1-7; Ruth 4:4-10; 2 Sam. 24:21-24; 1 Chron. 12:17; Ps. 41:9; 74:2; 78:54; Jer. 32:7-16,25,43-44; Hos. 3:2; Mt. 17:22; 13:46; 20:18; 24:10; 26:2,15,45-48; Mk. 13:12; Jn. 13:2,18; Acts 8:20; 1 Cor. 6:20; 7:23; 11:23; Eph. 1:14; 2 Pet. 2:1.

∞   ∞   ∞

𝔉𝔦𝔤

The fruitfulness of God's people

Key Scriptures: Is. 5:1-2; 38:21; Mt. 21:19-21; Jn. 15:1-16; Gal. 5:22-23; Col. 1:10.

Foundational Information ✐

The fig is a pear-shaped fruit often used for food and prized for its sweetness and flavor. The blooms of the fig tree (which can be either a tall tree or a low-spreading shrub) always appear in the spring before the leaves. Figs were eaten fresh, pressed into cakes, and used externally as a poultice. "Fig" is from the Hebrew *te'en* (Strong's #8384), which means "the fig (tree or fruit)." Compare the Greek words *suke* ("fig tree") and *sukon* ("fig").

Fulfilled in Christ ⵉ

Jesus Christ, the Tree of life and the true Vine, is the fruitful fig tree from Heaven (Gen. 2:9; Jn. 15:1-5; Rev. 22:14). Through Calvary's cross, He has been pressed into a corporate Man, the Body of Christ (1 Cor. 10:16-17). He was the lump of figs laid "for a plaster" upon mankind's boil, bringing healing from the sickness of sin (Is. 38:21). Jesus cursed a fig tree because it bore leaves without fruit (Mt. 21:19-21). He also used the fig tree in His parables (Lk. 13:6-7; 21:29-31). Our King is the well beloved who has a vine-yard (His Church) in the very fruitful hill of Zion (Is. 5:1; Heb. 12:22-24). Jesus chose and ordained the Church to bring forth fruit that remains (Jn. 15:16).

Applied to the Christian ⚖

Our new nature in Christ is the fruit of the Spirit, the divine nature of Jesus (Gal. 5:22-23; 2 Pet. 1:4). Canaan, a type of the heavenly places of Ephesians, was a "land of wheat, and barley, and vines, and fig trees, and pomegranates; a land of oil olive, and honey" (Deut. 8:8; see also Eph. 1:3; 2:6). Under the peaceful reign of Christ, every member of His Body is to be fruitful, each living under his own fig tree (1 Kings 4:25). Solomon wisely declared, "Whoso keepeth the fig tree shall eat the fruit thereof: so he that waiteth on his master shall be honoured" (Prov. 27:18). Paul prayed that God's people "might walk worthy of the Lord unto all pleasing, being fruitful in every good work..." (Col. 1:10).

Go Deeper 📖

See Gen. 1:22,28; 3:7; 9:1; 17:6; 41:52; 49:22; Num. 13:23; 1 Kings 4:25; 20:7; 1 Chron. 12:40; Neh. 13:15; Ps. 105:33; 128:3; Song 2:13; Is. 34:4; Jer. 8:13; 24:1-8; 23:3; Hos. 2:12; 9:10; Joel 1:7,12; 2:22; Amos 4:9; Mic. 4:4; Hab. 3:17; Mt. 7:16; 13:23; 24:32; Mk. 4:28; 11:13,20-21; Lk. 6:44; Jn. 1:48; Rev. 6:13.

∾ ∾ ∾

𝔉illet

Covenantal union

Key Scriptures: Num. 27:10-11; Ps. 133:1-3;
1 Cor. 6:17; Eph. 4:1-7,13; 1 Tim. 2:5.

Foundational Information ✍

Fillets were silver connecting rods that united the brass pillars in Moses' tabernacle. "Fillet" is from the Hebrew *chashuq* (Strong's #2838), which means "attached, a fence-rail or rod connecting the posts or pillars." Its root is *chashaq* (Strong's #2836), which means "to cling, join, (figuratively) to love, delight in." There was also a "fillet" circum-ferencing each of the two pillars in Solomon's Temple. This latter word is *chuwt* (Strong's #2339), and it means "to sew; a string; by implication, a measuring tape." It is also trans-lated in the King James Version as "cord, line, thread."

Fulfilled in Christ ☥

Jesus is Heaven's measuring tape—His Church is destined to come to His full meas-ure: into "the unity of the faith" (Eph. 4:13; compare Jn. 17:17-24). His righteous life is the canon, rule, and rod by which all men are to be judged (Jn. 5:22). Paul declared, "There is one mediator between God and men, the man Christ Jesus" (1 Tim. 2:5). All genuine human relationships and covenants must be horizontally mediated by Him. The fillets were made "of silver" (Ex. 27:10-11), a symbol for redemption. Jesus' blood of the New Covenant has made us one (Gal. 3:13-14,28; Rev. 1:5)! All true unity in the Body of Christ flows down from our exalted High Priest: "It is like the precious ointment [the anointing] upon the head...that went down to the skirts of [Aaron's] garments" (Ps. 133:2).

Applied to the Christian ⚖

Those joined covenantally to the Lord are one spirit with Him (1 Cor. 6:17). Unity cannot be created; it can only be kept, based on the seven absolutes revealed by the apostle Paul (Eph. 4:3-7). The psalmist declared, "Behold, how good and how pleasant it is for brethren to dwell together in unity!" (Ps. 133:1). Like the wings of the cherubim which were "joined one to another" (Ezek. 1:9,11), Christians are united in their prayer and praise (2 Chron. 5:13; Acts 4:24). Believers are joined to Jesus as a wife is to her husband in the covenant of marriage (Mt. 19:6; Eph. 5:31). Paul admonished us to be "perfectly joined together in the same mind and in the same judgment" (1 Cor. 1:10).

Go Deeper   📖

See Gen. 29:34; Ex. 28:7; 36:38; 38:10-12,17,19; Josh. 2:18; 1 Kings 7:15; Ps. 83:8; Eccles. 4:12; Song 4:3; Jer. 52:21; Ezek. 37:17; Zech. 2:11; Mk. 10:9; Lk. 15:15; Jn. 17:11; Acts 1:14; 2:1,46; 5:13,36; 8:29; 9:26; 18:7; 1 Cor. 6:16; Eph. 4:16; 5:31; Phil. 2:2.

∞   ∞   ∞

𝕱𝖎𝖑𝖙𝖍

The uncleanness of sin; moral depravity

Key Scriptures: Is. 4:4; 64:6; Ezek. 36:25; Rom. 3:10,23; 1 Jn. 1:7-9.

Foundational Information   ✎

Filth is foul or dirty matter; figuratively, it is ceremonial uncleanness or spiritual corruption. "Filth" is from the Hebrew *'alach* (Strong's #444), which means "to muddle, (figuratively and intransitive) to turn (morally) corrupt." The Greek word *rhupoo* (Strong's #4510) means "to soil, to become dirty (morally)." Its root *rhupos* means "dirt, (morally) depravity."

Fulfilled in Christ ✝

Jesus Christ is the sinless, spotless Lamb of God who died to cleanse mankind from the filth of sin (Jn. 1:29; Heb. 7:26). The changing of Joshua's filthy garments points to the changing of the law and the priesthood by the finished work of Christ (Zech. 3:3-4; Rom. 8:1-4; Heb. 7:12). Through the washing of regeneration, Jesus has sprinkled the water of His Word upon us, cleansing us from all filthiness and idolatry (Ezek. 36:25; Tit. 3:5). The blood of Jesus Christ cleanses us from all sin. If we will confess our sin, our great High Priest is faithful and just to forgive and cleanse us from all unrighteousness (1 Jn. 1:7-9). He declared, "Now ye are clean through the word which I have spoken unto you" (Jn. 15:3; compare Eph. 5:25-27).

Applied to the Christian ⚖

By nature, all men are morally depraved: "There is none righteous, no, not one...For all have sinned, and come short of the glory of God" (Rom. 3:10,23). Man, hopelessly and helplessly lost in his sin, cannot save himself by religious works, for "all our righteousnesses are as filthy rags" (Is. 64:6). Apart from Christ, men are abominably filthy, drinking iniquity like water (Job 15:16). Isaiah foresaw a day when God would cleanse His people and wash away the filth of the daughters of Zion (local churches) (Is. 4:4). Christians are to put away all "filthy communication" out of their mouths (Col. 3:8). The psalmist cried out to be cleansed from "secret faults" (Ps. 19:12). John concluded, "He...which is filthy, let him be filthy still: and he that is righteous, let him be righteous still..." (Rev. 22:11).

Go Deeper 📖

See Lev. 13–14; 2 Chron. 29:5; Ezra 6:21; 9:11; Ps. 14:3; 51:2; 53:3; 119:9; Prov. 30:12; Is. 6:5; 28:8; Lam. 1:9; Ezek. 16:36; 22:15; 24:11-13; Nahum 3:6; Zeph. 3:1; 1 Cor. 4:13; 2 Cor. 7:1; Gal. 5:19; Eph. 4:19; 5:3-4; 1 Tim. 3:3,8; Tit. 1:7,11; Jas. 1:21; 1 Pet. 3:21; 5:2; Jude 8; Rev. 17:4; 19:8,14.

∾ ∾ ∾

Fine Flour

The character of Christ; the balanced Word of God
Key Scriptures: Lev. 2:1-11; Jn. 1:1,14; 6:48; 1 Cor. 10:16-17; Heb. 3:14.

Foundational Information ✏

Flour is ground grain from which bread is baked, a fine substance made from wheat, with all the bran removed. "Flour" is from the Hebrew *coleth* (Strong's #5560), which means "to strip; flour (as chipped off)". It is translated in the King James Version as "(fine) flour, meal." The Greek word *semidalis* (Strong's #4585) means "fine wheaten flour."

Fulfilled in Christ ✝

Jesus Christ is the Bread of life, the Word made flesh (Jn. 1:1,14; 6:48). He "chipped off" His deity, took upon Himself the likeness of a servant, and was made in the likeness of men (Is. 42:1-5; Jn. 13:1-5; Phil. 2:7). Jesus was very God and very man, the two natures perfectly blended in the mystery of His incarnation (1 Tim. 3:16). Our Savior was the "express image" or "character" of the Father's person (Heb. 1:3). The law of the meal offering of fine flour was that oil (a symbol for the Holy Spirit) would be poured upon it (Lev. 2:1; compare Acts 10:38). The Messiah was anointed with the "oil of gladness" (Ps. 45:7; Heb. 1:9). Jesus is the continual, eternal meal offering by "perpetual ordinance" unto the Lord (Ezek. 46:14; see also Heb. 9:12-14).

Applied to the Christian ⚖

Paul declared, "The bread which we break, is it not the communion of the body of Christ? For we being many are one bread, and one body: for we are all partakers of that one bread" (1 Cor. 10:16b-17). We have become partakers of Jesus' divine nature (2 Pet. 1:4); His finished work has graced us with the privilege of sharing the "fine flour" of His balanced character and ministry in the following ways (Heb. 3:14):

1. The works of Christ (Mt. 11:2).
2. The Spirit of Christ (Rom. 8:9).
3. The love of Christ (Rom. 8:35).
4. The mind of Christ (1 Cor. 2:16).
5. The sufferings of Christ (2 Cor. 1:5).
6. The savour of Christ (2 Cor. 2:15).
7. The meekness and gentleness of Christ (2 Cor. 10:1).
8. The obedience of Christ (2 Cor. 10:5).
9. The power of Christ (2 Cor. 12:9).
10. The grace of Christ (Gal. 1:6).
11. The faith of Christ (Gal. 2:16).
12. The riches of Christ (Eph. 3:8).
13. The fulness of Christ (Eph. 4:13).
14. The knowledge of Christ (Phil. 3:8).
15. The name (nature) of Christ (1 Pet. 4:14).

Go Deeper 📖

See Ex. 29:2,40; 40:29; Lev. 5:11; 6:20; 7:12; 14:10,21; 23:17; Num. 4:16; 6:15; 7:13; 1 Sam. 1:24; 2 Sam. 17:28; 1 Kings 4:22; 8:64; 2 Kings 3:20; 1 Chron. 9:29; 21:23; 23:29; Ezra 7:17; Neh. 10:33; 13:5,9; Jer. 17:26; Ezek. 16:13,19; Joel 1:9,13; 2:14; Amos 5:22; Rev. 18:13.

∞ ∞ ∞

𝔉𝔦𝔫𝔢 𝔏𝔦𝔫𝔢𝔫

The righteousness of Christ; the righteous acts of saints

Key Scriptures: Lev. 6:10; Mt. 5:20; Rom. 5:18; 8:4; 14:17;
1 Cor. 1:30; Heb. 1:8-9; 7:2.

Foundational Information 📖

Fine linen is a cloth woven from fibers of the flax or hemp plant. It was used especially in the clothing of kings and priests. The Hebrew word meaning "whiteness" represents linen because bleached linen was so white. "Fine linen," also translated as "silk" in the King James Version, is from the Hebrew *shesh* (Strong's #8336), and it means "bleached stuff, white linen or (by analogy) marble." The Greek word *hussinos* (Strong's #1039) means "made of linen (neuter a linen cloth)." Its root *hussos* means "white linen."

The word for "righteousness" in Revelation 19:8 is *dikaioma* (Strong's #1345). It means "an equitable deed; by implication, a statute or decision." Also translated as "judgment, justification, ordinance" in the King James Version, it is taken from *dikaios* (Strong's #1342), which means "equitable (in character or act); by implication, innocent, holy."

Fulfilled in Christ ☀

Jesus is the King of righteousness, the heavenly Joseph arrayed in "vestures of fine linen" (Gen. 41:42; see also Heb. 7:2). The Father declared to the Son, "A sceptre of righteousness is the sceptre of Thy kingdom" (Heb. 1:8; compare Rom. 14:17). Paul described the fruit of Jesus' righteous act of complete obedience: "the free gift came upon all men unto justification of life" (Rom. 5:18). He added that Christ Jesus has been made unto us "wisdom, and righteousness, and sanctification, and redemption" (1 Cor. 1:30). Aaron was dressed in linen on the Day of Atonement (Lev. 16:4); Jesus, our great High Priest, has made atonement for sin through His blood (Lev. 17:11; Rom. 5:11; Heb. 9:22). The Master taught His disciples, "Except your righteousness shall exceed the righteousness of the scribes and Pharisees, ye shall in no case enter into the kingdom of heaven" (Mt. 5:20). Joseph of Arimathaea wrapped the body of Jesus in a clean linen cloth (Mt. 27:59; Mk. 15:46).

Applied to the Christian ⚖

John described the Church, the Lamb's wife: "And to her was granted that she should be arrayed in fine linen, clean and white: for the fine linen is the righteousness of saints" (Rev. 19:8). Because of Christ's finished work, the righteous acts of the law are fulfilled in those who walk after the Spirit (Rom. 8:4). The priests of the Old Testament were covered with fine linen prefiguring the priesthood of believers adorned with the righteousness of Christ (Ex. 28:42; 39:27-29; Lev. 6:10). The "woolen" garments of Adam (causing sweat) and the "linen" garments of our new nature in Christ are not to be worn together (Deut. 22:11; Ezek. 44:17-18; compare Rom. 6:1-14). Christ has made us to become kings and priests (Rev. 1:6; 5:10).

Go Deeper 📖

See Ex. 25:4; 26:1,31,36; 27:9,16,18; 28:5-8,15,39; 35:25,35; Lev. 16:23,32; Deut. 22:11; 1 Sam. 2:18; 22:18; 2 Sam. 6:14; 1 Chron. 4:21; 15:27; 2 Chron. 2:14; 3:14; Esther 1:6; 8:15; Prov. 7:16; 31:24; Jer. 13:1; Ezek. 9:2-3,11; 10:1-10; 16:13; Dan. 10:5; 12:6-7; Mk. 14:51-52; Lk. 24:12; Jn. 20:5-6; Rev. 15:6; 18:16; 19:14.

∞ ∞ ∞

𝔉inger

The power of the Holy Ghost to do God's work and will

Key Scriptures: Ex. 8:19; Deut. 9:10; Ps. 8:3; Mt. 12:28; Lk. 11:20; Acts 1:8; 10:38; 1 Cor. 4:20.

Foundational Information ✐

The finger is a part of the hand; figuratively, it refers to the power of God. "Finger" is from the Hebrew *'etsba'* (Strong's #676), which means "(in the sense of grasping) something to seize with, a finger; by analogy, a toe." The Greek word for "finger" is *daklutlos,* taken from the root *deka* ("ten").

Fulfilled in Christ ✝

In Matthew's Gospel, Jesus demonstrated His Kingdom by casting out demons "by the Spirit of God" (Mt. 12:28). In Luke's parallel text, the King explained this power to be done "with the finger of God" (Lk. 11:20). Jesus is the heavenly Moses who defeated the magicians of Pharaoh (a type of satan) with "the finger of God" (Ex. 8:19; see also Mk. 1:39; Jn. 1:17). The Pattern Son was birthed through the power of the Holy Spirit (Lk. 1:35). The life of the living Word (Jn. 1:1,14) was "written with the finger of God" (Ex. 31:18; Deut. 9:10). Through His resurrection, our King was declared to be the Son of God with power (Rom. 1:4). Jesus of Nazareth was anointed with the Holy Ghost and power to heal all who were oppressed by the devil (Acts 10:38). The blood of Jesus' sacrifice is applied by the "finger" (Spirit) of God (Lev. 8:15; 9:9).

Applied to the Christian ⚖

Believers have been filled with the power of the Holy Spirit, the same Spirit that raised Jesus from the dead (Acts 1:8; Rom. 8:11; Eph. 1:19)! Paul declared that "the kingdom of God is not in word, but in power" (1 Cor. 4:20). The Master commissioned His disciples to cast out demons through the power of His name (Mt. 10:8; Mk. 16:17). Jesus prophesied to His followers, "But ye shall receive power, after that the Holy Ghost is come upon you: and ye shall be witnesses unto Me..." (Acts 1:8). The Word of the Lord unto Zerubbabel still admonishes us that it is "not by might, nor by power, but by my spirit, saith the Lord of hosts" (Zech. 4:6).

Go Deeper 📖

See Ex. 29:12; Lev. 4:6,17,25,30,34; 14:16,27; 16:14,19; Num. 19:4; 1 Kings 12:10; 2 Chron. 10:10; Ps. 8:3; 144:1; Prov. 7:3; Song 5:5; Is. 58:9; Dan. 5:5; Mic. 3:8; Mk. 7:33; Lk. 1:17; 4:14; 16:24; Jn. 8:6; 20:25-27; Acts 8:19; Rom. 15:13,19; 1 Cor. 2:4; 5:4; 1 Thess. 1:5; 2 Tim. 1:7.

∞ ∞ ∞

𝕱𝖎𝖗

Stability, steadfastness, strength; the blessings of God

Key Scriptures: 1 Kings 5:8-10; Prov. 10:22; Is. 55:13; 60:13; 1 Cor. 15:58; Eph. 1:3; Heb. 6:19.

Foundational Information ✏

The fir is a tall, vigorous evergreen tree of uncertain identity, perhaps pine, cypress, juniper, or cedar. The Israelites valued the timber of the fir tree for building the temple, for ship building, and for making musical instruments. This tree symbolically represented the blessings of God toward His people. "Fir" is from the Hebrew *berowsh* (Strong's #1265), which means "of uncertain derivation; a cypress tree; hence a lance or a musical instrument (as made of that wood)."

Fulfilled in Christ ✝

Jesus, the true Vine and the Tree of life is the "choice fir" from Heaven (2 Kings 19:23; see also Jn. 15:1-5; Rev. 22:14). Isaiah declared, "Instead of the thorn shall come up the fir tree...and it shall be to the Lord for a name..." (Is. 55:13). Instead of Adam's thorn-infested curse, Jesus sprang forth in resurrection to bring new life and blessing (Jn. 10:10; Gal. 3:13-14). The Ark of the Covenant steadily ascended into its permament place in Zion (1 Kings 8:8)—so the greatest Son of David was the instrument "made of fir wood" that the Father joyously played all the way from Bethlehem unto His victorious ascension and coronation (2 Sam. 6:5; see also Acts 2:33-36; Heb. 2:9)! Paul declared that the Father had "blessed us with all spiritual blessings in heavenly places in Christ" (Eph. 1:3). Solomon added, "The blessing of the Lord, it maketh rich, and He addeth no sorrow with it" (Prov. 10:22). Jesus is the "sure and stedfast" Anchor of our soul (Heb. 6:19).

Applied to the Christian ⚖

Solomon's temple was assembled with "fir trees" (1 Kings 5:8-10); Paul described the New Testament Temple, the Church, as a "building fitly framed together" (Eph. 2:21). The Shulamite, a type of the Bride of Christ, declared, "The beams of our house are cedar, and our rafters of fir" (Song 1:17). Christians are to be as musical instruments unto the Lord, fir trees who "rejoice" and praise His name (Is. 14:8). Isaiah foresaw the unity of the Body of Christ: "The glory of Lebanon shall come unto thee, the fir tree, the pine tree, and the box together, to beautify the place of My sanctuary; and I will make the place of My feet glorious" (Is. 60:13; see also Is. 41:19; 61:3). Like the fir tree, the Christian is to be "stedfast, unmoveable, always abounding in the work of the Lord" (1 Cor. 15:58).

Go Deeper 📖

See Gen. 39:5; 49:25-26; Deut. 16:17; 28:1-2; 33:23; 1 Kings 6:15,34; 9:11; 2 Chron. 2:8; 3:5; Ps. 21:3; 104:17; Prov. 10:6; 28:20; Is. 37:24; Ezek. 27:5; 31:8; Hos. 14:8; Nahum 2:3; Zech. 11:2; Mal. 3:10; Rom. 15:29; 1 Cor. 7:37; 10:16; 2 Cor. 1:7; Heb. 2:2; 3:14; 1 Pet. 5:9; Rev. 5:12-13.

∞ ∞ ∞

𝔉ire

The Word of God, the Spirit of God;
purification; trials; judgment; angels

Key Scriptures: Ex. 13:21-22; Deut. 24:17; 1 Kings 18:24;
Jer. 23:29; Mt. 5:14; Jn. 8:12; Heb. 12:29; 1 Pet. 1:7.

Foundational Information ✐

Fire is the combustion of flammable materials, and often appears as a symbol of God's holy presence and power. "Fire" is from the Hebrew *'esh* (Strong's #784). It is also translated in the King James Version as "burning, fiery, flaming, hot." Genesis 15:17 represents God's presence as a "burning lamp" or "torch of fire." The Greek word *pur* (Strong's #4442) means "fire (literally or figuratively, specifically, lightning)."

Fulfilled in Christ ☀

Jesus is God (Jn. 1:1), and "our God is a consuming fire" (Heb. 12:29; compare Jer. 23:29; Mal. 3:2). Moses observed that the appearance of the Lord's glory was like a "devouring fire" on top of the mountain (Ex. 24:17). Comparing Himself to the "pillar of fire" (Ex. 13:21-22; Neh. 9:12,19) that guided "the church in the wilderness" (Acts 7:38), Jesus proclaimed, "I am the light of the world: He that followeth Me shall not walk in darkness, but shall have the light of life" (Jn. 8:12). Christ our Passover has been sacrificed for us, roasted with the fire of His Father's passion (Ex. 12:8; compare 1 Cor. 5:7). Jesus is the fiery answer from Heaven for every human problem (1 Kings 18:24). Daniel and John described the eyes of the Lord to be like lamps of fire (see Dan. 10:6; Rev. 1:14; 2:18; 19:12). Jesus is the One who baptizes men with the Holy Ghost and fire (Mt. 3:10-12; Acts 2:3).

Applied to the Christian ⚖

Jesus called the Church "the light of the world" (Mt. 5:14). God has promised, "When thou...walkest through the fire, thou shalt not be burned; neither shall the flame kindle upon thee" (Is. 43:2). The faith of the believer is "tried with fire" (1 Pet. 1:7; compare 1 Cor. 3:13-15). But God has sent His ministering angels to help us (Heb. 1:14); these spirits are like "a flame of fire" (Heb. 1:7; compare Ps. 104:4). There is a fire in Zion (Is. 31:9; compare Heb. 12:22-24), progressively impacting our lives in the following five ways:

1. We will be by the fire (Lk. 22:56).
2. We will be under fire (Ex. 9:23-24).
3. We will be in the fire (Dan. 3:24-25).
4. We will be on fire (2 Pet. 3:12).
5. We will be as fire (Joel 2:5).

Go Deeper 📖

See Gen. 22:6-7; Ex. 3:2; 29:18; 35:3; Lev. 1:17; 3:5; 10:2; Num. 28:2; Deut. 4:11; 5:22; 18:16; 1 Sam. 2:28; 2 Chron. 7:1; Ps. 18:13; 29:7; 50:3; 78:14; 97:3; Song 8:6; Is. 4:5; 10:17; 33:14; 54:16; 66:15; Ezek. 1:4,27; Dan. 3:25; Joel 2:3; Obad. 18; Lk. 12:49; Acts 28:3; 2 Thess. 1:8; 2 Pet. 3:7,12; Jude 7; Rev. 4:5.

∞ ∞ ∞

Firepans

Zeal, motivation; ignition, quickening; divine apprehension

Key Scriptures: Ex. 27:3; Lev. 16:12; Is. 9:7; Jer. 20:9;
Jn. 2:17; Rom. 8:11; Tit. 2:14.

Foundational Information ✎

A firepan was a bronze utensil used to transport live coals used in starting a fire. "Firepan" is from the Hebrew *machtah* (Strong's #4289), which means "the sense of removal; a pan for live coals." It is also translated in the King James Version as "censer, snuffdish." Its root *chathah* (Strong's #2846) means "to lay hold of; especially to pick up fire."

The Hebrew word for "zeal" is *qin'ah* (Strong's #7068), which means "jealousy, envy." The Greek word is *zelos* (Strong's #2205), meaning "heat, (figuratively) zeal (in a favorable sense, ardor." It is derived from the primary verb *zeo* (Strong's #2204), which means "to be hot (boil, of liquids; or glow, of solids); figuratively, be fervid (earnest)."

Fulfilled in Christ ☦

Jesus Christ the Messiah, the Firepan from heaven who carried the passion of the Father, declared, through the words of the psalmist, "The zeal of Thine house hath eaten Me up" (Ps. 69:9; Jn. 2:17; compare Is. 9:7). The firepans of the tabernacle were made according to the "pattern" of Jehovah (Ex. 25:40; 27:3). Similarly, Messiah's every step was ordered by the Father (Jn. 8:29; compare Ps. 37:23; 1 Pet. 2:21). Jesus is the One who ignites and motivates His people, for "in Him we live, and move, and have our being" (Acts 17:28a). He was the divine censer "full of burning coals" taken from the Father's altar and sent to bring atonement to mankind (Lev. 16:12). The Savior's ardent devotion redeemed and purified unto Himself a people zealous of good works (Tit. 2:14).

Applied to the Christian   ⚖

When a man hears the Word of the Lord, he picks up fire! Jeremiah declared, "But His word was in mine heart as a burning fire shut up in my bones..." (Jer. 20:9b). We have been "apprehended" by the Lord for the high calling (Phil. 3:12-14). Our firepans have been taken away by religious Babylon, but God's outpoured Spirit is restoring a divine zeal for the house of the Lord (2 Kings 25:15-26; Jer. 52:19 with Joel 2:25-26)! Nadab and Abihu's "strange fire" (Lev. 10:1) is what Paul described as zeal without knowledge (Rom. 10:2). The fire of the Holy Spirit, who raised Jesus from the dead, will "quicken" ("vitalize, make alive") the believer (Rom. 8:11). The apostolic declaration underlying every motivation was simple: "For me to live is Christ!" (Phil. 1:21a)

Go Deeper   📖

See Ex. 25:38; 37:23; 38:3; Num. 4:9,14; 16:37-39; 1 Kings 7:50; 2 Kings 25:15; Jer. 52:18; Rom. 4:17; 8:19; 12:11; 15:23; 1 Cor. 12:31; 14:12; 2 Cor. 5:2; 7:7,11; 8:16; 9:2; Gal. 1:14; Phil. 1:20; 3:6; Col. 4:13; 1 Thess. 2:17; 1 Tim. 6:12-13,19; Heb. 2:1; 6:18; Jas. 5:16-17; Rev. 3:19.

∞ ∞ ∞

𝔉irmament

The heavenly places; the realm of the Spirit

Key Scriptures: Gen. 1:6-8,14-20; Ps. 19:1; Dan. 12:3; Lk. 3:21-23; Eph. 1:3,20; 2:6.

Foundational Information   ✎

The firmament is the expanse of sky and space in which the stars and planets are set, reflecting the greatness of the God who made it. "Firmament" is from the Hebrew *raqiya'* (Strong's #7549), which means "an expanse, the firmament or (apparently) visible arch of the sky." Its root *raqa'* (Strong's #7554) means "to pound the earth (as a sign of passion); by analogy to expand (by hammering); by implication, to overlay (with thin sheets of metal)." It is translated in the King James Version as "beat, make broad, spread abroad (forth, over, out, into plates), stamp, stretch."

Fulfilled in Christ   ※

The Book of Genesis records, "And God called the firmament Heaven" (Gen. 1:8). Jesus Christ created all things, including the firmament and all that is in it; indeed, "all things were made by Him" (Jn. 1:3,10; compare Col. 1:16). When our Lord was baptized, the heavens opened and stayed opened. Jesus lived and ministered in an "open heaven"— the realm of the Spirit was the constant sphere wherein He operated His supernatural ministry (Lk. 3:21-23; Jn. 1:51). Our exalted King has been set at the right hand of the Father "in the heavenly places" (Eph. 1:20). His finished work on the cross rent the veil and opened Heaven's door to provide access for His creation (Mt. 27:51-52; Rev. 4:1). Our King is coming again, for John declared, "And I saw heaven opened, and behold a white horse; and He that sat upon him was called Faithful and True, and in righteousness He doth judge and make war" (Rev. 19:11).

Applied to the Christian

Believers are blessed, having been seated in "heavenly places" (Eph. 1:3; 2:6). The expanse of the New Testament "firmament" is described as being "in Christ." Christians are the seed of Abraham (Gal. 3:7-9,16,29), pictured as the "stars" of the heavens (Gen. 15:5; 22:17; 26:4). Daniel predicted, "And they that be wise shall shine as the brightness of the firmament; and they that turn many to righteousness as the stars for ever and ever" (Dan. 12:3). Paul explained our new creation in Christ, "As is the earthy, such are they also that are earthy: and as is the heavenly, such are they also that are heavenly. And as we have borne the image of the earthy, we shall also bear [put on and wear as a garment] the image of the heavenly" (1 Cor. 15:48-49). The psalmist declared, "The heavens declare the glory of God; and the firmament sheweth His handywork" (Ps. 19:1; compare Eph. 3:10).

Go Deeper

See Gen. 7:11; Deut. 28:12; Ps. 78:23; 150:1; Ezek. 1:22-26; 10:1; Mal. 3:10; Mt. 5:14; Jn. 3:12; 8:12; 14:2; Acts 10:11; 26:19; Rom. 8:9; 1 Cor. 14:2; Gal. 3:3; 5:16,25; Eph. 3:10; 6:18; Phil. 3:3; 1 Tim. 3:16; 2 Tim. 4:8; Heb. 3:1; 6:4; 8:5; 9:23; 11:16; 12:22; 1 Pet. 4:6; Rev. 1:10; 4:1; 13:6; 15:5.

∞ ∞ ∞

Firstborn

Jesus, the Pattern Son and Heir; the double portion; that which is most excellent

Key Scriptures: Ex. 13:11-13; Deut. 21:15-17; 2 Kings 2; Rom. 8:29; 1 Cor. 15:20; Col. 1:15,18; Heb. 12:23.

Foundational Information

God placed a special claim on the firstborn, the first offspring of human beings or animals. "Firstborn" is from the Hebrew *bekowr* (Strong's #1060), which means "firstborn; hence, chief." It is also rendered in the King James Version as "eldest (son)," and it is derived from the root *bakar* (Strong's #1069), which means "to burst the womb, (causatively) bear or make early fruit (of woman or tree); also to give the birthright." In the New Testament, "firstborn" is the word *prototokos* (Strong's #4416), rendered also as "firstbegotten" in the King James Version. It is a compound of two words: *protos* (Strong's #4413), which means "foremost (in time, place, order or importance)"; and *tikto* (Strong's #5088), meaning "to produce (from seed, as a mother, a plant, the earth, etc.)."

Fulfilled in Christ

Jesus Christ, the virgin Mary's "firstborn son" (Mt. 1:25; Lk. 2:7), is the Pattern Son, the Heir of all things (Heb. 1:2). According to Paul, our risen King is firstborn over all as follows:

1. "The firstborn among many brethren" (Rom. 8:29).
2. "The firstborn of every creature" (Col. 1:15).
3. "The firstborn from the dead" (Col. 1:18; compare 1 Cor. 15:20; Heb. 1:6; Rev. 1:5).

Jesus is the "beginning" of His Father's strength, the excellency of dignity and power (Gen. 49:3). The psalmist prophesied of Messiah, "Also I will make him My first-born, higher than the kings of the earth" (Ps. 89:27; compare Eph. 1:20-23). His is the "more excellent" name, ministry, and sacrifice (Heb. 1:4; 8:6; 11:4).

Applied to the Christian

New Testament believers all belong to the one true Church, "the general assembly and church of the firstborn" (Heb. 12:23). Paul declared that we are "heirs" of God and "joint-heirs" with Christ (Rom. 8:17). As the husband and the wife are "heirs together" of the grace of life (1 Pet. 3:7), so are Christ and His Church (Eph. 5:22-33). We have been redeemed with a Lamb (Ex. 13:13; 1 Pet. 1:18-19) and blessed with the "double portion" (Deut. 21:17)—literally, "the portion of the firstborn" (see 2 Kings 2:9; Is. 61:7; Zech. 9:12). John exclaimed, "Behold, what manner of love the Father hath bestowed upon us, that we should be called the sons of God" (1 Jn. 3:1)!

Go Deeper

See Gen. 27:19; 48:14; Ex. 4:22; 6:14; 12:12; Num. 3:12-13; Josh. 6:26; Neh. 10:36; Ps. 78:51; 105:36; 135:8; 136:10; Is. 14:30; Jer. 31:9; Mic. 6:7; Zech. 12:10; Mt. 2:15; 3:17; 17:5; 21:37-38; Lk. 3:22; Acts 13:33; Rom. 4:13; Gal. 3:29; 4:1-7; Tit. 3:7; Heb. 1:5,14; 5:5; 6:17; 11:7-9;28; Jas. 2:5; Rev. 21:7.

∞ ∞ ∞

𝔉irstfruits

That which matures early; the choice part; the tithe

Key Scriptures: Ex. 23:16-17; Lev. 23:9-22; Prov. 3:9; Rom. 8:23; 1 Cor. 15:20.

Foundational Information ✐

The firstfruits is the firstborn of the flocks or the first vegetables and grains to be gathered at harvest time. They were thought of as belonging to God in a special sense. "Firstfruits" is from the Hebrew *bikkuwr* (Strong's #1061), which means "the first-fruits of the crop," as well as "beginning, first, choicest." Its root *bakar* (Strong's #1069) means "to burst the womb, (causatively) bear or make early fruit (of woman or tree)." Compare *re'shiyth* (Strong's #7225), which means "the first, in place, time, order or rank (specifically, a firstfruit)." Its root is *ro'sh,* the Hebrew word for "head."

Fulfilled in Christ ⵙ

Christ is the "Head" of the Church (Eph. 1:22-23; 5:23), the "firstfruits" of them that slept (1 Cor. 15:20). John revealed Him as the "beginning" ("chief") of the new creation (Rev. 3:14). Our risen King is the antitype of the Old Testament "sheaf of the firstfruits" (Lev. 23:9-14)—this representative sheaf was a "forerunner" sheaf (Heb. 6:19-20). Waved before the Father in His resurrection and ascension, Jesus was accepted for us (Jn. 20:16-17; Eph. 1:6-7). The Father gave His "best" when He gave Jesus (Num. 18:12; compare Jn. 3:16). Our Savior is the "choice vine" (Gen. 49:11; compare Jn. 15:1-5). The apostle Peter described His Lord as "a living stone, disallowed indeed of men, but chosen of God, and precious" (1 Pet. 2:4).

Applied to the Christian ⚖

The Church is a called-out people for His name, the firstfruits of His creation (Acts 15:14-18). The term "firstfruits" also speaks of the resurrection power of the new creation manifested as believers arise to walk in newness of life (Rom. 6:4). After the resurrection of Jesus (as recorded in the Book of Acts), 120, then 3,000, then 5,000 persons soon followed their heavenly Head and passed from death unto spiritual life (Jn. 5:24; Col. 1:9-13). The term "firstfruits" is particular to the Old Testament Feast of Pentecost (Ex. 23:16-17; Lev. 23:15-22). This New Testament experience was described by Paul as the "firstfruits" of the Spirit and the "earnest" of our inheritance (Rom. 8:23; Eph. 1:13-14). Believers are to tithe their substance (Mal. 3:8-12), bringing unto the Lord the "firstfruits" of all their increase (Prov. 3:9). God's end-time Church will be full of overcomers, the "firstfruits" unto God and the Lamb (Rev. 14:1-5).

Go Deeper 📖

See Ex. 23:19; 34:22,26; Lev. 2:12-14; Num. 28:26; Deut. 12:11; 18:4; 26:10; 1 Sam. 9:2; 2 Sam. 10:9; 2 Kings 4:42; 19:23; 1 Chron. 7:40; 19:10; 2 Chron. 25:5; 31:5; Neh. 10:35-37; 12:44; 13:31; Prov. 8:10,19; Song 6:9; Jer. 2:3; Ezek. 20:40; 44:30; 48:14; Rom. 11:16; 16:5; 1 Cor. 15:23; 16:15; Jas. 1:18.

∞ ∞ ∞

𝕱𝖎𝖘𝖍 (𝕱𝖎𝖘𝖍𝖎𝖓𝖌)

Christians; evangelism

Key Scriptures: Jer. 16:16; Ezek. 47:9-10; Mt. 4:19; Mk. 1:17; 2 Tim. 4:5.

Foundational Information ✎

Though some 45 species of fish are found in the inland waters of Palestine, the Bible gives no specific details. Fish, just like other animals, were divided into categories of clean and unclean. Fish with fins and scales were considered clean, and they made a popular Sabbath meal. Unclean fish included catfish, eels, and probably sharks and lampreys, as well as shellfish. Fishing was a major industry. Jerusalem had a Fish Gate, and presumably a fish market. Fish were caught with nets, hooks, harpoons, and spears. The Hebrew word for "fish" is *dagah* (Strong's #1710), and it is taken from the root *dag* (Strong's #1709), which means "a fish (as prolific); or (in the sense of squirming, moving by the vibratory action of the tail)." Since the time of the early Church, the fish has been a symbol of Christianity. The Greek word for fish, *ichthus,* is an acrostic for "Jesus Christ, Son of God, Savior."

Fulfilled in Christ ⋆

Jesus Christ, the master Fisherman, instructed His disciples, "Follow ['come behind'] Me, and I will make you fishers of men" (Mt. 4:19; compare Mk. 1:17). He is the last Adam, the One with true dominion over "the fish of the sea" (Gen. 1:26-28). Jesus likened His death, burial, and resurrection to the story of Jonah and the fish (Jon. 1:17; 2:10; Mt. 12:39-41). In this great day of restoration, the Lord Himself is sending for "many fishers" (evangelists) to fish the nations of the earth (Jer. 16:16). The prophet Ezekiel foresaw the present outpouring of the Holy Spirit as God's river and described this great end-time catch as "a very great multitude of fish...exceeding many" (Ezek. 47:9-10; see also Jn. 7:38).

Applied to the Christian ⚖

There are two kinds of men (fish) on planet earth: Christians and soon-to-be Christians! We have been called to go "fishing" all over the world (Mt. 28:18-20; Mk. 16:15-20; Acts 1:8). The eyes (vision) of the Bride of Christ (typified by the Shulamite in the Song of Solomon) are geared for evangelism, aimed at the "fishpools" of Heshbon (Song 7:4). Born-again fish can talk, declaring the works of the Lord (Job 12:8). Some of them have money in their mouths, having learned their rights in Christ (Mt. 17:27; compare Deut. 8:18; Prov. 18:21)! It is imperative that we fish (evangelize) according to the instruction and word of the Lord (Lk. 5:1-11; Jn. 21:6-13). Paul admonished Timothy to go fishing, "Do the work ['deeds'] of an evangelist" (2 Tim. 4:5; compare Lk. 4:18; Acts 21:8; Eph. 4:11).

Go Deeper 📖

See Gen. 9:2; Ex. 7:18,21; Num. 11:5; Deut. 4:18; 1 Kings 4:33; 2 Chron. 33:14; Neh. 3:3; 12:39; Ps. 8:8; Eccles. 9:12; Is. 19:8-10; Ezek. 38:20; Hos. 4:3; Jon. 1:17; Hab. 1:14; Zeph. 1:3,10; Mt. 7:10; 14:17-19; Mk. 6:38-43; 8:7; 15:34-36; Lk. 24:42; Jn. 21:3; 1 Cor. 15:39.

∾ ∾ ∾

𝔉𝔩𝔞𝔤𝔬𝔫

The corporate joy of the Word and Spirit

Key Scriptures: 1 Chron. 12:39-40; Neh. 8:10; Song 2:5;
Is. 22:24; Rom. 14:17; Heb. 10:25.

Foundational Information ✐

"Flagons" is the King James word for "raisin cakes." It is the feminine Hebrew word 'ashiyshah (Strong's #809), which means "something closely pressed together, a cake of raisins or other comfits." It is derived from 'ashiysh ("pressing down firmly; a foundation") and 'esh, the Hebrew word for "fire." One could also picture a "flagon" of wine as a vessel of wine.

Fulfilled in Christ ☦

Jesus Christ was Heaven's raisin cake, squeezed in the fiery olive-press of Gethsemane until He qualified to become the Foundation of the Church (Heb. 5:7-9). Isaiah foresaw Messiah in the day when a corporate Man would be created in His image, "And they shall hang upon him all the glory of his father's house…even to all the vessels of flagons" (Is. 22:24). The greatest Son of David (Mt. 1:1) is ministering "a flagon of wine" to every man and woman in this day as He is restoring the Ark of His glory back to Zion—a picture of the end-time corporate joy expressed in the Feast of Tabernacles (2 Sam. 6:19; 1 Chron. 16:3; Joel 2:28-32). Jesus Christ is Lord of all. When all the men of war who could keep rank came up to Hebron with a perfect heart to make David "king over all Israel," they brought "bunches of raisins" (1 Chron. 12:39-40)—a picture of the glorious Church gathering unto the Lord in corporate worship centered in His Word and Spirit.

Applied to the Christian ⚖

There are some New Testament blessings that can only be found in the corporate expression of worship before the Lord (Heb. 10:25). Similarly, the new wine is only found in the "cluster" (Is. 65:8). The Shulamite, a type of the Bride of Christ, cried out for the sustaining strength of His Spirit ("flagons") and Word ("apples") (Song 2:5). God is pressing and shaping His people, processing us through a baptism of fire into one cake and one bread until only the Lord is our strength and foundation (1 Cor. 3:9-15; 10:16-17). Nehemiah declared, "The joy of the Lord is our strength" (Neh. 8:10). Paul added, "Rejoice in the Lord always: and again I say, rejoice" (Phil. 4:4).

Go Deeper 📖

See 1 Sam. 25:18; 30:12; 2 Sam. 16:1; 1 Chron. 15:25; 29:9; 2 Chron. 20:27; 30:26; Ezra 3:12-13; Neh. 8; Esther 8:16-17; Job 38:37; Ps. 16:11; 42:4; 65:13; 67:4; Is. 9:3; 12:3; 35:10; Jer. 33:11; Hos. 3:1; Lk. 6:38; Acts 8:8; 13:52; 18:5; 2 Cor. 1:8; 1 Thess. 1:6; 1 Pet. 1:8; 4:13; 2 Jn. 12.

∞ ∞ ∞

𝕱𝖑𝖆𝖙 𝕹𝖔𝖘𝖊

Lack of spiritual discernment; disgrace, dishonor

Key Scriptures: Lev. 21:17-21; Is. 52:14; Eph. 5:27;
Heb. 5:14; 1 Pet. 2:9; Rev. 1:6; 5:10.

Foundational Information ✐

Under the Levitical economy, a person with an outward blemish or defect could not serve as a priest. This list included a "flat nose" ("marred face" in the New King James

Version). "Flat nose" is from the Hebrew *charam* (Strong's #2763), which means "to seclude; specifically (by a ban) to devote to religious uses (especially destruction); physical and reflexive, to be blunt as to the nose."

"Discern" is from the Hebrew *nakar* (Strong's #5234), which means "to scrutinize, look intently at; hence (with recognition implied), to acknowledge, be acquainted with, care for, respect, revere, or (with suspicion implied), to disregard, ignore, be strange toward, reject, resign, dissimulate (as if ignorant or disowning)." Compare *biyn* (Strong's #995), which means "to separate mentally (to distinguish), understand." The Greek word for "discern" is *diakrino* (Strong's #1252), which means "to separate thoroughly; to discriminate," then "to determine, decide." It literally means "to judge through."

Fulfilled in Christ ☥

Jesus Christ, our great High Priest, is sinless, without "blemish" ("stain, fault") (Lev. 21:17; compare Heb. 7:26; 1 Pet. 1:19). To accomplish this, He suffered and died for our sins; Isaiah declared of Him, "His visage ['appearance'] was so marred ['disfigured, ruined'] more than any man" (Is. 52:14; see also Is. 53:2-3). Jesus is the greatest Son of David, and "as an angel of God" is able "to discern good and bad" (2 Sam. 14:17). He is the righteous Judge, the King-Priest with perfect discernment (Jn. 5:22; Acts 10:42). Jesus is our merciful and faithful High Priest in things pertaining to God; His priesthood is immutable, made after the power of His endless life (Heb. 2:17; 7:16).

Applied to the Christian ⚖

The Church is a "royal priesthood" (1 Pet. 2:9), and believers have been made "kings and priests" in Christ (Rev. 1:6; 5:10). As such, we must cleanse ourselves from idolatrous images and strange gods that mar our land (1 Sam. 6:5; compare 1 Cor. 7:1). We have been called to be His glorious Church, "not having spot, or wrinkle, or any such thing," a holy people without blemish (Eph. 5:27). Let us cry out with Solomon, "Give therefore thy servant an understanding heart...that I may discern between good and bad" (1 Kings 3:9). Using the example of righteous Zadok, Ezekiel described this end-time priesthood, "And they shall teach My people the difference between the holy and profane, and cause them to discern between the unclean and the clean" (Ezek. 44:23; compare Mal. 3:18; Heb. 5:14).

Go Deeper 📖

See Lev. 19:27; Num. 11:20; Ruth 4:6; 1 Chron. 12:32; Ezra 3:13; 4:14; Neh. 8:8; Job 30:13; Ps. 69:19; Prov. 6:33; Eccles. 8:4-5; Jer. 13:7-9; 14:21; 18:4; Jon. 4:11; Mic. 7:6; Mal. 2:8-9; Mt. 16:3; Mk. 2:22; Jn. 8:49; Rom. 9:21; 13:11-14; 1 Cor. 2:14; 11:29-31; 14:29; 12:10; 2 Tim. 2:20.

∞ ∞ ∞

Flax

Righteousness

Key Scriptures: Jer. 33:16; Jn. 16:8; Rom. 3:10,23;
2 Cor. 5:17-21; Heb. 1:8; 7:2; Rev. 19:8.

Foundational Information ✐

Flax was a plant used for making linen cloth and wicks for lamps. "Flax" is from the feminine *pishtah* (#6594), and it means "flax; by implication, a wick." Also translated as "tow" in the King James Version, it is taken from *pishteh* (Strong's #6593), which means "linen (the thread, as carded)."

"Righteousness" is from the Hebrew *tsedaqah* (Strong's #6666), which means "rightness (abstractly), subjectively (rectitude), objectively (justice), morally (virtue) or figuratively (prosperity)." The Greek word *dikaiosune* (Strong's #1342) means "equity (of character or act); specially (Christian) justification." Formerly spelled "rightwiseness," righteousness is the character or quality of being right or just.

Fulfilled in Christ ☦

Jesus Christ, who fulfilled all righteousness (Mt. 3:15), is the righteousness of God expressed in these ways:

1. Righteousness is the girdle of His loins (Is. 11:5).
2. He is the Sun (Son) of righteousness (Mal. 4:2).
3. He is the King of righteousness (Heb. 7:2).
4. His Kingdom is righteousness (Rom. 14:17).
5. The sceptre of His kingdom is righteousness (Heb. 1:8).
6. He has provided the gift of righteousness (Rom. 5:17-18).
7. He is the end of the law for righteousness (Rom. 10:4).
8. He is made unto us righteousness (1 Cor. 1:30).
9. He judges and makes war in righteousness (Rev. 19:11).

Applied to the Christian ⚖

John affirmed the Bride of Christ, "And to her was granted that she should be arrayed in fine linen, clean and white; for the fine linen is the righteousness ['equitable deeds'] of saints" (Rev. 19:8). As the two spies were hidden in the flax on Rahab's roof, so we have died to sin, and our lives are "hid with Christ in God" (Col. 3:3). The name or nature of the Lord has been invoked over us: Jehovah-Tsidkenu, "The Lord our righteousness" (Jer. 33:16). Jesus taught us to seek first the kingdom of God, "and ['even'] His righteousness" (Mt. 6:33). The same Holy Spirit who convicts men of their need of the Savior also convinces us that we are the righteousness of God in Christ (Jn. 16:8). Like the virtuous woman who sought "flax" (Prov. 31:13), we are to hunger and thirst after righteousness (Mt. 5:6). God's righteousness is imputed or reckoned to our account (our position) and imparted into our spirits to enable us (our practical lifestyle).

Go Deeper 📖

See Gen. 15:6; 30:33; Ex. 9:31; Judg. 15:14; 16:9; 2 Sam. 22:21; 1 Kings 8:32; Ps. 4:1; 22:31; 50:6; 103:17; Is. 1:31; 41:10; 42:3; 43:17; 46:13; Ezek. 18:22-26; 40:3; Hos. 2:5,9; Mt. 5:20; 12:20; Lk. 1:75; Acts 10:35; Rom. 1:17; 3:25-26; 8:4; 10:3; 2 Cor. 6:7; Gal. 2:21; Eph. 4:24; 5:9; 6:14; Phil. 1:11; Tit. 3:5; 1 Jn. 2:29; 3:7.

∾ ∾ ∾

𝔉lea

Insignificance; little things

Key Scriptures: 1 Sam. 24:14; 26:20; Prov. 15:33; Is. 53:2-3; 60:22; Phil. 2:5-11.

Foundational Information ✏

Fleas were parasites that flourished in the sand and dust. "Flea" is from the Hebrew *par'osh*, which means "a flea (as the isolated insect)." Its root is *para'* (Strong's #6544), meaning "to loosen; by implication, to expose, dismiss; figuratively, absolve, begin." Compare *'ash* (Strong's #6211), which means "a moth." Its root means "to shrink, fail."

Fulfilled in Christ ✝

David, though apprehended to rule in Zion, felt as insignifcant as a "flea" when running from King Saul (1 Sam. 24:14; 26:20). Jesus Christ, the greatest Son of David, received unto Himself all of mankind's sense of insignificance. Paul revealed that God's Son took upon Himself the form of a servant and was made in the likeness of men—Jesus stooped very low and "humbled" ("depressed, humiliated") Himself (Phil. 2:7-8). The Spirit of Messiah prophesied through David, "But I am a worm ['maggot'], and no man; a reproach of men, and despised of the people" (Ps. 22:6). In His humiliation, His justice was taken away (Acts 8:32-33). Isaiah predicted Jesus' "insignificance"—"He hath no form nor comeliness...there is no beauty that we should desire Him. He is despised and rejected of men; a man of sorrows, and acquainted with grief..." (Is. 53:2b-3).

Applied to the Christian ⚖

Our total identity, significance, and sense of worth is in Christ—"in Him we live, and move, and have our being" (Acts 17:28; see also Eph. 1:6-7; Col. 1:9-13). Little is much when God is in it. Solomon advised, "The fear of the Lord is the instruction of wisdom, and before honour is humility" (Prov. 15:33). "Little" things are important to God as seen in these items:

1. Samuel's little coat (1 Sam. 2:19).
2. Jonathan's little taste of honey (1 Sam. 14:29).
3. Solomon's sense of little wisdom (1 Kings 3:7).
4. The widow's little cruse of oil (1 Kings 17:12).
5. The little cloud like a man's hand (1 Kings 18:44).
6. Elisha's little chamber (2 Kings 4:10).
7. The little maid who served Naaman's wife (2 Kings 5:2).
8. The promise made to the little one (Is. 60:22).
9. The little sanctuary that God is to us (Ezek. 11:16).
10. The few little fishes (Mt. 15:34).
11. Zacchaeus' little stature (Lk. 19:3).
12. The little book open (Rev. 10:2).

Go Deeper 📖

See Ex. 12:4; 23:30; 30:36; 2 Sam. 12:3; Job 36:27; Ps. 8:5; 68:27; Prov. 15:16; 16:8; Eccles. 9:14; Is. 11:6; 40:15; 50:5; 52:14; 53:2-3; Ezek. 40:36; Zech. 4:10; 9:9; Mt. 10:42; 18:3; Mk. 4:36; 9:12; Jn. 6:9; Rom. 15:3; 1 Cor. 4:3; 2 Cor. 8:9; Gal. 5:9; Heb. 2:7-18; 12:2; Jas. 3:4-5; Rev. 3:8.

∞ ∞ ∞

𝔉leece

Testing the spirits; inquiry

Key Scriptures: Judg. 6:37-40; Ps. 72:6; Jn. 16:13; Acts 8:32-33;
1 Thess. 5:21; 1 Jn. 4:1-6.

Foundational Information ✐

Fleece is the coat of wool shorn from a sheep. The judge Gideon used a fleece in a test to determine if God would deliver the nation of Israel from their enemies. "Fleece" is from the Hebrew *gez* (Strong's #1488), which means "a fleece (as shorn); also mown grass." It is taken from *gazaz* (Strong's #1494), meaning "to cut off; specifically to shear a flock or shave the hair; figuratively to destroy an enemy."

Fulfilled in Christ ✝

Jesus Christ was the sacrificial Lamb from Heaven who was sheared at the cross for man's sins. "He was led as a sheep to the slaughter; and like a lamb dumb before his shearer [the Father]" (Acts 8:32). The dew on Gideon's fleece, a symbol for God's favor and anointing (Gen. 27:28; Deut. 33:28), is a picture of the anointing resting upon Judge Jesus (typified by Gideon) and His Church (the 300). Calvary preceded Pentecost— blood predicates oil—Jesus died, rose again, then sent His Spirit to guide the Church (Acts 2). Like mown grass, our Savior's flesh was plowed to release His Spirit like rain upon the earth (Ps. 72:6). Jesus Himself declared, "He that is of God heareth God's words" (Jn. 8:47a).

Applied to the Christian ⚖

The Holy Spirit (who authored the Scriptures) is now our basis for all spiritual inquiry (Jn. 16:13-14; 1 Cor. 2:9-16). Gideon's two fleeces were not for guidance, but for confirmation. Those who "throw out a fleece" may get fleeced! Moreover, Gideon's fleece was doubly impossible. John cautioned, "Beloved, believe not every spirit, but try the spirits whether they are of God" (1 Jn. 4:1a). Paul added, "Prove all things; hold fast that which is good" (1 Thess. 5:21). As we grow in grace, "the king's mowings" produce the wisdom and life of Christ (Amos 7:1; Gal. 5:17; Heb. 4:12) that we might hear the still small voice of His Spirit (1 Kings 19:12). The Shulamite, a picture of the Bride of Christ, is described as "a flock of sheep that are even shorn" (Song 4:2).

Go Deeper 📖

See Gen. 31:19; 38:13; Lev. 13:34; Deut. 13:3; 15:19; 18:4,21; 1 Sam. 25:4,7,11; Neh. 6:12; Job 26:4; 31:20; Ps. 27:4; Prov. 19:27; Is. 9:15; 53:7; Mic. 2:11; Mk. 13:5-6; Lk. 12:57; Jn. 6:45; Acts 17:11; 18:18; Rom. 16:19; 1 Cor. 11:6; 14:29,32; 2 Cor. 11:3; Eph. 4:14; 5:6; Phil. 1:10; 4:8; Rev. 2:2; 16:13.

∞ ∞ ∞

𝔉𝔩𝔢𝔰𝔥𝔥𝔬𝔬𝔨

Religious legalism and manipulation

Key Scriptures: Ex. 27:3; 38:3; 1 Sam. 2:13-14; Ezek. 34;
Mk. 10:42-45; Jn. 10:1-11; 1 Pet. 5:2-3.

Foundational Information ✎

A fleshhook was an implement with three prongs used by the priests (as exampled by Hophni and Phineas, the evil sons of the priest Eli) to handle meat provided for sacrifices in the tabernacle. "Fleshhook" is from the Hebrew *mazleg* (Strong's #4207) that means "to draw up; a fork."

Fulfilled in Christ

Jesus Christ is the gentle Shepherd, our great and merciful High Priest (see Is. 40:11; Ezek. 34; Jn. 10:1-11; Heb. 2:17). The fleshhooks were made of brass, the symbol for judgment (Ex. 27:3). Jesus the righteous Judge exposed religious legalism, "hooking" the Pharisees of His day (Mt. 23). Although He was God Almighty in the flesh (1 Tim. 3:16), He taught His followers, "Ye know that they which are accounted to rule over the Gentiles exercise lordship over them; and their great ones exercise authority upon them. But so shall it not be among you: but whosoever will be great among you, shall be your minister: And whosoever of you will be the chiefest, shall be servant of all. For even the Son of man came not to be ministered unto, but to minister, and to give his life a ransom for many" (Mk. 10:42-45).

Applied to the Christian

Hophni and Phineas made their own rules and customs, taking the best for themselves (1 Sam. 2:13-14). The apostle Peter addressed Christian leaders, "Feed the flock which is among you, taking the oversight thereof, not by constraint, but willingly; not for filthy lucre, but of a ready mind; neither as being lords over God's heritage, but being ensamples to the flock" (1 Pet. 5:2-3). The fleshhooks were used at the brazen altar, a type of the cross—fleshly arrogance and manipulation must be crucified (Ex. 38:3; Gal. 5:19-21). There are others in the Bible who ruled with force and cruelty (Ezek. 34:4). Consider these:

1. Pharoah (Ex. 1–12).
2. Korah (Num. 16).
3. Rehoboam (1 Kings 12).
4. The Pharisees (Mt. 23).
5. Saul of Tarsus (Acts 8:3; 9:1-4).

Go Deeper

See Gen. 49:15; Num. 4:14; 11:12; Deut. 1:31; 24:17; 1 Chron. 28:17; 2 Chron. 4:16; 10:4; Ps. 18:35; Jer. 5:30-31; Lam. 5:13; Mt. 11:28; 20:25-26; 23:4,8-10; Lk. 22:24-27; Jn. 2:16; Acts 15:10,28; 1 Cor. 3:5; 2 Cor. 1:17,24; 4:5; Gal. 5:1; 1 Pet. 2:25; 2 Pet. 2:3; 3 Jn. 9-10; Rev. 7:17; 18:11-13.

∞ ∞ ∞

𝔉lies

Evil, unclean demon spirits; impurities

Key Scriptures: Ex. 8:24; Ps. 78:45; Eccles. 10:1; Mt. 12:24-27; 23:24.

Foundational Information ✐

The "flies" of the Bible included the common housefly, and other two-winged insects, many of which were biting insects. "Flies" is from the Hebrew *'arob* (Strong's #6157), which means "a mosquito (from its swarming)." Rendered in the King James Version as "divers sorts of flies, swarm," its root is *'arab* (Strong's #6148), which means "to braid, intermix; technically, to traffic (as if by barter); also or give to be security (as a kind of exchange)." Compare *zebuwb* (Strong's #2070), which means "(to flit); a fly (especially one of a stinging nature)."

Fulfilled in Christ ✝

One of the names Jesus used for the devil in the gospels is "Beelzebub" (Mt. 10:25; 12:24-27), which means "Baal ['lord'] of the flies; dung-god." The "flies" that infest the foul kingdom of this unclean prince are evil demon spirits. Satan rules from the "dung-hill" (1 Sam. 2:8; Erza 6:11; Ps. 113:7); but our risen King rules from the "holy hill" of Zion (see Ps. 2:6; 3:4; 15:1; 24:3; 43:3; 99:1). Jesus and His apostles took dominion over "unclean spirits" (see Mt. 10:1; Mk. 1:27; 3:11; 5:13; 6:7; Lk. 4:36; 6:18; Acts 5:16; 8:7). Jesus called the Pharisees "blind guides, which strain at a gnat" (Mt. 23:24). This referred to the custom of straining wine to take out the impurities before it was served.

Applied to the Christian ⚖

The world (typified by Egypt) and all that is in it (1 Jn. 2:15-17) has been "corrupted" ("decayed, ruined") by a swarm of flies (Ex. 8:24). Only the Lord can take care of these pests (Ex. 8:31; Mk. 16:17). Paul declared, "For the wages of sin is death; but the gift of God is eternal life through Jesus Christ our Lord" (Rom. 6:23). Solomon's "fly in the ointment" proverb indicates that these spirits can even show up in our churches to bring damage to our corporate witness! The wise man explained, "Dead flies cause the ointment ['anointing'] of the apothecary ['perfume'] to send forth a stinking savour ['moral offense']: so doth a little folly him that is in reputation for wisdom and honour" (Eccles. 10:1; see also Mk. 1:23; Lk. 4:33; Acts 6:9-10; Rev. 2:9; 3:9).

Go Deeper 📖

See Ex. 8:21-31; Lev. 17:7; Deut. 32:17; 2 Kings 1:16; 2 Chron. 11:15; Ps. 78:45; 105:31; 106:37; Is. 7:18; Zech. 13:2; Mt. 4:24; 7:22; 8:28-31; 10:8; 12:43; Mk. 1:26,34; 3:22,30; 5:2,8; 7:25; Lk. 8:2,27-39; 9:1,42; 10:17; 11:15-19,24; 13:32; 1 Cor. 10:20-21; Eph. 6:12; 1 Tim. 4:1; Jas. 2:19; Rev. 9:20; 16:13-14; 18:2.

∽ ∽ ∽

𝔉lint

Christ the Rock; determination; circumcision

Key Scriptures: Ex. 17:6; Is. 50:7; Ezek. 3:9;
Jn. 4:10,14; 7:37-39; 1 Cor. 10:1-4.

Foundational Information

Flint, a very hard variety of quartz, has a sharp edge when broken. Therefore, it was used to make tools such as knives, weapons, saws, sickles, and many other implements. "Flint" is from the Hebrew *challamiysh* (Strong's #2496), which means "(in the sense of hardness); flint." Its root *chalam* means "to bind firmly." Compare *tsor* (Strong's #6864), which means "a stone (as if pressed hard or to a point); (by implication, of use) a knife." Its root *tsuwr* means "to cramp, confine."

Fulfilled in Christ

Jesus Christ is the smitten Rock (Ex. 17:6). The apostle Paul recounted the Old Testament Church in the wilderness (Acts 7:38), "And did all drink the same spiritual drink: for they drank of that spiritual Rock that followed them: and that Rock was Christ" (1 Cor. 10:4). Jesus said to the woman of Samaria, "If thou knewest the gift of God, and who it is that saith to thee, Give me to drink; thou wouldest have asked of Him, and He would have given thee living water...But whosoever drinketh of the water that I shall give him shall never thirst; but the water that I shall give him shall be in him a well of water springing up into everlasting life" (Jn. 4:10,14; compare Jn. 7:37-39). Because of His cross, Jesus is the stone of stumbling and the rock of offence (Rom. 9:33; 1 Pet. 2:8).

Applied to the Christian

Paul taught about five experiences for the Christian in First Corinthians 10:1-4. The first three are once-and-for-all, and the other two are ongoing in the life of the believer:

1. Blood—the Passover (Jn. 1:29; Rom. 3:25; 5:9).
2. Baptism in water—the Red Sea (Acts 2:38).
3. Baptism in Spirit—the cloud (1 Cor. 12:13).
4. Bread—the manna (Mt. 4:4; 6:11).
5. Beverage—the water from the rock (Jn. 7:38-39).

Daily, we must eat God's Word and drink from Christ, from His Spirit within (Col. 1:27). The flinty rock was also used for circumcision (Ex. 4:25; Josh. 5:2; compare Rom. 8:28-29; Phil. 3:3; Col. 2:11-12). Flint also speaks of determination, as exampled by the prophets Isaiah and Ezekiel (Is. 50:7; Ezek. 3:9).

Go Deeper 📖

See Ex. 33:21-22; Num. 20:8-11; Deut. 8:15; 32:4,13,18,30-31; 1 Sam. 2:2; 2 Sam. 22:2-3,32,47; 23:3; Neh. 9:15; Ps. 78:15,20,35; 81:16; 94:22; 95:1; 105:41; 114:8; Song 2:14; Is. 2:10; 32:2; 42:11; 43:20; 48:21; Hab. 3:9; Mt. 7:24-25; 16:18; Lk. 6:48; Rev. 22:17.

∞ ∞ ∞

𝔉lock

The Body of Christ, the Family of God

Key Scriptures: Ps. 68:6; Ezek. 34:1-31; Mic. 4:8; Jn. 10:1-11; Eph. 3:15; Heb. 13:20; 1 Pet. 5:4.

Foundational Information ✎

A flock is a herd or group of animals that consisted of a mixture of sheep and goats. In biblical times both of these animals grazed and traveled together. The size of one's flocks and herds was a measure of wealth. "Flock" is from the Hebrew *tso'n* (Strong's #6629), which means "to migrate; a collective name for a flock (of sheep or goats); also figuratively (of men)." The Greek word for "flock" is *poimne,* contracted from *poimaino* (Strong's #4165), which means "to tend as a shepherd of (figuratively, superviser)." The latter is rendered in the King James Version as "feed (cattle), rule."

Fulfilled in Christ ✝

Jesus Christ is the Head of His Body, the Church (see Eph. 1:22-23; 2:16; 3:6; 4:4; 5:23; Col. 1:18); He is the Head of the Family (Eph. 3:15). Our Savior is the good Shepherd, the great Shepherd, and the chief Shepherd (Jn. 10:11; Heb. 13:20; 1 Pet. 5:4). Jesus is the delivering prophet like unto Moses (Deut. 18:15; Acts 3:22-23) who waters His flock (Ex. 2:19). God made His own people to go forth like sheep and guided them in the wilderness like a flock (Ps. 78:52). When Jesus saw the multitudes, He was moved with compassion because they fainted, and were scattered abroad, as sheep having no shepherd (Mt. 9:36). Isaiah prophesied of Messiah's gentle care, "He shall feed His flock like a shepherd: He shall gather the lambs with His arm, and carry them in His bosom, and shall gently lead those that are with young" (Is. 40:11). Jesus said, "My sheep hear My voice, and I know them, and they follow Me" (Jn. 10:27).

Applied to the Christian ⚖

The psalmist declared that "we are His people, and the sheep of His pasture" (Ps. 100:3b; see also Ps. 79:13; 95:7; Jer. 23:1). We are members of His Body, of His flesh and of His bones (Eph. 5:30). God promised to restore His end-time people, "And I will gather the remnant of My flock out of all countries whither I have driven them, and will bring them again to their folds; and they shall fruitful and increase" (Jer. 23:3). Micah added, "And thou, O tower of the flock, the strong hold of the daughter of Zion, unto thee shall it come, even the first dominion; the kingdom shall come to the daughter of Jerusalem" (Mic. 4:8; compare Zech. 9:16). Every Christian needs to be part of a local flock, a local church—"God setteth the solitary in families" (Ps. 68:6).

Go Deeper 📖

See Gen. 4:4; Job 21:11; Ps. 65:13; 77:20; 80:1; 107:41; Prov. 27:23; Song 1:7-8; 4:1-2; Is. 65:10; Jer. 31:10-12; 33:12-13; Ezek. 34:31; 36:37-38; Mic. 2:12; 7:14; Mt. 27:58; Lk. 2:8; 12:32; 15:4-6; Jn. 10:7; 21:16-17; Acts 20:28-29; Rom. 7:4; 8:36; 12:4-5; 1 Cor. 9:7; 10:16-17; 11:29; 12:12-27; Heb. 10:5; 1 Pet. 2:25.

∽ ∽ ∽

Flood

Judgment; blessing; water baptism

Key Scriptures: Gen. 6–8; Mt. 24:37-41; Lk. 17:26-27; Heb. 11:7; 1 Pet. 3:20-21; 2 Pet. 2:5.

Foundational Information ✐

The Flood was the Lord's destruction of the world by water during the time of Noah. The same Flood that took away the wicked elevated and delivered Noah and His family. The Flood was used to illustrate God's wrath against man's wickedness and His salvation for His people. "Flood" is from the Hebrew *mabbuwl* (Strong's #3999), which means "flowing; a deluge." Its root means "to flow; causatively, to bring (especially with pomp)." Compare *nahar* (Strong's #5104), meaning "a stream (including the sea; the Nile, Euphrates, etc.); figuratively, prosperity." Translated in the King James Version as "flood, river," its root means "to sparkle, (figuratively) be cheerful; hence (from the sheen of a running stream) to flow, (figuratively) assemble." The Greek word for "flood" is *kataklusmos* (Strong's #2627), which means "an inundation" (English, *cataclysm*). Its root means "to dash (wash) down, to deluge, overflow."

Fulfilled in Christ �

Jesus is the heavenly Noah, the righteous One who walked with the Father (Gen. 6:9). As Noah built the ark, so our Lord is building His Church (Mt. 16:18). The prophet Jesus likened Noah's day to the endtimes in which the wicked would be taken away in judgment and the righteous would be left to inherit the earth. He described how the Flood came "and took them [the wicked] all away" and "destroyed them all" (Mt. 24:39; Lk. 17:27). The psalmist described Messiah's might, "The Lord sitteth upon the flood; yea, the Lord sitteth King for ever" (Ps. 29:10). When the enemy shall come in, like a flood "the Spirit of our Lord shall lift up a standard against him" (Is. 59:19).

Applied to the Christian ⚖

The Day of the Lord is like day and night at the same time in the earth (Is. 60:1-5; Joel 2:1-14; Mal. 4:1-2). The Spirit of the Lord is being poured out like a flood, simultaneously blessing the righteous and judging the wicked. The writer to the Hebrews declared that Noah "prepared an ark to the saving of his house; by the which he condemned the world, and became heir of the righteousness which is by faith" (Heb. 11:7). The Flood was also a picture of New Testament water baptism; eight souls (the biblical number of a new beginning) were saved by water, "the like figure whereunto even baptism doth also now save us" (1 Pet. 3:20-21). God destroyed our old, ungodly Adamic order (*cosmos*) with water, "bringing in the flood upon the world of the ungodly" (2 Pet. 2:5). God has promised to pour out "floods" of blessing (Is. 44:3).

Go Deeper 📖

See Gen. 6:17; 7:6-10,17; 9:11,15,28; 10:1,32; 11:10; Ex. 15:8; Josh. 24:2-3,14-15; 2 Sam. 22:5; Job 14:11; 20:17; 22:16; 28:4,11; Ps. 24:2; 32:6; 66:6; 69:2; 90:5; 93:3; Song 8:7; Is. 28:2; Jer. 46:7-8; Dan. 9:26; Amos 8:8; 9:5; Jon. 2:3; Nahum 1:8; Mt. 7:24-27; Lk. 6:48; Rev. 12:15-16.

∞ ∞ ∞

𝔉𝔩𝔬𝔴𝔢𝔯

Beauty; resurrection life; the fading glory of men

Key Scriptures: Ps. 103:15; Song 2:1; 5:13; Is. 28:1-4;
2 Cor. 3:7–4:6; Jas. 1:10-11; 1 Pet. 1:24.

Foundational Information

"Flower" is from the Hebrew *perach* (Strong's #6525), which means "a calyx (natural or artificial); generally, bloom." It is also translated as "blossom, bud" in the King James Version. Its root is *parach* (Strong's #6524), and it means "to break forth as a bud, bloom; generally, to spread; specifically, to fly (as extending the wings); figuratively, to flourish." The Greek word is *anthos* (Strong's #438), which means "a blossom."

Fulfilled in Christ

Jesus Christ is the Flower from Heaven who has bestowed upon men the fragrance and beauty of His resurrection life (Jn. 11:25; Phil. 1:21; Col. 3:1-4). Our King is the light of the world (Jn. 8:12); the flowers on the golden candlestick (lampstand) in the Mosaic tabernacle were "his flowers" (Ex. 25:31). They were the blossoms of the almond plant ("the hastener"), a firstfruits plant which pictures Jesus' resurrection (1 Cor. 15:20). The Shulamite described the Bridegroom's beauty and radiance, "His cheeks are as a bed of spices, as sweet flowers: his lips like lilies, dropping sweet smelling myrrh" (Song 5:13). God is changing us "from glory to glory"—out of the dissipating glory that was in the face of Moses into the unfading glory of God revealed in the face of Jesus Christ (2 Cor. 3:7–4:6). Jesus' priesthood and kingship are immutable and eternal, energized by the power of His own endless life (Heb. 7:16; compare Dan. 7:14).

Applied to the Christian

In the Song of Songs, the Bride, not the Bridegroom, announces that she is "the rose of Sharon, and the lily of the valleys." (Song 2:1 is in the feminine gender.) The flowers on the Mosaic lampstand were "beaten work" ("molded by hammering"); so the Lord is fashioning the beauty of His life into us by His Word and Spirit (Num. 8:4; Jer. 23:29). The carved cedar "open flowers" in Solomon's temple point to the manifestation and expression of the Christ-life in the midst of His sons (1 Kings 6:18; compare Rom. 8:19). From another perspective, the psalmist knew that man's days, like the grassy flowers, were passing, not permanent (Ps. 103:15). James understood that earthly riches would fade and pass away (Jas. 1:10-11). Peter confirmed this, declaring that "all flesh is as grass, and all the glory of man as the flower of grass…" (1 Pet. 1:24).

Go Deeper 📖

See Ex. 25:33-34; 37:17-20; 2 Sam. 22:46; 1 Kings 6:29,32,35; 7:26,49; 2 Chron. 4:5,21; Job 6:15; 14:2; 15:33; Ps. 144:4; Eccles. 1:4; Song 2:12; Is. 1:30; 18:5; 24:4; Is. 28:1,4; 40:6-8; 64:6; Jer. 8:13; Ezek. 47:12; Nahum 1:4; Mt. 24:35; 1 Cor. 7:31; 1 Pet. 1:4; 5:4; 2 Pet. 3:10; 1 Jn. 2:17.

∾ ∾ ∾

𝔉𝔬𝔞𝔩

Mature, overcoming sons of God

Key Scriptures: Gen. 49:11; Zech. 9:9; Mt. 21:1-7;
Rom. 8:29; 1 Jn. 5:4; Rev. 21:7.

Foundational Information ✏

A foal is the young offspring of a donkey. The Hebrew word for "colt" in Genesis 49:11 and Zechariah 9:9 is *ben*, which means "son." In Matthew 21:5, the word for "colt" is *polos* ("foal; young ass"), but the word for "foal" is *huios* (Strong's #5207), the Pauline word for "mature son." This word primarily signifies the relationship of offspring to parent. The Greek word for "overcome" is *nikao* (Strong's #3528), which means "to subdue." Also translated in the King James Version as "conquer, prevail, get the victory," its root is the Greek word for "victory"—*nike* (Strong's #3529) means "conquest; the means of success."

Fulfilled in Christ ☀

As prophesied by Zechariah, Jesus' triumphal entry into Jerusalem was upon a donkey, "Rejoice greatly, O daughter of Zion; shout, O daughter of Jerusalem: behold, thy King cometh unto thee: He is just, and having salvation; lowly, and riding upon an ass, and upon a colt the foal of an ass" (Zech. 9:9). A careful reading of Matthew 21:1-7 ("thereon" in verse 7 is plural) indicates that Jesus may have been riding the mother and the foal. Jesus, the prevailing Pattern Son, declared, "I have overcome the world" (Jn. 16:33; see also Rev. 5:5). Paul explained, "For whom He [the Father] did foreknow, He also did predestinate to be conformed to the image of His Son, that He [Jesus] might be the firstborn among many brethren" (Rom. 8:29).

Applied to the Christian ⚖

In Matthew 21:1-7, Jesus could have been sitting on the mother donkey with His feet on her son (a portable throne). Accordingly, the mother donkey pictures the Church, and her foal (*huios* or "mature son") can represent the overcomers within the Church (Rev. 2–3). Jesus said through John, "He that overcometh shall inherit all things; and I will be his God, and he shall be My son [*huios*]" (Rev. 21:7). *Huiothesia,* a compound of *huios* ("son") and *tithemi* ("to place"), is the Pauline word for "adoption." It pertains to the full development of the heirs of God (see Rom. 8:15,23; 9:4; Gal. 4:5; Eph. 1:5). This "high calling" unto rulership in Zion (Phil. 3:12-14; compare 1 Cor. 13:10-11; Eph. 4:13) was described by the patriarch Jacob when he prophesied over his son Judah (Mt. 2:6; Heb. 7:14; Rev. 5:5), "Binding his foal unto the vine, and his ass's colt ['son'] unto the choice ['richest, most noble'] vine" (Gen. 49:11a). John affirmed, "For whatsoever is born of God overcometh the world: and this is the victory that overcometh the world, even our faith" (1 Jn. 5:4).

Go Deeper 📖

See 1 Sam. 26:25; Is. 42:13; Mt. 1:1,23-25; 3:17; 5:9; 16:18; Lk. 11:22; Acts 19:20; Rom. 3:4; 8:3,14,32; 12:21; Gal. 1:16; 2:20; 4:1-7; Col. 1:13; 1 Thess. 5:5; Heb. 1:2,8; 3:6; 5:5-9; 7:3,28; 1 Jn. 2:13-14; 3:8; 4:4; 5:11-13,20; Rev. 6:2; 12:5,11; 14:14; 15:2; 17:14.

∞ ∞ ∞

𝕱𝖔𝖑𝖉

The local church; holy habitation

Key Scriptures: Num. 32:16; 1 Chron. 17:7; Ps. 23:1; 125:1;
Is. 32:18; Jer. 23:3; Ezek. 34:14; Jn. 10:1-16.

Foundational Information ✐

A fold ("sheepcote" in the King James Version) is a pen or shelter for protecting sheep; permanent sheepfolds were enclosed by stone walls. "Fold" is from the Hebrew *gederah* (Strong's #1448), which means "enclosure (especially for flocks)." It is taken from the noun *gader* ("a circumvallation; an inclosure") and the verb *gadar* ("to wall in or around." Compare *naveh* (Strong's #5116), which means "at home; hence (by implication of satisfaction) lovely; also a home, of God (temple), men (residence), flocks (pasture), or wild animals (den)." Also translated as "court, sheepfold, hall, palace" in the King James Version, the Greek word for "fold" is *aule* (Strong's #833). It means "a yard (as open to the wind); by implication, a mansion."

Fulfilled in Christ ✝

Jesus Christ is the good Shepherd, the great Shepherd, and the chief Shepherd over the Church (Jn. 10:11; Heb. 13:20; 1 Pet. 5:4). He is the greatest son of David (Mt. 1:1). Our Savior was taken from the "sheepcotes" of Bethlehem and Nazareth to rule the people of God (2 Sam 7:8; 1 Chron. 17:7). Jesus promised concerning His Body comprised of both Jew and Greek (Eph. 2:13-18), "And other sheep I have, which are not of this fold: them also I must bring, and they shall hear My voice; and there shall be one fold, and one shepherd" (Jn. 10:16). The psalmist described Messiah's holy habitation, "Clouds and darkness are round about Him; righteousness and judgment are the habitation of His throne" (Ps. 97:2). Jesus Christ is the Head of the Church, locally and universally (Eph. 1:22; 4:15; 5:23).

Applied to the Christian ⚖

The psalmist declared, "The Lord is my shepherd; I shall not want" (Ps. 23:1). God promised through His prophet Isaiah, "And My people shall dwell in a peaceable habitation, and in sure dwellings, and in quiet resting places" (Is. 32:18; compare Jer. 23:3; Ezek. 34:14). Every Christian needs to be covered and protected by a local church according to divine order (Ps. 68:6; 1 Cor. 12:18,28; Heb. 10:25). David rejoiced in God's protection, "The angel of the Lord encampeth round about them that fear Him, and delivereth them" (Ps. 34:7). God's power and love surrounds us, for "as the mountains are round about Jerusalem, so the Lord is round about His people from henceforth even for ever" (Ps. 125:1; compare Phil. 4:7).

Go Deeper 📖

See Ex. 15:13; Num. 32:24,36; 1 Sam. 24:3; 1 Chron. 4:23; Ps. 18:11; 48:12; 50:9; 121:3-4; Prov. 21:20; 24:12,15; Is. 13:20; 33:20; 65:10; Jer. 25:30; 31:23; 33:12; Ezek. 1:27-28; 34:26; 43:12; Mic. 2:12; Hab. 3:17; Zeph. 2:6; Zech. 2:5; Acts 22:6; Phil. 4:7; 1 Pet. 1:5; 2:25; Rev. 4:3.

∞ ∞ ∞

𝕱𝖔𝖔𝖙 (𝕱𝖊𝖊𝖙)

Our walk with God; foundation

Key Scriptures: See Gen. 5:22-24; 6:9; Ps. 119:105;
Eccles. 5:1; 1 Cor. 3:10-12; Eph. 1:22; 1 Pet. 2:21; Rev. 1:15.

Foundational Information ✏

The foot is the lower extremity of the leg. The Bible uses the word both literally and symbolically. "Foot" is from the Hebrew *regel* (Strong's #7272), which means "a foot (as used in walking); by implication, a step."

Fulfilled in Christ ☀

Jesus Christ, our sinless Savior, walked perfectly before the Father (Jn. 8:29; Heb. 4:15). Peter declared concerning the Pattern Son, "Christ also suffered for us, leaving us an example, that ye should follow His steps ['accompany His tracks']" (1 Pet. 2:21; compare 1 Jn. 2:6). Jesus is the "foot" of the Laver (Ex. 30:28)—His blood, Word and Spirit are the ground and basis of our sanctification (Eph. 5:25-27; Heb. 13:11-12). The Savior's feet were pierced at Calvary (see Ps. 22:16; Zech. 12:10; Jn. 19:37; Rev. 1:7). The Father "hath put all things under His feet, and gave Him to be the head over all things to the church" (Eph. 1:22). Daniel and John described the feet of the risen Christ as fine, polished brass (a symbol for judgment) (Dan. 10:6; Rev. 1:15). Jesus Christ is the "foundation" of the Church (Lk. 6:48-49; 1 Cor. 3:10-11; Eph. 2:20).

Applied to the Christian ⚖

Scripture records that the patriarchs Enoch and Noah "walked with God" (Gen. 5:22-24; 6:9). The Bible uses various expressions with regard to "feet": To remove the sandals from one's feet demonstrated worship and reverence (Ex. 3:5; Josh. 5:15); to put something under the feet was a symbol of conquest (Josh. 10:24); to fall at the feet was a gesture of humility (1 Sam. 25:24); to wash a guest's feet was a sign of hospitality and humility (Lk. 7:44; Jn. 13:4-15). Our feet (walk) must be anointed with blood (Lev. 8:23; Heb. 9:22; 10:19-22). Like Ruth, we need to "uncover" (reveal) the feet of the Kinsman-redeemer (Ruth 3:4-8; see also Gal. 3:13-14). Solomon admonished, "Keep ['guard, attend to'] thy foot when thou goest to the house of God…" (Eccles. 5:1). The psalmist declared, "Thy word is a lamp unto my feet, and a light unto my path" (Ps. 119:105).

Go Deeper 📖

See Gen. 8:9; Ex. 24:10; Deut. 8:4; Josh. 1:3; 3:13; 1 Sam. 2:9; 1 Kings 5:17; Ps. 8:6; 11:3; 18:33-38; 26:12; 31:8; 38:16; 40:2; 47:3; 56:13; 91:12-13; 116:8; 121:3; Prov. 1:15; 3:23; 4:27; 10:25; Song 5:3; 7:1; Is. 58:12; Zech. 4:9; 1 Cor. 12:15; 15:25-27; Eph. 6:15; 1 Tim. 5:10; 2 Tim. 2:19; Heb. 2:8; 11:10; 12:13; Rev. 10:1-2.

∞ ∞ ∞

𝕱ootmen

Soldiers of the Lord; messengers; evangelists

Key Scriptures: Jer. 12:5; 2 Tim 2:3-4; 4:5; Heb. 6:19-20; Rev. 19:11.

Foundational Information ✐

Footmen were runners, messengers, or couriers. The King James Version often uses footmen to refer to foot soldiers or infantrymen. "Footman" is from the Hebrew *ragliy* (Strong's #7273), which means "a footman (soldier)." A soldier was a member of a military force. "Soldier" is from the Hebrew *tsaba'* (Strong's #6635), which means " a mass of persons organized for war (an army)." The Greek word is *stratiotes* (Strong's #4757), which means "a camper-out, a (common) warrior." It is taken from *stratia* (Strong's #4756), meaning "(an army, as encamped); camp-likeness, an army, (figuratively) the angels, the celestial luminaries." The latter Greek word is translated as "host" in the King James Version.

Fulfilled in Christ ☧

Jesus Christ was Heaven's Footman, the divine Forerunner and Scout who has entered the Most Holy Place for us (Heb. 6:19-20). He was Jehovah-Tsebaoth (the Lord of all the armies in Heaven and earth) in the flesh (Jn. 1:14). Our risen King is our heavenly Joshua, "the captain ['chief leader'] of [our] salvation" (Heb. 2:10; compare Josh. 4:14). John described General Jesus, "And I saw heaven opened, and behold a white horse; and He that sat upon him was called Faithful and True, and in righteousness He doth judge and make war" (Rev. 19:11). Like the centurion, our Leader has "soldiers" under His authority (Mt. 8:9; compare 1 Chron. 12:21-22). The night Jesus was born, all the "hosts" of Heaven sang and rejoiced (Lk. 2:13).

Applied to the Christian ⚖

Paul declared that good Christian soldiers must learn to endure "hardness" or "hardship." He then added, "No man that warreth entangleth ['entwines, involves'] himself with the affairs of this life; that he may please Him who hath chosen him to be a soldier" (2 Tim. 2:3-4). Every child of God needs to learn how to pull out his sword (Judg. 20:2; Eph. 6:17; Heb. 4:12). The prophet Jeremiah challenged every believer with regard to spiritual warfare, "If thou hast run with the footmen, and they have wearied ['tire, make disgusted'] thee, then how canst thou contend with horses? And if in the land of peace, wherein thou trustedst, they wearied thee, then how wilt thou do in the swelling of Jordan?" (Jer. 12:5; see also Lk. 18:1; Gal. 6:9; Eph. 6:18) Evangelists are the "foot-soldiers" in the Body of Christ (see Lk. 4:18; Acts 21:8; Eph. 4:11; 2 Tim. 4:5).

Go Deeper 📖

See Gen. 2:1; Ex. 12:37-41; Num. 1:52; 11:21; 1 Sam. 1:11; 4:10; 15:4; 22:17; 2 Sam. 6:2; 8:4; 10:6-7; 1 Kings 20:29; 22:19; 2 Kings 13:7; 1 Chron. 7:4,11; 9:19; 18:4;

19:18; 2 Chron. 25:13; Ezra 8:22; Neh. 9:6; Ps. 24:10; 27:3; 33:6; Is. 6:3; 9:7; 13:4; 15:4; 54:5; Hag. 2:8-9; Zech. 4:6; Mal. 3:10; Lk. 3:14; Acts 10:7.

∞   ∞   ∞

𝔉ootstool

The earth; the place of God's rest

Key Scriptures: 1 Chron. 28:2; 2 Chron. 9:18; Is. 66:1;
Mt. 5:5; Acts 7:47-49; Heb. 3–4; Rev. 5:10.

Foundational Information ✐

A footstool is a piece of furniture designed for the resting of a person's feet. "Footstool" is from the Hebrew *hadom* (Strong's #1916), which means "to stamp upon; a footstool." The Greek word is *hupopodion* (Strong's #5286), a compound of *hupo* ("under") and *pous* ("foot"), meaning "something under the feet, a foot-rest."

"Rest" is from the Hebrew *menuwchah* (Strong's #4496), which means "repose or (adverbially) peacefully; figuratively, consolation (specifically, matrimony); hence (concretely) an abode." It is akin to *manowach* (Strong's #4494), meaning "quiet, a settled spot, or a home," and it is from a root meaning "to rest, settle down." The Greek word is *katapausis* (Strong's #2663), which means "reposing down, abode."

Fulfilled in Christ ☦

The Lord declared through His prophet, "The heaven is My throne, and the earth is My footstool: where is the house that ye build unto Me? And where is the place of My rest?" (Is. 66:1; compare Acts 7:49) The place of Jesus' "rest" will literally be on this earth, and spiritually, it will be in the hearts of His Church, the corporate new creation (Mt. 6:10 with Heb. 3–4). When He walked this earth, Jesus was the "footstool of gold," ever showing forth the divine nature (2 Chron. 9:18; compare Jn. 14:6-9). Jehovah (the Father) said to David's Lord (the Son), "Sit thou at My right hand, until I make Thine enemies Thy footstool" (Ps. 110:1). This one-of-a-kind Messianic promise is repeated seven times in the New Testament (see Mt. 22:44; Mk. 12:36; Lk. 20:43; Acts 2:35; 1 Cor. 15:25; Heb. 1:3; 10:12-13). The latter passage explains that our Savior, "after He had offered one sacrifice for sins for ever, sat down on the right hand of God; from henceforth expecting ['waiting'] till His enemies be made His footstool" (compare Acts 3:19-21; Eph. 4:13; Jas. 5:7).

Applied to the Christian   ⚖

Jesus promised, "Blessed are the meek: for they shall inherit the earth" (Mt. 5:5). John affirmed that the finished work of Christ "hast made us unto our God kings and priests: and we shall reign on the earth" (Rev. 5:10). The Church is God's "house of rest," the building of God (1 Chron. 28:2; see also Eph. 2:19-22). When the Church is fully formed into the image of Christ, she will be a "footstool of gold" in the earth (2 Chron. 9:18; see also Gal. 4:19; 2 Pet. 1:3-4)! When Moses and the elders saw the God of Israel, there was "under His feet" a picture of this glorious Church, "the body of heaven in His clearness ['brightness']" (Ex. 24:10 with Prov. 4:18; Heb. 1:3). The apostle Paul admonished the Church, "And the God of peace shall bruise ['crush completely, shatter'] satan under your feet shortly" (Rom. 16:20a)! The psalmist saw this end-time revival through the Church, "He shall subdue the people under us, and the nations under our feet" (Ps. 47:3; compare Mal. 4:2-3).

Go Deeper   📖

See Gen. 49:15; Num. 10:33; Deut. 12:9; Ruth 1:9; 2 Sam. 22:10,37-39; 1 Kings 5:3; 2 Kings 9:33; 1 Chron. 22:9; Ps. 8:6; 18:9,38; 91:13; 99:5; 132:7-14; Is. 11:10; 14:19,25; 18:7; 28:3; Jer. 12:10; Lam. 1:15; 2:1; 3:34; Dan. 8:13; Mt. 5:13,35; Mk. 6:11; 1 Cor. 15:27; Eph. 1:22; Heb. 2:8; 10:29; Jas. 2:3; Rev. 11:2; 12:1.

∞   ∞   ∞

𝕱𝖔𝖗𝖊𝖍𝖊𝖆𝖉

The mind; the identifying seal of God

Key Scriptures: Ex. 28:38; Jn. 6:27; Rom. 8:27; 12:1-2; 1 Cor. 2:16; Phil. 2:5; Rev. 14:1-5.

Foundational Information   ✐

The forehead is the area of the face above the eyes. "Forehead" is from the Hebrew *metsach* (Strong's #4696), which means "to be clear, conspicuous; the forehead (as open and prominent)." The Greek word for "forehead" is *metopon* (Strong's #3359), taken from *meta* ("with") and *ops* ("an eye").

Fulfilled in Christ   ☥

The mind that was in Christ Jesus was the mind of the Father (Phil. 2:5), typified by the golden plate (with the words, "holiness to the Lord") on the forehead of Aaron the

High Priest (Ex. 28:36-38; compare Heb. 7:26). "Him hath [God] the Father sealed" (Jn. 6:27). The suffering Servant "thought it not robbery to be equal with God; but made Himself of no reputation ['emptied Himself']..." (Phil. 2:6-7; compare Acts 8:33; 2 Cor. 8:9). Jesus, the heavenly David, slew satan (typified by Goliath) at Golgotha (1 Sam. 17:49), the place of the "skull" (Jn. 19:17; compare Judg. 4:21; 5:26). Peter declared, "Forasmuch then as Christ hath suffered for us in the flesh, arm yourselves likewise with the same mind: for he that hath suffered in the flesh hath ceased from sin" (1 Pet. 4:1).

Applied to the Christian ⚖

Paul admonished, "Let this mind be in you, which was also in Christ Jesus" (Phil. 2:5). Believers have been gifted with the mind of the Holy Spirit, who makes "intercession for the saints according to the will of God" (Rom. 8:27). Paul declared that "we have the mind of Christ" (1 Cor. 2:16). The overcomers who stand with the Lamb on Mount Zion have "His Father's name" (the same kind of relationship that Jesus had with the Father) in their forehead (Rev. 14:1-5; 22:4; compare 1 Cor. 1:10)! Paul admonished, "And be not conformed to this world: but be ye transformed by the renewing ['renovating'] of your mind, that ye may prove what is that good, and acceptable, and perfect, will of God" (Rom. 12:2; compare Eph. 4:23). Leprosy in the forehead is a picture of the spiritual mark of the beast (Lev. 13:41-44; 2 Chron. 26:19-20; compare Rev. 13:16-18).

Go Deeper 📖

See Lev. 24:12; Deut. 6:8; Is. 48:4; Jer. 3:3; Ezek. 3:8-9; 16:12; Rom. 1:28; 7:23-25; 8:5-7; 11:34; 12:16; 15:6; 2 Cor. 7:7; 8:12,19; 9:2; 13:11; Eph. 2:3; 4:17; Phil. 1:27; 2:2-3; 3:16,19; 4:2; Col. 1:21; 2:18; 3:2; 2 Thess. 2:2; 2 Tim. 1:7; Tit. 1:15; 3:1; Heb. 8:10; 1 Pet. 1:13; 3:8; 5:2; Rev. 7:1-4; 14:9; 17:5,9,13.

∞　∞　∞

𝔉orerunner

Jesus our example; one who prepares the way

Key Scriptures: Ps. 19:5; Is. 40:3; Mal. 3:1; Jn. 14:6;
1 Cor. 9:24; Heb. 6:19-20.

Foundational Information ✑

A forerunner is one who goes or runs before. "Forerunner" is from the Greek *prodromos* (Strong's #4274), which means "a runner ahead, scout (figuratively, precursor)."

Also translated as "running forward, going in advance," it refers to those who were sent ahead as military scouts to make observations. It may also refer to those who were sent before a king to prepare a way for Him. *Prodromos* is taken from *protrecho* (Strong's #4390), which means "to run forward, outstrip, precede." It is translated as "outrun, run before" in the King James Version. This latter word is a compound of *pro* ("fore; in front of, prior, superior to") and *trecho* ("to run or walk hastily"). In the Septuagint, the "first-ripe" grapes of Numbers 13:20 are "the forerunners (of the grape)."

Fulfilled in Christ ☼

Jesus Christ is both the Runner and the Road! The writer to the Hebrews declared Him to be "the forerunner" who entered into the Most Holy Place for us (Heb. 6:19-20). Jesus Himself said, "I am the way ['road, route'], the truth, and the life; no man cometh unto the Father, but by Me" (Jn. 14:6). The psalmist revealed that Messiah would be like a Bridegroom coming out of His chamber, rejoicing as a strong man "to run a race" (Ps. 19:5). John the Baptist was the forerunner who prepared the way for His divine Cousin (see Is. 40:3; Mt. 3:1-3; 11:10; Jn. 1:23). Malachi prophesied the coming of both John and Jesus, "Behold, I will send my messenger, and he shall prepare the way before Me: and the Lord, whom ye seek, shall suddenly come to His temple, even the messenger of the covenant, whom ye delight in: behold, He shall come, saith the Lord of hosts" (Mal. 3:1).

Applied to the Christian ⚖

As revealed by the "pattern" of Moses' tabernacle (Ex. 25:40), a people will follow Jesus from the Outer Court (where He is Savior), through the Holy Place (where He is Baptizer), into the Most Holy Place (where He is Lord, King, Overcomer, and Head of the Church). Let us run the way of His commandments, hastening from the land of sin (Ex. 12:11,33; Ps. 119:32). The army of God runs like horsemen through the earth with the good news of His resurrection (Joel 2:4-9; Mt. 28:8). Paul admonished, "So run, that ye may obtain" (1 Cor. 9:24; compare Heb. 12:1). Those who praise the Lord like David can say, "For by Thee I have run through a troop; and by my God have I leaped over a wall" (Ps. 18:29). The Shulamite exclaimed, "Draw me, and we will run after thee" (Song 1:4).

Go Deeper 📖

See Deut. 19:3; 2 Sam. 18:19-23; 1 Kings 1:5; 2 Kings 4:22,26; Ps. 78:16; 104:10; Is. 40:31; 57:14; 62:10; Ezek. 46:2; Nahum 2:4; Hab. 2:2; Hag. 1:9; Zech. 2:4; 4:10; Mt. 26:17; Mk. 1:2-3; Lk. 1:76; 3:4; 7:27; 9:52; 19:4; Jn. 14:2-3; 20:4; 1 Cor. 9:26; Gal. 2:2; 5:7; Phil. 2:16.

∞ ∞ ∞

𝔍oreskin

The flesh; the uncircumcised heart

Key Scriptures: Gen. 17:10-25; Deut. 10:16; 30:6; Is. 52:1;
Jn. 6:63; Rom. 2:25-29; Gal. 5:6; 6:15; Phil. 3:3.

Foundational Information ✑

Foreskin is skin that covers the end of the male sex organ. As a sign of the Abrahamic Covenant, the foreskin was cut off in the rite of circumcision eight days after the child's birth. (The number eight denotes a new beginning.) "Foreskin" is from the Hebrew *'orlah* (Strong's #6190), which means "prepuce." It is akin to *'arel* (Strong's #6189), meaning "exposed, projecting loose (as to the prepuce); used only technically, uncircumcised (still having the prepuce uncurtailed)." Its root means "to strip; to expose or remove the prepuce."

Fulfilled in Christ ☦

Jesus Christ is the living Word, the sharp knife from Heaven who came to circumcise the hearts of men (Jn. 1:1; Heb. 4:12). The "hill of the foreskins" foreshadowed the hill of Calvary (Josh. 5:3). Paul declared, "Now I say that Jesus Christ was a minister of the circumcision for the truth of God, to confirm ['establish, make firm or secure'] the promises made unto the fathers [Abraham, Isaac, and Jacob]" (Rom. 15:8; compare Acts 3:13). In Jesus Christ neither circumcision nor uncircumcision avails anything, but faith which works by love—the reality of the new creation (Gal. 5:6; 6:15). Moses declared, "And the Lord thy God will circumcise thine heart, and the heart of thy seed, to love the Lord thy God with all thine heart, and with all thy soul, that thou mayest live" (Deut. 30:6). Jesus reminded us that the spirit is willing, but the flesh is weak (Mt. 26:41; Mk. 14:38); He added, "The flesh profiteth nothing..." (Jn. 6:63).

Applied to the Christian ⚖

Paul exclaimed, "For we are the circumcision, which worship God in the spirit, and rejoice in Christ Jesus, and have no confidence in the flesh" (Phil. 3:3). The apostle revealed that a spiritual "Jew" was the man or woman who had experienced a circumcision of his heart (Rom. 2:25-29). Christians are the seed of Abraham (Gal. 3:7,9,16,29). Even the early Torah (the Law) asserted, "Circumcise therefore the foreskin of your heart, and be no more stiffnecked" (Deut. 10:16; compare Jer. 4:4). God will cleanse His Church from those who are "uncircumcised and unclean" (Is. 52:1; compare Ezek. 44:7-9; Acts 7:51). Circumcision in the Old Testament (Gen. 17:11,14,23-25; Lev. 12:3) is a type of water baptism in the New (Rom. 6:1-14; Col. 2:11-12; 1 Pet. 3:21).

Go Deeper   📖

See Gen. 21:4; 34:14-15; Ex. 4:25-26; 6:30; 12:48; 1 Sam. 18:27; 2 Sam. 3:14; Jer. 9:25; Hab. 2:16; Lk. 1:59; Jn. 7:22-23; Acts 7:8; 10:45; 11:2; 15:1,5,24; 16:3; 21:21; Rom. 3:30; 4:9-12; 8:1-9; 1 Cor. 7:18-19; 2 Cor. 7:1; Gal. 2:3,7-12; 3:3; 5:1-3,13-21; 6:8,12-13; Eph. 2:3,11-12; Phil. 3:2,5; Col. 3:11; 4:11; Tit. 1:10; 2 Pet. 2:10.

∞ ∞ ∞

𝔉𝔬𝔯𝔢𝔰𝔱 (𝔗𝔯𝔢𝔢𝔰)

The planting of the Lord; a new humanity in Christ

Key Scriptures: Gen. 2:8; Neh. 10:37; Song 2:3; Is. 41:19; 44:23; 60:21; 61:3; Jer. 17:8; Mt. 15:13.

Foundational Information   ✏

A forest is a grove or thicket of trees. Wood is a biblical symbol for humanity. "Forest" is from the Hebrew *ya'ar* (Strong's #3293), which means "to thicken with verdure; a copse of bushes; hence, a forest; hence, honey in the comb (as hived in trees)." "Trees" is from the Hebrew *'ets* (Strong's #6086), which means "a tree (from its firmness); hence, wood (plural sticks)." The Greek word is *dendron* (Strong's #1186), and it means "(an oak); a tree."

Fulfilled in Christ   ✝

Jesus is Heaven's Cedar, the King of the trees—He is the "tree of life" (see Gen. 2:9; 3:22-24; Prov. 3:18; 11:30; 13:12; 15:4; Rev. 2:7; 22:2,14). Our King is "the apple tree among the trees of the wood" (Song 2:3), the Son among the sons (Heb. 1:9; 2:11). "The Lord God planted a garden" (Gen. 2:8); similarly, the Lord has planted us "as cedar trees beside the waters" (Num. 24:6; compare Ps. 1:1-3; Jer. 17:8). The trees of the forest were used to build the Temple—the Lord alone can build His House (Ps. 127:1; Mt. 15:13; 16:18). Jehovah promised through Isaiah, "I will plant in the wilderness the cedar, the shittah tree, and the myrtle, and the oil tree; I will set in the desert the fir tree, and the pine, and the box tree together" (Is. 41:19)—these seven trees (the Bible number denoting perfection) point to the mature, glorious Church (Eph. 4:13; 5:27)!

Applied to the Christian   ⚖

Isaiah described the people of God as "trees of righteousness, the planting ['garden, vineyard'] of the Lord..." (Is. 61:3). He prophesied, "Thy people also shall be all righteous; they shall inherit the land for ever, the branch of My planting, the work of My hands, that I may be glorified" (Is. 60:21). Trees sing, shout, and clap their hands (see 1 Chron. 16:33; Ps. 96:12; Is. 44:23; 55:12). The woods are full of honey and sap (1 Sam. 14:25-26; Ps. 19:9-10; 119:103)—the life of Christ (Ps. 104:16). The outpouring of the Holy Spirit is causing the Church to become a place of luxurious growth, fruitfulness, and glory (Ps. 92:13; Is. 32:15; 35:1-2)—trees are "moved with the wind" of revival (Is. 7:2; see also Song 4:16; Ezek. 37:9-10; Jn. 3:8; Acts 2:2)! The record of Church history is like "the forest of Lebanon," wherein hang all the golden shields (mighty acts of faith) (1 Kings 10:17; compare Eph. 6:16). The Body of Christ has great diversity (Rom. 12; 1 Cor. 12), bringing forth "the fruit of all manner of trees" (Neh. 10:37; compare Lev. 19:23).

Go Deeper 📖

See Gen. 3:2,8; Lev. 26:4; 1 Sam. 22:5; 2 Sam. 18:6-8,17; 1 Kings 7:2; 10:21; 2 Kings 19:23; 2 Chron. 9:16,20; Neh. 2:8; Ps. 50:10; 104:20; 132:6; Eccles. 2:5-6; Song 4:14; Is. 9:18; 10:18-19,34; 21:13; 22:8; 29:17; 32:19; 37:24; 44:14; Jer. 5:6; 12:8; 26:18; Ezek. 15:1-6; 20:47; Hos. 2:12; Joel 1:12; Amos 3:4; Mic. 3:12; 7:14; Zech. 11:2.

∾ ∾ ∾

𝔉ormer 𝔕ain

The Pentecostal outpouring of the Holy Spirit

Key Scriptures: Lev. 23:15-22; Deut. 11:11; Jer. 5:24; Hos. 6:3; Joel 2:23; Rom. 8:23; Eph. 5:17-18; Jas. 5:7.

Foundational Information ✎

Rain is liquid precipitation that provides essential moisture for plants, animals, and man. Rain was a sign of blessing; the withholding of rain was a sign of warning or judgment. The rainy season in Palestine begins in October and November with the "early" or "former" rains. It lasts until the "latter" rains of April and May (June through September constitute the hot summer months). Winter and rain are synonomous. The former rain is for plowing and sowing; the latter rain is for harvest and increase.

"Former rain" is from the Hebrew *yowreh* (Strong's #3138), which means "sprinkling; hence, a sprinkling (or autumnal showers)." Its root is *yarah* (Strong's #3384), which means "to flow as water (to rain); transitively, to lay or throw (especially an arrow, to shoot); figuratively, to point out (as if by aiming the finger), to teach." The latter is the same root word for *mowreh* (Strong's #4175), which means "an archer; also teacher or teaching; also the early rain." The Greek word for "early rain" is *proimos*, and it means "dawning, (by analogy) autumnal (showering, the first of the rainy season)." It is derived from *proi* ("the daybreak watch") and *pro* ("fore, in front of, prior").

Fulfilled in Christ

The Lord Himself is the "rain of heaven" (Deut. 11:11; compare Ps. 72:6; Acts 14:17)! Hosea prophesied that "His going forth is prepared as the morning; and He shall come unto us as the rain, as the latter and former rain unto the earth" (Hos. 6:3). In the former rain, Jesus is Baptizer (Acts 1:5); in the time of latter rain, He is Lord (Eph. 4:13; Phil. 2:11)! He promised through His prophet, "And I will make them and the places round about My hill [Zion, a type of the Church] a blessing; and I will cause the shower to come down in his season; there shall be showers of blessing" (Ezek. 34:26). James revealed that Jesus will not return to earth until He has poured out and received the fruit of the early and latter rains (Jas. 5:7; compare "the times of refreshing" mentioned in Acts 3:19-21)!

Applied to the Christian

Historically, the "early" rain points back to the outpouring of the Holy Spirit upon the Church at the beginning of this age (Acts 1–12); the "latter" rain began to fall around the year 1900, and was most pronounced from 1948-1956; the Lord continues to rain His presence upon us, bringing the Church to the full stature of the King's favor (Prov. 16:15; Eph. 4:13).

We are recipients of the former rain, having been filled with His Spirit (Acts 2:1-4; Eph. 5:17-18). The former rain is "the first rain" (Deut. 11:14)—the Pentecostal experience is the "firstfruits" of the Spirit (Rom. 8:23; compare Eph. 1:13-14). Joel predicted an end-time revival, "Be glad then, ye children of Zion, and rejoice in the Lord your God: for He hath given you the former rain moderately ['in righteousness'], and He will cause to come down for you the rain, the former rain, and the latter rain in the first month" (Joel 2:23; compare Jer. 5:24). The former rain is the "teaching" rain, when the seed is planted in the earth (Deut. 32:2)—the purpose of the Holy Spirit is to reveal the Son, Jesus the Word (see Prov. 1:22-23; Jn. 14:26; 15:26; 16:13)! A true Feast of Pentecost is the writing of the law of God upon our hearts (Ex. 19:1; Lev. 23:15-22). It rains in proportion to the ascending "vapour" of our praise (Job 36:27).

Go Deeper

See Gen. 2:5; 8:2; Ex. 23:16-17; Lev. 26:4; Deut. 11:17; 16:9-12; 28:12,24; 1 Sam. 12:17-18; 2 Sam. 23:4; 1 Kings 8:35-36; 17:1,14; 18:1,41-45; Ezra 10:9,13; Job 5:10; 28:26; 29:23; 37:6-13; Ps. 65:9-13; 68:9; 84:6; 135:7; 147:8; Eccles. 11:3; Song 2:11; Is. 55:10; Jer. 14:22; Ezek. 1:28; Zech. 10:1; Acts 2:4; 8:18,21; 10:44-46; 19:6; 28:2; Heb. 6:7; Jas. 5:17-18; Rev. 11:6.

𝕱𝖔𝖚𝖓𝖉𝖆𝖙𝖎𝖔𝖓

Jesus Christ our ground; apostolic truth and practice

Key Scriptures: Ps. 11:3; 82:5; Prov. 11:25; Is. 28:16; Mt. 7:24-27; Lk. 6:48-49; 1 Cor. 3:9-15; Heb. 5:11–6:3.

Foundational Information   ✐

A foundation is the strong, stable base upon which a building is built. The Hebrew word for "foundation" is *yecowd* (Strong's #3247), also rendered in the King James Version as "bottom, repairing." Its root is *yacad* (Strong's #3245), which means "to set; to found; to sit down together, settle, consult." The Greek word is *themelios* (Strong's #2310), which means "something put down, a substructure (of a building)." It is derived from *tithemi,* which means "to place."

Fulfilled in Christ   ⋇

The apostle Paul declared, "For other foundation can no man lay than that is laid, which is Jesus Christ" (1 Cor. 3:11). Furthermore, the Church is built upon the literary foundation of the apostles (who wrote the New Testament) and prophets (who wrote the Old Testament), "Jesus Christ Himself being the chief corner stone" (Eph. 2:20). The Father laid the foundation of the Church with the death of His firstborn Son (Josh. 6:26; 1 Kings 16:34). Jesus, the righteous One, is our everlasting Foundation (Prov. 10:25). Isaiah said of Messiah, "Behold, I lay in Zion for a foundation a stone, a tried stone, a precious corner stone, a sure foundation..." (Is. 28:16). The hands of Jesus (pierced on the cross) laid the foundation of the Church, and the "hand" ministry of Jesus (Eph. 4:11) will complete the work (Zech. 4:9; see also Ps. 138:8; Jer. 29:11; Phil. 1:6)!

Applied to the Christian   ⚖

Believers are to build their lives, homes, and ministries upon Him who is our sure foundation (Mt. 7:24-27; Lk. 6:48-49). The writer to the Hebrews details this solid New Testament "foundation," the first principles of the doctrine of Christ, the reality of apostolic faith and practice (Heb. 6:1-2; compare Acts 2:42). They are:

1. Repentance from dead works (Acts 2:38).
2. Faith toward (upon) God (Heb. 11:6).
3. The laying on of hands (Acts 8:18; 13:3).
4. The doctrine of baptisms (Acts 1:5; 2:41).
5. The resurrection of the dead (Acts 4:2,33).
6. Eternal judgment (1 Cor. 6:1-3).

The psalmist cried out, "If [these] foundations be destroyed, what can the righteous do?" (Ps. 11:3; compare Ps. 82:5). A revival of praise has begun in the earth that will destroy the foundations of every human bondage (Acts 16:26)! Paul declared, "Nevertheless the foundation of God standeth sure, having this seal, The Lord knoweth them that are His..." (2 Tim. 2:19).

Go Deeper 📖

See Ex. 9:18; Deut. 32:22; 2 Sam. 22:8,16; 1 Kings 5:17; 6:37; 7:9-10; 2 Chron. 8:16; 23:5; 31:7; Ezra 3:6-12; 4:12; 5:16; 6:3; Job 38:4; Ps. 18:7,15; 87:1; 102:25; 137:7; Prov. 8:29; Is. 44:28; 51:13,16; 54:11; 58:12; Lam. 4:11; Hag. 2:18; Zech. 8:9; Lk. 14:29; Rom. 15:20; Eph. 1:4; 1 Tim. 6:19; Heb. 4:3; 11:10; Rev. 13:8; 21:14,19.

∾   ∾   ∾

𝔉ountain

Christ, the source of God's life; cleansing

Key Scriptures: Deut. 8:7; Ps. 36:9; Jer. 2:13; Zech. 13:1; Jn. 11:25; Col. 1:27.

Foundational Information ✎

A fountain is a source of water. These were either man-made wells (cisterns) or natural springs. "Fountain" is from the Hebrew *ma'yan* (Strong's #4599), which means "a spring; a fountain; figuratively, a source (of satisfaction)." Its root is *'ayin* (Strong's #5869), which means "an eye; by analogy, a fountain (as the eye of the landscape)." Also translated as "well" in the King James Version, the Greek word for "fountain" is *pege* (Strong's #4077), meaning "through (the idea of gushing plumply); a fount (literally or figuratively), source or supply (of water, blood, enjoyment)."

Fulfilled in Christ ☦

Jesus, the Source of all God-life, announced, "I am the resurrection, and the life" (Jn. 11:25). All divine life is "of Him," literally, "out of Him" (Rom. 11:36) who is "the fountain of life" (Ps. 36:9; Prov. 13:14; 14:27). Jesus is the New Testament "fountain gate ['door']" (Neh. 12:37; see also Jn. 10:7,9; 14:6). The Master declared to the woman of Samaria, "But whosoever drinketh of the water that I shall give him shall never thirst; but the water that I shall give him shall be in him a well of water springing up into everlasting life" (Jn. 4:14). Zechariah prophesied of Messiah's cleansing blood, "In that day there shall be a fountain opened to the house of David and to the inhabitants of Jerusalem for sin and for uncleanness" (Zech. 13:1; see also Acts 20:28; Heb. 9:12; 13:12; Rev. 1:5).

Applied to the Christian ⚖

Believers have been raised from the state of spiritual death, then "quickened" and made alive in Christ (Eph. 2:1; compare Jn. 5:24). The New Testament "fountain" is described by Paul as "Christ in you" (Col. 1:27)! As with weary Hagar, the Lord found all of us "by a fountain" in the way to Shur ("going round about"), mundanely wandering in the desert of life (Gen. 16:7). The Lord promises to bring His people "into a good land, a land of brooks of water, of fountains and depths that spring out of valleys and hills" (Deut. 8:7; compare Is. 41:18; Joel 3:18). There is no place for the beast nature at "the king's pool" (Neh. 2:14; compare Eph. 4:27). Jeremiah lamented, "For My people have committed two evils; they have forsaken Me the fountain of living waters, and hewed them out cisterns, broken cisterns, that can hold no water" (Jer. 2:13). Rebellious, lawless sons of disobedience, void of the life of Christ, are described as "wells without water" (2 Pet. 2:17).

Go Deeper 📖

See Gen. 7:11; 8:2; Lev. 11:36; 14:52; Num. 8:7; 33:9; Deut. 33:28; Josh. 15:9; 1 Sam. 29:1; 1 Kings 18:5; 2 Chron. 32:3-4; Neh. 3:15; Ps. 68:26; 114:8; Prov. 5:18; 8:28; 25:26; Eccles. 12:6; Song 4:12,15; Jer. 6:7; 9:1; 17:13; Ezek. 36:25; Hos. 13:15; Jn. 4:6; Eph. 5:27; Col. 1:15-18; Jas. 3:11-12; Rev. 7:17; 8:10; 14:7; 16:4; 21:6.

∞ ∞ ∞

𝔉𝔬𝔴𝔩𝔢𝔯

The devil; scheming spiritual entrapments

Key Scriptures: Josh. 23:13; Ps. 91:3; 124:7; Prov. 6:5; Hos. 9:8; Jer. 5:26; Mt. 22:15; 2 Cor. 2:11; Gal. 5:1.

Foundational Information ✐

A fowler is one who hunts and captures birds, using all kinds of implements and devices, such as decoys, traps, nets, bait, bows and arrows, slings, lures, setting dogs, and bird lime smeared on branches. "Fowler" is from the Hebrew *yaquwsh* (Strong's #3353), which means "entangled, (intransitively) a snare, or (transitive) a snarer." "Snare" is from the Hebrew *mowqesh* (Strong's #4170), which means "a noose (for catching animals); a hook (for the nose)." The Greek word is *pagis* (Strong's #3803) and means "a trap (as fastened by a noose or notch); figuratively, a trick or stratagem (temptation)."

Fulfilled in Christ ⚸

Satan had no power over Heaven's Eagle, the high-flying Son of God; Jesus declared, "I will not talk with you much more, for the prince (evil genius, ruler) of the world is coming. And he has no claim on Me. [He has nothing in common with Me; there is nothing in Me that belongs to him, he has no power over Me.]" (Jn. 14:30 AMP). The Pharisees tried to "entangle" or "ensnare" the Master in His speech (Mt. 22:15). Our King delivered mankind from the power of the evil one at the cross—"the snare is broken ['bursted; shattered, smashed, crushed']" (Ps. 124:7): "it is finished" (Jn. 19:30; compare Col. 2:15; Heb. 2:14-15; 1 Jn. 3:8)! Jesus warned His people about the coming Day of the Lord, "For as a snare shall it come on all them that dwell on the face of the whole earth [the lower realms]. Watch ye therefore, and pray always, that ye may be accounted worthy ['prevail, overpower'] to escape all these things that shall come to pass, and to stand before the Son of man" (Lk. 21:35-36).

Applied to the Christian ⚖

We are not to be ignorant of satan's scheming "devices" (2 Cor. 2:11). The prophet Jeremiah warned us about the devil and his crowd, "For among my people are found wicked men: they lay wait, as he that setteth snares; they set a trap, they catch men" (Jer. 5:26). Believers are not to make covenant (intermarry) with the world (Ex. 34:12; Deut. 7:16 with 2 Cor. 6:14-18; 1 Jn. 2:15-17). Joshua warned that these ill-advised relationships would become "snares and traps unto you, and scourges in your sides, and thorns in your eyes…" (Josh. 23:13). The psalmist lamented, "They also that seek after my life lay snares for me: and they that seek my hurt speak mischievous things, and imagine deceits all the day long" (Ps. 38:12). God has promised to deliver His people from the snare of the fowler (Ps. 91:3). Solomon admonished, "Deliver thyself…from the hand of the fowler" (Prov. 6:5; compare Acts 2:40). The devil especially loves to prey upon prophets (Hos. 9:8; compare Amos 3:4-8). Those captured by the fowler can "recover themselves" (2 Tim. 2:26).

Go Deeper 📖

See Ex. 10:7; 14:3; 23:33; Judg. 2:3; 8:27; 1 Sam. 18:21; 28:9; 2 Sam. 22:6; Job 18:8-10; 22:10; Ps. 11:6; 64:5; 119:110; 140:5; 141:9; 142:3; Prov. 7:23; 13:14; 14:27; 18:7; 20:25; 22:5,25; 29:6,8,25; Eccles. 7:26; 9:12; Is. 8:14; 24:17-18; 29:21; Jer. 18:22; Lam. 3:47; Rom. 11:9; 1 Cor. 7:35; 1 Tim. 3:7; 6:9; 2 Tim. 2:4; 2 Pet. 2:20.

∞ ∞ ∞

𝔉𝔬𝔵𝔢𝔰

Deceivers, cowards; false prophets

Key Scriptures: Gen. 32:24-32; Song 2:15; Ezek. 13:3-6;
Mt. 8:20; Lk. 13:32; Rom. 8:1-9; 2 Jn. 7.

Foundational Information

Foxes were common predators in Bible times. A problem to grape farmers, they often settled in holes and burrows. These shrewd animals prey at night and will pretend to be dead when captured. When hunted, they are cunning and devious, misleading their pursuers. "Fox" is from the Hebrew *shuw'al* (Strong's #7776), which means "a jackal (as a burrower)." Its root is *sho'al* (Strong's #8168), and it means "to hollow out; the palm; by extension, a handful." The Greek word is *alopex* (Strong's #258), which means "a fox, (figuratively) a cunning person."

"Deceiver" is from the Hebrew *ta'a'* (Strong's #8591), which means "to cheat, to maltreat, misuse." Compare *shagah* (Strong's #7686), which means "to stray (causatively, mislead), to mistake, to transgress, to reel, be enraptured;" and *nakal* (Strong's #5230), which means "to defraud, act treacherously." The latter is also translated in the King James Version as "beguile, conspire, deal subtilly." The Greek word for "deceiver" is *planos* (Strong's #4108), and it means "roving (as a tramp), an impostor or misleader."

Fulfilled in Christ

Jesus Christ is the Truth, the antithesis of lies and deception (Jn. 1:1; 14:6; 17:17). He sternly addressed devious King Herod, "Go ye, and tell that fox, Behold, I cast out devils, and I do cures to day and to morrow, and the third day I shall be perfected" (Lk. 13:32; compare Hos. 6:1-3). Jesus warned about the deception of false ministry and counterfeit anointings, "For there shall arise false Christs, and false prophets, and shall shew great signs and wonders; insomuch that, if it were possible, they shall deceive ['cause to roam from safety, truth, or virtue'] the very elect" (Mt. 24:24; compare Mt. 7:15; 24:4-5,11; Lk. 6:26). The apostle John declared, "For many deceivers are entered into the world, who confess not that Jesus Christ is come in the flesh. This is a deceiver and an antichrist" (2 Jn. 7). Jesus said, "The foxes have holes ['burrows, lurking-places'], and the birds of the air have nests; but the Son of man hath not where to lay his head" (Mt. 8:20).

Applied to the Christian

Believers have been delivered from the old Adamic man, the scheming, manipulative Jacob nature ("Jacob" means "heel-catcher, supplanter") (Gen. 32:24-32; Rom. 8:1-9). The Bridegroom urged the Shulamite, "Take us the foxes, the little foxes, that spoil the vines: for our vines have tender grapes" (Song 2:15). Ezekiel exposed false prophets who followed their own spirits, "O Israel, thy prophets are like the foxes in the deserts...they have seen vanity and lying divination..." (Ezek. 13:3-6). Whenever Mount Zion is desolate, these "foxes" will operate their ministry (Lam. 5:18). Deceivers are cursed and slain by sin (Mal. 1:14; Rom. 7:11). Moses admonished, "Take heed to yourselves, that your heart be not deceived, and ye turn aside, and serve other gods, and worship them" (Deut. 11:16; compare Jer. 49:16). Paul added, "Let no man deceive you with vain words: for because of these things cometh the wrath of God upon the children of disobedience" (Eph. 5:6; compare 2 Tim. 3:13).

Go Deeper 📖

See Gen. 27:12; 31:7; Lev. 6:2; Judg. 15:4; 1 Sam. 13:17; Neh. 4:3; Job 12:16; Ps. 63:10; Prov. 20:1; 24:28; Jer. 9:5; 29:8; Ezek. 14:9; Zech. 13:4; Mt. 27:63; Lk. 9:58; Acts 13:6; Rom. 16:18; 1 Cor. 3:18; 6:9; 15:33; 2 Cor. 6:8; Gal. 6:7; Eph. 4:14; Tit. 1:10; 3:3; 2 Pet. 2:1; 1 Jn. 3:7; 4:1; Rev. 18:23; 19:20; 20:3,10.

∾ ∾ ∾

Frankincense

Acceptable, pure worship

Key Scriptures: Ex. 30:1-10,34; Lev. 24:5-9; Song 3:6; 4:6,14; Mt. 2:11; Jn. 4:19-24; Rom. 12:1-2; Phil. 3:3.

Foundational Information ✎

Frankincense, an aromatic gum resin obtained by cuttings, was called "frank" because of the freeness with which, when burned (with a constant, steady flame), it gives forth its sweet odor. A divinely prescribed ingredient of the incense used in the Mosaic tabernacle, frankincense was placed upon the 12 loaves of showbread for seven days, then consumed on the golden altar on the weekly Sabbath during the priests' covenantal meal. "Frankincense" is from the Hebrew *lebownah* (Strong's #3828), which means "frankincense (from its whiteness or perhaps that of its smoke)." Its root is *laban,* the Hebrew word for "white." The Greek word *libanos* (Strong's #3030) means "the incense-tree, incense itself."

Fulfilled in Christ ✝

Jesus Christ was the consummate worshiper (Jn. 4:19-24). He who was the antitype of the showbread covered with frankincense declared Himself to be the "bread of life"

(Jn. 6:35,48). The "mountain of myrrh" pictures Mount Calvary (His death); the "hill of frankincense" reveals worship in Mount Zion (His resurrection) (Song 4:6)! Jesus proclaimed the "acceptable" year of the Lord (Lk. 4:19). The brazen altar (His blood) and the golden altar (His intercession) reveal that the way to God is through Jesus' sacrifice (Jn. 14:6). Peter affirmed that God's priestly people have been called to "offer up spiritual sacrifices, acceptable ['well-received, approved'] to God by ['through'] Jesus Christ" (1 Pet. 2:5). Wise men still bring frankincense, bowing down to King Jesus (Mt. 2:11; Phil. 2:9-11; compare Lev. 2:1-2,15-16).

Applied to the Christian ⚖

One's entire life is to be worship—"...a living sacrifice, holy, acceptable unto God..." (Rom. 12:1). The tried-and-true Church, the Bride of Christ, has been "perfumed" with worship (Song 3:6; 4:14). The sweet odor of "pure ['clear, clean, transparent'] frankincense" (Ex. 30:34) on the weekly Sabbath revealed that God had accepted priestly worship, "an offering made by fire unto the Lord" (Lev. 24:5-9). Accordingly, the New Testament reveals these four kinds of worship:

1. Vain worship (Mt. 15:9).
2. Ignorant worship (Acts 17:23).
3. Will worship (Col. 2:23).
4. Worship that is in spirit and in truth (Jn. 4:23-24).

Some are chosen to "oversee" worship in the house of the Lord (1 Chron. 9:29). As in the restoration days of Nehemiah, God is cleansing our worship (Neh. 13:5,9; compare Rev. 11:1). New Testament priests are not to be "negligent" in their worship (2 Chron. 29:11; see also Rev. 1:6; 5:10). Paul declared, "For we are the circumcision, which worship God in the spirit, and rejoice in Christ Jesus, and have no confidence in the flesh" (Phil. 3:3). Isaiah saw an end-time revival during which the nations of the earth would bring their wealth and their worship into the house of the Lord (Is. 60:5-6; compare Rev. 21:23-27).

Go Deeper 📖

See Lev. 5:11; 6:15; Num. 5:15; Deut. 33:10; 1 Sam. 2:28; 1 Kings 9:25; 2 Kings 22:17; 1 Chron. 28:18; 2 Chron. 2:4; 26:16-19; Is. 43:23; Jer. 6:20; 17:26; 41:5; Mt. 4:9-10; Mk. 7:7; Acts 24:14; Rom. 14:18; 15:16; 1 Cor. 14:25; Eph. 5:10; Phil. 4:18; 1 Tim. 2:3; Heb. 1:6; 1 Pet. 2:20; Rev. 4:10; 9:20; 13:8; 14:7; 15:4; 18:13.

∾ ∾ ∾

Freewill Offering

Spontaneous worship

Key Scriptures: Lev. 3:1-17; 7:11-21; Deut. 23:23; Ps. 54:6; 110:3; Mt. 10:8; Eph. 2:14.

Foundational Information

These three kinds of peace offerings (sweet-savor offerings of worship) were given under the Levitical economy:

1. Thank offerings in response to an unsolicited special divine blessing.
2. Votive (vowed) offerings promised as part of a petitition or pledge to God.
3. Freewill offerings spontaneously presented in worship to God on the basis of who He is, not what He has done.

"Freewill" is from the Hebrew *nebadah* (Strong's #5071), which means "spontaneity, or (adjectively) spontaneous; also a spontaneous or (by inference, in plural) abundant gift." Its root is *nadab* (Strong's #5068), meaning "to impel; hence, to volunteer (as a soldier), to present spontaneously."

Fulfilled in Christ

Jesus Christ is our peace (Eph. 2:14), the living Word (Jn. 1:1,14-18). He is the freewill offering who went forth from the lips of the Father (Deut. 23:23; Ps. 19:6; Is. 55:11)! He was the perfect "voluntary offering," sinless, and "without blemish" (Lev. 7:16; 22:21). Our Savior prayed to the Father in Gethsemane, "Nevertheless not as I will, but as Thou wilt" (Mt. 26:39). Jesus was the "prince" who prepared Himself for His death on the cross (Ezek. 46:12; see also Is. 9:6; Acts 3:15; 5:31; Rev. 1:5)—"and after his going forth one shall shut the gate" (His finished work on the cross slammed the door in the devil's face) (Mic. 5:2; Jn. 19:30; Rev. 13:8)! The Pattern Son declared, "I seek not Mine own will, but the will of Him that sent Me" (Jn. 5:30; compare John 6:38; 14:31; Rom. 15:1-3; Phil. 2:8). The Master ever admonishes His disciples, "Freely ye have received, freely give" (Mt. 10:8).

Applied to the Christian

Each of us is to be "a willing offering" unto the Lord (Ex. 35:29), tendering Him our lives "every morning" (Ex. 36:3). Moses defined the freewill offering this way, "That which is gone out of thy lips thou shalt keep and perform..." (Deut. 23:23; compare Ps. 119:108). The psalmist rejoiced, "I will freely sacrifice unto thee: I will praise thy name, O Lord; for it is good" (Ps. 54:6). God's end-time Church will be "freewill offerings" in the day of His power (Ps. 110:3). The Holy Spirit, the One who enables us to worship (see Zech. 4:6; Jn. 4:23-24; Rom. 5:5; 1 Cor. 2:12), is the "rain" of God, plenteous and free (Ps. 68:9). Those who are thirsty are ever invited to come and worship, taking the water of life freely (Rev. 21:6; 22:17).

Go Deeper 📖

See Gen. 2:16; Lev. 22:18-23; 23:38; Num. 15:3; 29:39; Deut. 12:6,17; 16:10; 1 Sam. 14:30; 2 Chron. 29:31; 31:4; 35:8; Ezra 1:4; 2:68; 3:5; 7:13-16; 8:28; Ps. 51:12; Hos. 14:4; Amos 4:5; Jn. 8:32,36; Acts 2:29; 26:26; Rom. 3:24; 5:15-18; 6:7; 8:32; 2 Cor. 11:7; Gal. 4:26-31; 5:1.

∞ ∞ ∞

𝔉retting 𝔏eprosy

The sin of worry; anxiety; carefulness; bitterness

Key Scriptures: Lev. 13:51-52; 14:44-45; Ps. 37:1-8; Lk. 10:41;
Rom. 3:14; Eph. 4:31; Phil. 4:6; Heb. 12:15.

Foundational Information ✐

A leper was a person who suffered from a slowly progressing and incurable skin disease. "Fretting" is from the Hebrew *ma'ar* (Strong's #3992), meaning "to be bitter or (causatively) to embitter, be painful." It is also rendered in the King James Version as "picking." The Greek word for "bitterness" is *pikria* (Strong's #4088), which means "acridity (especially poison)." Compare *pikros* (Strong's #4089), which means "(through the idea of piercing) sharp (pungent), acrid."

"Careful" is from the Hebrew *charad* (Strong's #2729), which means "to shudder with terror; hence, to fear; also to hasten (with anxiety)." Compare *da'ag* (Strong's #1672), which means "anxious." The Greek word is *phrontizo* (Strong's #5431), meaning "to exercise thought, be anxious." Taken from *phren* ("mind"), it also means "to think, consider, be thoughtful." Compare *merimnao* (Strong's #3309), which means "to be anxious about." Rendered as "take thought" in the King James Version, the latter is taken from *merimna* (Strong's #3308), which means "(through the idea of distraction); solicitude."

Fulfilled in Christ ✝

Jesus healed the lepers (see Mt. 8:2; 10:8; 11:5; 26:6; Mk. 1:40; 14:3; Lk. 4:27; 7:22; 17:11-15). Jesus Christ is man's only Savior, the One who has delivered us from fretting leprosy (Acts 4:12). He alone is the Priest who inspects the leper, for "all things are naked and opened ['laid bare'] unto the eyes of Him with whom we have to do" (Heb. 4:13). Zechariah prophesied concerning Messiah, God's only Son, "And I will pour upon the house of David, and upon the inhabitants of Jerusalem, the spirit of grace and of supplications: and they shall look upon Me whom they have pierced, and they shall mourn for Him, as one mourneth for his only son, and shall be in bitterness for Him, as one that is in bitterness for his firstborn" (Zech. 12:10; see also Jn. 3:16-18; Heb. 11:17; 1 Jn. 4:9). Jesus taught, "Take therefore no thought for the morrow...Sufficient unto the day is the evil thereof" (Mt. 6:34).

Applied to the Christian ⚖

The unclean, foul "plague" or "spot" of worry is sin—we must not let it "spread," else it must be burned with fire (Lev. 13:51-52). "Fretting leprosy" has caused the breakdown of lives, homes, churches, and nations (Lev. 14:44-45). Paul admonished, "Be careful for nothing..." (Phil. 4:6)—The Living Bible renders this, "Don't worry about anything." Martha was "careful" on the inside and "troubled" on the outside about many things (Lk. 10:41). The mouth of the wicked is full of cursing and bitterness (Rom. 3:14). The "root of bitterness" troubles the believer and defiles the Church (Heb. 12:15). Paul admonished, "Let all bitterness, and wrath, and anger, and clamour, and evil speaking, be put away from you, with all malice" (Eph. 4:31). Those delivered from the fretting leprosy of worry are like trees planted by the water (Jer. 17:8). "Fret not" (Ps. 37:1-8; Prov. 24:19).

Go Deeper 📖

See 1 Sam. 1:10; 15:32; 2 Sam. 2:26; Job 7:11; 9:18; 10:1; 21:25; Prov. 14:10; 17:25; Is. 8:21; 38:15-17; Lam. 1:4; 3:15; Ezek. 3:15; 21:6; 27:31: 28:24; Mt. 6:25-34; 10:19; Lk. 12:11,22-26; Acts 8:23; 1 Cor. 7:32-34; 12:25; Phil. 2:20; Col. 3:19; Jas. 3:11-14; Rev. 8:11.

∞ ∞ ∞

𝔉𝔯𝔦𝔢𝔫𝔡 (𝔬𝔣 𝔱𝔥𝔢 𝔅𝔯𝔦𝔡𝔢𝔤𝔯𝔬𝔬𝔪)

The prophetic ministry of the sons of God;
the fivefold ministries; the Holy Spirit

Key Scriptures: Prov. 18:24; Is. 54:5; Jn. 3:29; 15:13-15; 16:13; Eph. 4:11.

Foundational Information ✑

The friend of the bridegroom, the "best man" in the wedding ceremony of the ancient world, was the one who assisted in planning and arranging the marriage.

"Friend" is from the Greek *philos* (Strong's #5384), which means "dear, a friend; actively, fond, friendly (still as a noun, an associate, neighbor, etc.)." The Hebrew word for "friend" is *rea'* (Strong's #7453), which means "an associate (more or less close)." It is also translated in the King James Version as "brother, companion, fellow, husband, lover, neighbor."

Fulfilled in Christ ☦

Jesus Christ is the heavenly Bridegroom, the Head and Husband of the Church (Is. 54:5; Mt. 25:1-10; Eph. 5:23). Jesus defined His "friends" as those who completely obeyed Him and who knew His secrets (Jn. 15:13-15). John the Baptist, the prophetic forerunner of Jesus who came in the spirit and power of Elijah (Mal. 4:5-6; Lk. 1:17), declared, "He that hath the bride is the bridegroom; but the friend of the bridegroom, which standeth and heareth him, rejoiceth greatly because of the bridegroom's voice: this my joy therefore is fulfilled" (Jn. 3:29). Jesus, the greatest son of David, has shared the spoils of Calvary's triumph with His "friends" (1 Sam. 30:26; compare Is. 53:12; Mt. 1:1). Jesus is the Friend who sticks closer than a brother (Prov. 18:24; compare Song 5:16). The psalmist described the Messiah "as a bridegroom coming out of his chamber, [who rejoices] as a strong man to run a race" (Ps. 19:5).

Applied to the Christian ⚖

The Church is the Bride of Christ (Eph. 5:30-32; Rev. 21:2,9). The "friend of the bridegroom" of John 3:29 is marked by three distinctive traits: He stands, He hears, He rejoices. This term has various applications: it can describe an end-time prophetic Elijah ministry of the sons of God (compare the "mighty men" of David in First Samuel 25), the fivefold ministries of Ephesians 4:11, or the ministry of the Holy Spirit. Abraham was called "the Friend of God" (Jas. 2:23; compare Ex. 33:11; Is. 41:8). Jesus taught His disciples that "greater love hath no man than this, that a man lay down his life for his friends" (Jn. 15:13). The Book of Proverbs teaches these things about friendship:

1. The rich have many friends (Prov. 14:20).
2. A friend loves at all times (Prov. 17:17).
3. He who loves purity is the king's friend (Prov. 22:11).
4. Faithful are the wounds of a friend (Prov. 27:6).
5. A friend's counsel rejoices the heart (Prov. 27:9).
6. Friends keep each other sharp (Prov. 27:17).

Go Deeper 📖

See Job 6:14; 19:21; 42:10; Ps. 41:9; Prov. 17:9; 19:6; Is. 49:18; 61:10; 62:5; Jer. 2:32; 7:34; 16:9; 25:10; 33:11; Hos. 3:1; Joel 2:16; Zech. 13:6; Mt. 9:15; 11:19; 26:50; Mk. 2:19-20; 5:19; Lk. 5:34-35; 11:5-8; 14:10; 15:6,9; Jn. 2:9; 11:11; Jas. 4:4; 3 Jn. 14; Rev. 18:23; 22:17.

∞ ∞ ∞

𝔉𝔯𝔦𝔫𝔤𝔢𝔰

Our witness to the world

Key Scriptures: Num. 15:38-39; Is. 43:10; Mt. 18:16; 24:14;
Acts 1:8; Jas. 4:4; Rev. 1:5.

Foundational Information ✐

"Fringes" (also translated as "lock") is the word used in the King James Version to mean "tassel." "Fringe" is from the Hebrew *tsiytsith* (Strong's #6734), which means "a floral or wing-like projection, a forelock of hair, a tassel." It is the feminine form of *tsiyts* (Strong's #6731), which means "glistening, a burnished plate; also a flower (as bright-colored); a wing (as gleaming in the air)." The root *tsuwts* (Strong's #6692) means "to twinkle, glance; by analogy, to blossom (figuratively, flourish)." Compare *gedil* (Strong's #1434), which means "(in the sense of twisting); thread, a tassel or festoon." Also translated as "wreath" in the King James Version, its root *gadal* means "to twist, to make large."

"Witness" is from the Hebrew *'edah* (#5713), which means "testimony." Its root *'uwd* (Strong's #5749) means "to duplicate or repeat; by implication, to protest, testify (as by reiteration); intensively, to encompass, restore (as a sort of reduplication)." The Greek word is *martureo* (Strong's #3140), which means "to be witness, testify." Its root is *martus* (English, *martyr*), meaning "one who bears witness by his death." A "witness" is one who says or does whatever he has seen, heard, or knows.

Fulfilled in Christ ☀

John revealed Jesus to be "the faithful witness" (Rev. 1:5) who cannot lie (Prov. 14:5,25; compare Jn. 14:6; Heb. 6:18). Our King is the heavenly "tabernacle of witness" (Num. 17:7-8; 18:2), the Word made flesh (Jn. 1:14). He is the greatest Son of David, the Leader and Commander of His people (Is. 55:4; Mt. 1:1). Those who touched the "hem" of His garment were healed (Mt. 9:20; Mk. 14:36). Our heavenly Abel offered unto God a more excellent sacrifice and obtained witness that He was righteous (Heb. 11:4). Jesus taught "that in the mouth of two or three witnesses every word may be established" (Mt. 18:16b). He declared, "I am one that bear witness of Myself, and the Father that sent Me beareth witness of Me" (Jn. 8:18).

Applied to the Christian ⚖

The people of God were told to make "fringes" with a blue ribband (the biblical color denoting Heaven or the Holy Spirit) in the borders (edges) of their garments—this was to remind themselves to obey God's Word in their witness to the heathen (Num. 15:38-39). The Holy Spirit empowers our witness to others (Acts 1:8). God wants to "hem" us in, to surround us with His will. Moreover, Moses commanded, "Thou shalt make thee fringes upon the four quarters of thy vesture, wherewith thou coverest thyself"

(Deut. 22:12): We are to carry the witness of the gospel to the "four corners" (Rev. 7:1) of the earth (Mt. 28:18-20; Mk. 16:15-20). Jehovah affirmed through Isaiah, "Ye are my witnesses" (Is. 43:10). The Gospel of the Kingdom shall be proclaimed in all the world for a witness unto all nations (Mt. 24:14).

Go Deeper 📖

See Gen. 31:52; Ex. 28:33-34; 39:25-26; Deut. 19:15; Josh. 22:27; 24:27; Ruth 4:9-10; 2 Chron. 24:6; Ps. 89:37; Is. 44:8; Jer. 32:10; 42:5; Jn. 1:7-8; 5:32; Acts 2:32; 4:33; 5:32; 7:44; 10:43; 14:17; 22:15; 26:16; 2 Cor. 13:1; 1 Tim. 6:12; Heb. 12:1; 1 Pet. 5:1; 1 Jn. 1:2; 5:8; 3 Jn. 6; Rev. 3:14; 11:3; 20:4.

∞ ∞ ∞

𝔉𝔯𝔬𝔤𝔰

Unclean spirits

Key Scriptures: Ex. 8:1-13; Ps. 105:30; Ezek. 47:11; Mt. 10:1; Jude 11; Rev. 16:13.

Foundational Information ✑

Excepting Revelation 16:13, every mention of frogs in the Bible refers to the plague of frogs in Egypt (where frogs were connected with fertility and thus deemed sacred). "Frog" is from the Hebrew *tsephardea'* (Strong's #6854), which means "a swamp; a marsh-leaper, frog." Its root *tsaphar* (Strong's #6852) means "to skip about, return," and it is translated in the King James Version as "depart early." Quacks and charlatans were represented as "frogs" and were metaphorically associated with serpents.

The Greek word for "unclean," also translated as "foul" in the King James Version, is *akathartos* (Strong's #169), which means "impure (ceremonially, morally [lewd] or specially, [demonic])." Compare *kathairo* ("to cleanse, prune, expiate, purge") and *katharos* ("clean"). The Hebrew word for "unclean" is *tame'* (Strong's #2931), and it means "foul in a religious sense. " This latter word denotes a state of being ceremonially unfit, defiled, and polluted.

Fulfilled in Christ ✝

Jesus delivered men from the power of unclean spirits (Mt. 10:1; Mk. 1:23-27; Lk. 6:18). The One who mediated grace and truth (Jn. 1:17) is the heavenly Moses with authority over frogs (Ex. 8:12-13; Lk. 4:36). Jesus revealed, "When the unclean spirit is gone out of a man, he walketh through dry places, seeking rest, and findeth none" (Mt. 12:43). Knowing that our Lord is holy, Paul instructed, "For this ye know, that no whore-monger, nor unclean person, nor covetous man, who is an idolater, hath any inheritance in the kingdom of Christ and of God" (Eph. 5:5). Men could find "no fault" ("a reason or crime; cause") in the spotless Passover Lamb (Lk. 23:4,14; Jn. 18:38; 19:4-6).

Applied to the Christian ⚖

Egypt, a type of the world, was plagued with frogs (Ex. 8:1-13; 1 Jn. 2:15-17). The river of God cannot bring new life into miry places and marshes, the habitation of frogs (Ezek. 47:11). Uncleanness in the life of the believer will cause him to "hop" and "skip" from church to church, often departing early from the purposes, will, and timing of God. The three "unclean spriits" of Revelation 16:13 are revealed in the Book of Jude, "Woe unto them! For they have gone in the way of Cain, and ran greedily after the error of Balaam for reward, and perished in the gainsaying of Core" (Jude 11). These three "frog-men" have diminished the glory of God and sought the honor of men:

1. Cain is the brother-killer, jealous of those who have been accepted (Gen. 4).
2. The spirit of Balaam is snared by the love of money, the wages of unrighteous-ness; his divided heart refuses to obey God's Word instantly (Num. 22–24).
3. The spirit of Core (Korah) hates and disputes authority, demanding equality, though he has praise (his censer) in him (Num. 16).

Go Deeper 📖

See Ex. 2:3; Lev. 5:2; 2 Chron. 23:19; Ezra 9:11; Job 8:11; 40:21; Ps. 78:45; 105:30; Is. 6:5; 18:2; 19:6-7; 35:7-8; 52:1,11; 64:6; Ezek. 22:26; 44:23; Zech. 13:2; Mk. 3:11,30; 5:2,8,13; 6:7; 7:25; 9:25; Lk. 4:33-36; 8:29; 9:42; 11:42; Acts 5:16; 8:7; 10:14, 28; 11:8; 1 Cor. 7:14; 2 Cor. 6:17; Rev. 18:2.

∞ ∞ ∞

Frost

Divine dealings and judgments

Key Scriptures: Gen. 31:40; Ex. 16:14; Lk. 6:12; Jn. 5:22,27; 1 Cor. 6:1-3.

Foundational Information ✑

Frost is a covering of small ice crystals formed from frozen water vapor that falls over the land at night during the winter months. "Frost" is from the Hebrew *qerach* (Strong's #7140), which means "ice (as if bald, smooth); hence, hail; by resemblance, rock crystal." It is also translated in the King James Version as "crystal, ice." Its root *qarach* means "to depilate," and it is translated as "make bald." Compare *kephowr* (Strong's #3713), which means "a cover, (by implication) a tankard (or covered goblet); also white frost (as covering the ground)." Its root *kaphar* means "to cover; to expiate, to cancel."

Fulfilled in Christ ☥

All "judgment" has been committed unto the divine Son (Jn. 5:22,27; Acts 10:42; Rom. 2:16). Moses described the manna as "a small round thing, as small as the hoar frost on the ground" (Ex. 16:14). Jesus was the antitype, the Bread of life (Jn. 6:35,48). The Pattern Son had many night seasons of communion with the Father—Luke records that the Man of sorrows "went out into a mountain to pray, and continued all night in prayer to God" (Lk. 6:12; compare Lk. 21:37). Joseph took Mary and Jesus to Egypt "by night" to escape the wiles of Herod (Mt. 2:14). Jesus the Word was birthed at night (Lk. 2:14). Our King liked to go walking at night (Mt. 14:25; Mk. 6:48).

Applied to the Christian ⚖

There will come a day when the Church will judge the world and angels (1 Cor. 6:1-3). God used frost to judge Egypt, a type of the world (Ps. 78:47; 1 Jn. 2:15-17). The judgments of God are past, present, and future (Jn. 16:11; 1 Cor. 11:31; Rev. 20:12-13). Frost comes "by night" (Gen. 31:40): There are "night seasons" in the life of the believer (Job 30:17; Ps. 22:2) The prophetess Anna fasted and prayed "night and day" (Lk. 2:37). The psalmist declared, "I will bless the Lord, who hath given me counsel; my reins ['heart'] also instruct me in the night seasons" (Ps. 16:7). God loves to open prison doors by night (Acts 5:19). There are times when the frost comes out of the north by the breath (Spirit) of God (Job 37:10; compare Job 37:9; Song 4:16). Each of us must experience those night deposits, "treasures of darkness" (Is. 45:3).

Go Deeper 📖

See Gen. 1:5; 8:22; 28:11; Job 6:15-16; 24:7; 30:17; 38:29; Ps. 134:1; 147:16-17; Prov. 20:4; 25:13,20,25; 31:18; Song 3:1; Is. 4:5; Jer. 18:14; 36:30; Ezek. 1:22; Nahum 3:17; Mt. 10:42; 24:12; Lk. 18:7; Jn. 18:18; Acts 9:25; 17:10; 23:31; 28:2; 2 Cor. 11:27; Rev. 3:15-16.

∾ ∾ ∾

𝔉𝔯𝔲𝔦𝔱

The divine nature; children; the words of our mouths

Key Scriptures: Gen. 1:11-12; Ps. 1:3; 127:3; Prov. 18:21;
Jn. 15:1-16; Gal. 5:22-23; Heb. 13:15; 2 Pet. 1:3-4.

Foundational Information 📝

Fruit is that which is produced by the inherent energy in the seed of a living organism, the visible expression of power working inwardly and invisibly, the character of the "fruit" being evidence of the character of the power producing it. The fruits most often mentioned in Scripture are the grape, pomegranate, fig, olive, and apple. Also translated as "bough, firstfruit, fruitful, reward," in the King James Version, the Hebrew word for "fruit" is *periy* (Strong's #6529). The verb *parah* (Strong's #6509) means "to bear fruit (literally or figuratively)." The Greek word *karpos* (Strong's #2590) means "fruit (as plucked), literally or figuratively." Compare *harpazo* ("to seize") and *haireomai* ("to take for oneself, to prefer, choose").

Fulfilled in Christ ✝

The "fruit of the Spirit" is the divine nature and character of Jesus Christ—His life is marked by "love, joy, peace, longsuffering, gentleness, goodness, faith, meekness, temperance" (Gal. 5:22-23; compare Eph. 5:9). The fruit of the Bridegroom, like "the apple tree," is sweet to the Bride (Song 2:3). Jesus Christ is the divine Seed—"in Him was life" (Jn. 1:4). He is the Seed of the Woman, the Seed of Abraham, and the Seed of David (Gen. 3:15; Mt. 1:1); this reveals respectively His pain, promise, and power as He relates to mankind racially, redemptively, and royally. Children are the fruit of the womb (Ps. 127:3; 128:3); so the Pattern Son was planted in death and reproduced through resurrection into a vast family of children in His image and likeness (Rom. 6:1-14; 8:29; 1 Cor. 15:44-49). Jesus declared, "I am the vine, ye are the branches: He that abideth in Me, and I in him, the same bringeth forth much fruit: for without Me ye can do nothing" (Jn. 15:5).

Applied to the Christian ⚖

The apostle Peter declared that the "divine power" of the Holy Spirit ministers to us the things of God, "whereby are given unto us exceeding great and precious promises [through the Scriptures]; that by these [we] might be partakers of the divine nature" (2 Pet. 1:3-4). The law of reproduction in Genesis 1:11-12 declares that all fruit is replicated after its "kind" ("sort, species")—"fruit trees with seeds inside the fruit, so that these seeds will produce the kinds of plants and fruits they came from" (TLB). The psalmist revealed that the righteous man would be like a tree "that bringeth forth his fruit in his season," even unto "old age" (Ps. 1:3; 92:14). Solomon taught, "Death and life are in the power of the tongue: and they that love it shall eat the fruit thereof" (Prov. 18:21; compare Is. 57:19; Heb. 13:15). Believers are to be fruitful in every good work (Col. 1:10).

Go Deeper 📖

See Gen. 1:28-29; Lev. 19:24; 23:39; 25:3; Num. 13:20; Deut. 7:13; 28:4; Josh. 5:12; 2 Kings 19:30; Ps. 72:16; 127:3; 132:11; Prov. 11:30; 12:14; Song 8:11-12; Is. 5:1-2; 27:6; 32:15; Jer. 23:3; Mt. 3:10; 7:17-18; 13:8,23; Mk. 4:28; Acts 2:30; Rom. 1:3; 6:22; 1 Cor. 9:7; Phil. 4:17; Heb. 12:11; Jas. 3:18; 5:7; Rev. 22:12.

∞ ∞ ∞

𝔉uel

That which is to be burned; slanderous talebearing; the source of heat and light

Key Scriptures: Prov. 26:20; Is. 9:5,19; Ezek. 15:4,6; 21:32; 1 Cor. 3:9-15; Heb. 12:29.

Foundational Information ✐

Fuel is any material burned to produce heat or light. In Palestine, wood and other fuel sources were scarce. Grass and dung were used for cooking food, and olive oil was used for lamps. "Fuel" is from the Hebrew *ma'akoleth* (Strong's #3980), which means "something eaten (by fire), fuel." It is derived from *'akal* (Strong's #398), which means "to eat." From the same root, compare *'oklah* (Strong's #402), which means "food." The latter is also translated as "consume, devour, eat, meat" in the King James Version. Compare *'Ukal*, which means "devoured."

"Talebearer" is from the Hebrew *rakiyl* (Strong's #7400), which means "a scandalmonger (as travelling about)." Compare *nirgan* (Strong's #5372), which means "to roll to pieces; a slanderer."

Fulfilled in Christ ✝

The Bible reveals that our God is a "consuming fire" (Heb. 12:29). Wood is a symbol for humanity. Jesus Christ was the fuel from Heaven, totally consumed by the Father on a wooden cross to produce the energy of divine light and life in His resurrection.

Jesus declared Himself to be "the light of the world" (Jn. 8:12; compare Lk. 2:32). The Father accepted the sacrificial offering of His only Son, and He subsequently sent the Holy Spirit to empower the Church (2 Chron. 7:1; Acts 2:1-4). Luke explained in the Book of Acts "that Christ should suffer, and that He should be the first to rise from the dead, and should show light unto the people" (Acts 26:23).

Applied to the Christian   ⚖

The oil of the Holy Spirit is the fuel that makes the Church the light of the world (Ex. 25:6; Mt. 5:14; Phil. 2:15). As believers, we must build our lives with gold, silver, and precious stones, and not with "wood, hay, stubble" (1 Cor. 3:12). These latter three are to be "cast into the fire for fuel" (Ezek. 15:4). Job warned, "For the congregation of hypocrites shall be desolate, and fire shall consume the tabernacles of bribery" (Job 15:34). Those who utter slanderous words are foolish (Prov. 10:18), and those who spread gossip "shall surely make restitution" (Ex. 22:6). Solomon taught, "Where no wood [fuel] is, the fire goeth out: so where there is no talebearer, the strife ceaseth" (Prov. 26:20; compare Prov. 11:13; 18:8; 20:19; 26:22).

Go Deeper   📖

See Ex. 3:2; 20:16; 22:6; Lev. 9:24; 19:16; Num. 11:1; 14:36; 16:35; 21:28; Deut. 4:24; 5:25; 9:3; 32:22; Judg. 6:21; 1 Kings 18:38; 2 Kings 1:10-12; Neh. 2:3,13; Job 1:16; 20:26; Ps. 31:13; 78:63; Jer. 6:29; 49:27; Ezek. 4:15; 19:12; 22:31; 24:10; Lk. 9:54; 12:28; Eph. 4:29-32.

∞   ∞   ∞

Fuller

Cleansing; transfiguration

Key Scriptures: 2 Kings 18:17; Is. 7:3; 36:2; Jer. 2:22; Mal. 3:2; Mt. 17:2; Mk. 9:2-3; Rom. 12:2; 2 Cor. 3:18.

Foundational Information   ✏

A fuller is one who cleans, shrinks, thickens, and sometimes dyes newly cut wool or cloth. Garments were washed in some alkaline, such as white clay or nitre, then washed out by treading on the material repeatedly in clean, running water. The material was then dried and bleached by the sun. "Fuller" is from the Hebrew *kabac* (Strong's #3526), which means "to trample; hence, to wash (properly by stamping with the feet), whether literal (including the fulling process) or figurative." It is translated as "bathe, wash," in the King James Version. Compare the Hebrew *rachats* (Strong's #7364), which means "to lave (the whole or a part of the thing)." The Greek word is *gnapheus* (Strong's #1102), and it means "(to tease cloth); a cloth-dresser." The launderer's or bleacher's process created an unpleasant odor, and was usually done outside the city gates in an area named Fuller's Field.

"Transfiguration" is from the Greek *metamorphoo* (Strong's #3339), which means "to transform (literally or figuratively, 'metamorphose')." Also rendered as "change, transform" in the King James Version, *metamorphoo* means "to change into another form," taken from *meta* (implying "change") and *morphe* ("form"). Compare the Greek word *katharos* (Strong's #2513), translated as "clean, clear, pure" in the King James Version.

Fulfilled in Christ ✝

Jesus Christ is the heavenly Fuller, the One who sanctifies His people (Heb. 2:11). Malachi prophesied that Messiah's coming would be "like a refiner's fire, and like fullers' soap" (Mal. 3:2). Jacob described the coming Deliverer, "He washed his garments in wine, and his clothes in the blood of grapes" (Gen. 49:11). Jesus "cleansed" the lepers (Mt. 11:5; Mk. 1:42; Lk. 7:22). At Jesus' Transfiguration, "...His raiment became shining, exceeding white as snow; so as no fuller on earth can white them" (Mk. 9:2-3; compare Mt. 17:2). God promised to sprinkle "clean water" upon His people, to cleanse us from our filthiness (Ezek. 36:25). Jesus affirmed this to His disciples, "Now ye are clean through the word which I have spoken unto you" (Jn. 15:3). His many-membered Bride is arrayed in linen, clean and white (Rev. 19:8,14). The fear of the Lord is "clean" (Ps. 19:9).

Applied to the Christian ⚖

No human agency can cleanse from sin, even with "much soap" (Jer. 2:22; compare Prov. 20:9). Like unwashed Mephibosheth, all of us were unclean (2 Sam. 19:24). Believers have been "sanctified" ("set apart") by the blood of Jesus and the water of His Word (Eph. 5:25-27; Heb. 13:12). The Day of the Lord has dawned, the day for God's people to "wash their clothes" (Ex. 19:10,14; compare Num. 8:21; 31:24). Christians are "transformed" by the renewing or renovating of their minds (Rom. 12:2). We are "changed" from glory to glory as we worship the Lord (2 Cor. 3:18). Let us cry out with the psalmist, "Wash me throughly from mine iniquity, and cleanse me from my sin...Purge me with hyssop, and I shall be clean: wash me, and I shall be whiter than snow" (Ps. 51:2,7). John affirmed, "But if we walk in the light, as He is in the light, we have fellowship with one another, and the blood of Jesus Christ His Son cleanseth us from all sin" (1 Jn. 1:7).

Go Deeper 📖

See Lev. 6:27; 10:10; 11:25,28,40; 13:6,34,54-58; 14:8-9,47; 15:5-27; 16:26-28; 17:15-16; Num. 8:7; 19:7-10; 2 Kings 5:10-14; 2 Chron. 29:18; 34:5; Neh. 13:30;

Ps. 24:4; 51:7,10; Is. 52:11; Jer. 4:14; Ezek. 44:23; Joel 3:21; Mt. 8:1-3; 23:25-26; 27:59; Lk. 4:27; 11:39-41; 17:14-17; Jn. 13:10-11; Acts 10:15; 11:9; 18:6; 2 Pet. 2:18.

∾ ∾ ∾

𝔉urnace

God, the consuming fire; the trial of faith

Key Scriptures: Job 23:10; Ps. 12:6; Prov. 17:3; 27:21; Is. 48:10; Dan. 3:1-30; Heb. 12:29; 1 Pet. 1:7; 4:12.

Foundational Information

Furnaces made of stone or brick were used mostly by potters and metalsmiths. Household furnaces were called ovens. "Furnace" is from the Hebrew *kibshan* (Strong's #3536), which means "a smelting furnace (as reducing metals)." Its root *kabash* (Strong's #3533) means "to tread down; hence, negatively, to disregard; positively, to conquer, subjugate, violate." Compare *kuwr* (Strong's #3564), which means "to dig through; a pot or furnace (as if excavated)"; and *'attuwm* (Strong's #861), which means "a fire-place, furnace." The root of the latter is *'esh,* the Hebrew word for "fire." It is also translated in the King James Version as "burning, fiery, flaming, hot." The Greek word for "furnace, oven, kiln" is *kaminos* (Strong's #2575), taken from *kaio* (Strong's #2545), which means "to set on fire, kindle or (by implication) consume." Compare the English *chimney.*

Fulfilled in Christ

Jesus Christ was God Almighty in the flesh (Jn. 1:1,14; 1 Tim. 3:16), and "our God is a consuming fire" (Heb. 12:29). Our sinless Savior is the pure Word who was "tried in a furnace of earth" (Ps. 12:6). He was the "fiery law" of the Father (Deut. 33:2). The "smoking furnace" and the "burning lamp" that sealed the covenant with Abraham symbolize the Father and the Son (Gen. 15:17; see also Heb. 13:20). The Lord prophesied through Isaiah, "Behold, I have refined thee, but not with silver; I have chosen thee in the furnace of affliction" (Is. 48:10). Jesus protects His servants in the fiery furnace; Nebuchadnezzar exclaimed, "Lo, I see four men loose ['free'], walking in the midst of the fire, and the form of the fourth is like the Son of God" (Dan. 3:25). John described the risen Christ as One whose were "like unto fine brass, as if they burned in a furnace" (Rev. 1:15).

Applied to the Christian

The apostle Peter declared that the trial of our faith is more precious than gold, "though it be tried with fire" (1 Pet. 1:7; compare 1 Pet. 4:12). The Lord has brought us forth out of the "iron furnace" to be His people (Deut. 4:20; compare 1 Kings 8:51). Solomon declared, "The fining pot is for silver, and the furnace for gold: but the Lord trieth the hearts…As the fining pot for silver, and the furnace for gold; so is a man to his praise" (Prov. 17:3; 27:21). Those who refuse to worship false gods are tried in "a burning fiery furnace" (Dan. 3:6-15). Paul assured our being victorious in Christ, "Above all, taking the shield of faith, wherewith ye shall be able to quench all the fiery darts ['missiles'] of the wicked" (Eph. 6:16). Job declared, "But He knoweth the way that I take: when He hath tried me, I shall come forth as gold" (Job 23:10).

Go Deeper 📖

See Gen. 19:28; Ex. 9:8-10; 19:18; 29:18; Lev. 1:9; Num. 8:6-8; 15:10; Deut. 8:15; 18:1; 33:2; Josh. 13:14; 1 Sam. 2:28; 1 Kings 18:24; 1 Chron. 21:26; Neh. 3:11; 12:38; Ps. 21:9; Is. 14:29; 30:6; 31:9; 66:16; Jer. 11:4; Ezek. 22:18-22; Dan. 7:9-10; Amos 7:4; Zech. 13:9; Mal. 3:3; Mt. 13:42,50; 1 Cor. 3:13-15; Heb. 10:27; Rev. 9:2.

∞ ∞ ∞

𝔉urniture (𝔗abernacle)

The ministry of Christ and His Church

Key Scriptures: Ex. 18–40; 1 Chron. 17:5; Jn. 1:14; Eph. 2:19-22; 1 Jn. 4:17.

Foundational Information ✐

Although the furniture in a typical house in Palestine in Bible times included a bed, table, chair, and lampstand, this word is used to describe the "furniture" of the Mosaic tabernacle. "Furniture" is from the Hebrew *keliy* (Strong's #3627), which means "something prepared, any apparatus (as an implement, utensil, dress, vessel or weapon)." It can also mean "receptacle, stuff, clothing, tool, instrument, ornament or jewelry, armor."

"Tabernacle" is from the Hebrew *mishkan* (Strong's #4908), and it means "a residence (including a shepherd's hut, the lair of animals, figuratively, the grave; also the temple); specifically, the tabernacle (properly, its wooden walls)." Also translated as "dwelleth, dwelling (place), habitation, tent" in the King James Version, its root is *shakan* (Strong's #7931), which means "lodging; to reside or permanently stay (literally or figuratively)."

Fulfilled in Christ ✝

God gave the tabernacle plan to Moses by divine "pattern" (Ex. 25:9,40), and it pictures Jesus as the Pattern Son. Jesus Christ was the Word made flesh who "tabernacled" among men (Jn. 1:14). Each piece of furniture in Moses' tabernacle typifies the Son of God as follows:

1. The brazen altar reveals Jesus as Savior and Healer (Ex. 27:1-8; Acts 4:12; 1 Pet. 2:24).
2. The brazen laver reveals Jesus as Sanctifier (Ex. 30:17-21; Heb. 2:11).
3. The golden lampstand reveals Jesus as the Light of the world (Ex. 25:31-40; Jn. 8:12).
4. The table of showbread reveals Jesus as the Bread of Life (Ex. 25:23-30; Jn. 6:35,48).
5. The golden altar of incense reveals Jesus as our Intercessor, our Great High Priest (Ex. 30:1-10; Rom. 8:34; Heb. 7:25).
6. The mercy-seat reveals Jesus as our Propitiation (Ex. 25:17-22; Rom. 3:25).
7. The ark of the Covenant reveals Jesus as the Head of the Church, Lord and King, the Overcomer (Ex. 25:10-22; Eph. 1:20-23; Rev. 3:21; 19:16).

Applied to the Christian ⚖

John declared, "As He is, so are we in this world" (1 Jn. 4:17). The "pattern" or "model" given to Moses was God's divine order for His people (Ex. 25:9,40). Each piece of furniture in Moses' tabernacle reveals an aspect of our Christian walk:

1. The brazen altar pictures the cross of Christ and our justification (Gal. 2:20; Heb. 9:22).
2. The brazen laver pictures water baptism and our sanctification (Acts 2:38; Eph. 5:25-27).
3. The golden lampstand pictures the Church as the light of the world (Mt. 5:14; Phil. 2:15).
4. The table of showbread pictures the new covenant, the Lord's Supper, and the fivefold ministries (1 Cor. 11:23-30; Eph. 4:8-16).
5. The golden altar of incense pictures the Church's ministry in prayer, praise, and worship (Ps. 141:2; 150:1-6; Jn. 4:23-24).
6. The mercy-seat pictures the word and ministry of reconciliation (2 Cor. 5:17-21; Heb. 8:1-6).
7. The ark of the covenant pictures the full stature and maturity of the overcoming Church (1 Cor. 13:8-13; Eph. 4:13; Rev. 3:21; 14:1-5; 21:7).

Go Deeper 📖

See Ex. 25:9; 40:33-38; Lev. 8:10; 15:31; 17:4; 26:11; Num. 1:50-53; 3:7-8; 9:15-22; Josh. 22:19; 2 Sam. 7:6; 1 Chron. 6:32,48; 15:1; 16:39; 21:29; 23:26; 2 Chron. 1:5; 29:6; Ps. 26:8; 43:3; 46:4; 78:60; 84:1; 132:5-7; Is. 32:18; 40:3; Ezek. 37:27; Jn. 14:2-3,23; Rom. 9:33; 2 Tim. 2:20-21; Heb. 10:5; 11:6,17; Rev. 21:2.

∾ ∾ ∾

𝔉urrows

The deep dealings of God

Key Scriptures: Ps. 65:10; 129:3; Is. 28:24; Hos. 10:4; Mic. 3:12; 1 Cor. 9:10.

Foundational Information

A furrow is a long, narrow trench in the ground made by a plow. "Furrow" is from the Hebrew *deduwd* (Strong's #1417), which means "a furrow (as cut)." Its root *gadad* (Strong's #1413) means "to crowd; also to gash (as if by pressing into)." Compare *ma'anah* (Strong's #4618), which means "in the sense of depression or tilling; a furrow." Its root *'anah* means "to depress."

Fulfilled in Christ

The back of Jesus Christ was plowed for our healing (Is. 53:5; 1 Pet. 2:24). Messiah declared through the psalmist, "The plowers plowed upon my back: they made long their furrows" (Ps. 129:3). Jonathan and his armorbearer, like "a yoke of oxen," picture Jesus working and walking with the believer (1 Sam. 14:14; Mt. 11:28-30; Eph. 6:10-18). The Lord plows His people "in hope" that they will be changed into His glorious image (1 Cor. 9:10; see also 2 Cor. 3:18; 4:17-18; Col. 1:27). The psalmist declared of the Lord, "In His hand are the deep places of the earth" (Ps. 95:4). Daniel affirmed that God alone "revealeth the deep and secret things: He knoweth what is in the darkness, and the light dwelleth with Him" (Dan. 2:22).

Applied to the Christian

Those who press on to know Him as Lord will experience deep dealings (Hos. 6:3; Phil. 3:12-14). Hosea described God's disciplines, "They have spoken words, swearing falsely in making a covenant: thus judgment springeth up as hemlock in the furrows of the field" (Hos. 10:4,10). Furrows have a voice; they cause us to "complain" (Job 31:38). The psalmist promised God's comfort, "Thou waterest the ridges thereof abundantly: Thou settlest the furrows thereof: Thou makest it soft with showers..." (Ps. 65:10). Zion will be plowed like a field (Mic. 3:12; compare Heb. 12:22-24). But God is merciful; He will not plow us forever (Is. 28:24). Judah, which means "praise," is a plow (Hos. 10:11).

Go Deeper

See Gen. 7:11; Deut. 8:5; 22:10; Judg. 14:18; Job 4:8; 12:22; 39:10; Ps. 36:6; 42:7; 64:6; 69:14; 73:14; 80:9; 89:30-34; 92:5; 119:75; 135:6; Prov. 3:12; 13:24; 20:4; 23:27; Eccles. 7:24; Is. 2:4; Jer. 48:37; Ezek. 7:7; Hos. 12:11; Joel 3:10; Amos 6:12; Mic. 4:3; Lk. 6:48; Heb. 12:5-11; Jas. 1:12; 5:11; Rev. 3:19.

Coming Soon—
Understanding Types, Shadows, and Names, Vol. 3!

Subsequent volumes in this series, *Understanding Types, Shadows, and Names*, are scheduled to be released semi-annually.

For a complete listing of Destiny Image titles, contact:

Destiny Image Publishers
P.O. Box 310
Shippensburg, PA 17257-0310
1-800-722-6774
Or reach us on the Internet: **http://www.reapernet.com**

Destiny Image Books by Kelley Varner

Prevail—A Handbook for the Overcomer
TPB-196p. ISBN 0-938612-06-9 Retail $8.99

The More Excellent Ministry
TPB-280p. ISBN 0-914903-60-8 Retail $9.99

The Priesthood Is Changing
TPB-238p. ISBN 1-56043-033-8 Retail $8.99

The Issues of Life
TPB-182p. ISBN 1-56043-075-3 Retail $8.99

Rest in the Day of Trouble
TPB-294p. ISBN 1-56043-119-9 Retail $9.99

Unshakeable Peace
TPB-252p. ISBN 1-56043-137-7 Retail $8.99

Whose Right It Is
TPB-322p. ISBN 1-56043-151-2 Retail $10.99

The Time of the Messiah
TPB-182p. ISBN 1-56043-177-6 Retail $8.99

The Three Prejudices
TPB-246p. ISBN 1-56043-187-3 Retail $9.99

Understanding Types, Shadows, and Names—Vol.1
TPB-276p. ISBN 1-56043-165-2 Retail $16.99

These books and other materials may also be obtained through the author's ministry:

Pastor Kelley Varner
Praise Tabernacle
P.O. Box 785
Richlands, NC 28574

Church phone: 910-324-5026
Fax: 910-324-1048
E-mail: kvarner@nternet.net
Reach us on the Internet: http://www.reapernet.com/ptm

Or call Destiny Image at 1-800-722-6774.